ATTACK ON TITAN

10

HAJIME ISAYAMA

"Attack on Titan" Character Introductions

104th Corps

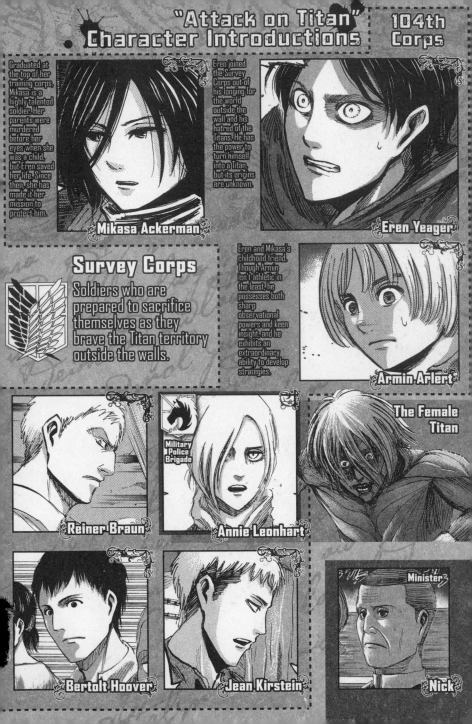

Graduated at the top of her training corps, Mikasa is a highly talented soldier. Her parents were murdered before her eyes when she was a child, but Eren saved her life. Since then, she has made it her mission to protect him.

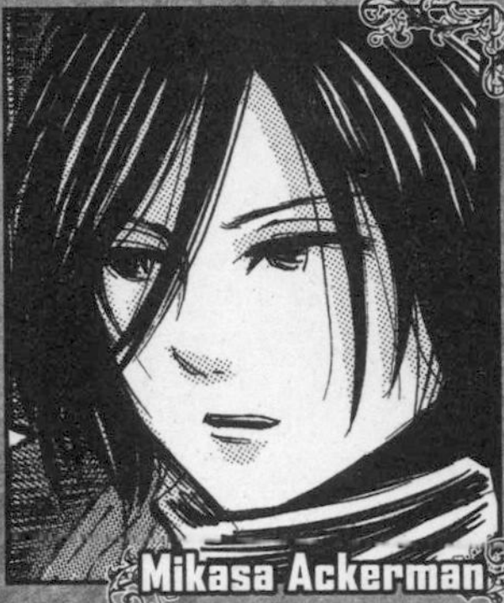

Mikasa Ackerman

Eren joined the Survey Corps out of his longing for the world outside the wall and his hatred of the Titans. He has the power to turn himself into a Titan, but its origins are unknown.

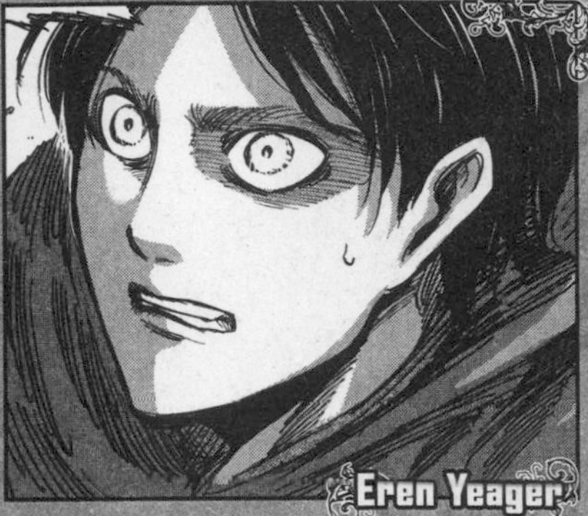

Eren Yeager

Survey Corps

Soldiers who are prepared to sacrifice themselves as they brave the Titan territory outside the walls.

Eren and Mikasa's childhood friend. Though Armin isn't athletic in the least, he possesses both sharp observational powers and keen insight, and he exhibits an extraordinary ability to develop strategies.

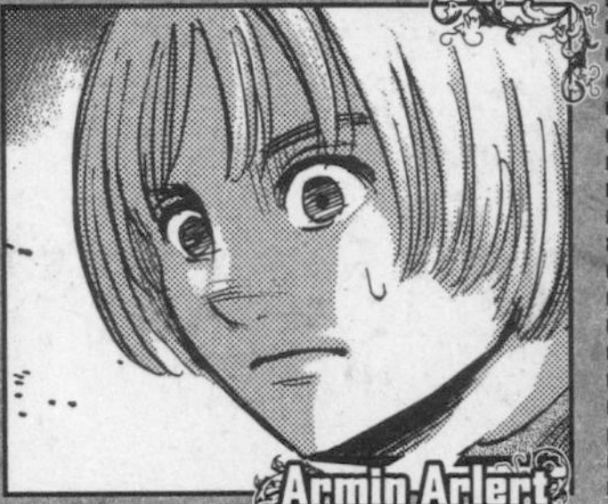

Armin Arlert

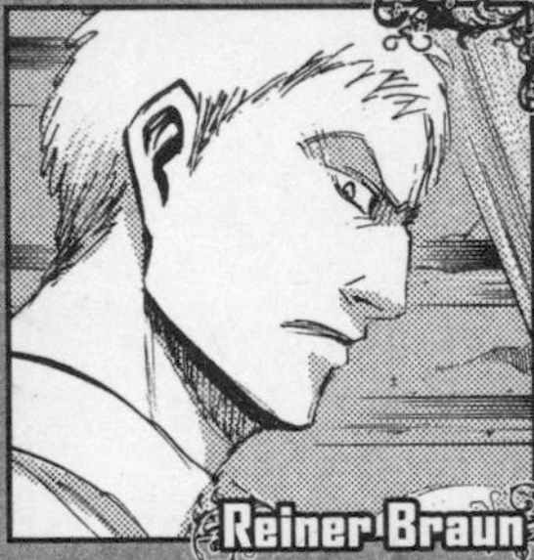

Reiner Braun

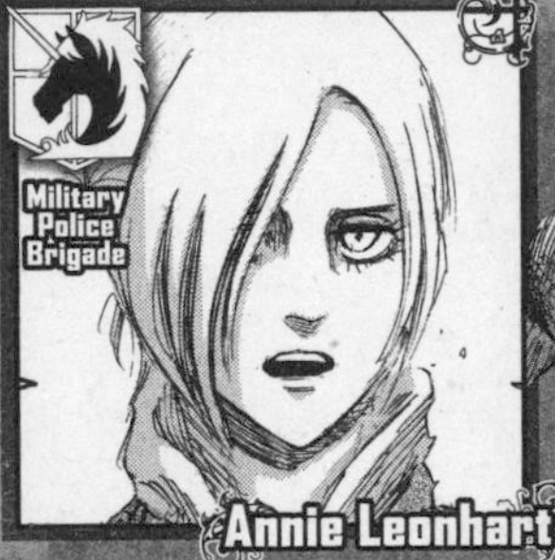
Military Police Brigade

Annie Leonhart

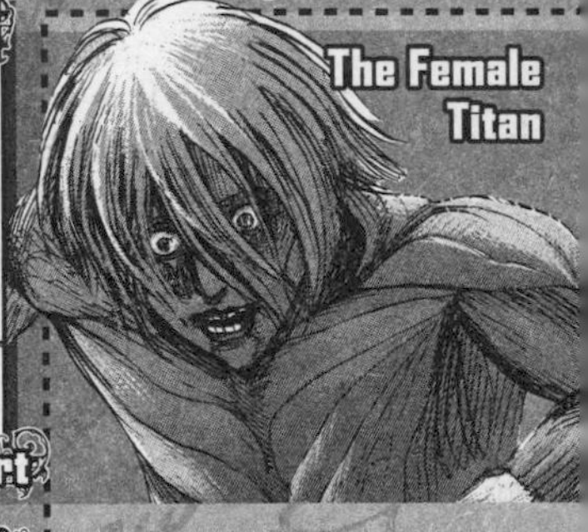

The Female Titan

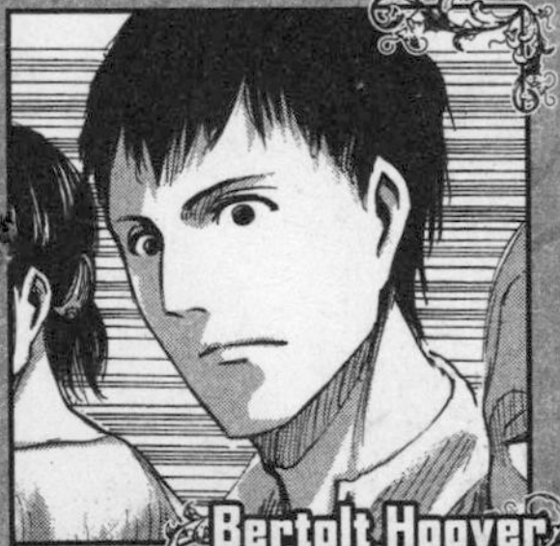

Bertolt Hoover

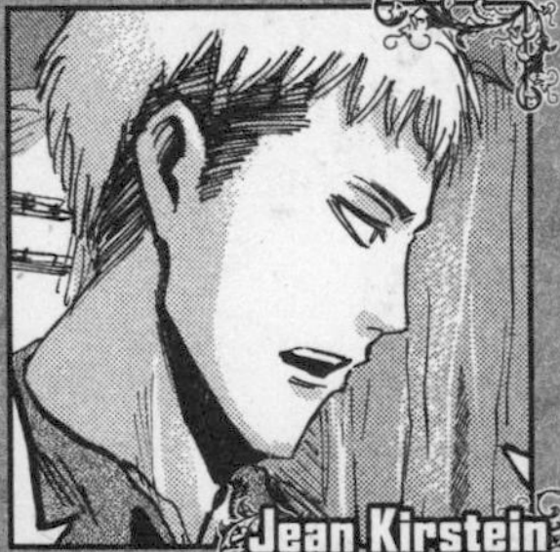

Jean Kirstein

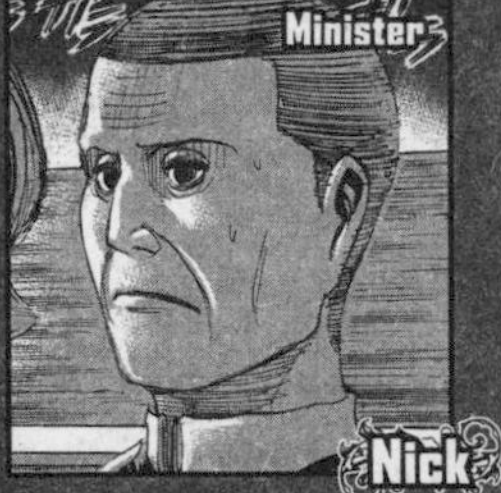

Minister

Nick

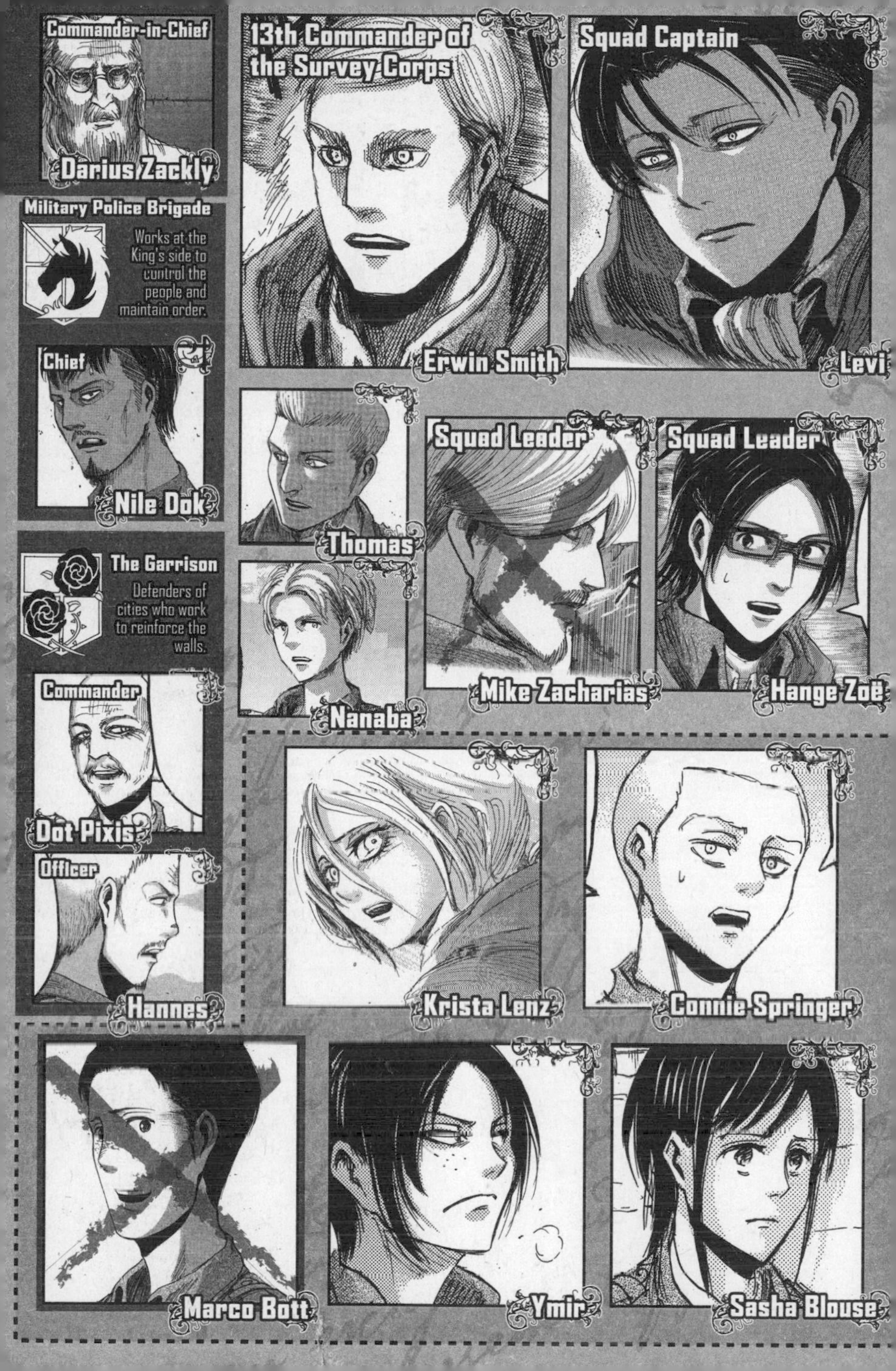
Squad Captain
Levi
13th Commander of the Survey Corps
Erwin Smith
Squad Leader
Hange Zoë
Squad Leader
Mike Zacharias
Thomas
Nanaba
Connie Springer
Krista Lenz
Commander-in-Chief
Darius Zackly
Military Police Brigade
Works at the King's side to control the people and maintain order.
Chief
Nile Dok
The Garrison
Defenders of cities who work to reinforce the walls.
Commander
Dot Pixis
Officer
Hannes
Sasha Blouse
Ymir
Marco Bott

ATTACK on TITAN

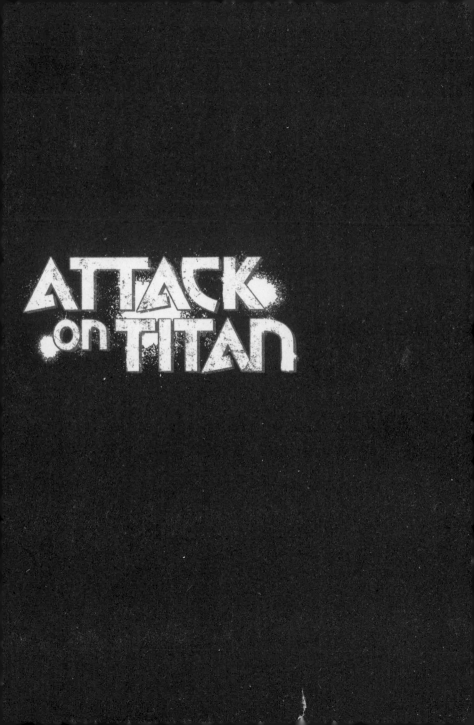

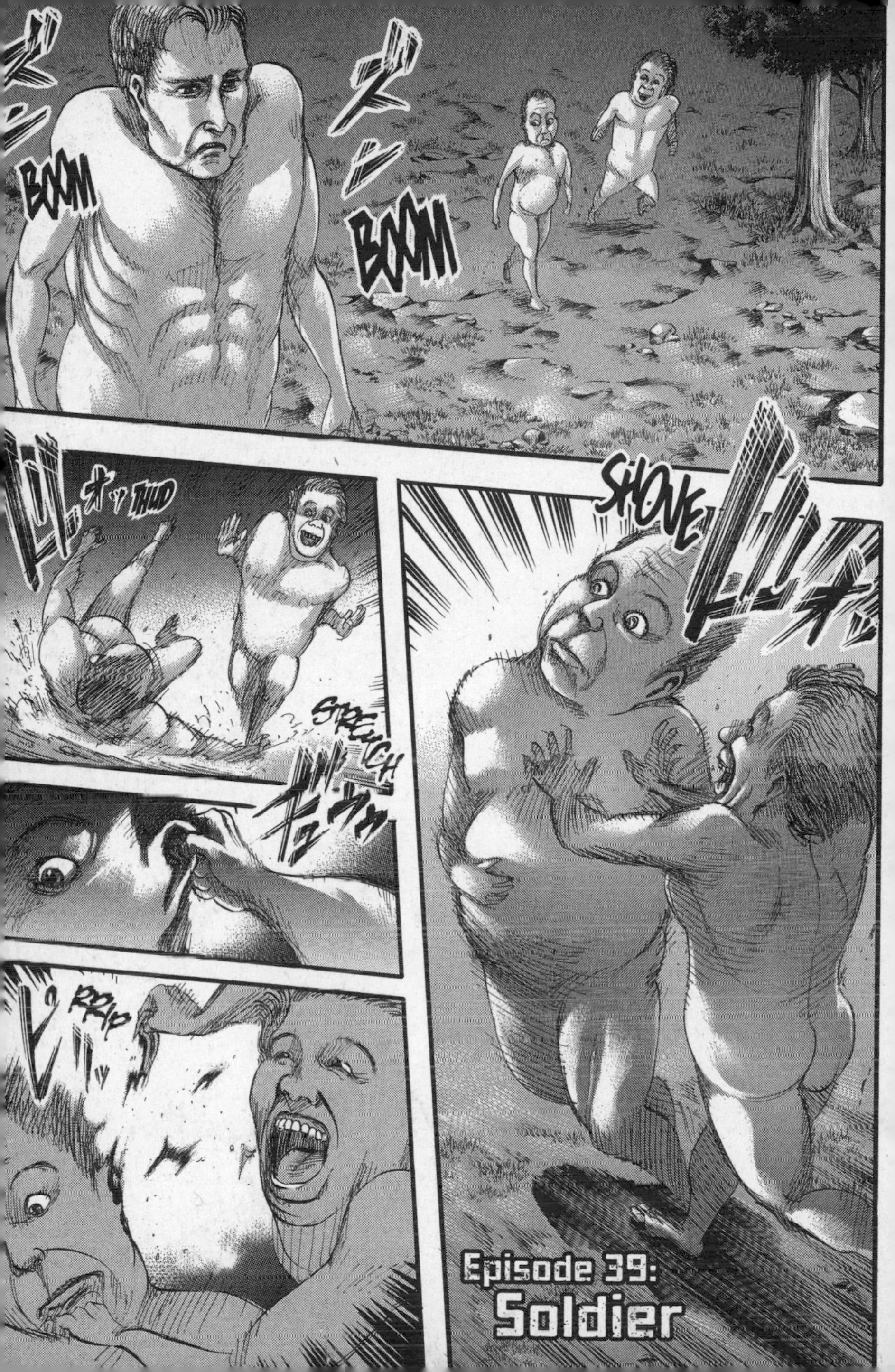
BOOM
BOOM
SHOVE
Episode 39:
Soldier
THUD
STRETCH
RRIP

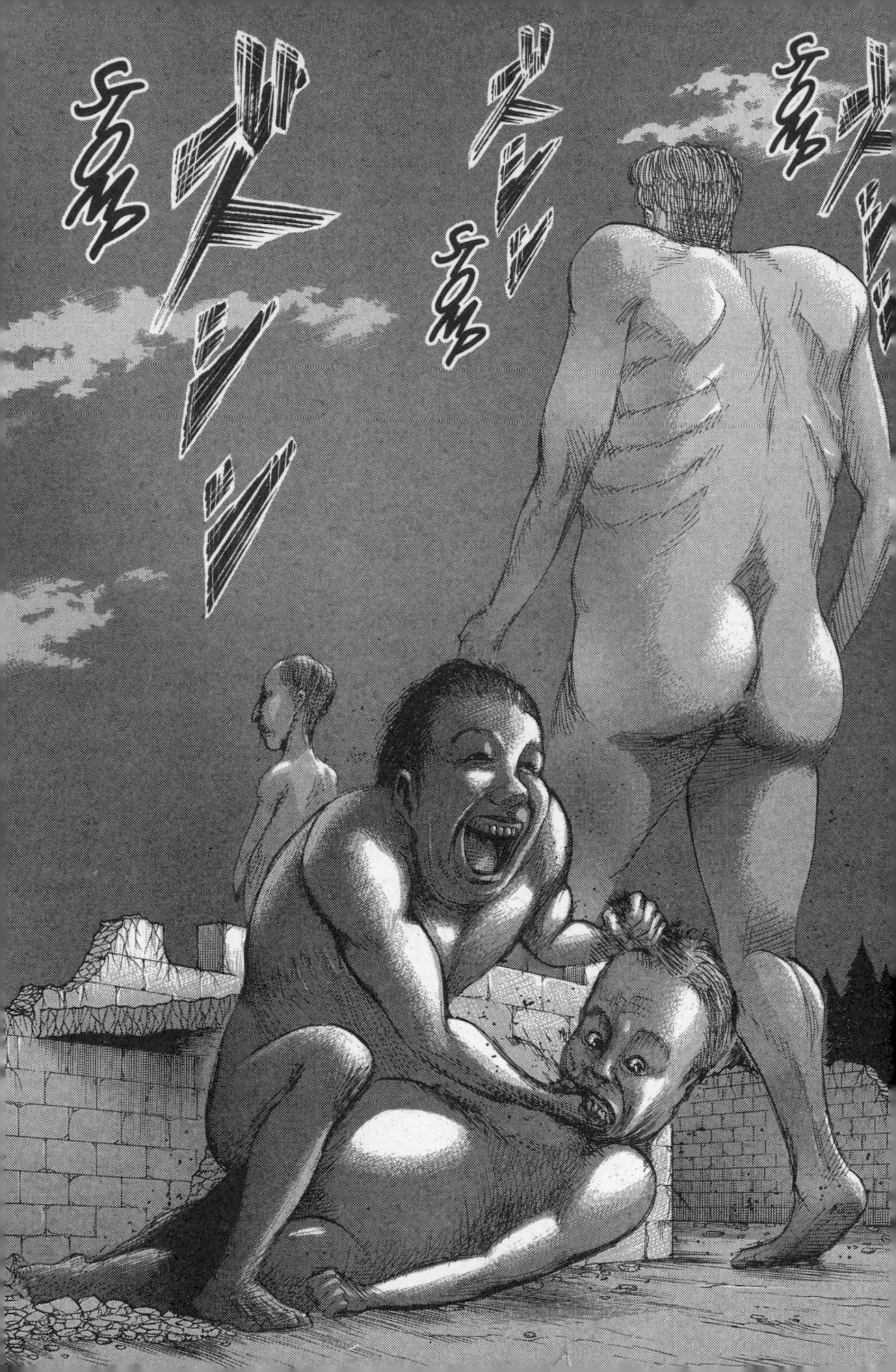
ズシン
ズシン

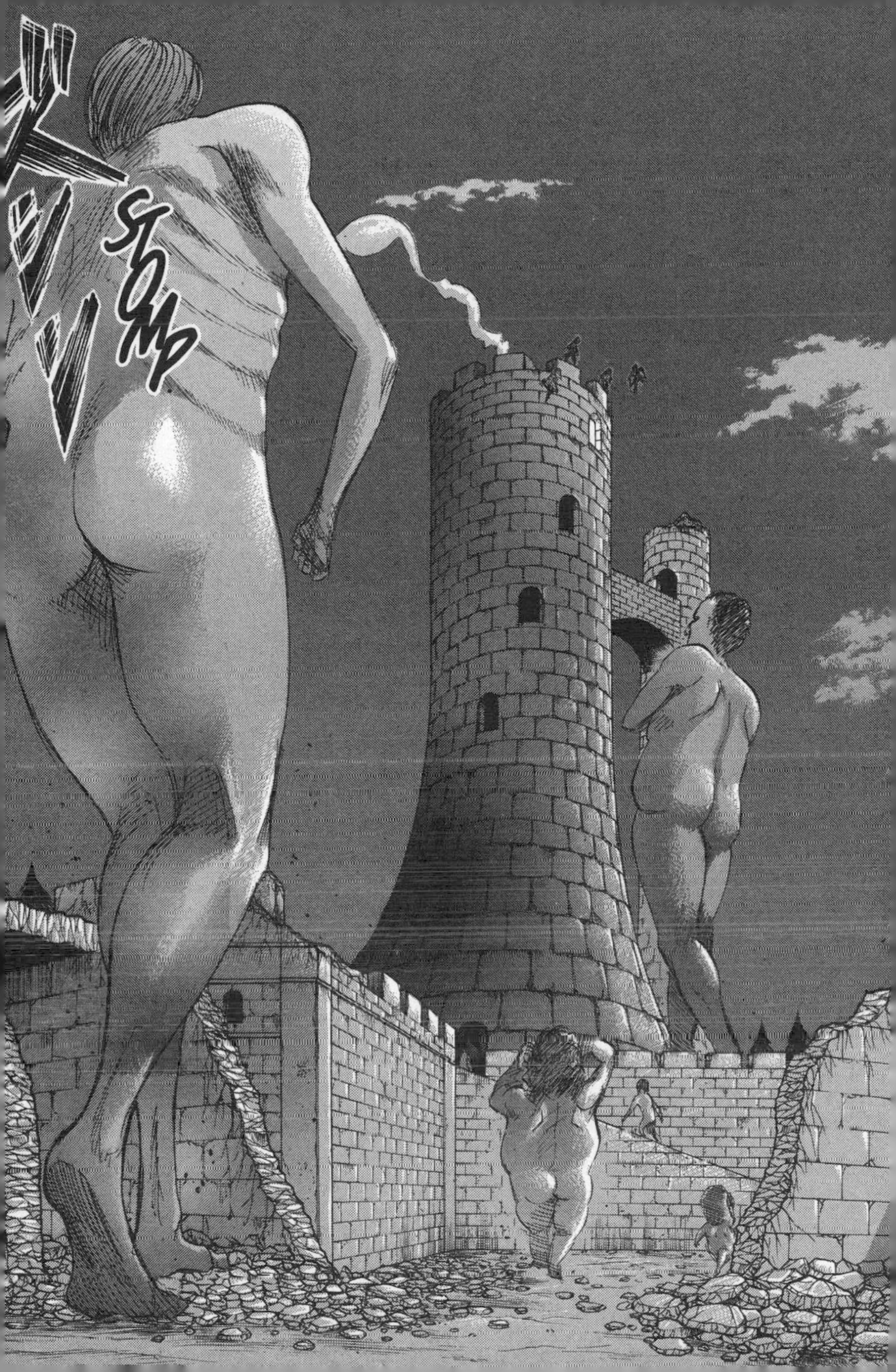
STOMP

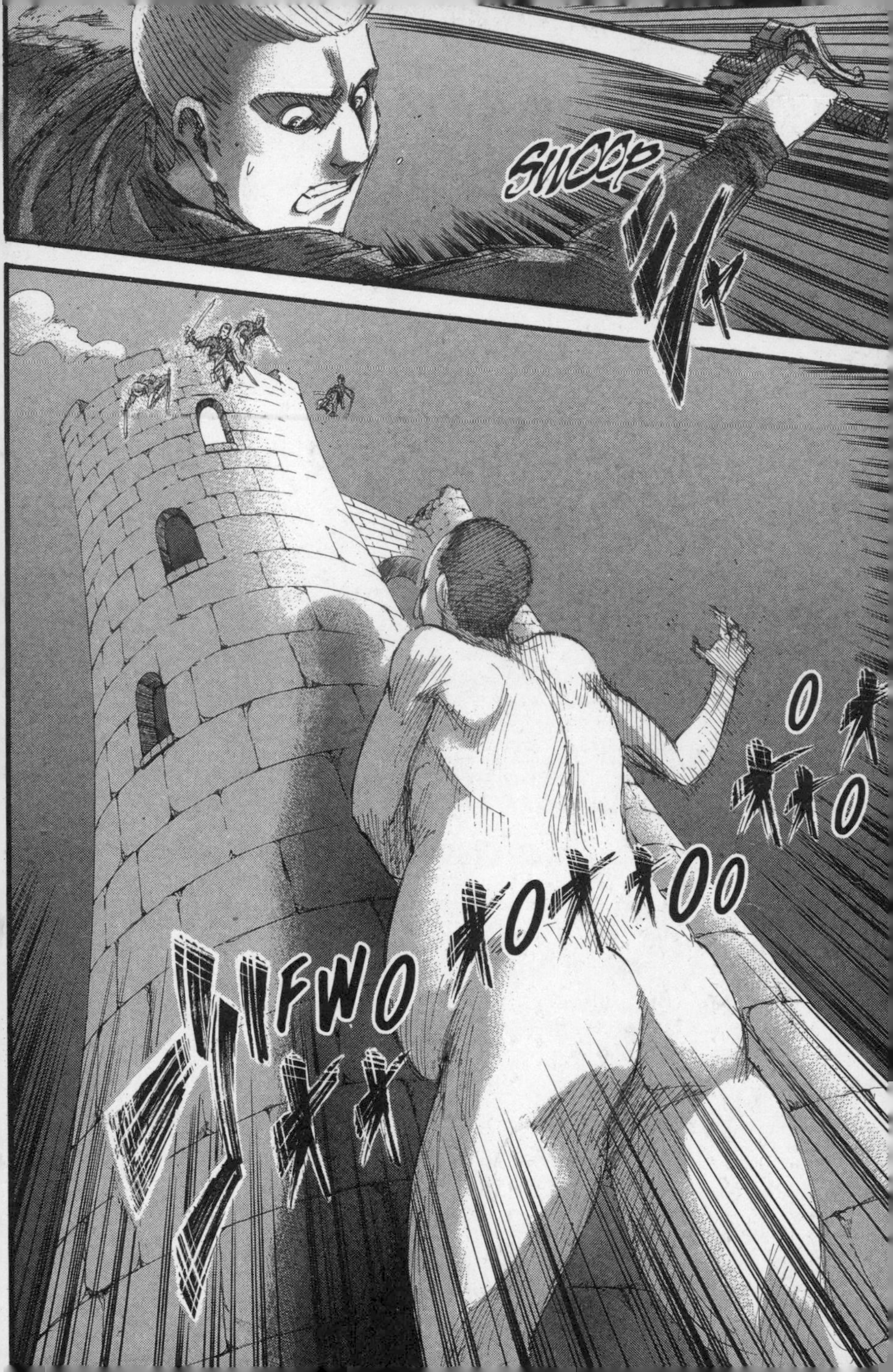
SWOOP
FWOOOOOO

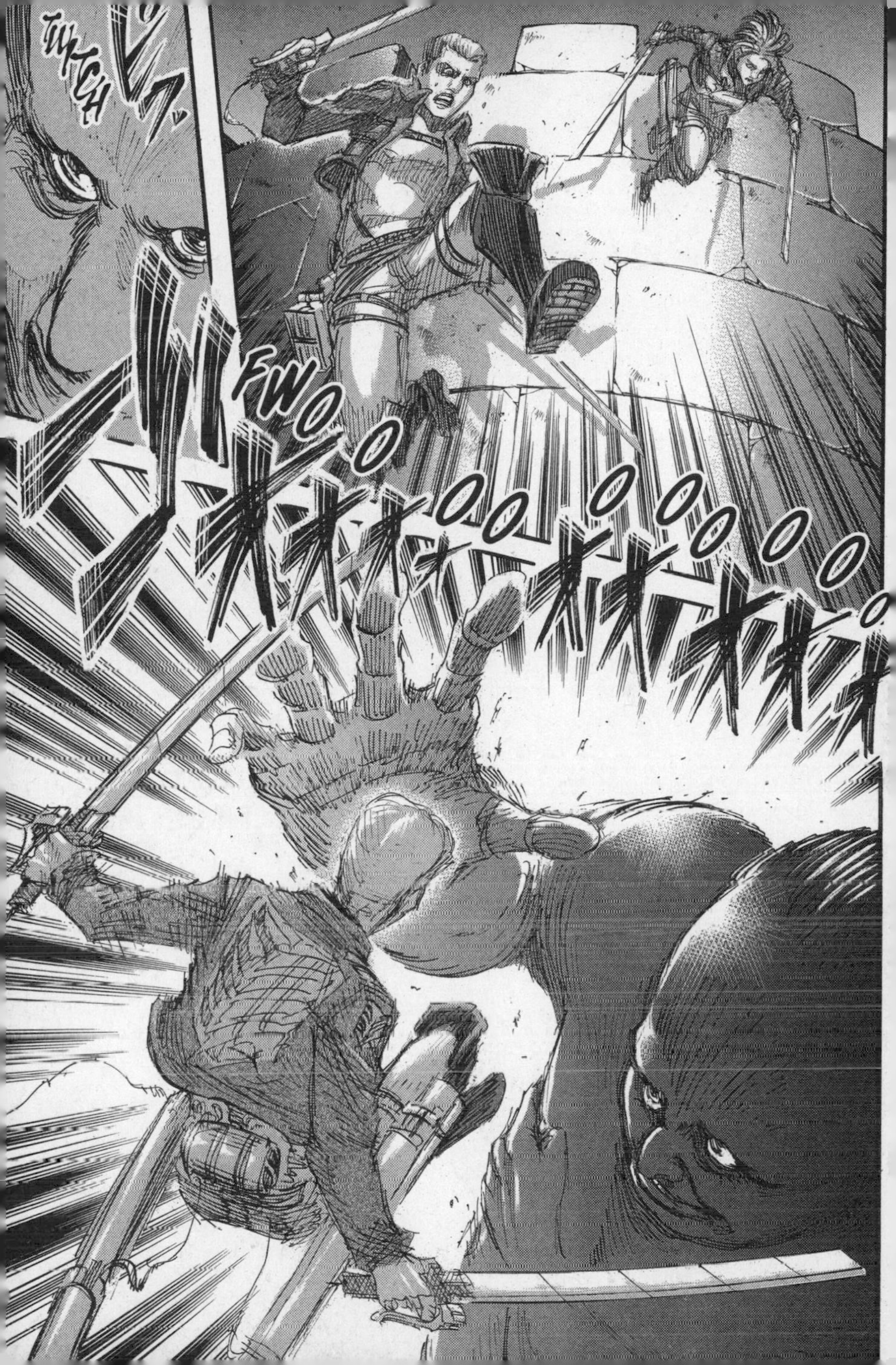
TWITCH
FWOOOOOOOOOOO

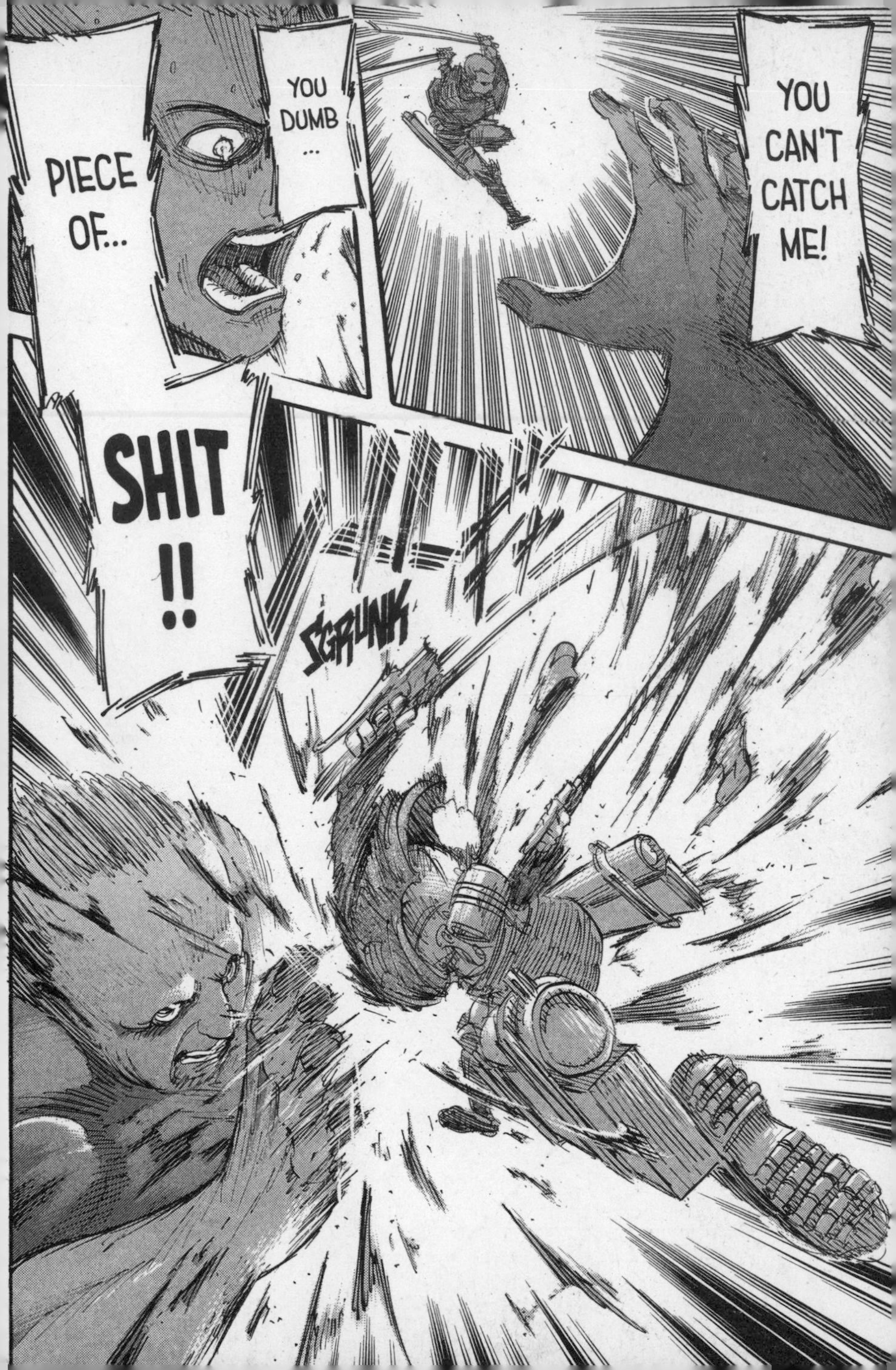
YOU CAN'T CATCH ME!
YOU DUMB ...
PIECE OF...
SHIT !!
SGRUNK

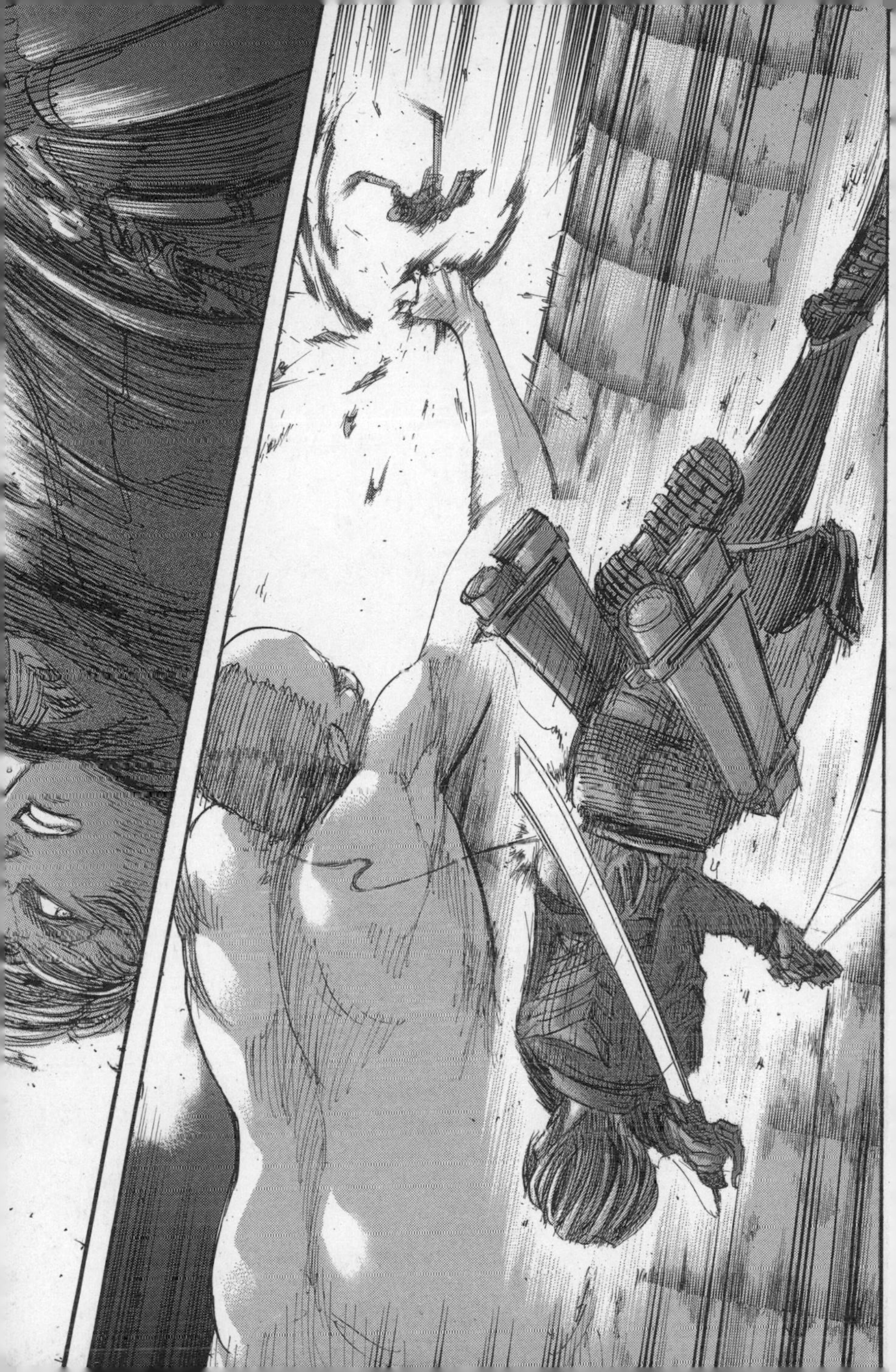

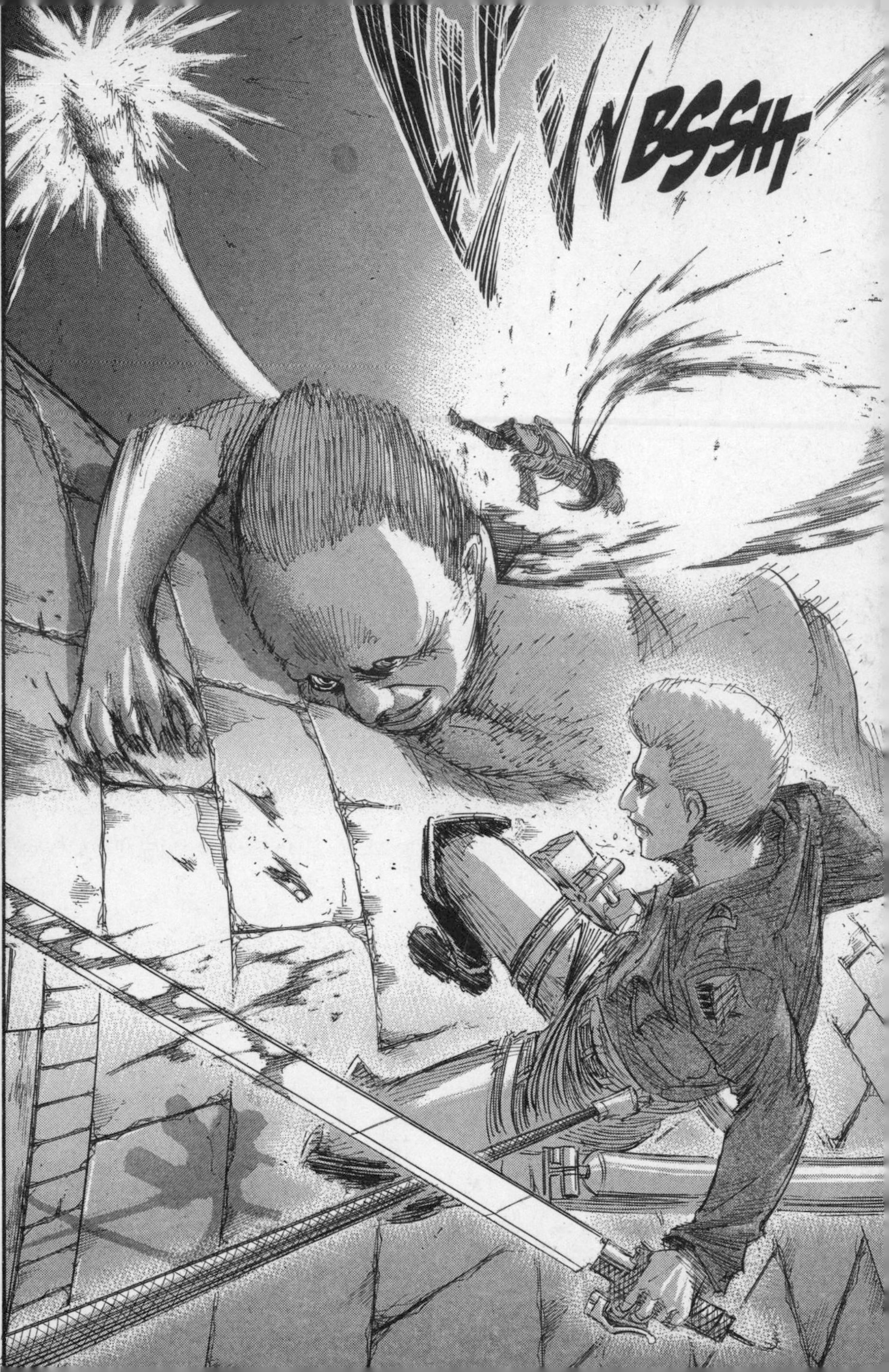
BSSHT

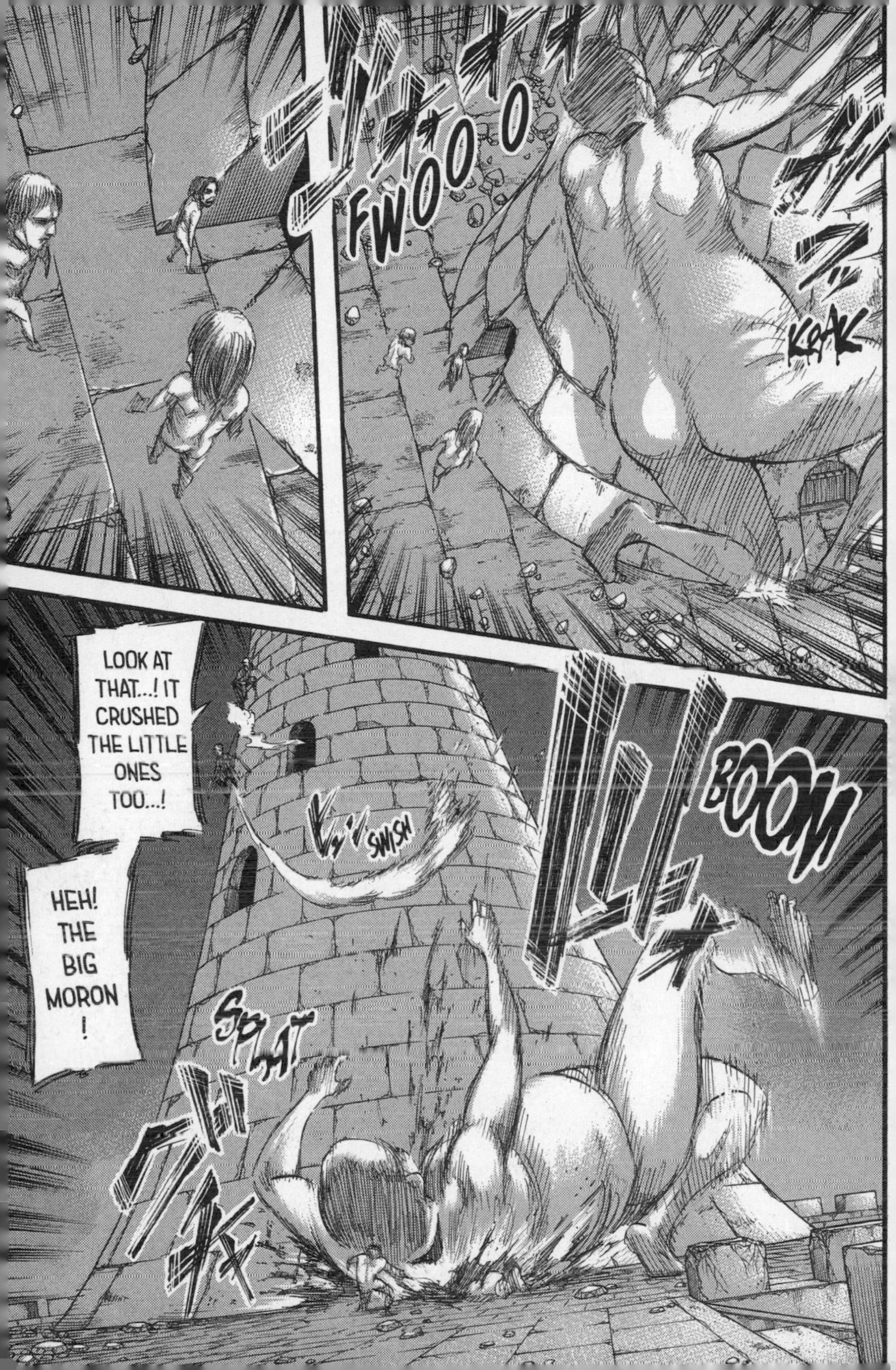
FWOOO
KRAK
BOOM
LOOK AT THAT...! IT CRUSHED THE LITTLE ONES TOO...!
SWISH
HEH! THE BIG MORON!
SPLAT

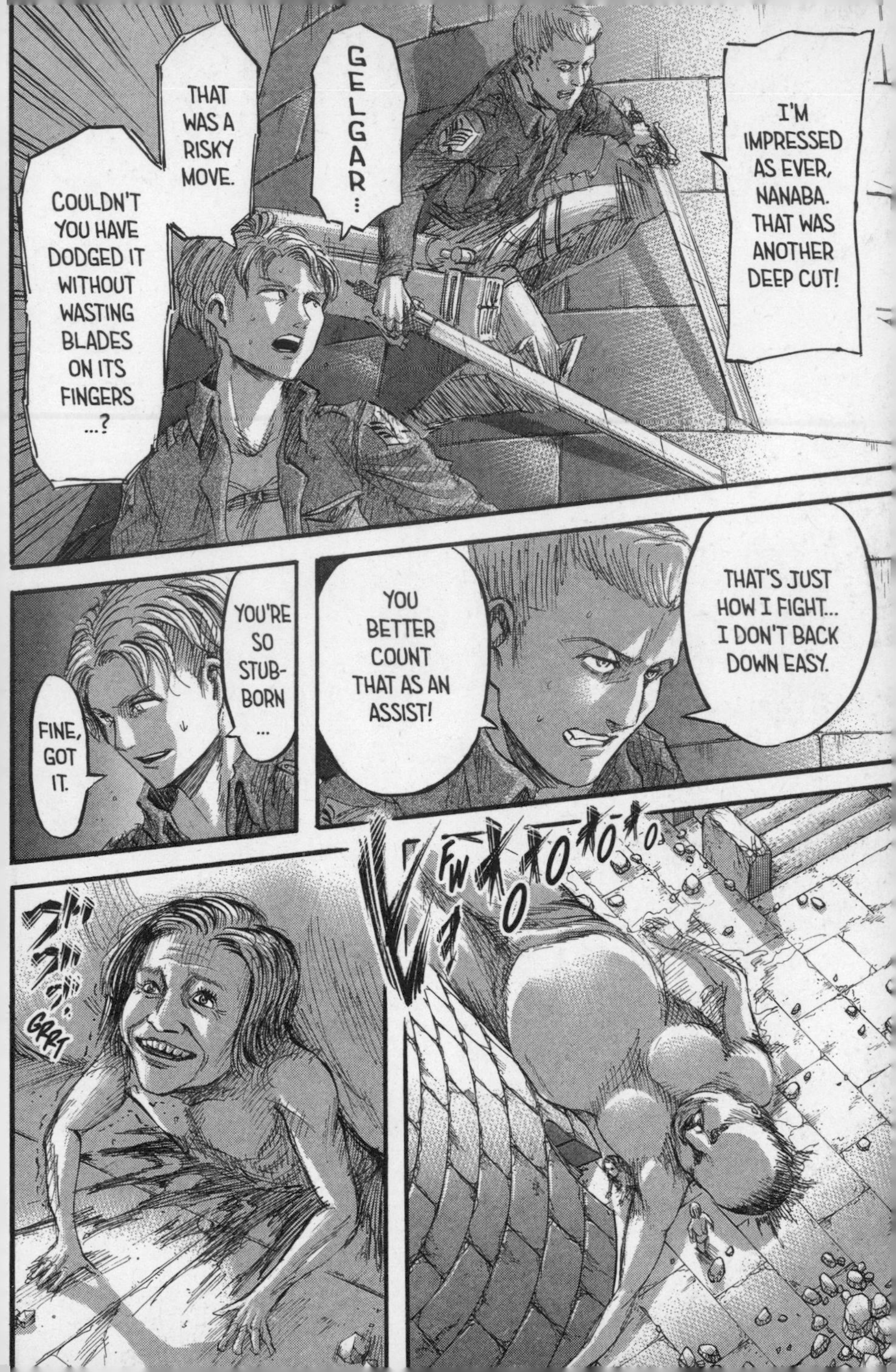
I'M IMPRESSED AS EVER, NANABA. THAT WAS ANOTHER DEEP CUT!
GELGAR...
THAT WAS A RISKY MOVE.
COULDN'T YOU HAVE DODGED IT WITHOUT WASTING BLADES ON ITS FINGERS ...?
THAT'S JUST HOW I FIGHT... I DON'T BACK DOWN EASY.
YOU BETTER COUNT THAT AS AN ASSIST!
YOU'RE SO STUBBORN ...
FINE, GOT IT.
FWOOOOO
GRR

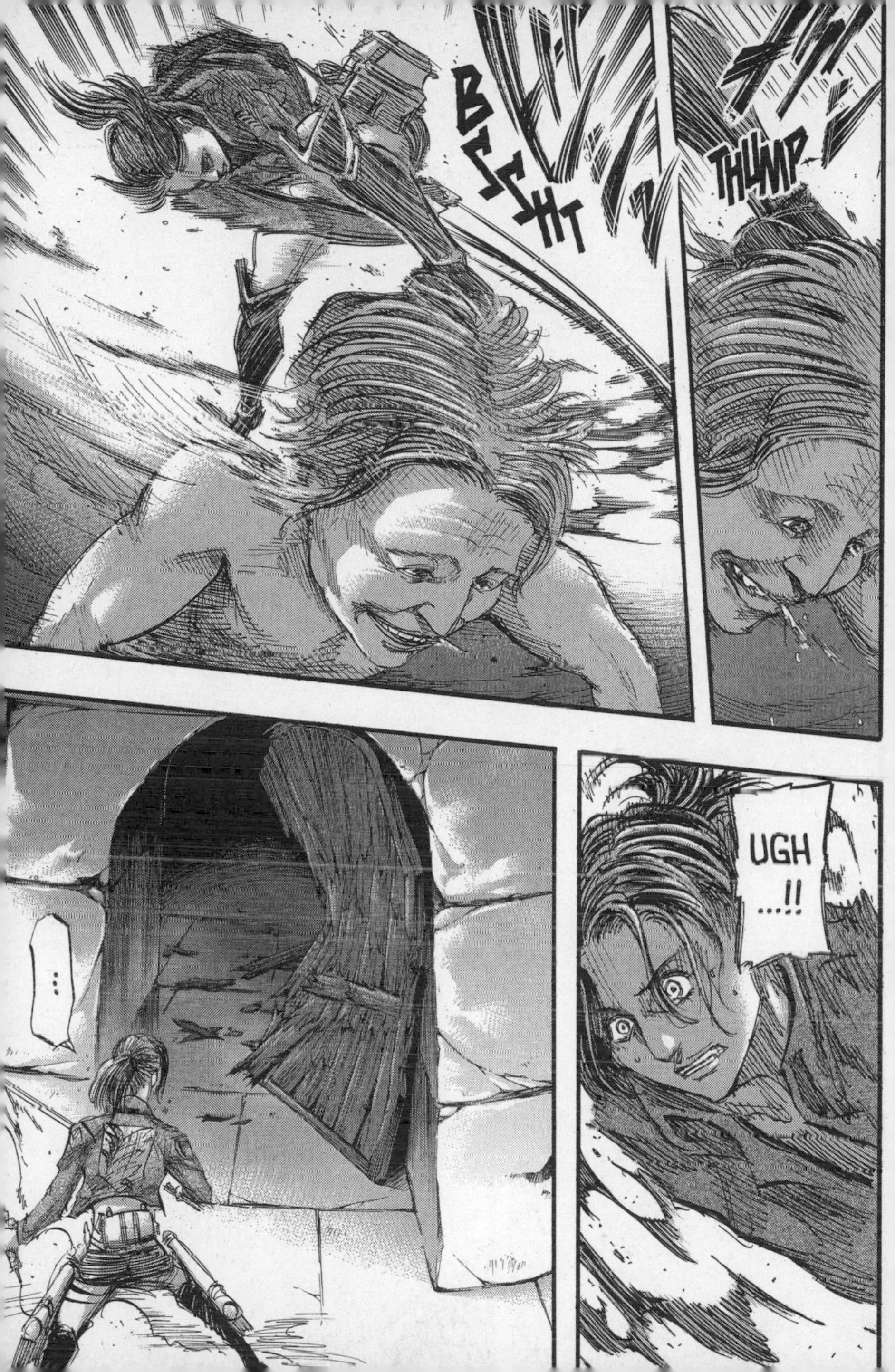
THUMP
BSSHT
UGH ...!!
...

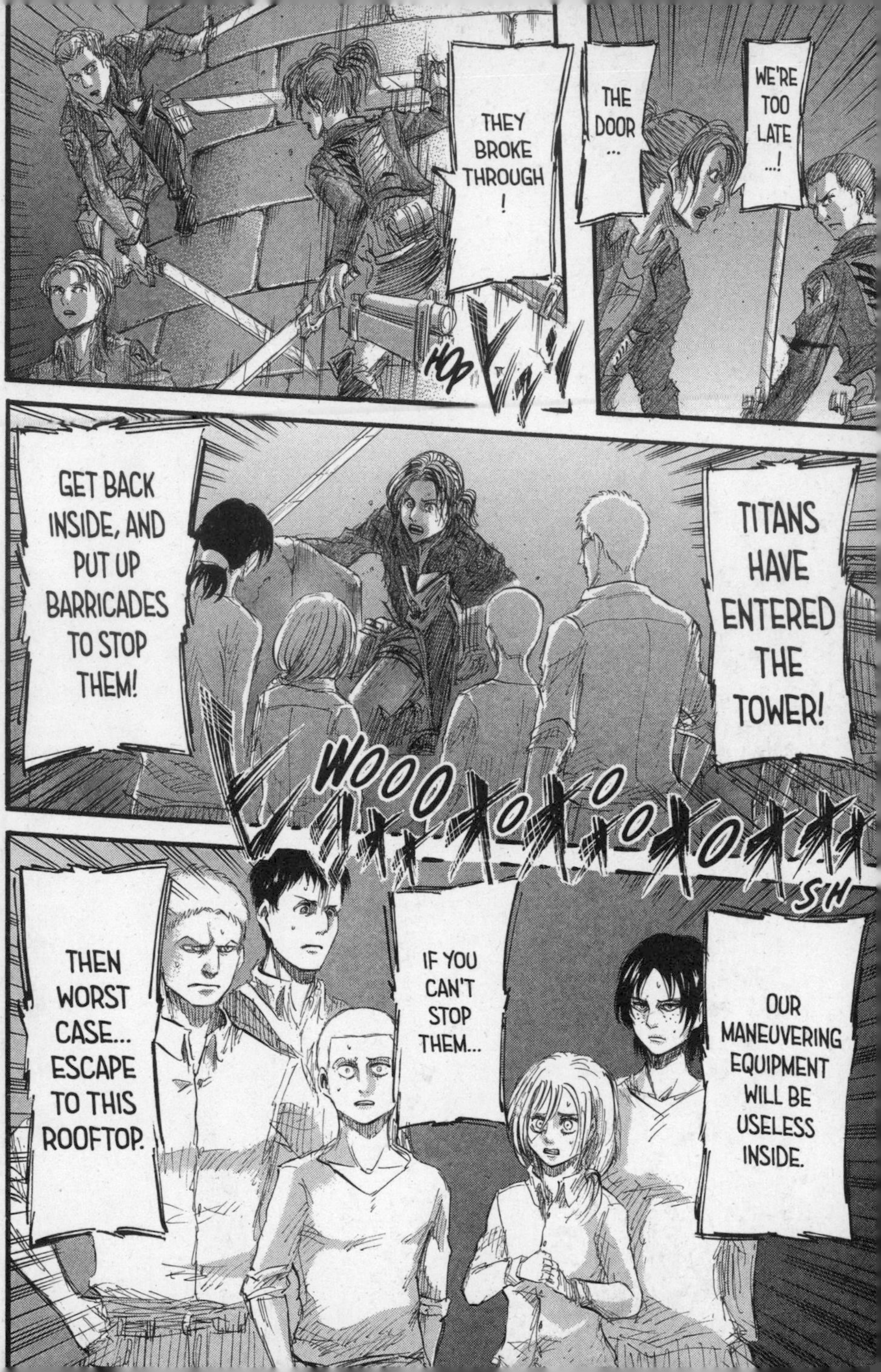
WE'RE TOO LATE ...!
THE DOOR ...
THEY BROKE THROUGH !
HOP
TITANS HAVE ENTERED THE TOWER!
GET BACK INSIDE, AND PUT UP BARRICADES TO STOP THEM!
WOOOOOO
SH
OUR MANEUVERING EQUIPMENT WILL BE USELESS INSIDE.
IF YOU CAN'T STOP THEM...
THEN WORST CASE... ESCAPE TO THIS ROOFTOP.

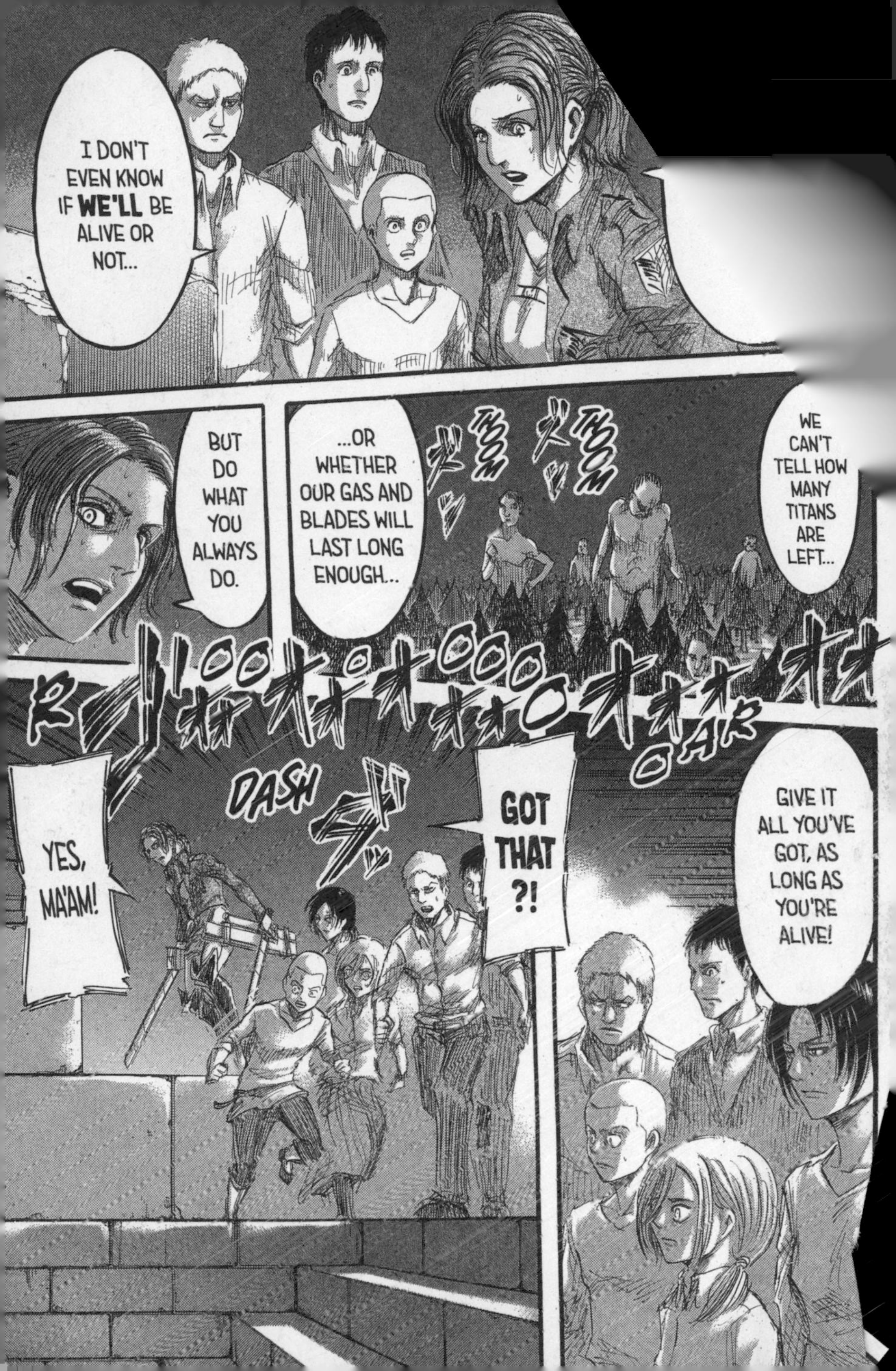
I DON'T EVEN KNOW IF **WE'LL** BE ALIVE OR NOT...
WE CAN'T TELL HOW MANY TITANS ARE LEFT...
THOOM
THOOM
...OR WHETHER OUR GAS AND BLADES WILL LAST LONG ENOUGH...
BUT DO WHAT YOU ALWAYS DO.
ROOOOOOOOOOAR
GIVE IT ALL YOU'VE GOT, AS LONG AS YOU'RE ALIVE!
GOT THAT?!
DASH
YES, MA'AM!

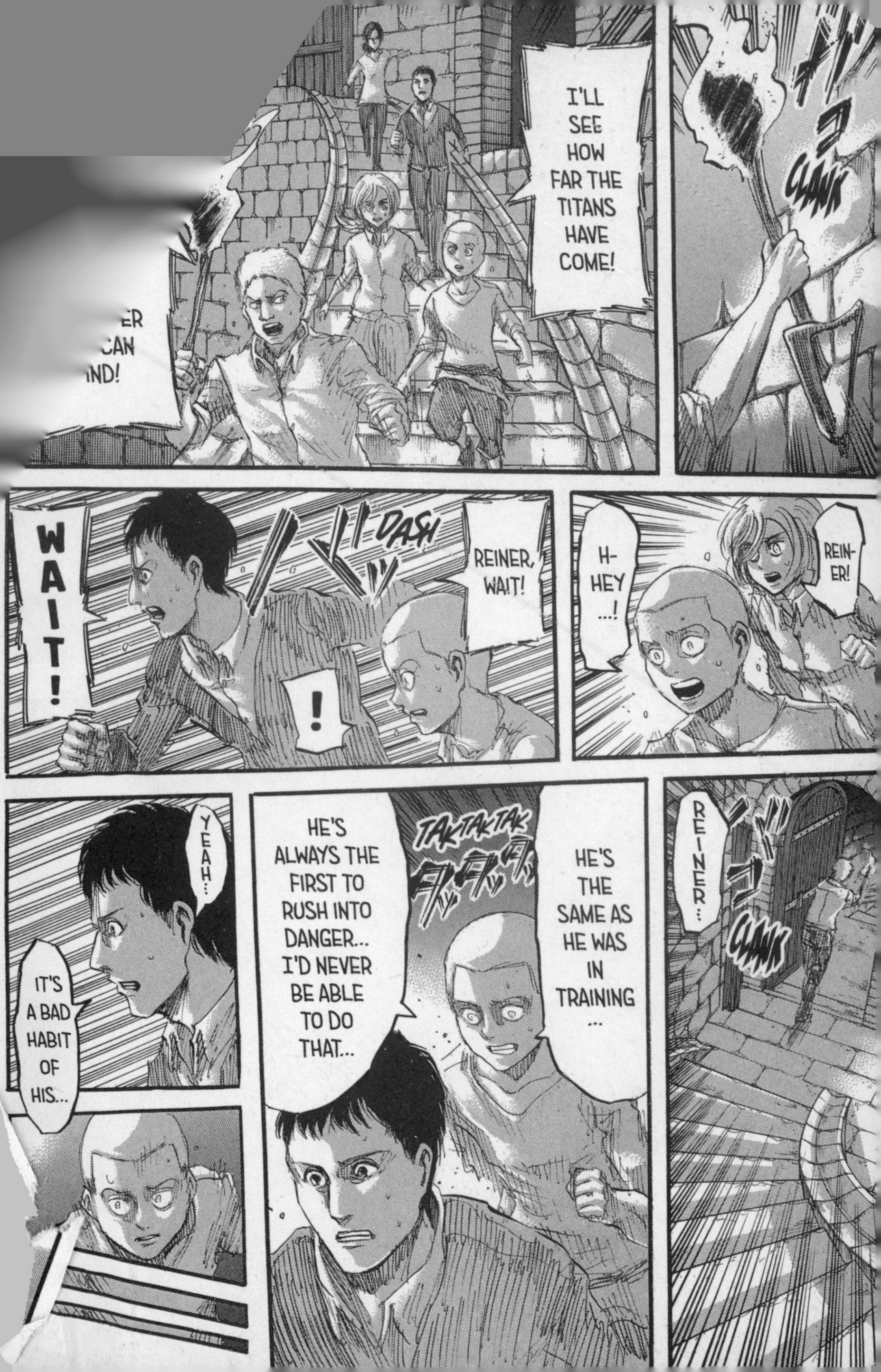
CLANK
I'LL SEE HOW FAR THE TITANS HAVE COME!
ER CAN IND!
REIN-ER!
H-HEY...!
REINER, WAIT!
DASH
!
WAIT!
REINER...
CLANK
HE'S THE SAME AS HE WAS IN TRAINING...
TAKTAKTAK
HE'S ALWAYS THE FIRST TO RUSH INTO DANGER... I'D NEVER BE ABLE TO DO THAT...
YEAH...
IT'S A BAD HABIT OF HIS...

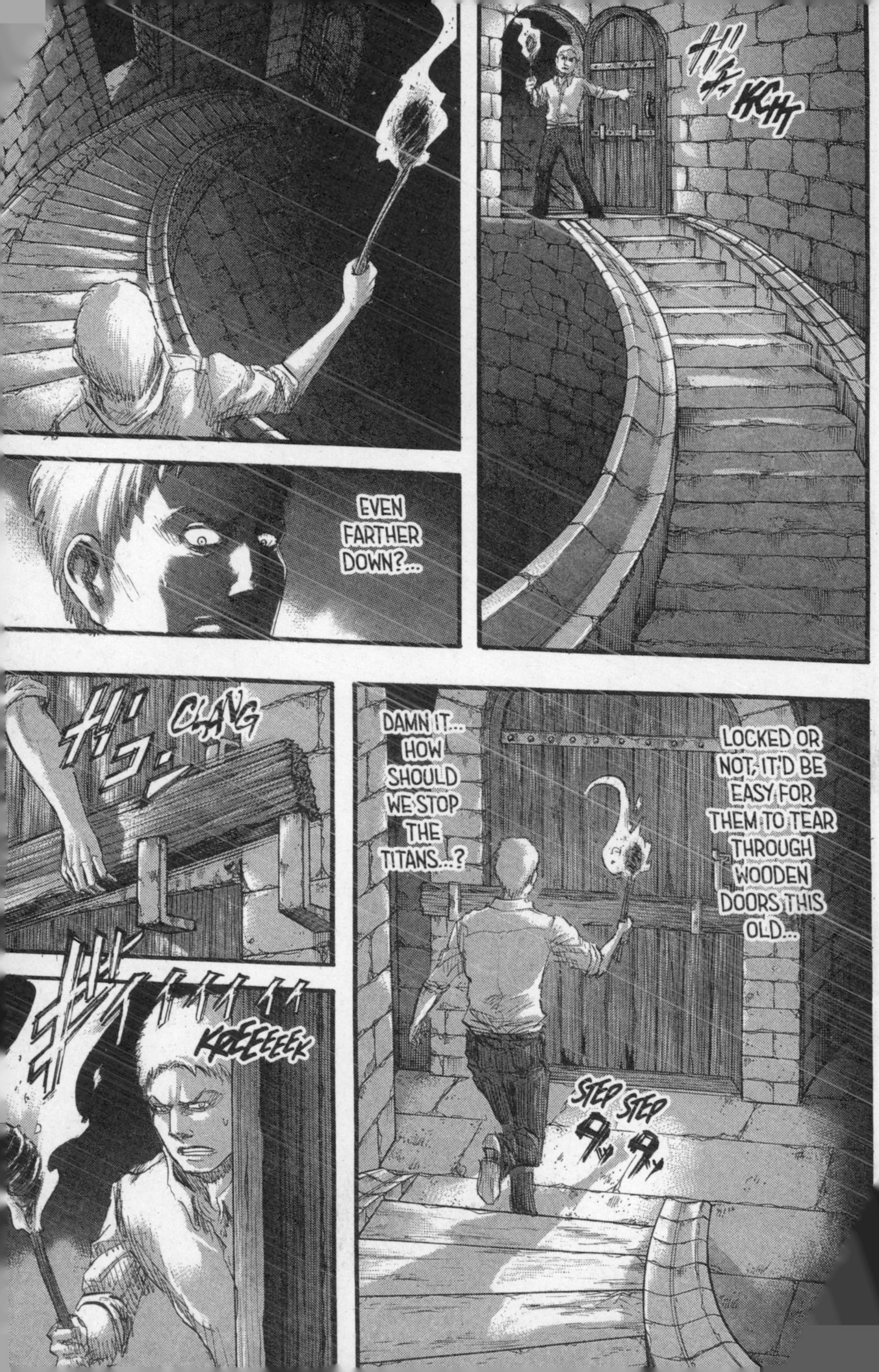
KCHK
EVEN FARTHER DOWN?...
LOCKED OR NOT, IT'D BE EASY FOR THEM TO TEAR THROUGH WOODEN DOORS THIS OLD...
DAMN IT... HOW SHOULD WE STOP THE TITANS...?
STEP STEP
CLANG
KREEEEEK

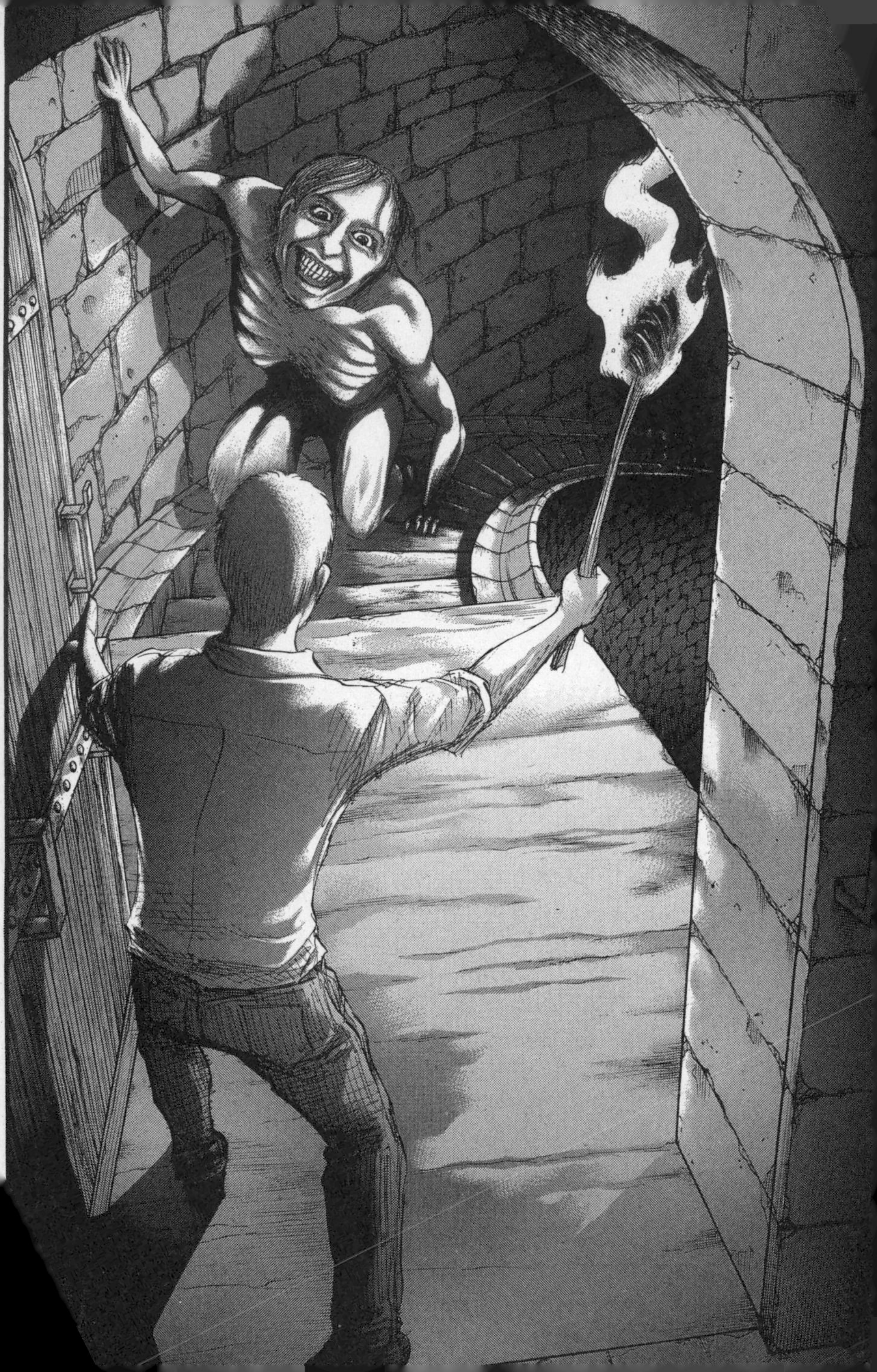

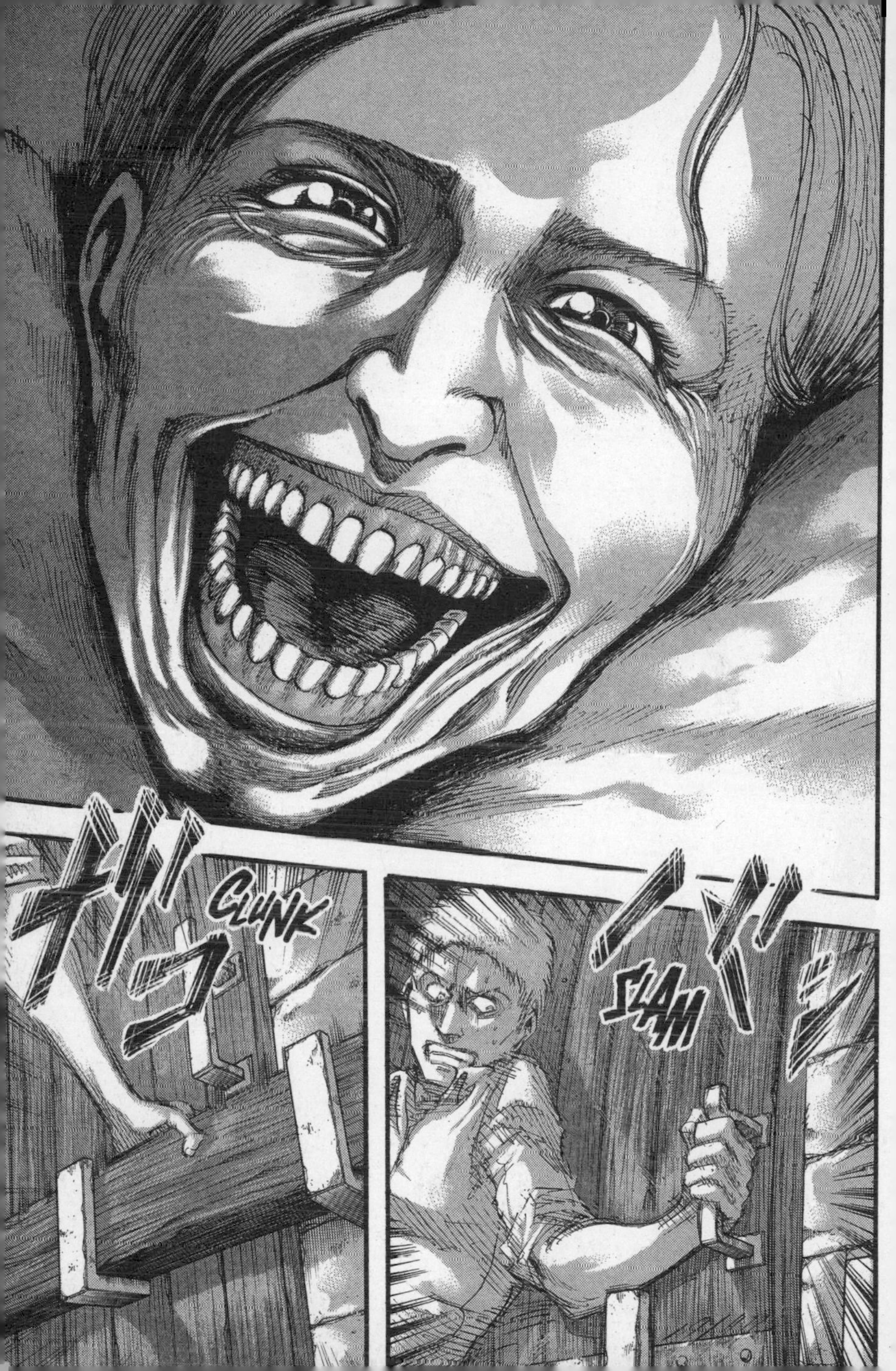
SLAM
CLUNK

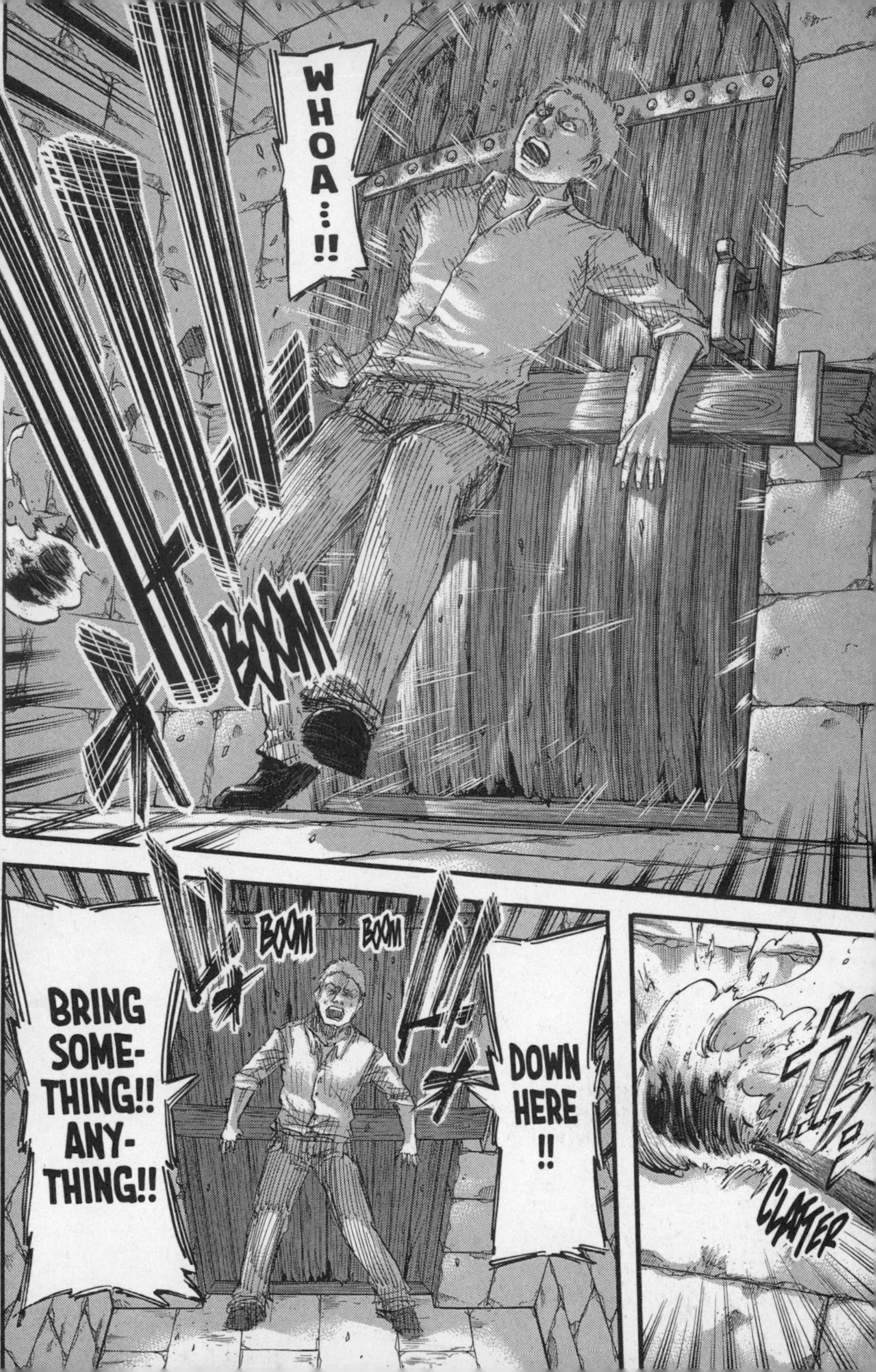
WHOA...!!
BOOM
CLATTER
BOOM
BOOM
DOWN HERE!!
BRING SOMETHING!! ANYTHING!!

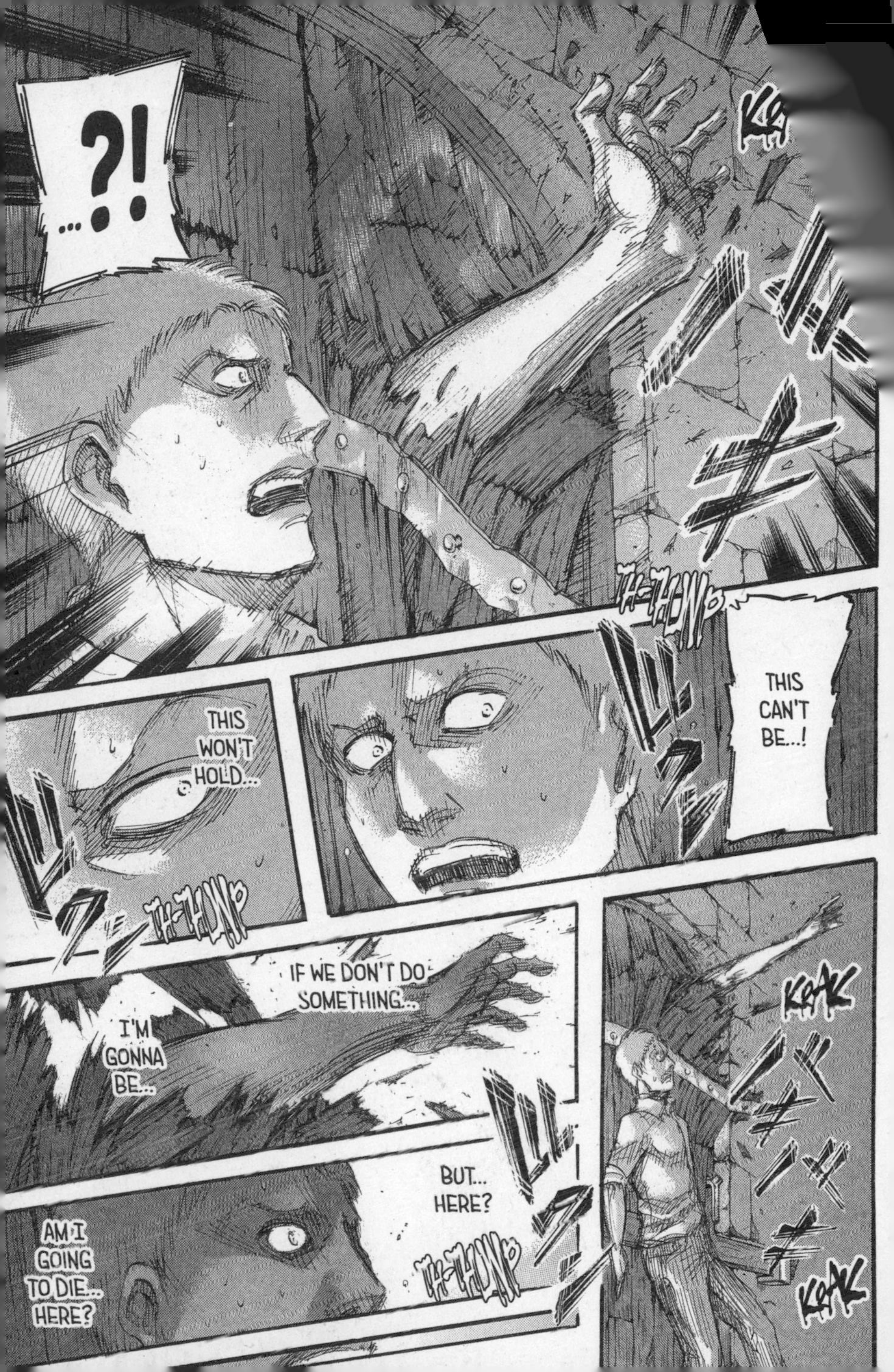

...?!
TH-THUNK
THIS CAN'T BE...!
THIS WON'T HOLD...
TH-THUNK
KRAK
KRAK
IF WE DON'T DO SOMETHING...
I'M GONNA BE...
BUT... HERE?
AM I GOING TO DIE... HERE?
TH-THUNK

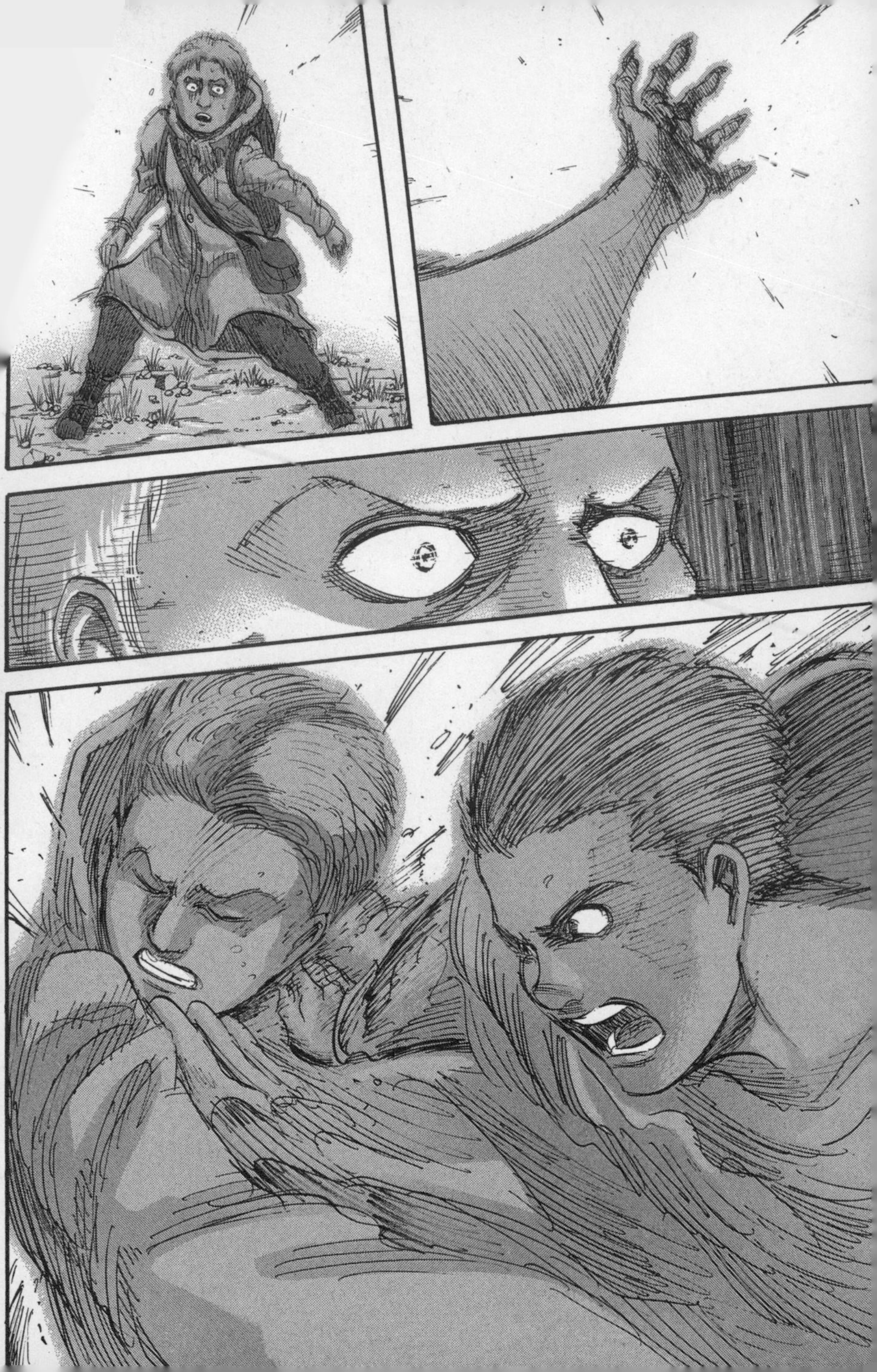

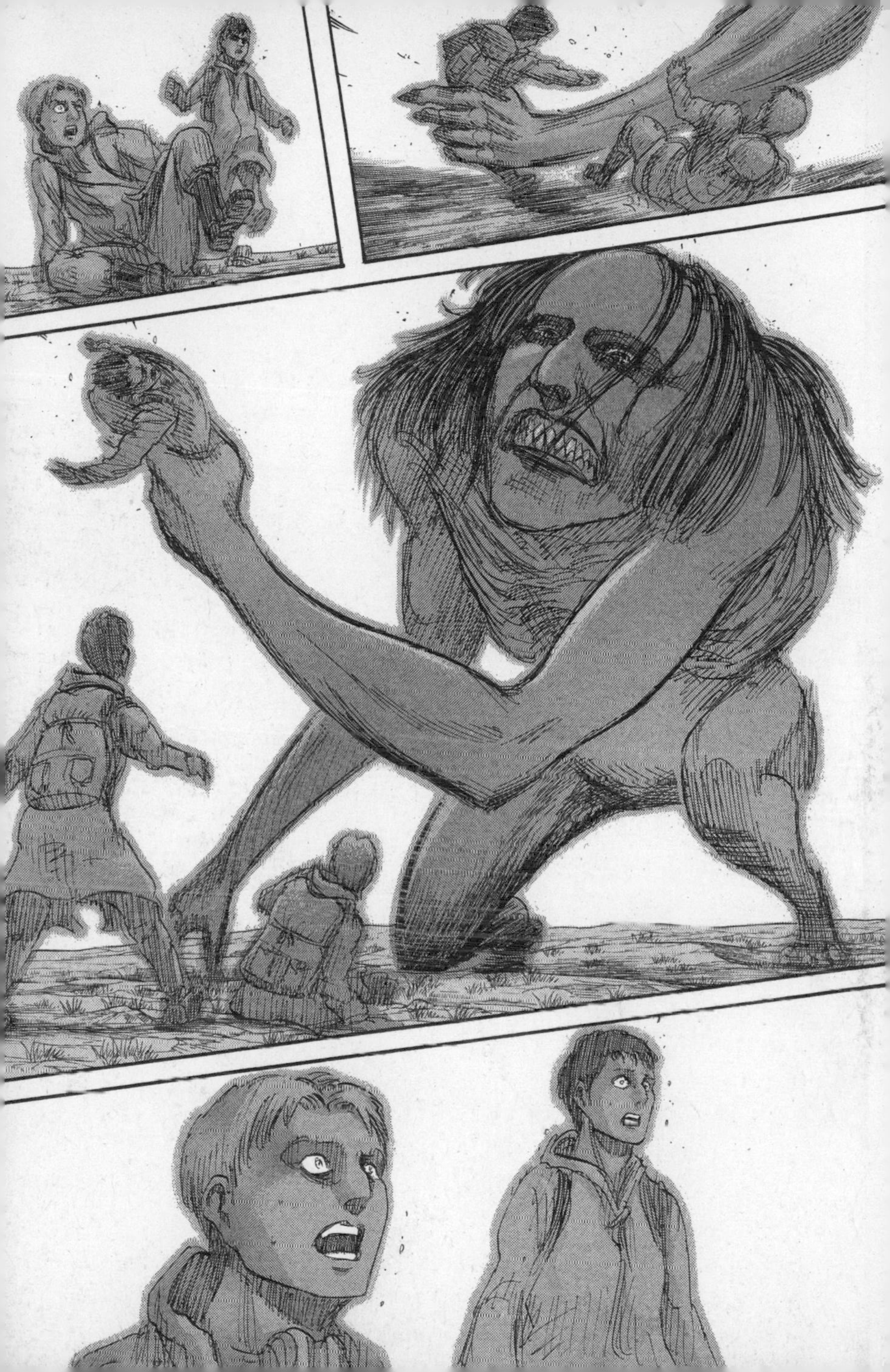

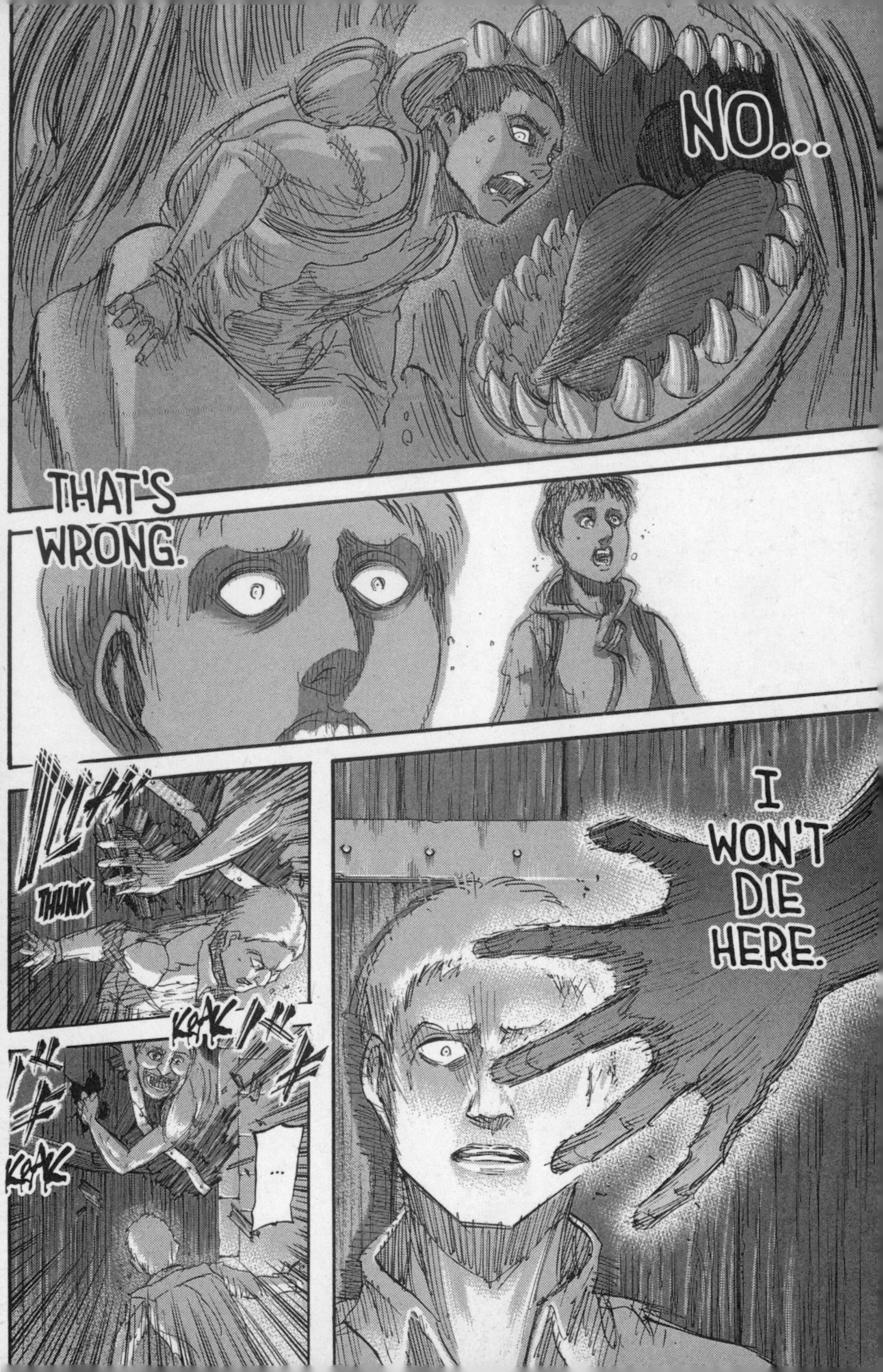
NO...
THAT'S WRONG.
I WON'T DIE HERE.
THUNK
KRAK
KRAK
...

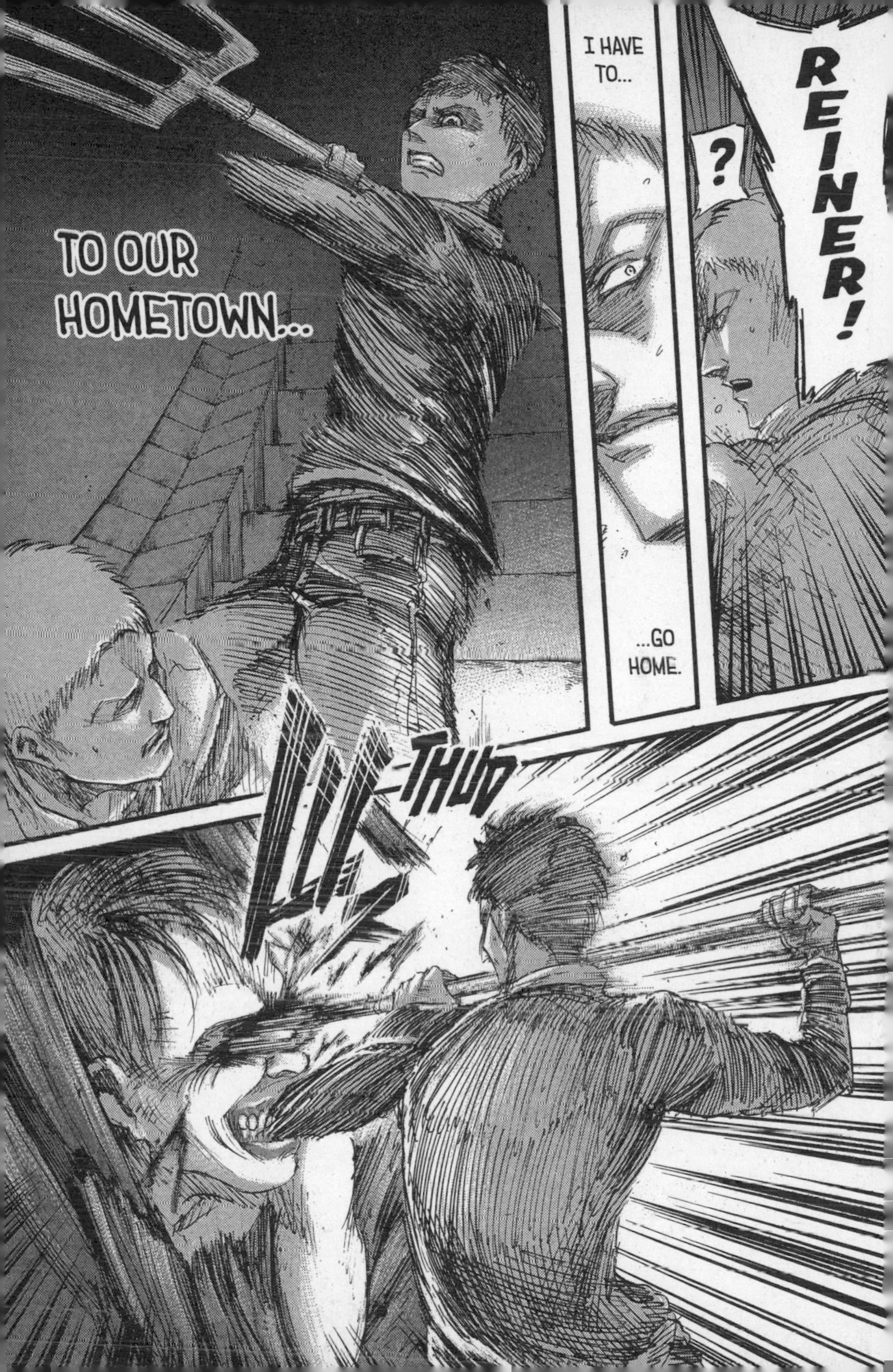
REINER!
?
I HAVE TO...
...GO HOME.
TO OUR HOMETOWN...
THUD

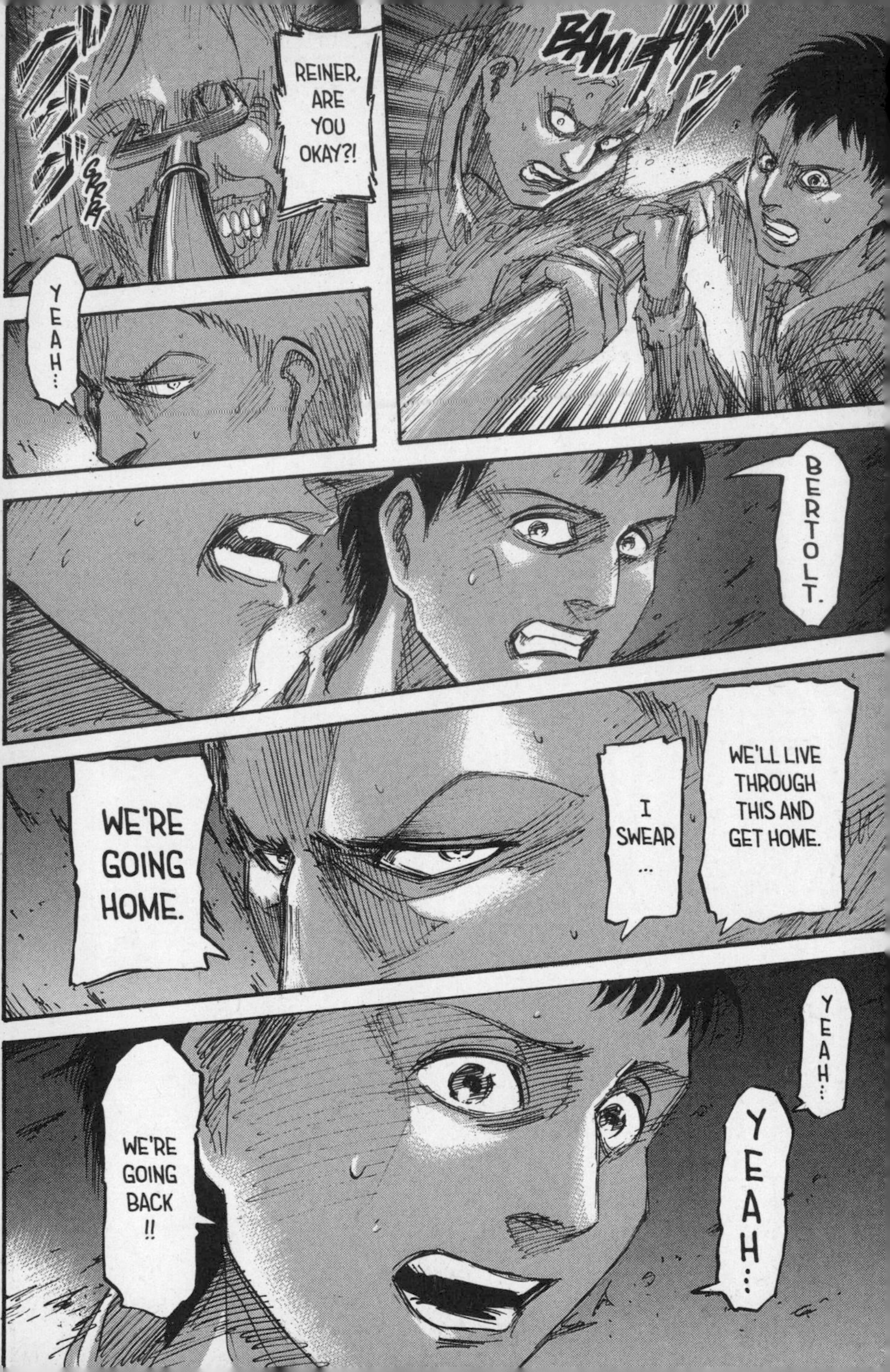
BAM
REINER, ARE YOU OKAY?!
YEAH...
BERTOLT.
WE'LL LIVE THROUGH THIS AND GET HOME.
I SWEAR ...
WE'RE GOING HOME.
YEAH...
YEAH...
WE'RE GOING BACK !!

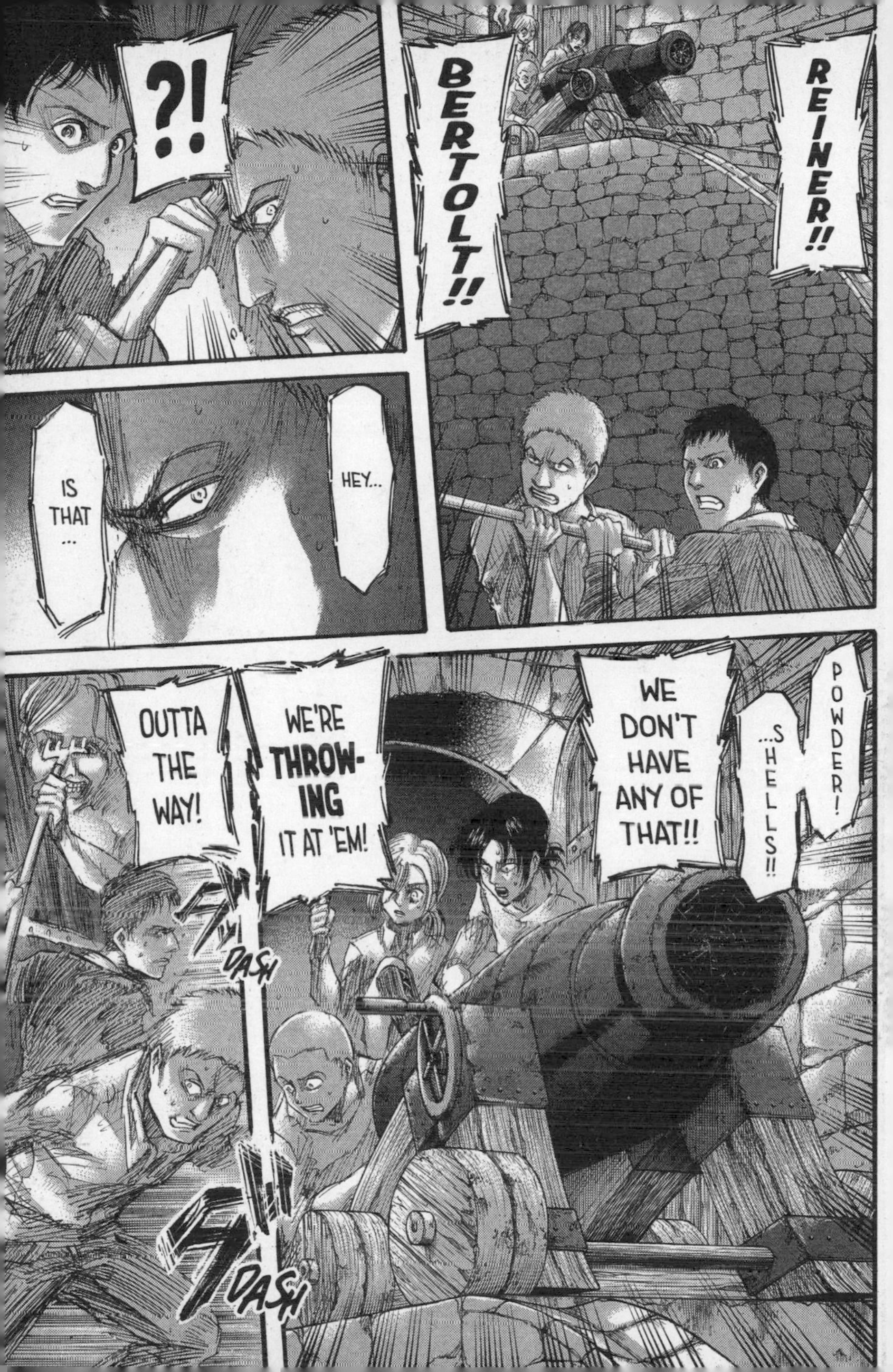
REINER!!
BERTOLT!!
?!
HEY...
IS THAT ...
POWDER!
...SHELLS!!
WE DON'T HAVE ANY OF THAT!!
WE'RE THROWING IT AT 'EM!
OUTTA THE WAY!
DASH
DASH

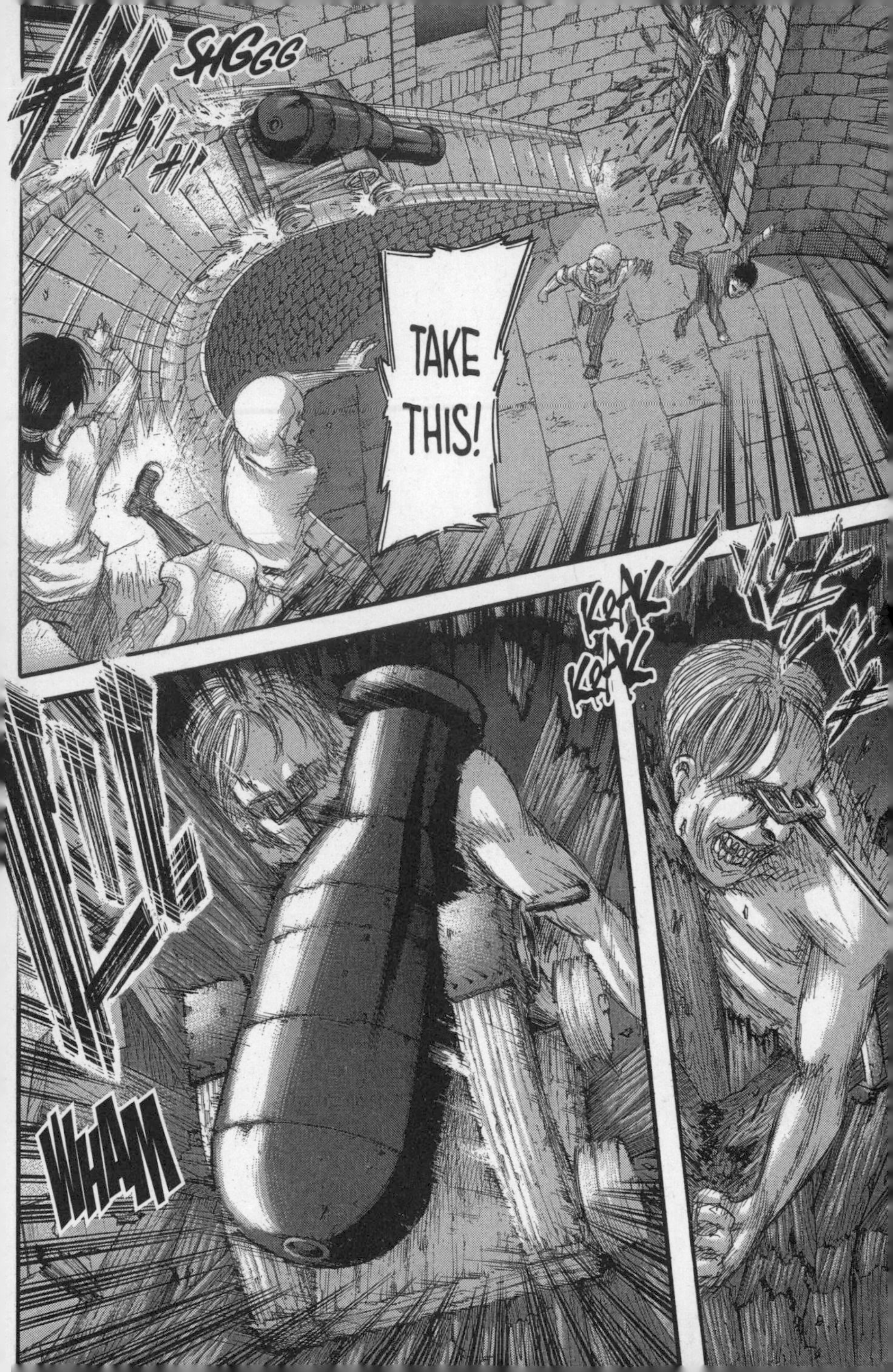
TAKE THIS!
SHGGG
KRAK KRAK
WHAM

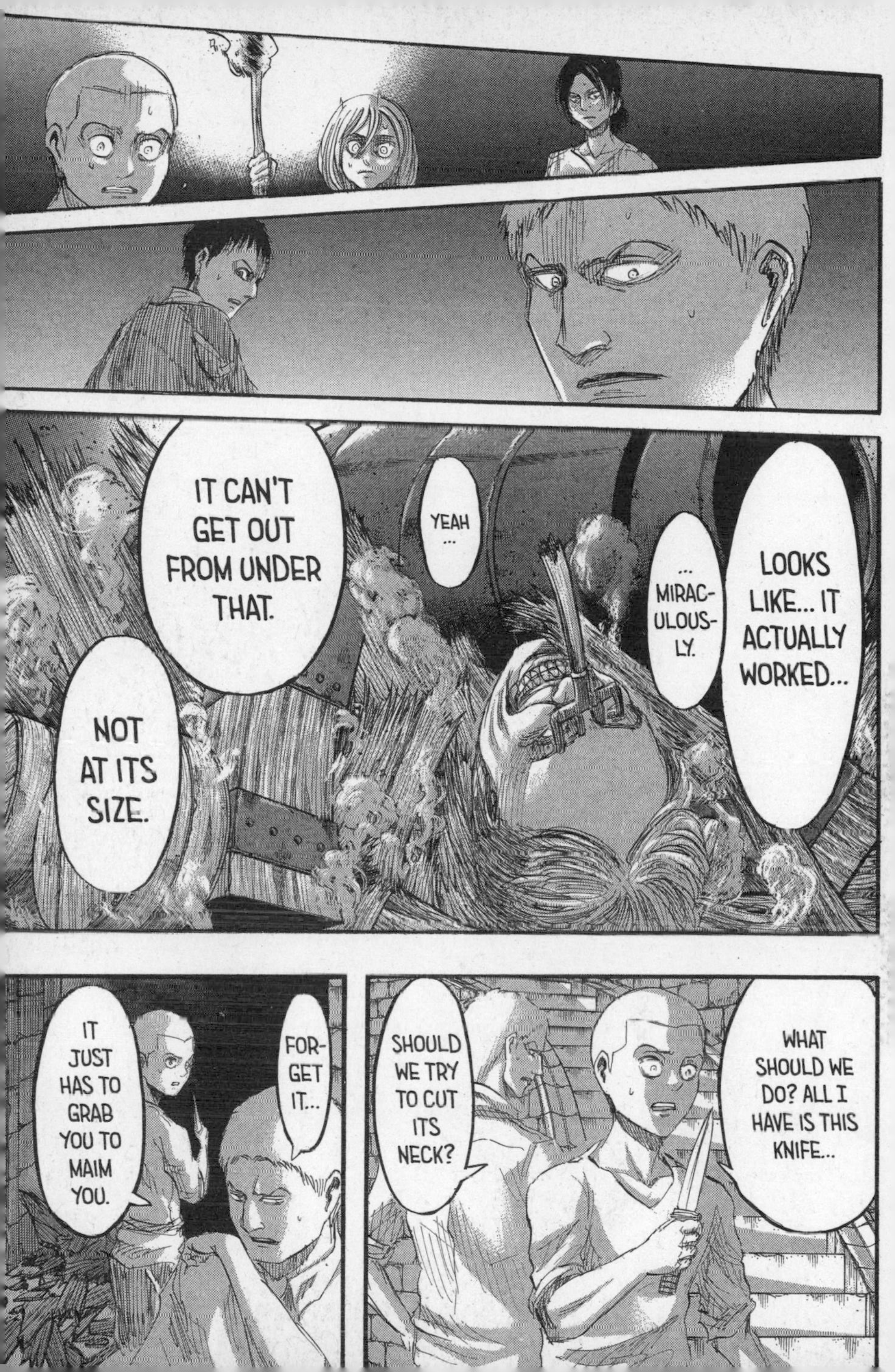
LOOKS LIKE... IT ACTUALLY WORKED...
... MIRACULOUSLY.
YEAH ...
IT CAN'T GET OUT FROM UNDER THAT.
NOT AT ITS SIZE.
WHAT SHOULD WE DO? ALL I HAVE IS THIS KNIFE...
SHOULD WE TRY TO CUT ITS NECK?
FORGET IT...
IT JUST HAS TO GRAB YOU TO MAIM YOU.

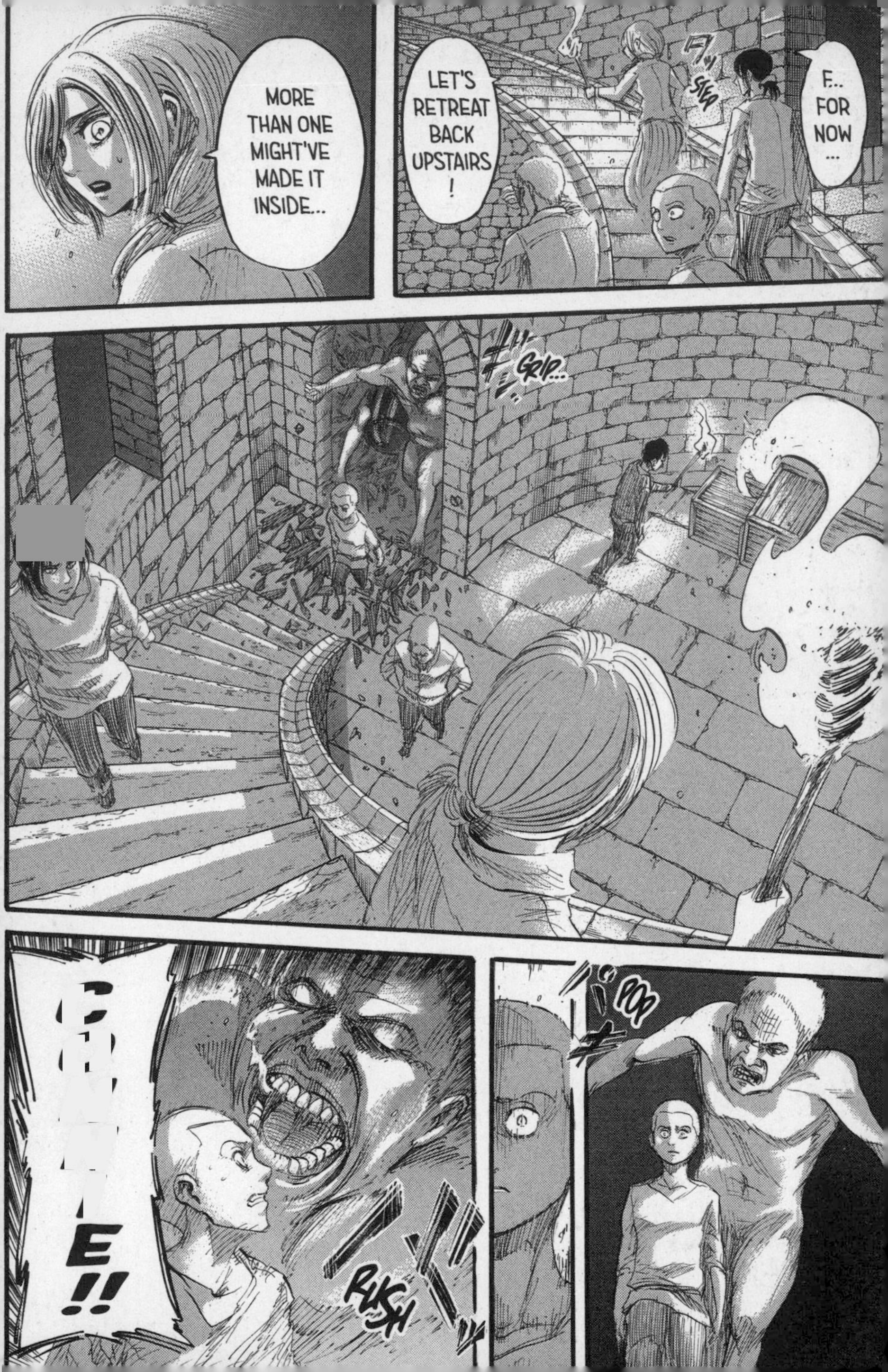
F... FOR NOW ...
STEP
LET'S RETREAT BACK UPSTAIRS !
MORE THAN ONE MIGHT'VE MADE IT INSIDE...
GRIP...
POP
RUSH

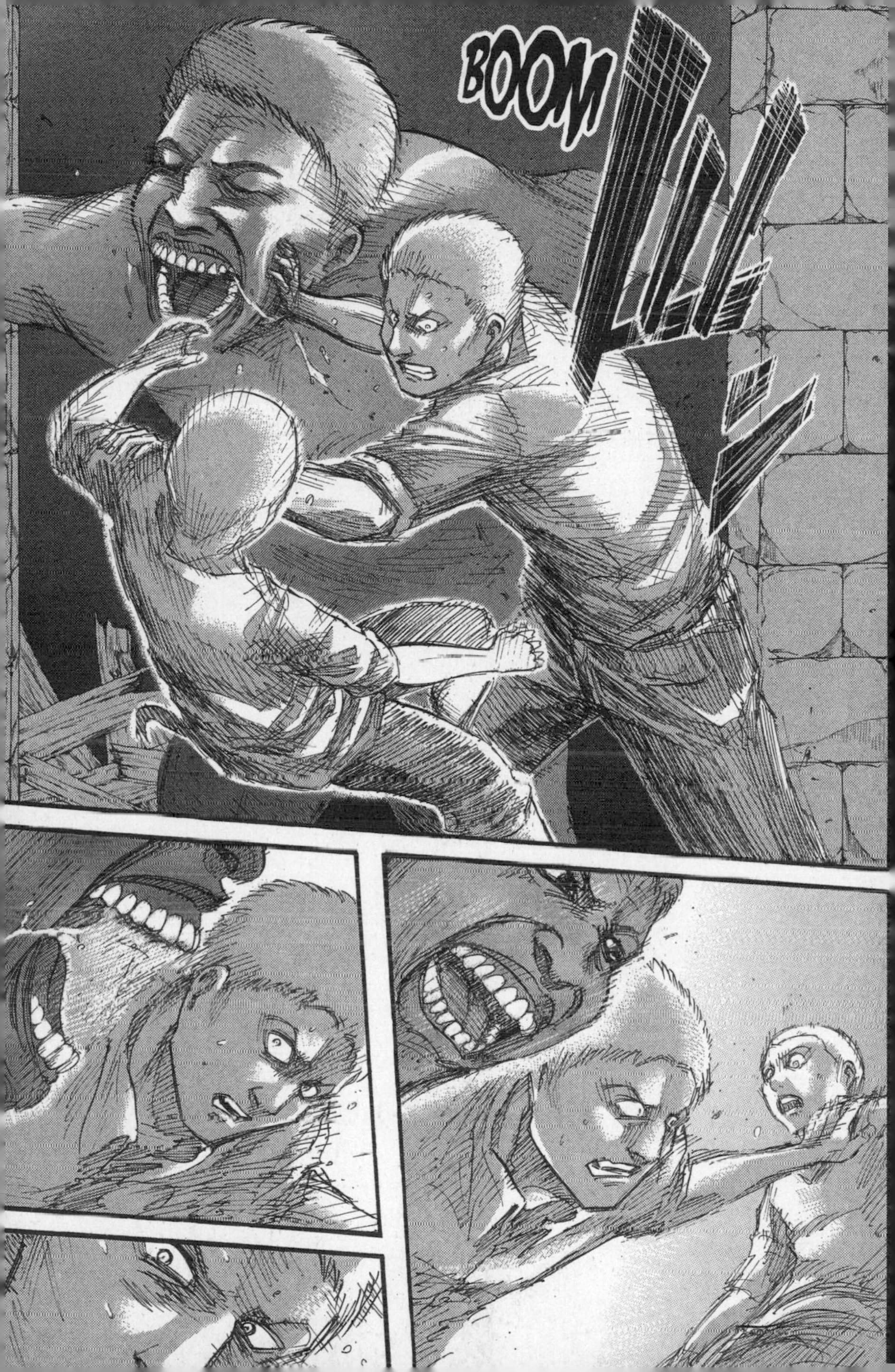
BOOM

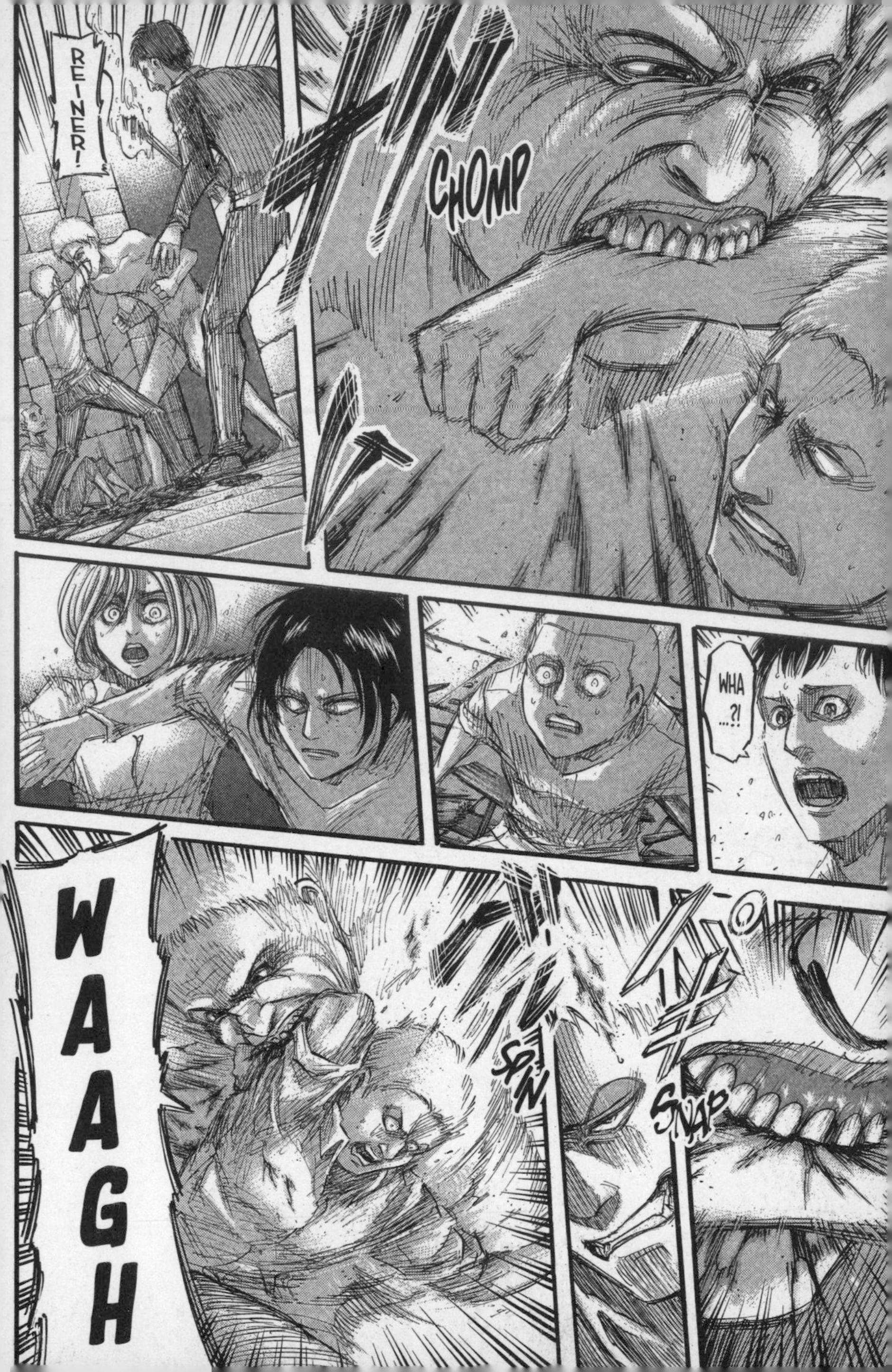
CHOMP
REINER!
WHA ...?!
SNAP
SPIN
WAGH

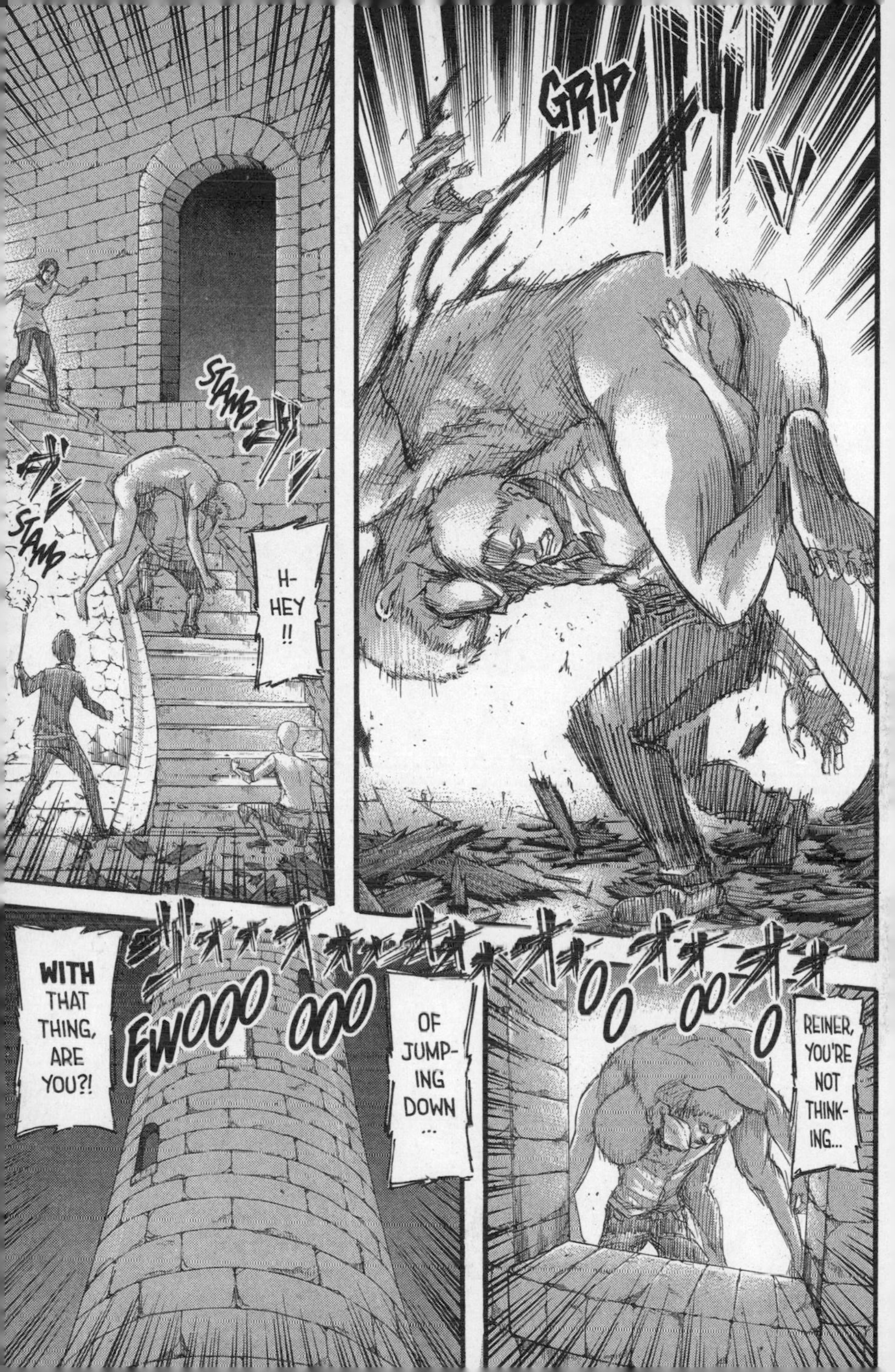
GRIP
SLAM
SLAM
H-HEY!!
REINER, YOU'RE NOT THINKING...
OF JUMPING DOWN...
WITH THAT THING, ARE YOU?!
FWOOO OOO

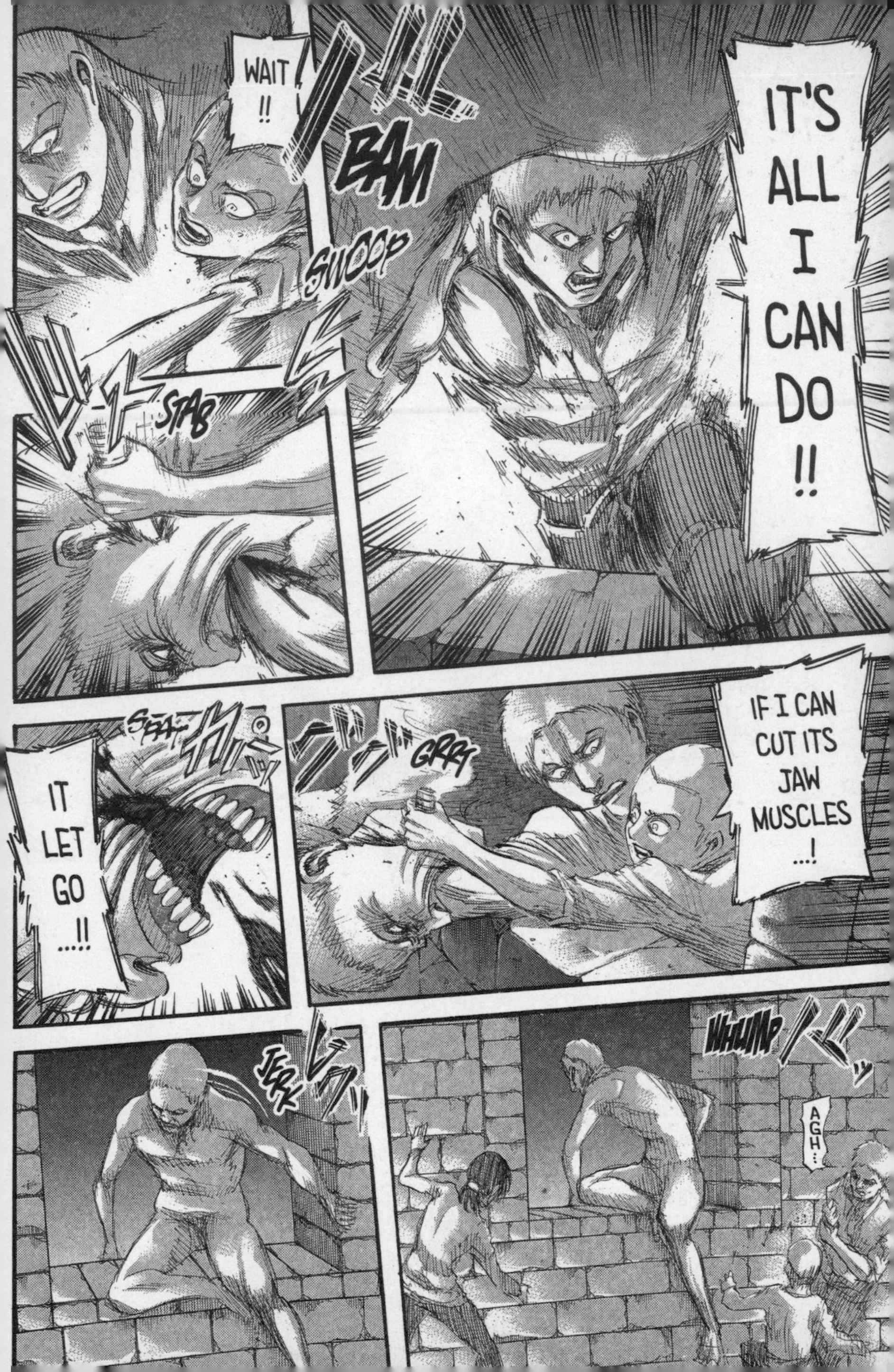

IT'S ALL I CAN DO!!
WAIT!!
BAM
SWOOP
STAB
IF I CAN CUT ITS JAW MUSCLES ...!
GRRR
IT LET GO ...!!
WHUMP
AGH...
JERK

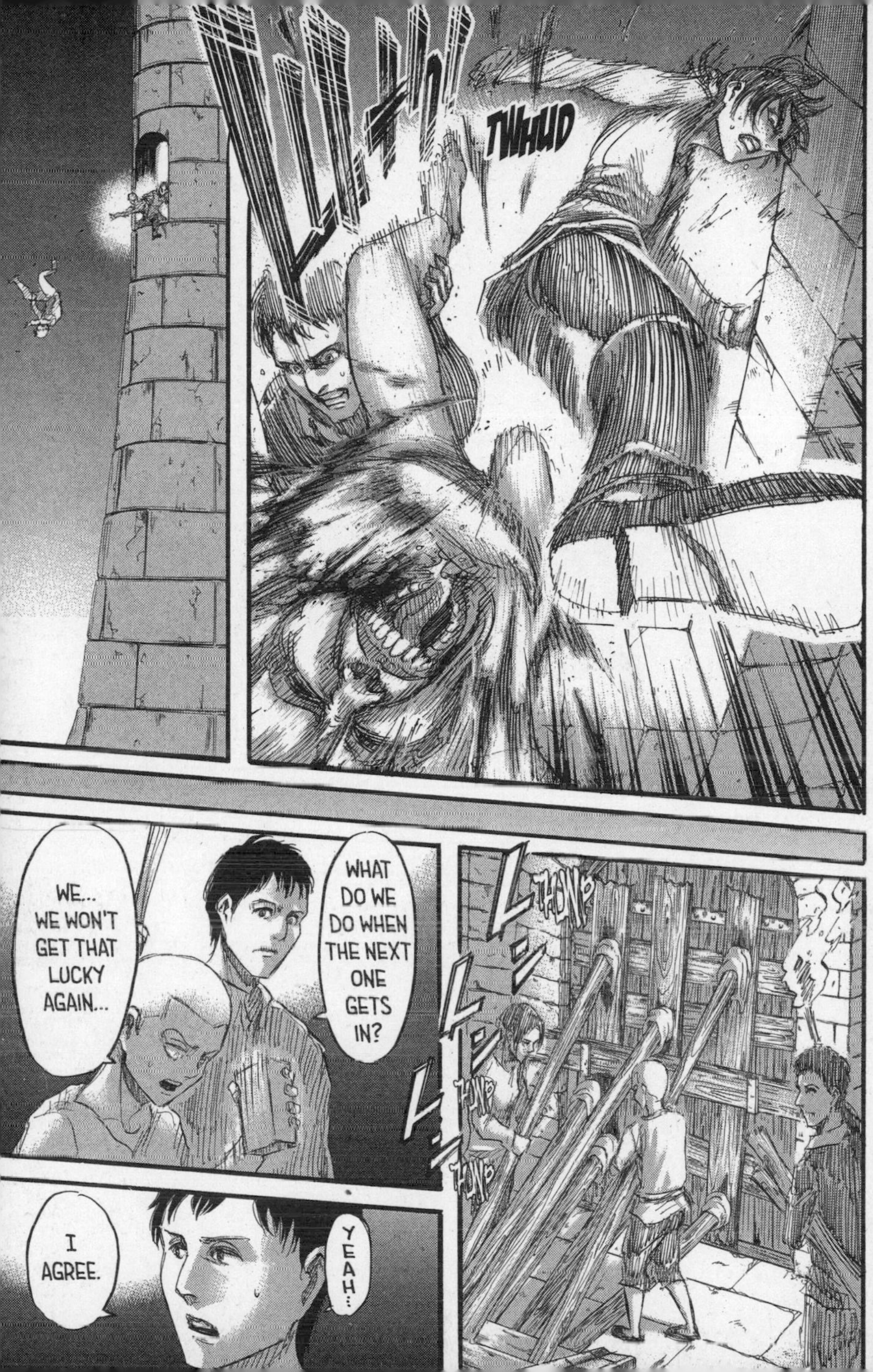
TWHUD
THUMP
THUMP
THUMP
WHAT DO WE DO WHEN THE NEXT ONE GETS IN?
WE... WE WON'T GET THAT LUCKY AGAIN...
YEAH...
I AGREE.

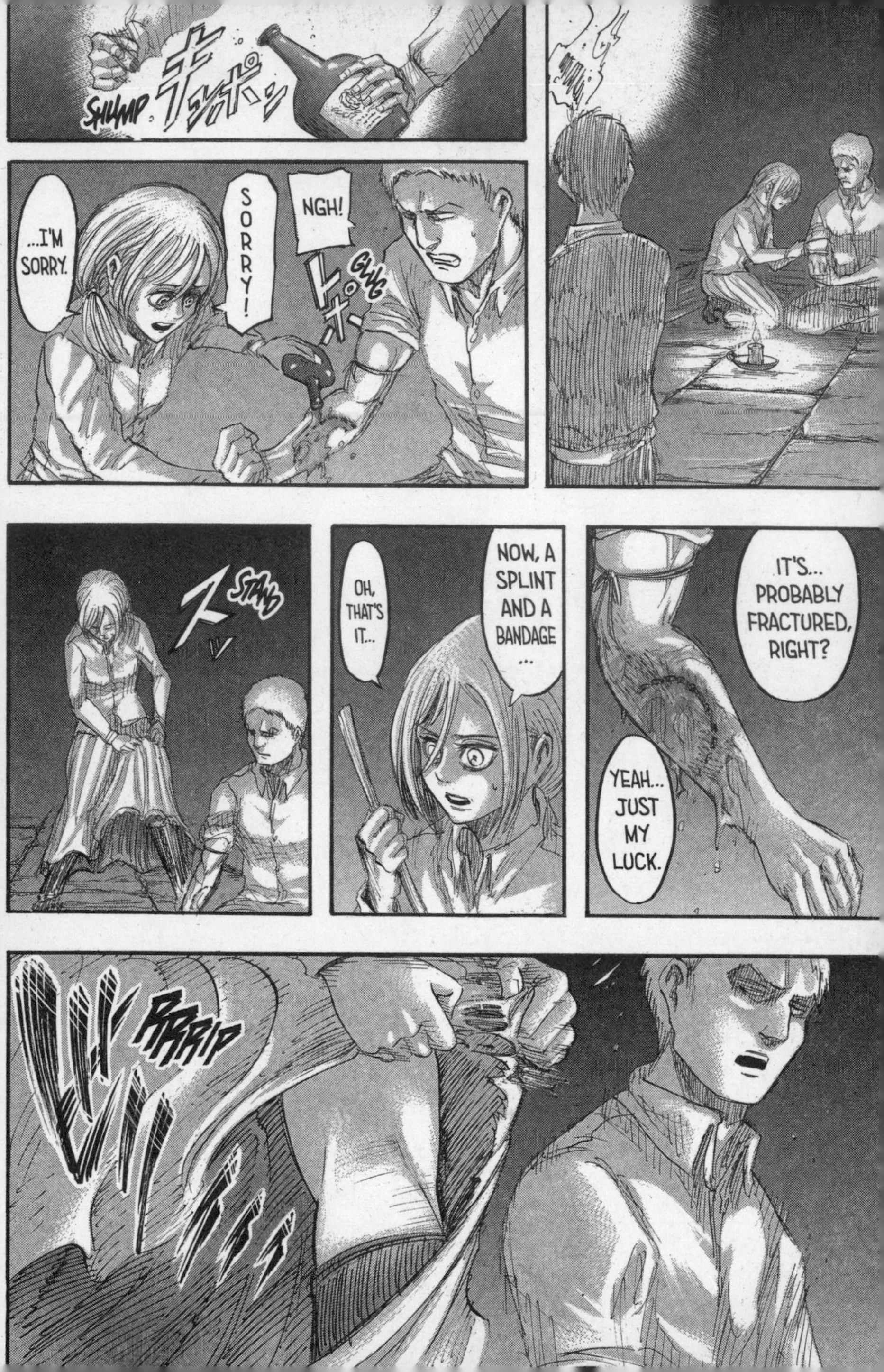

SHUMP
NGH!
GLUG
SORRY SORRY!
...I'M SORRY.
IT'S... PROBABLY FRACTURED, RIGHT?
YEAH... JUST MY LUCK.
NOW, A SPLINT AND A BANDAGE ...
OH, THAT'S IT...
STAND
RRRIP

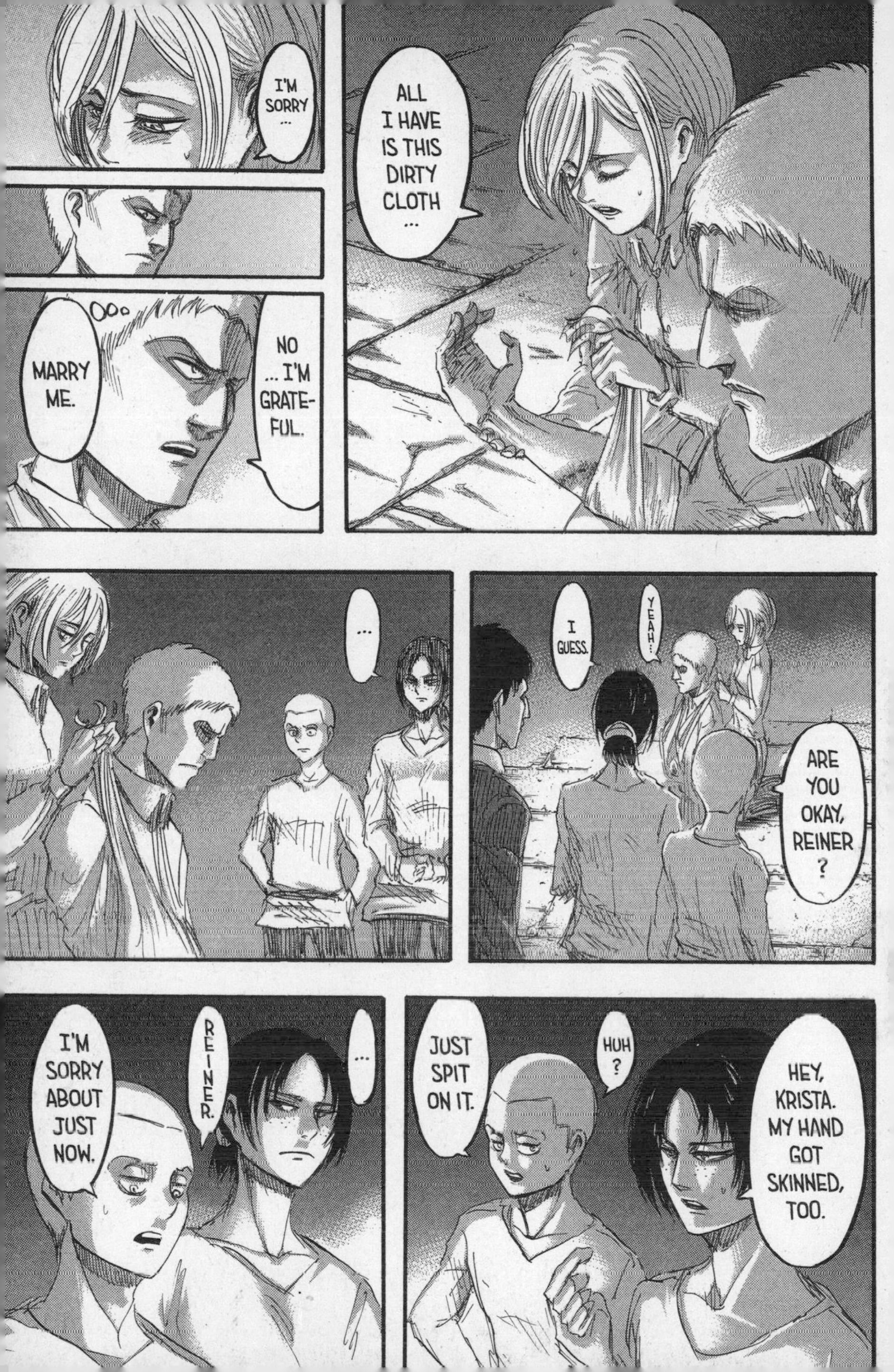
ALL I HAVE IS THIS DIRTY CLOTH...
I'M SORRY...
NO ...I'M GRATEFUL.
MARRY ME.
ARE YOU OKAY, REINER?
YEAH...
I GUESS.
...
HEY, KRISTA. MY HAND GOT SKINNED, TOO.
HUH?
JUST SPIT ON IT.
...
REINER.
I'M SORRY ABOUT JUST NOW.

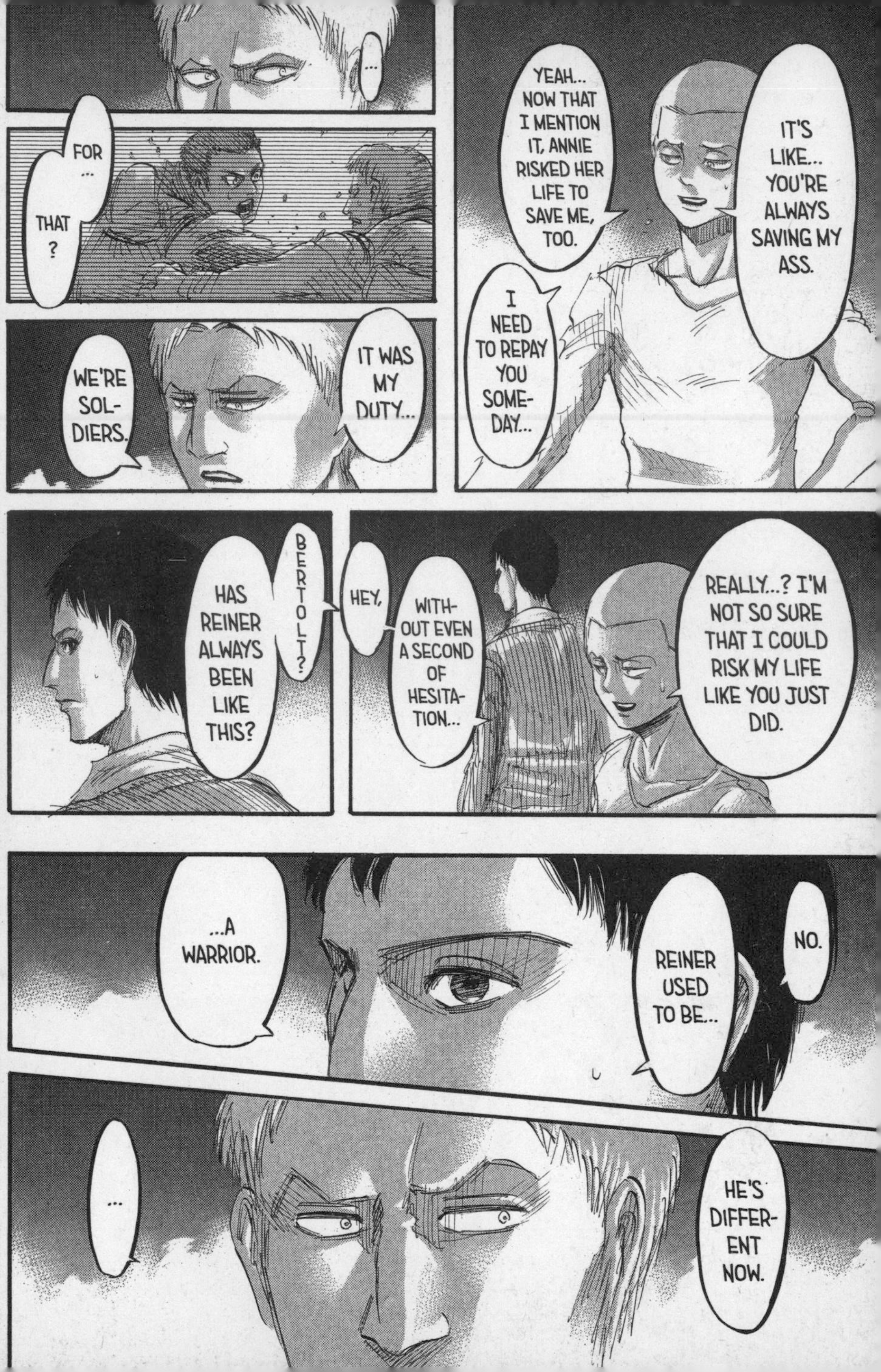
IT'S LIKE... YOU'RE ALWAYS SAVING MY ASS.
YEAH... NOW THAT I MENTION IT, ANNIE RISKED HER LIFE TO SAVE ME, TOO.
I NEED TO REPAY YOU SOME-DAY...
...
FOR ... THAT ?
IT WAS MY DUTY...
WE'RE SOL-DIERS.
REALLY...? I'M NOT SO SURE THAT I COULD RISK MY LIFE LIKE YOU JUST DID.
WITH-OUT EVEN A SECOND OF HESITA-TION...
HEY,
BERTOLT?
HAS REINER ALWAYS BEEN LIKE THIS?
NO.
REINER USED TO BE...
...A WARRIOR.
HE'S DIFFER-ENT NOW.
...

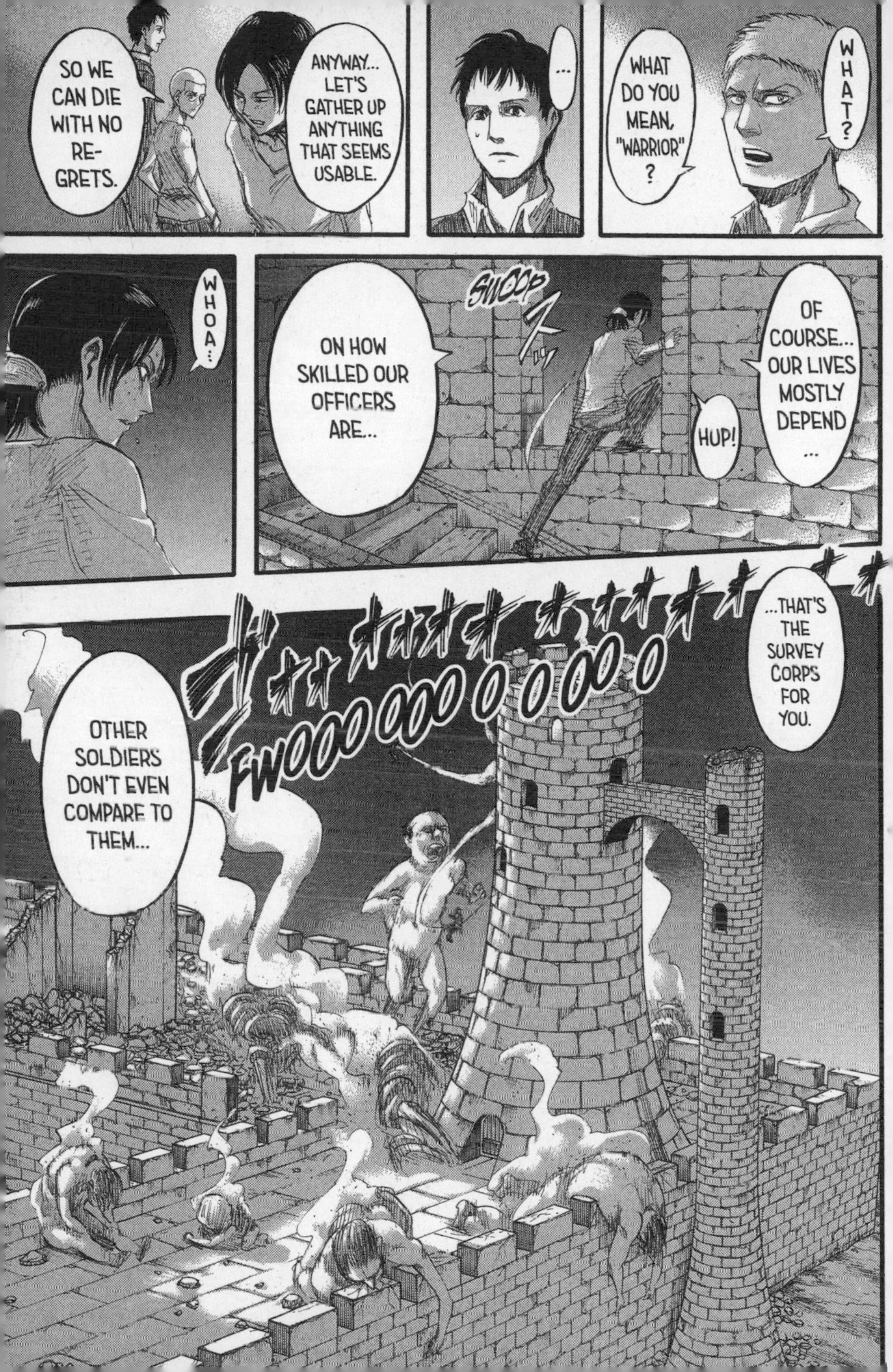
WHAT?
WHAT DO YOU MEAN, "WARRIOR"?
...
ANYWAY... LET'S GATHER UP ANYTHING THAT SEEMS USABLE.
SO WE CAN DIE WITH NO RE-GRETS.
OF COURSE... OUR LIVES MOSTLY DEPEND ...
HUP!
SWOOP
ON HOW SKILLED OUR OFFICERS ARE...
WHOA...
...THAT'S THE SURVEY CORPS FOR YOU.
FWOOOO OOO O O OO O
OTHER SOLDIERS DON'T EVEN COMPARE TO THEM...

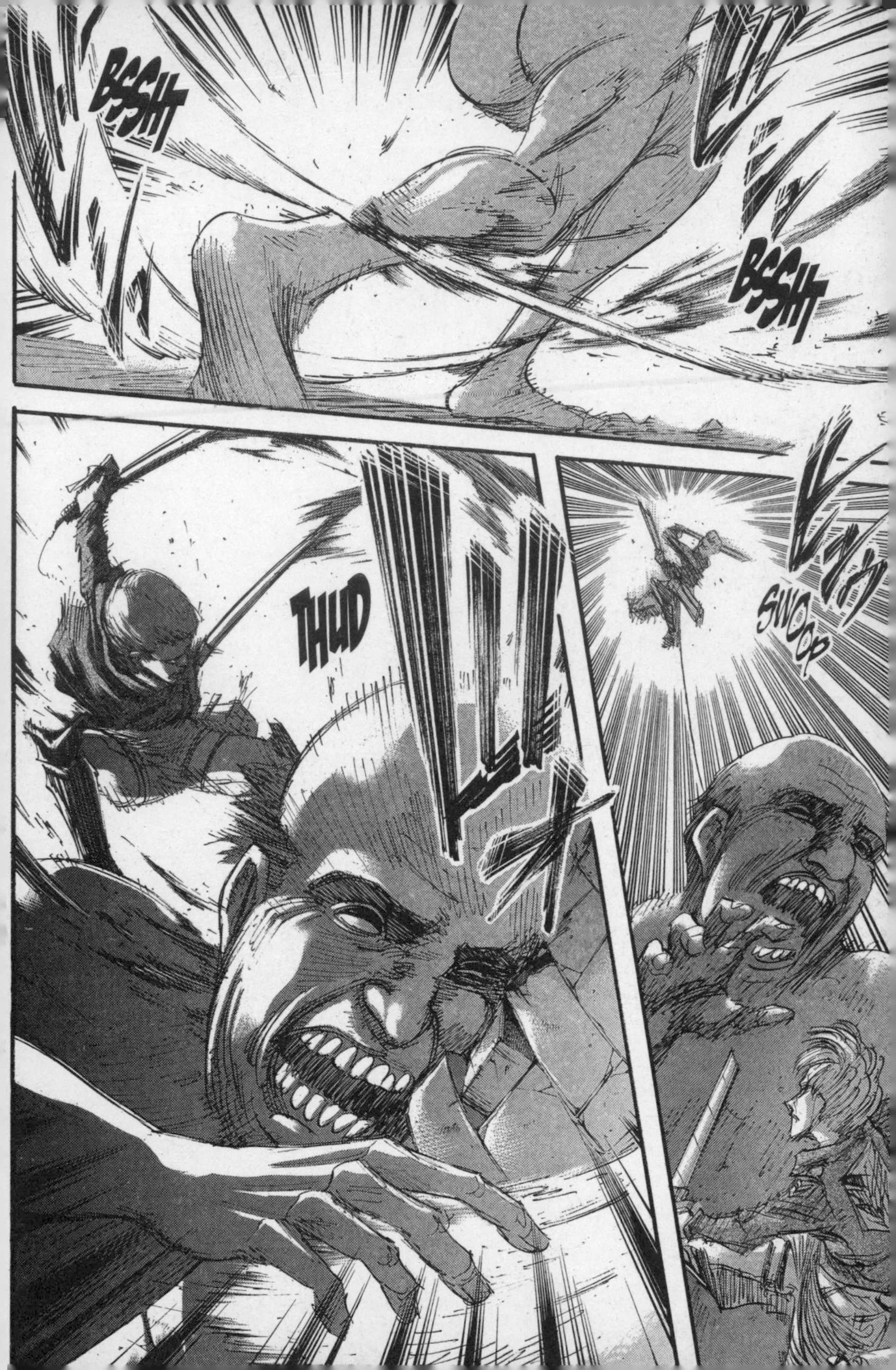
BSSHT
BSSHT
SWOOP
THUD

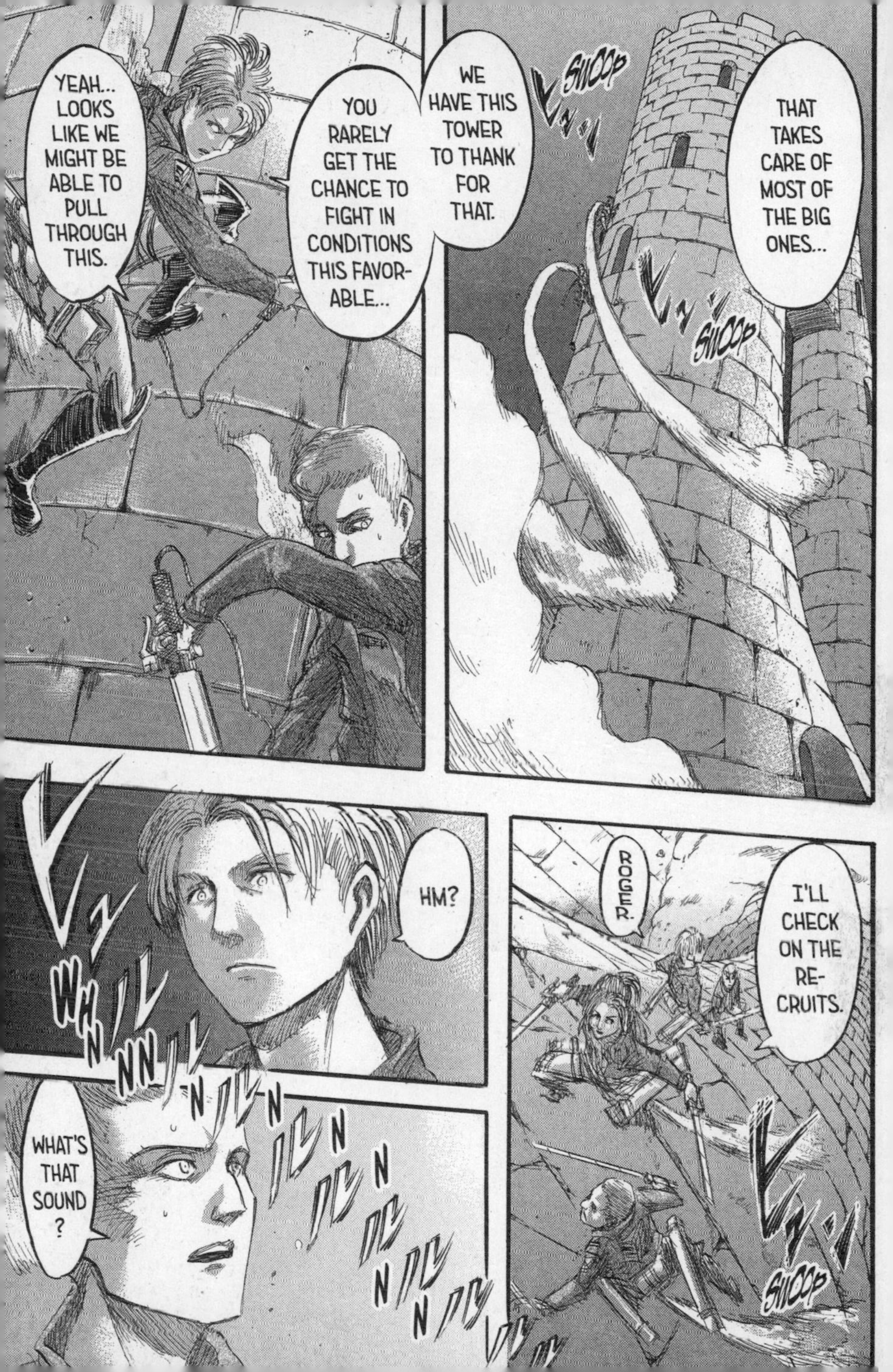
THAT TAKES CARE OF MOST OF THE BIG ONES...
SWOOP
SWOOP
WE HAVE THIS TOWER TO THANK FOR THAT.
YOU RARELY GET THE CHANCE TO FIGHT IN CONDITIONS THIS FAVOR-ABLE...
YEAH... LOOKS LIKE WE MIGHT BE ABLE TO PULL THROUGH THIS.
I'LL CHECK ON THE RE-CRUITS.
ROGER.
SWOOP
HM?
WHNNNNNNNNNN
WHAT'S THAT SOUND?

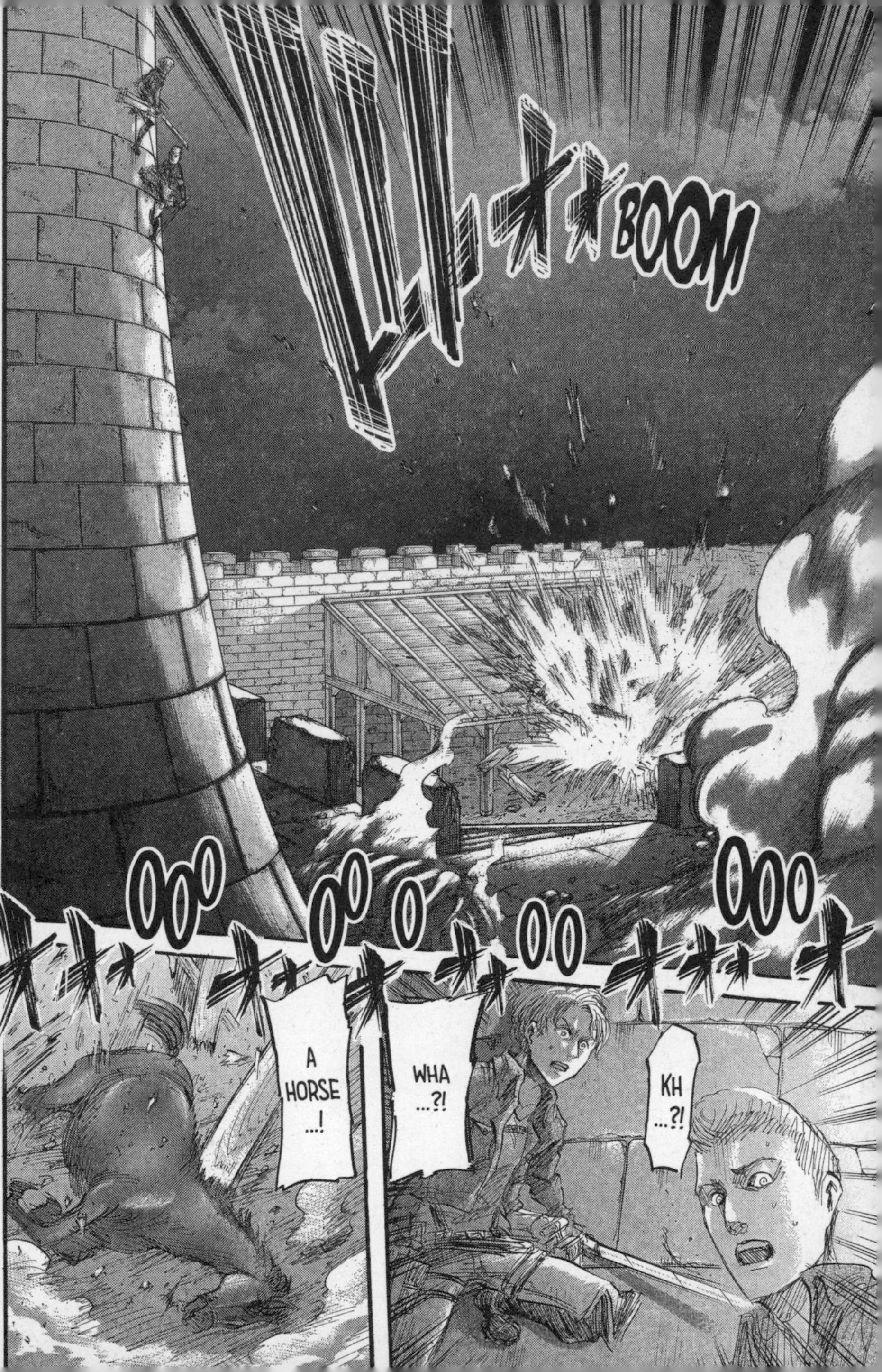
BOOM
OOO
KH ...?!
WHA ...?!
A HORSE ...!

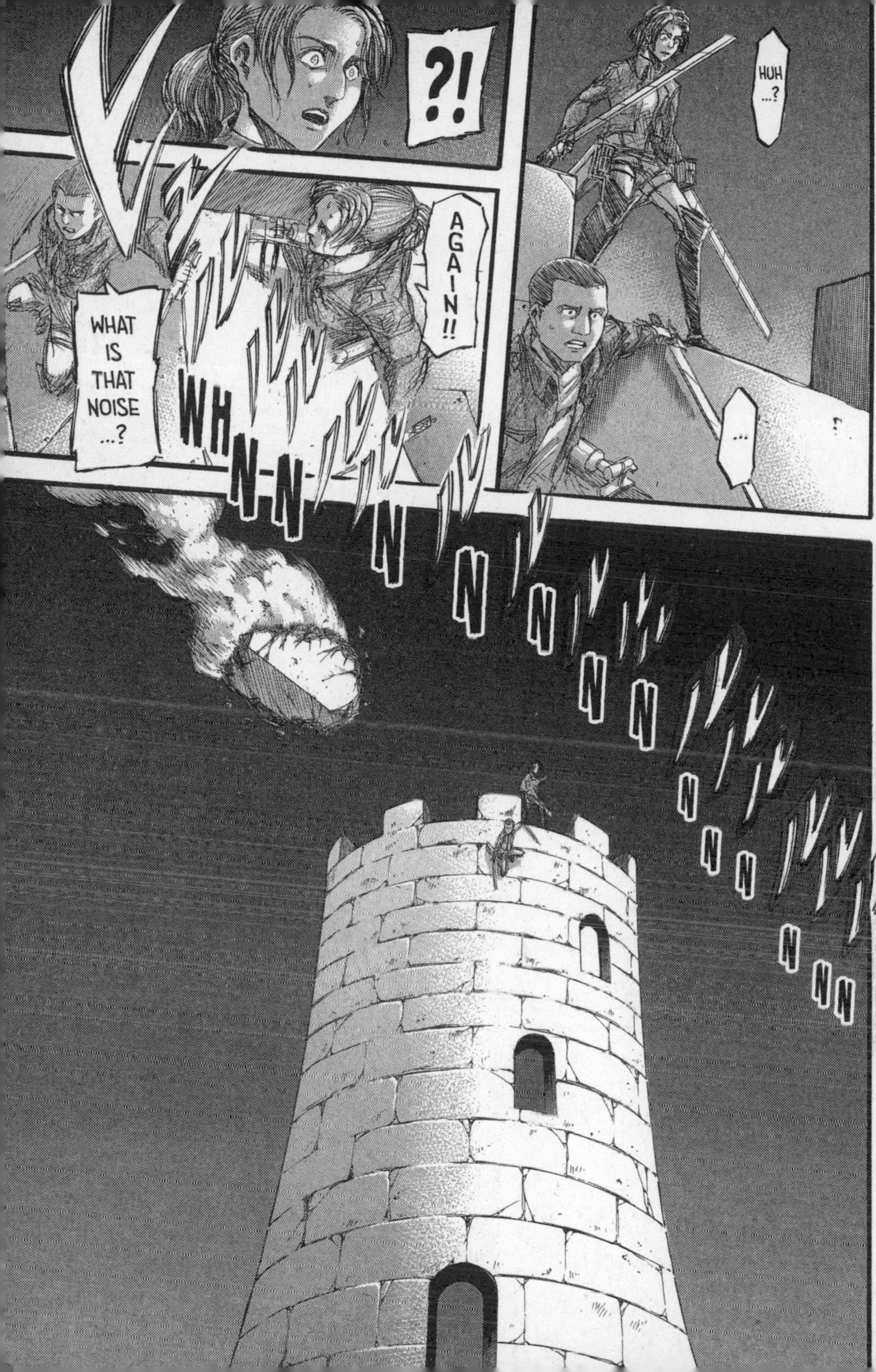
HUH ...?
...
?!
AGAIN!!
WHAT IS THAT NOISE ...?
WHN-N-NNNNNNNNNNN

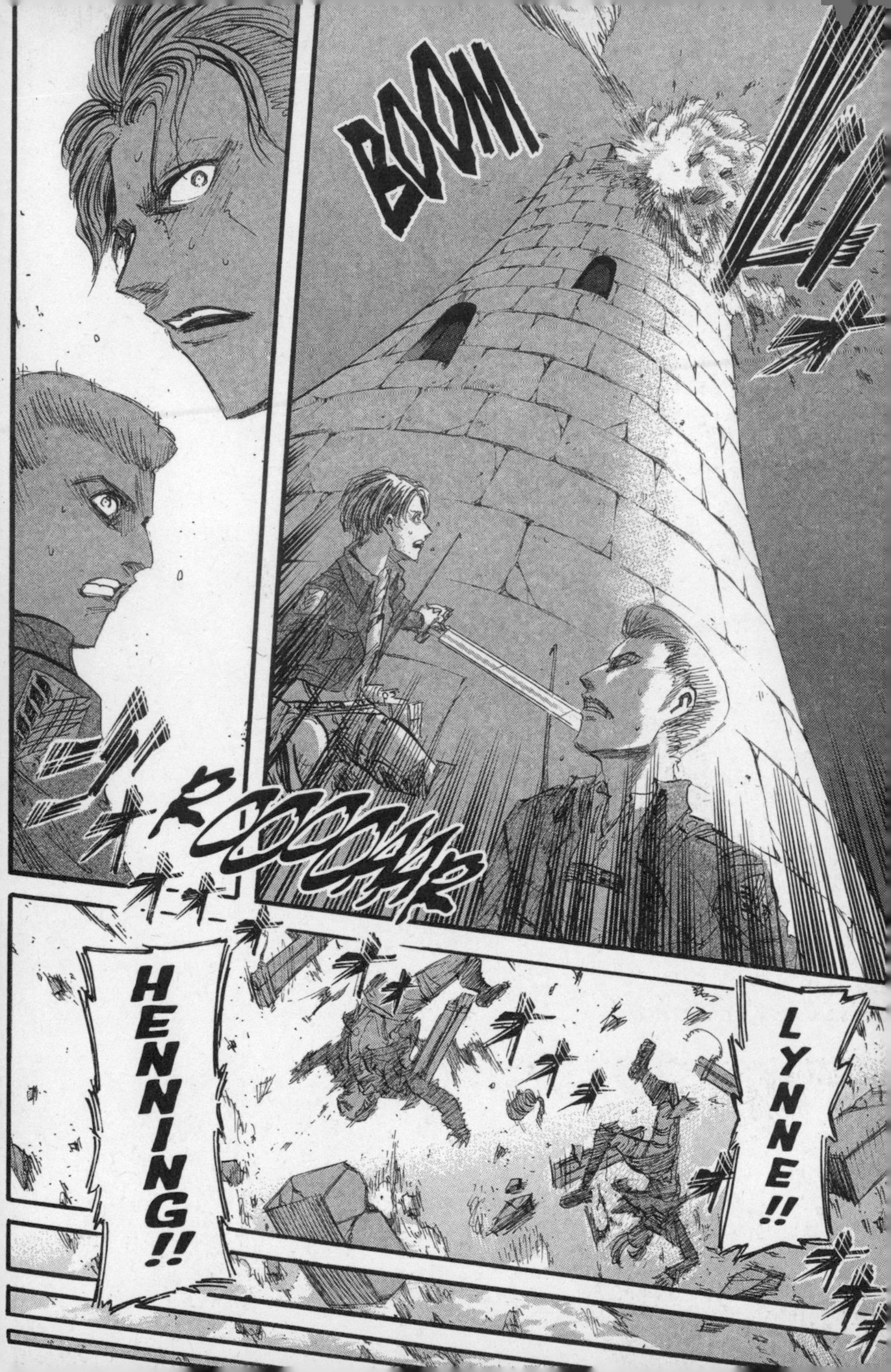
BOOM
ROOOAR
LYNNE!!
HENNING!!

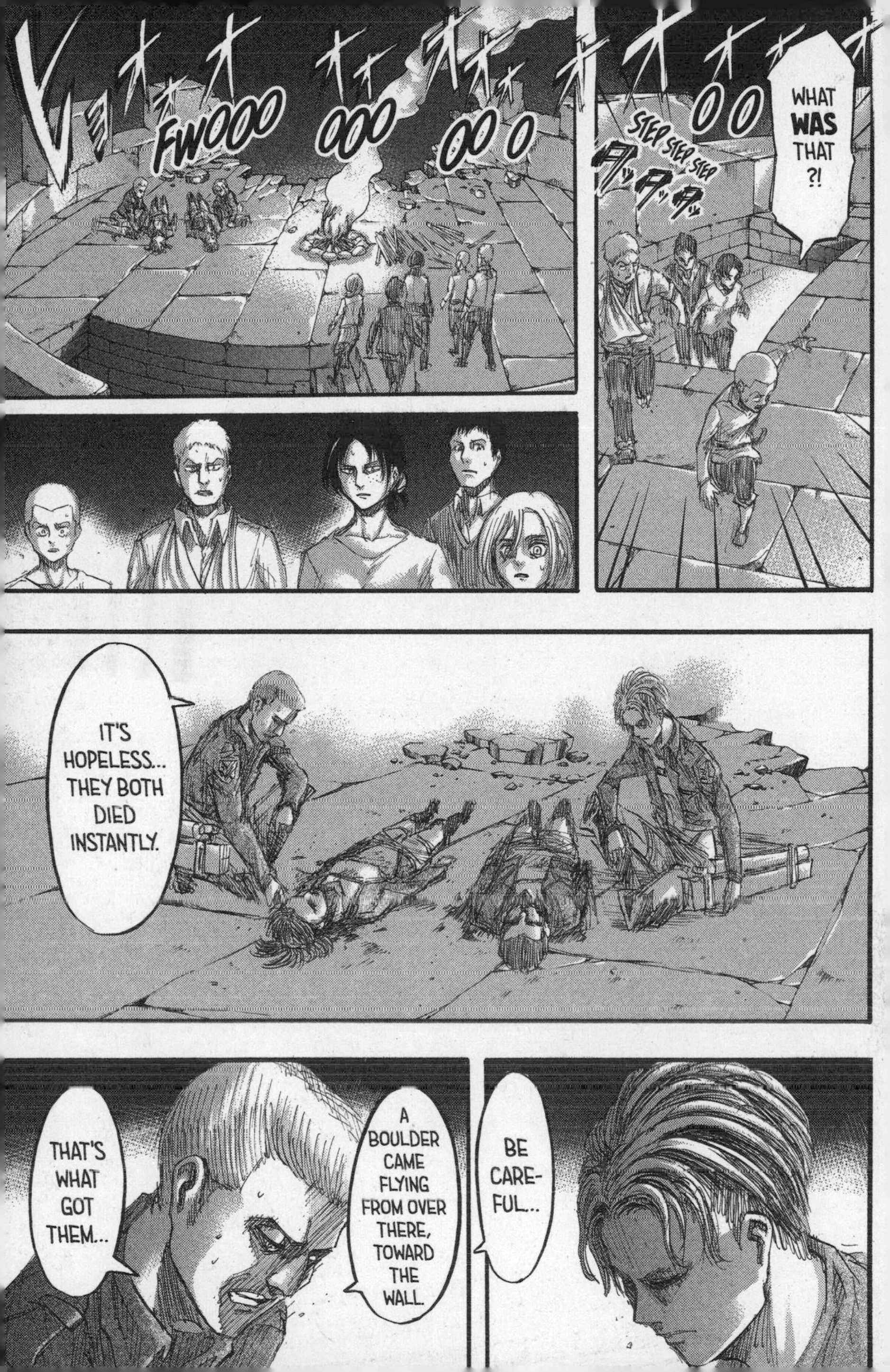

STEP STEP STEP
WHAT WAS THAT ?!
FWOOO OOO OO O OO
IT'S HOPELESS... THEY BOTH DIED INSTANTLY.
BE CARE-FUL...
A BOULDER CAME FLYING FROM OVER THERE, TOWARD THE WALL.
THAT'S WHAT GOT THEM...

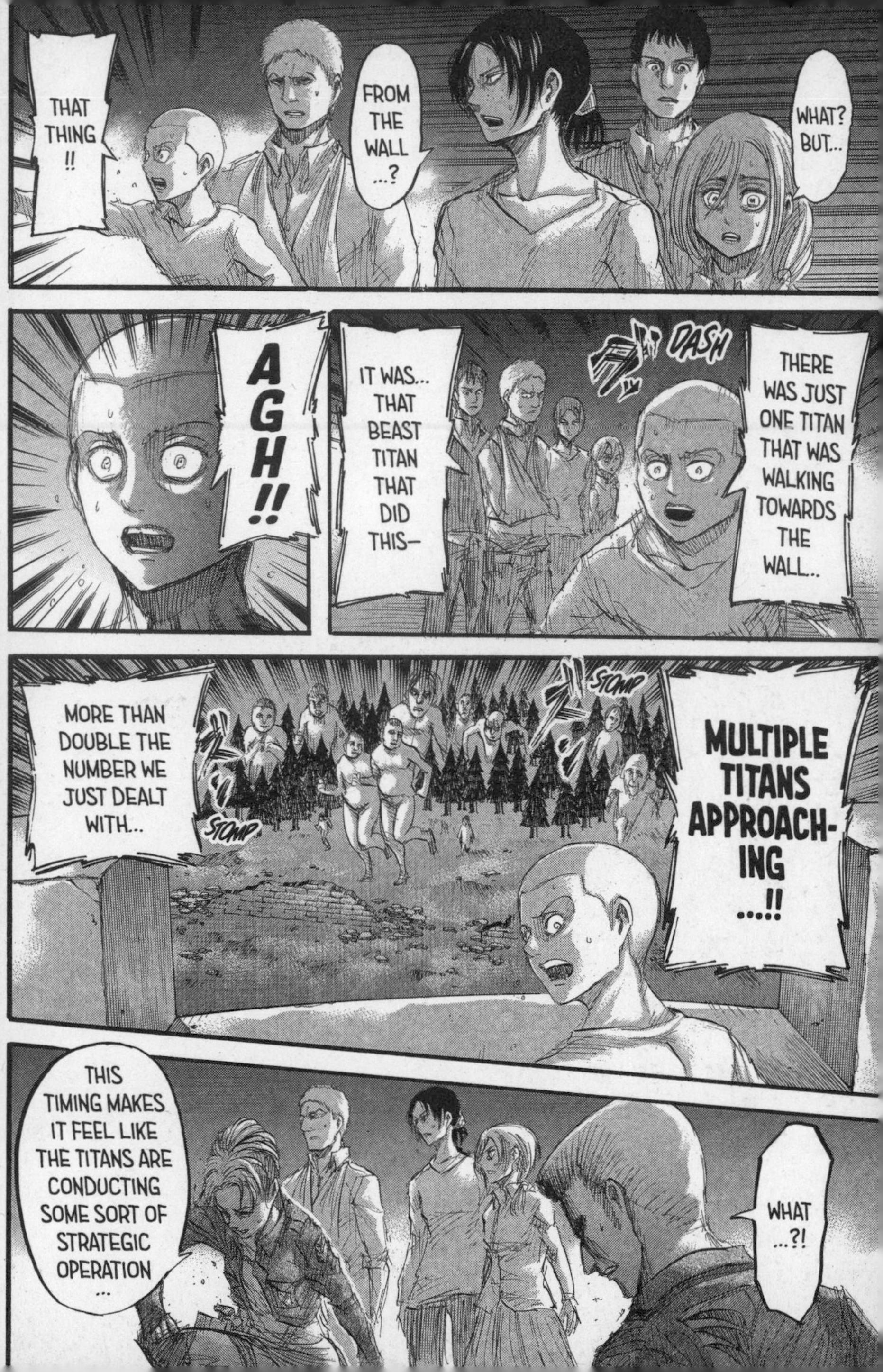
WHAT? BUT...
FROM THE WALL ...?
THAT THING !!
DASH
THERE WAS JUST ONE TITAN THAT WAS WALKING TOWARDS THE WALL..
IT WAS... THAT BEAST TITAN THAT DID THIS—
AGH!!
STOMP
MULTIPLE TITANS APPROACH-ING ...!!
MORE THAN DOUBLE THE NUMBER WE JUST DEALT WITH...
STOMP
WHAT ...?!
THIS TIMING MAKES IT FEEL LIKE THE TITANS ARE CONDUCTING SOME SORT OF STRATEGIC OPERATION ...

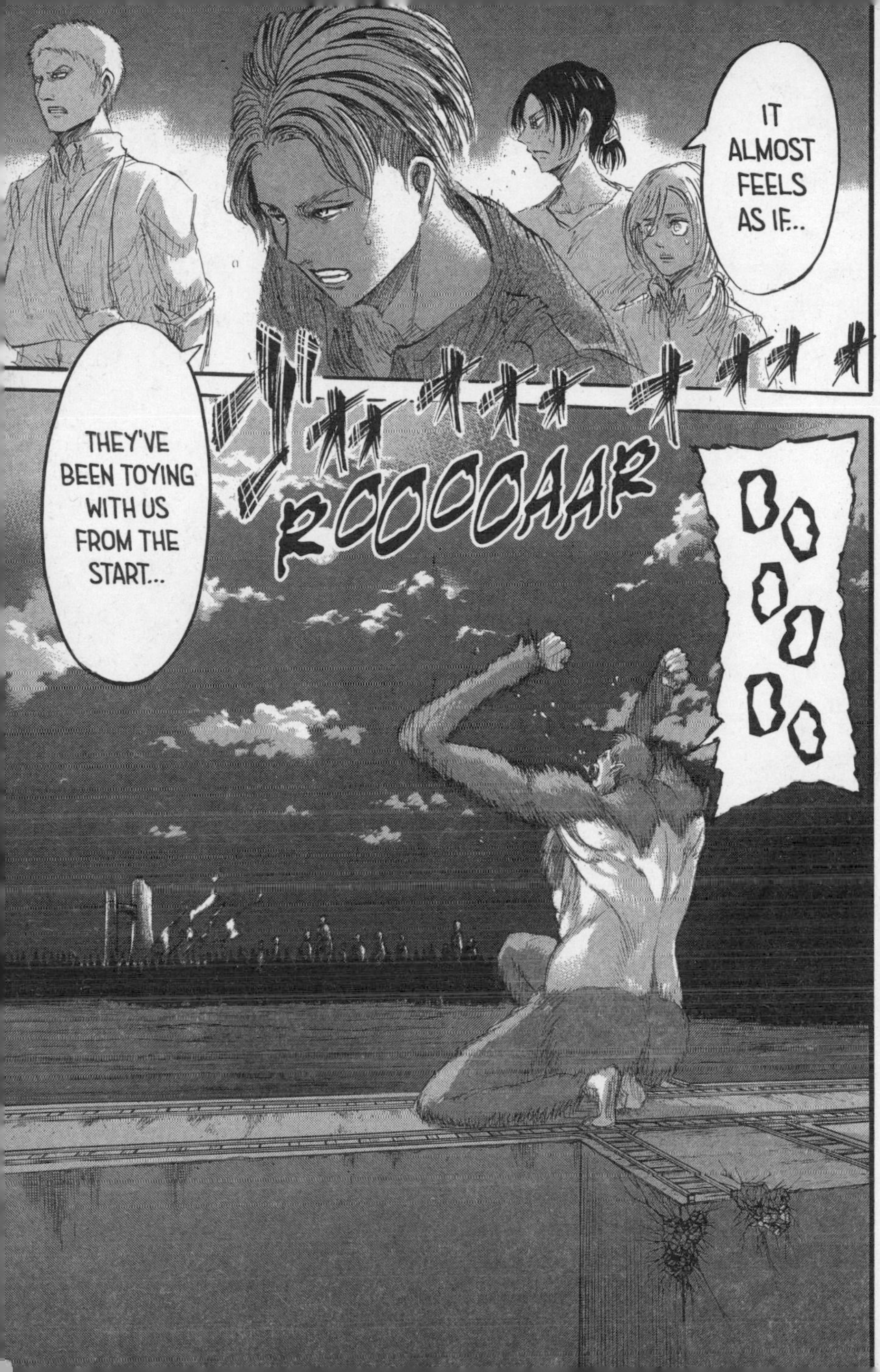
IT ALMOST FEELS AS IF...
THEY'VE BEEN TOYING WITH US FROM THE START...
ROOOOAAR
OOOOOOOO

ATTACK on TITAN

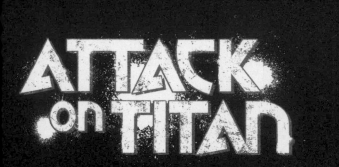

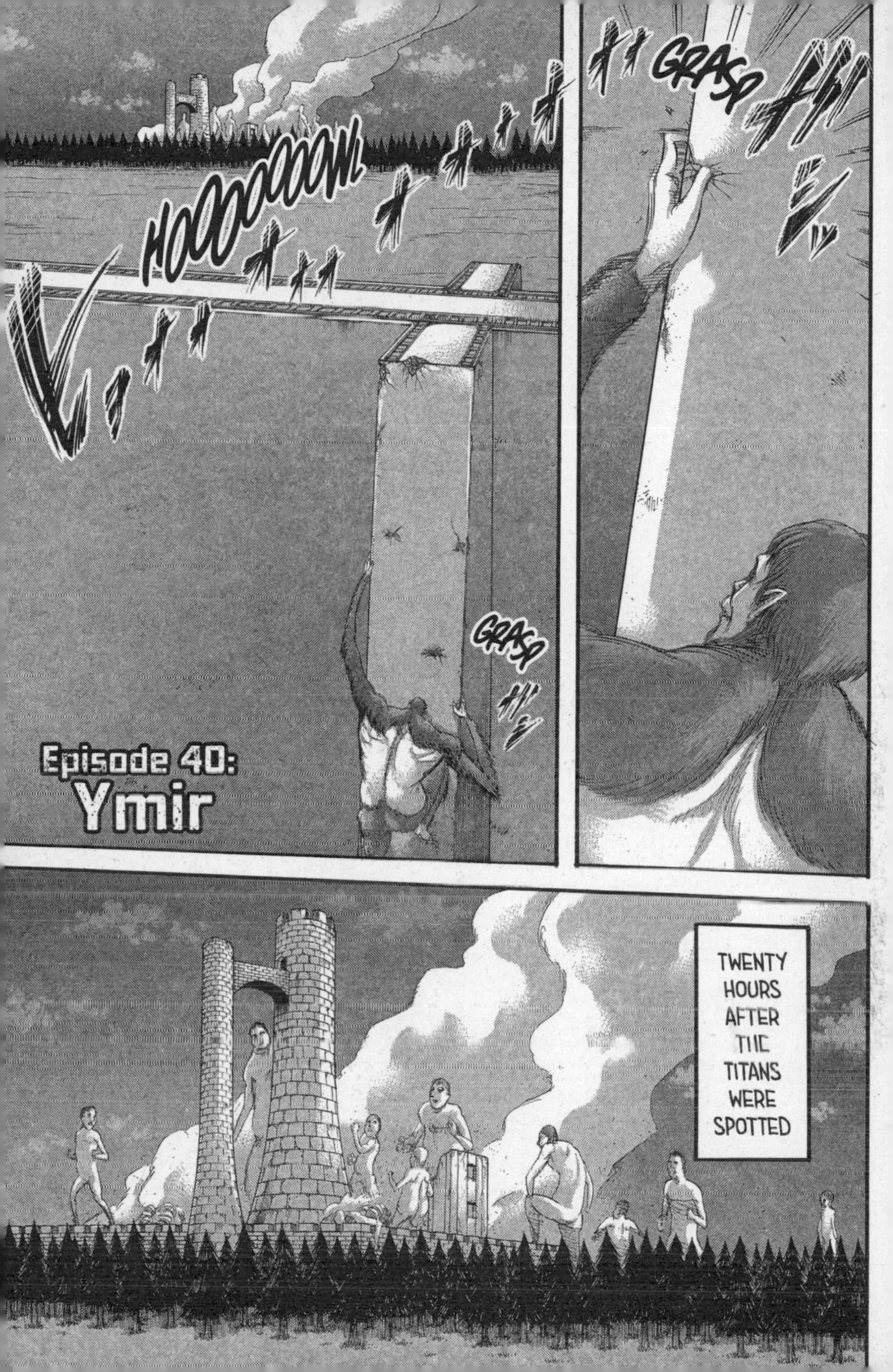
GRASP
VHOOOOOOOM
GRASP
Episode 40:
Ymir
TWENTY HOURS AFTER THE TITANS WERE SPOTTED

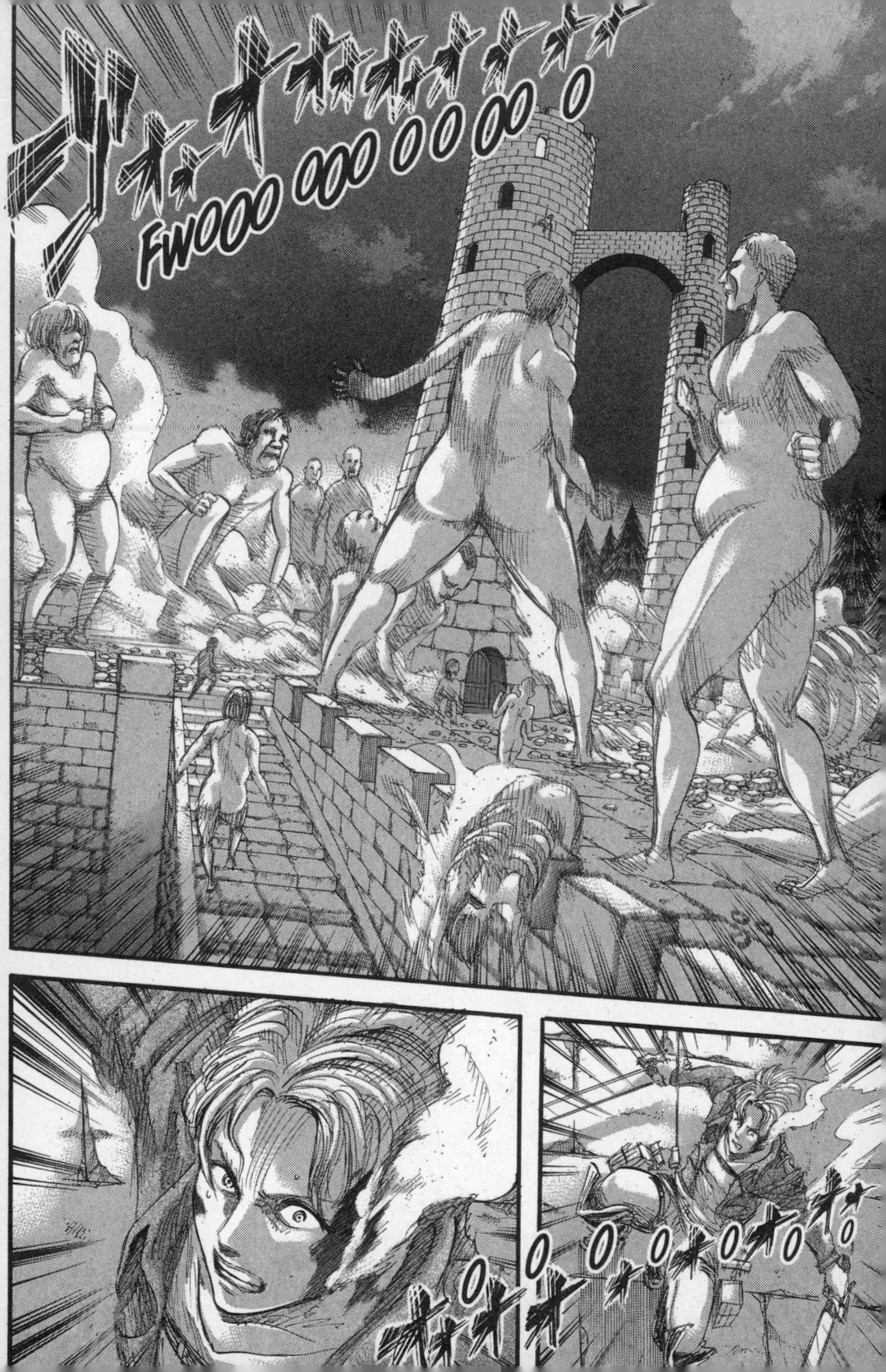
FWOOO OOO OO OO O
O O O O O O O

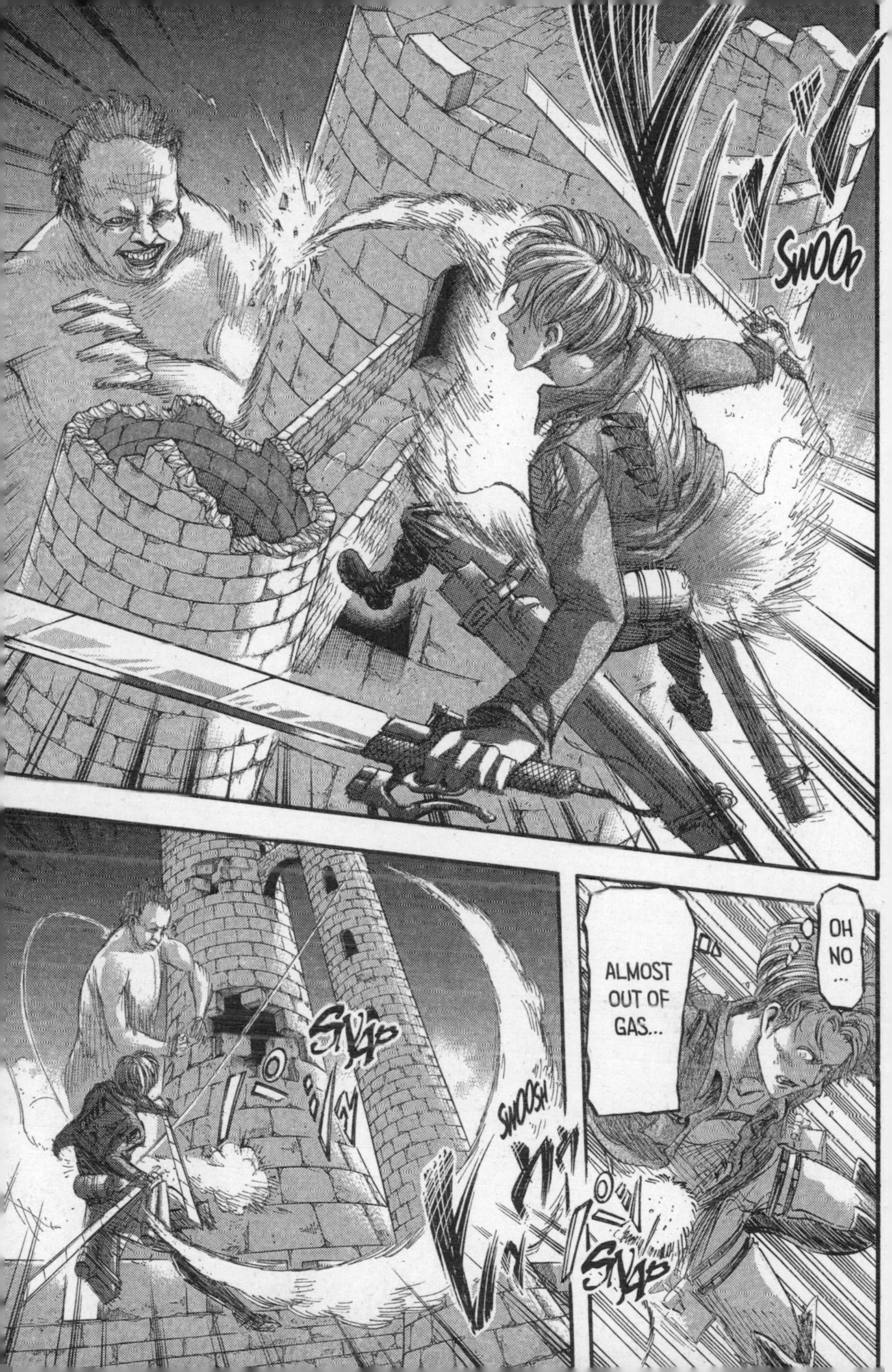
SWOOP
OH NO...
ALMOST OUT OF GAS...
SWOOSH
SNAP
SNAP

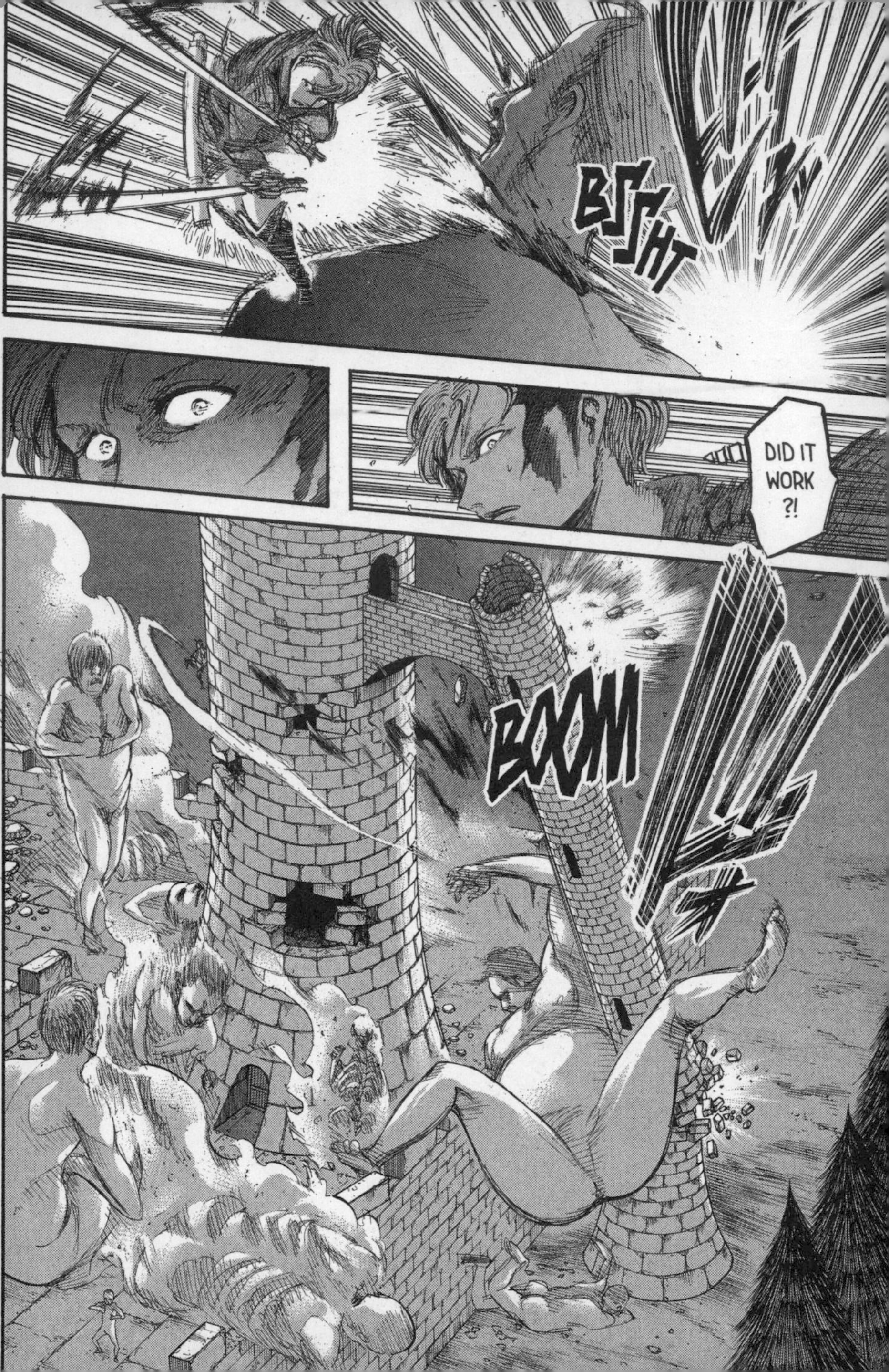
BSSHT
DID IT WORK ?!
BOOM

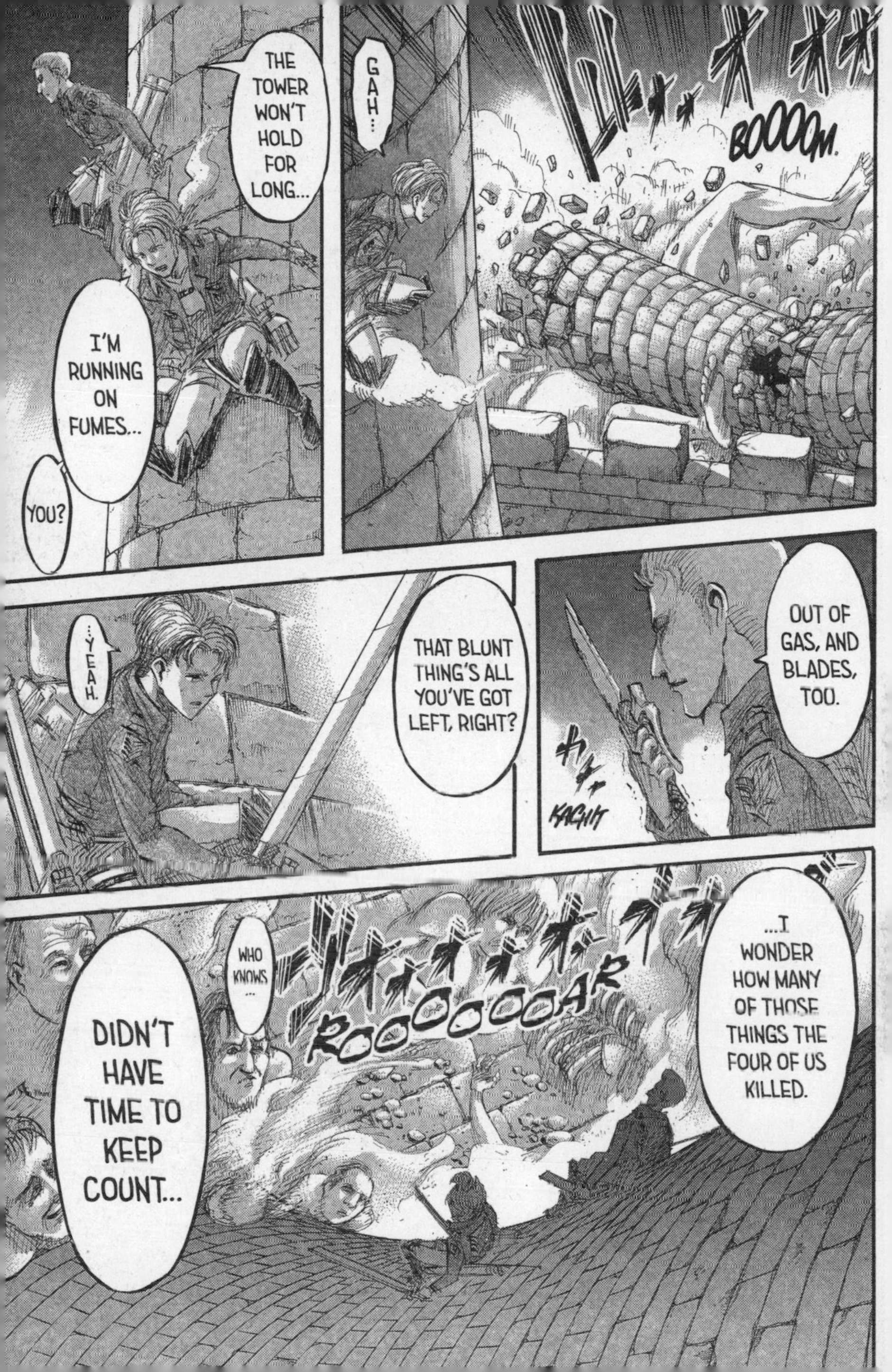
BOOOOM.
GAH...
THE TOWER WON'T HOLD FOR LONG...
I'M RUNNING ON FUMES...
YOU?
OUT OF GAS, AND BLADES, TOO.
KACHIT
THAT BLUNT THING'S ALL YOU'VE GOT LEFT, RIGHT?
...YEAH.
...I WONDER HOW MANY OF THOSE THINGS THE FOUR OF US KILLED.
ROOOOOOAR
WHO KNOWS...
DIDN'T HAVE TIME TO KEEP COUNT...

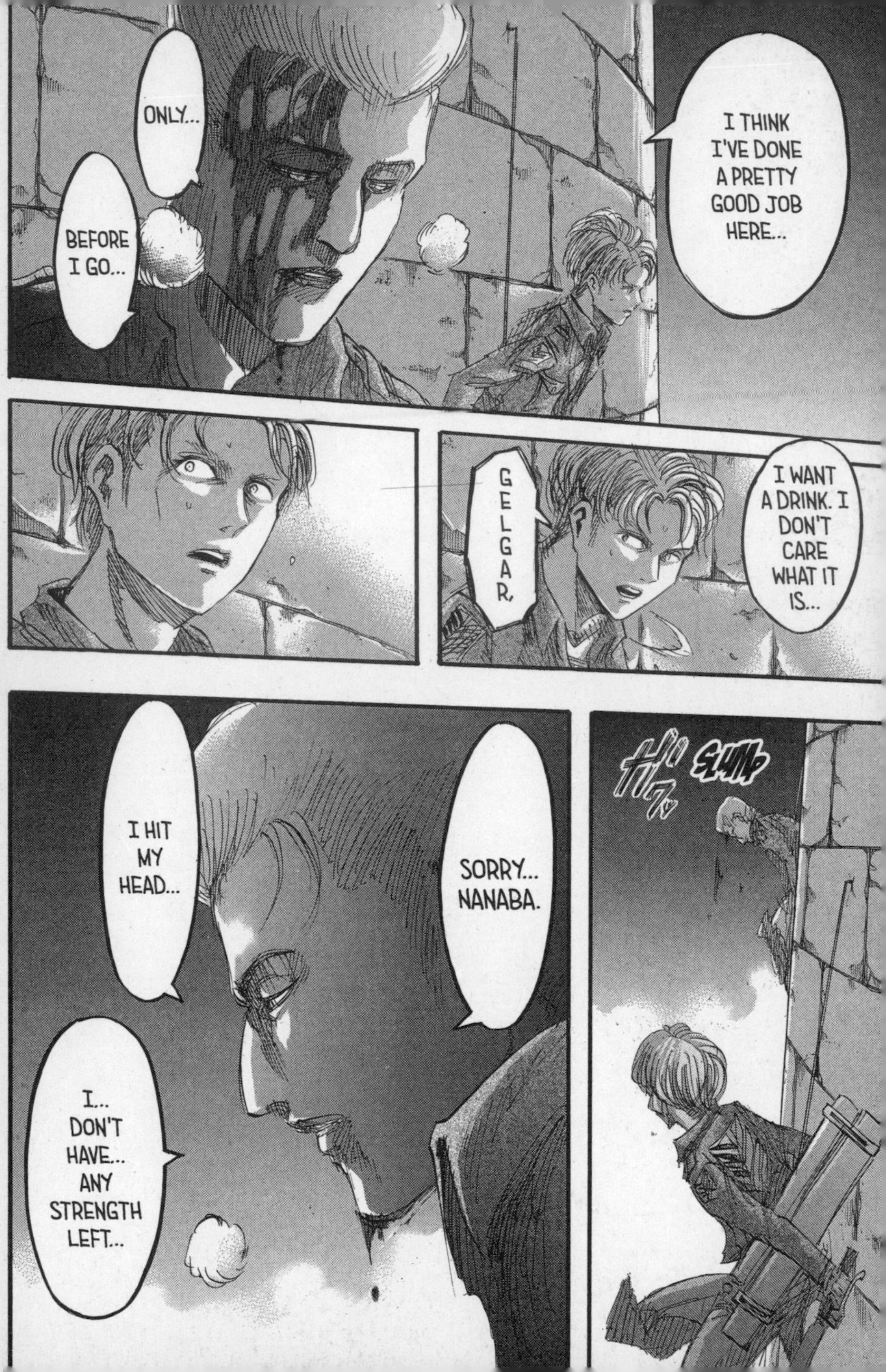
I THINK I'VE DONE A PRETTY GOOD JOB HERE...
ONLY...
BEFORE I GO...
I WANT A DRINK. I DON'T CARE WHAT IT IS...
GELGAR,
SLUMP
SORRY... NANABA.
I HIT MY HEAD...
I... DON'T HAVE... ANY STRENGTH LEFT...

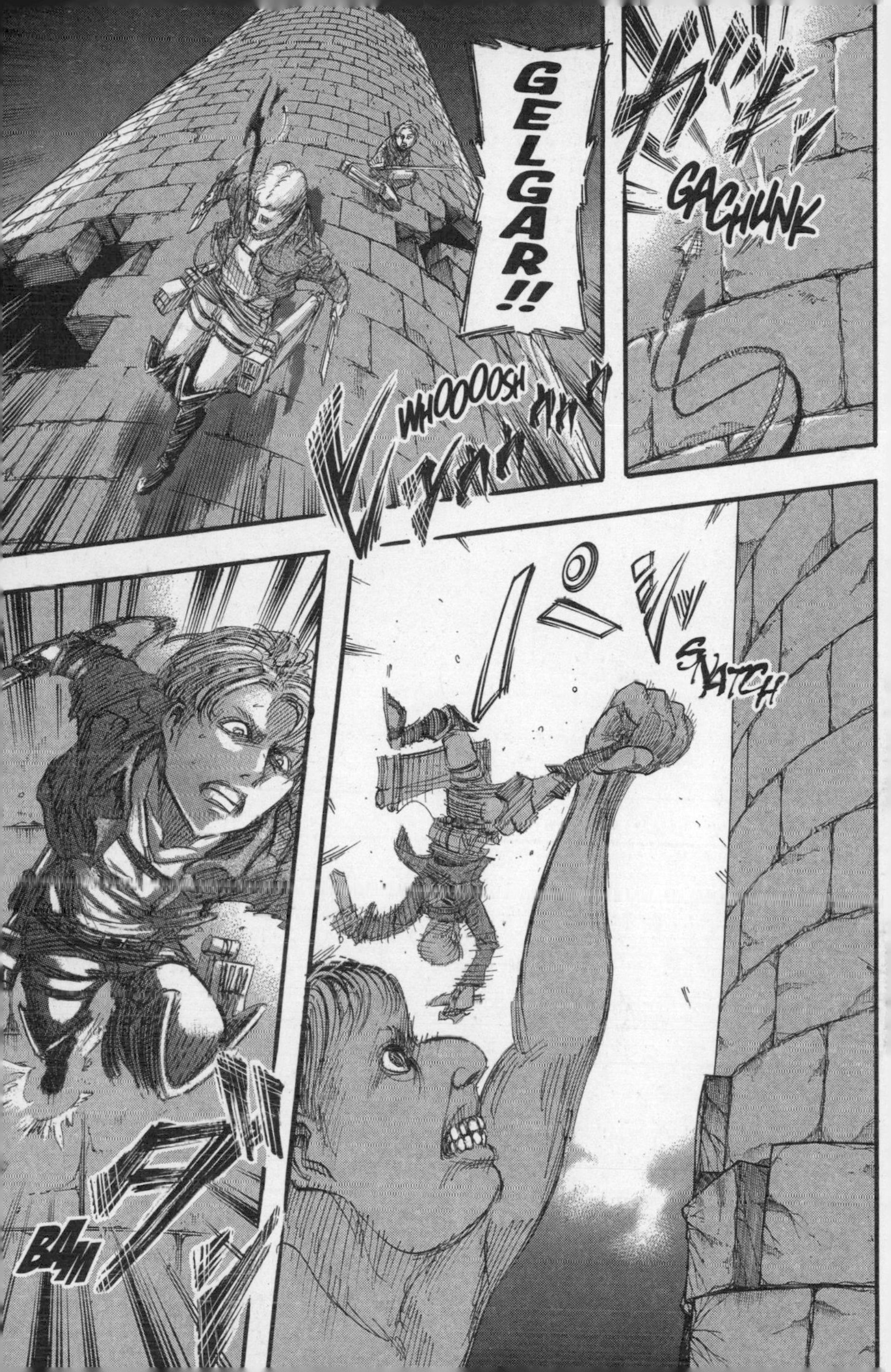
GACHUNK
GELGAR!!
WHOOOOSH
SNATCH
BAM

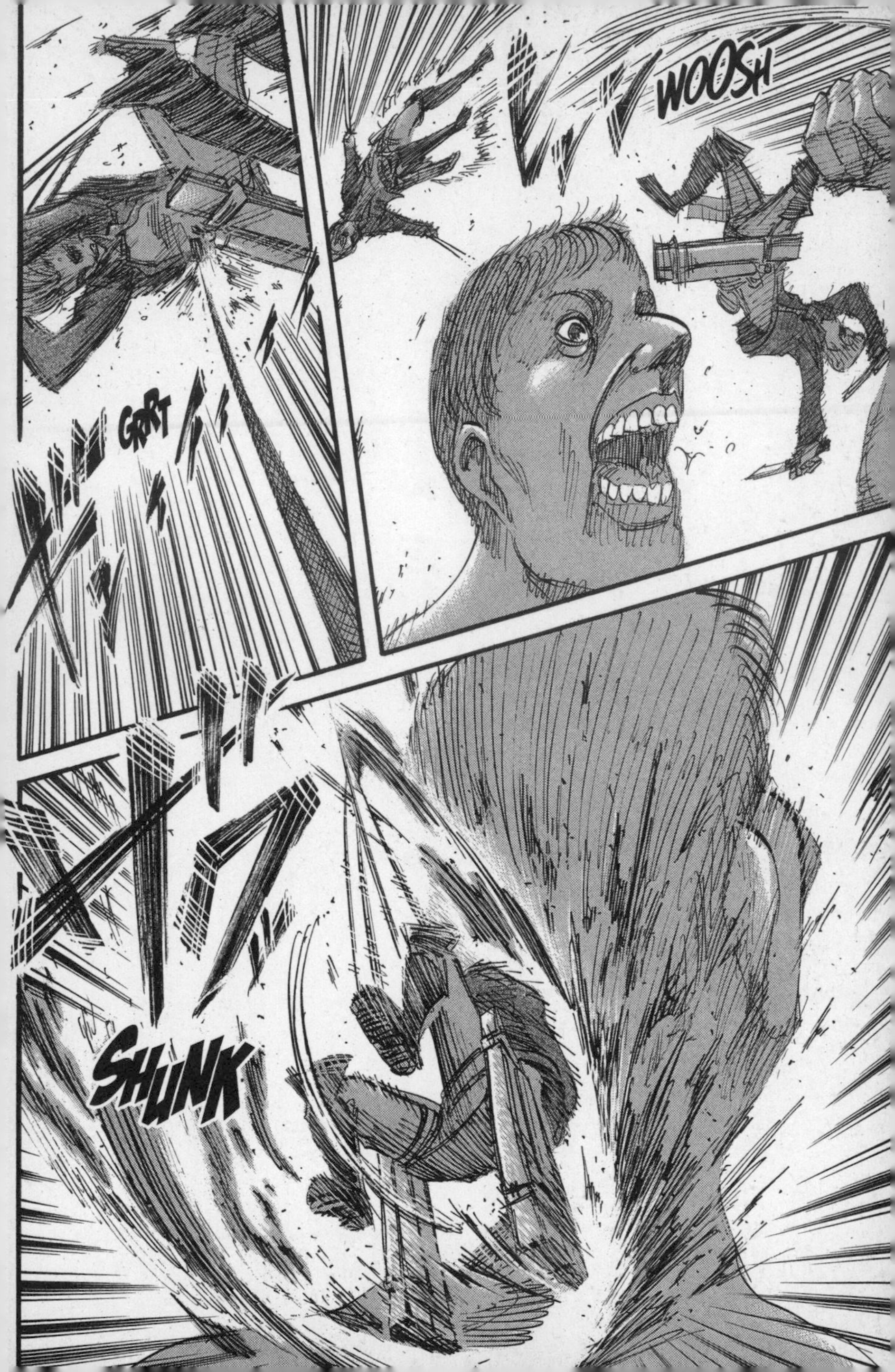
WOOSH
GRRT
SHUNK

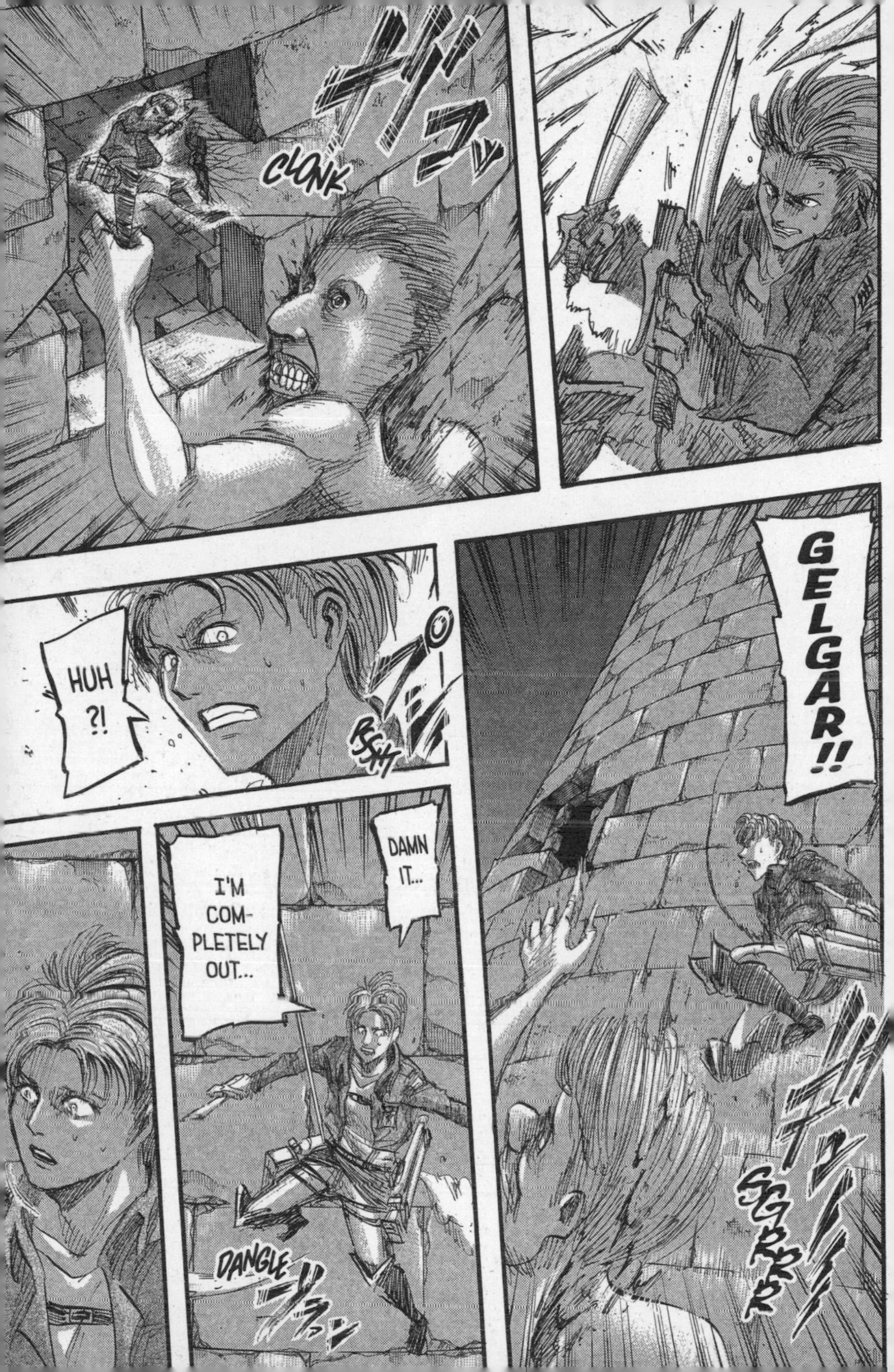
CLONK
GELGAR!!
SCRRRR
HUH ?!
RSHH
DAMN IT...
I'M COMPLETELY OUT...
DANGLE

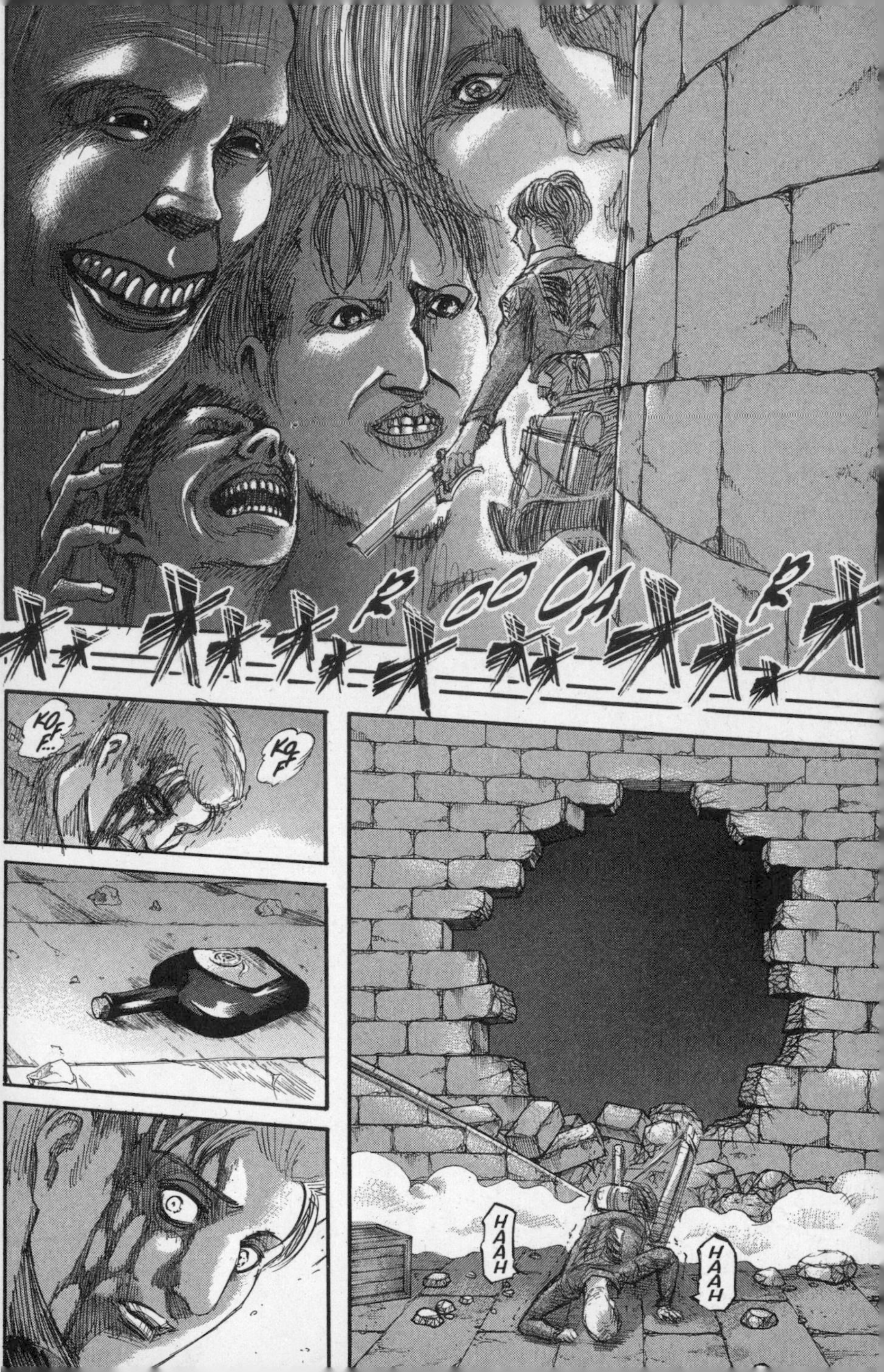
ROOOAR
HAAH
HAAH
KOFF
KOFF...

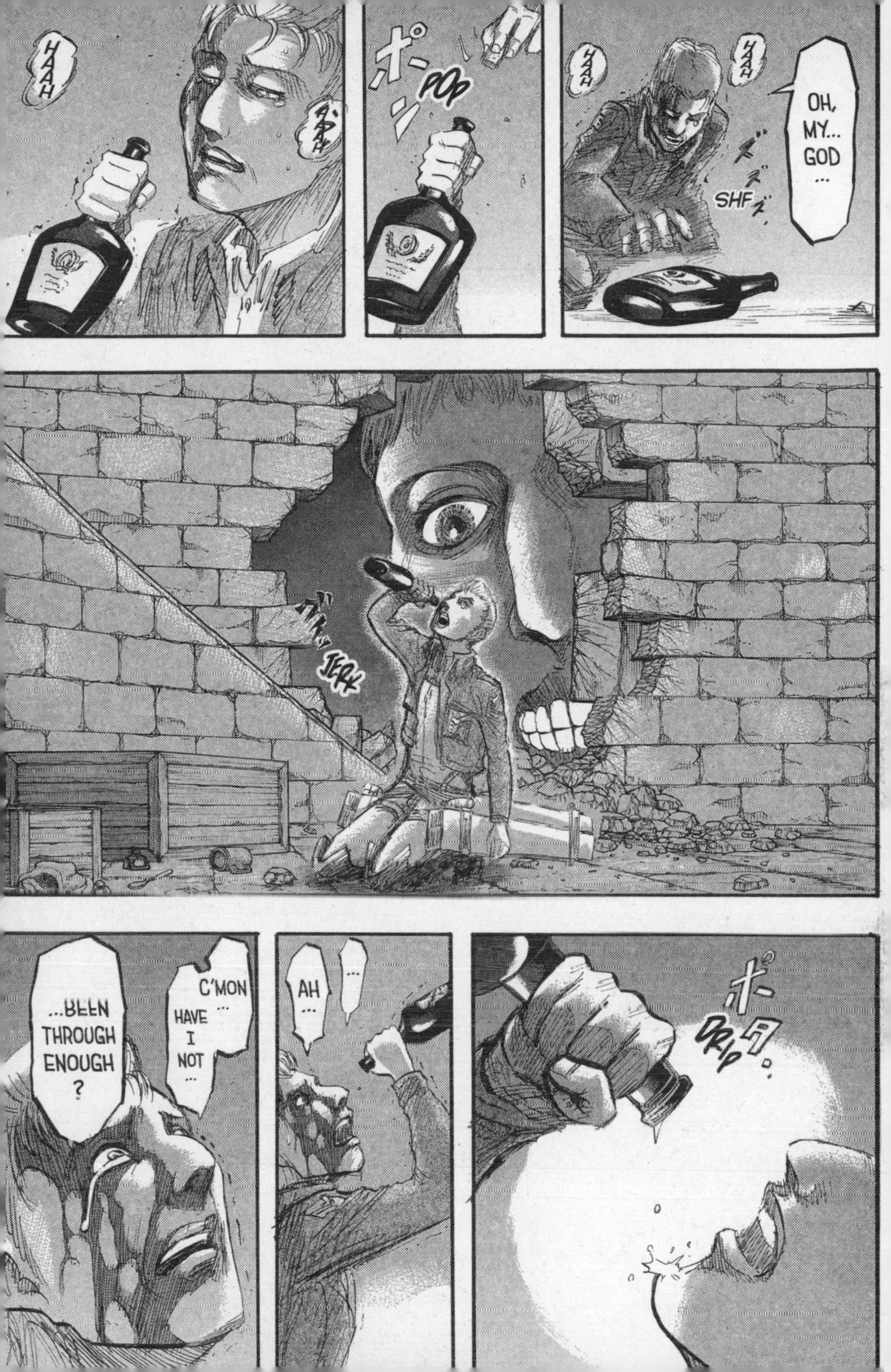

HAAH
OH, MY... GOD ...
SHF
POP
HAAH
HAAH
JERK
DRIP
...
AH ...
C'MON ...
HAVE I NOT ...
...BEEN THROUGH ENOUGH ?

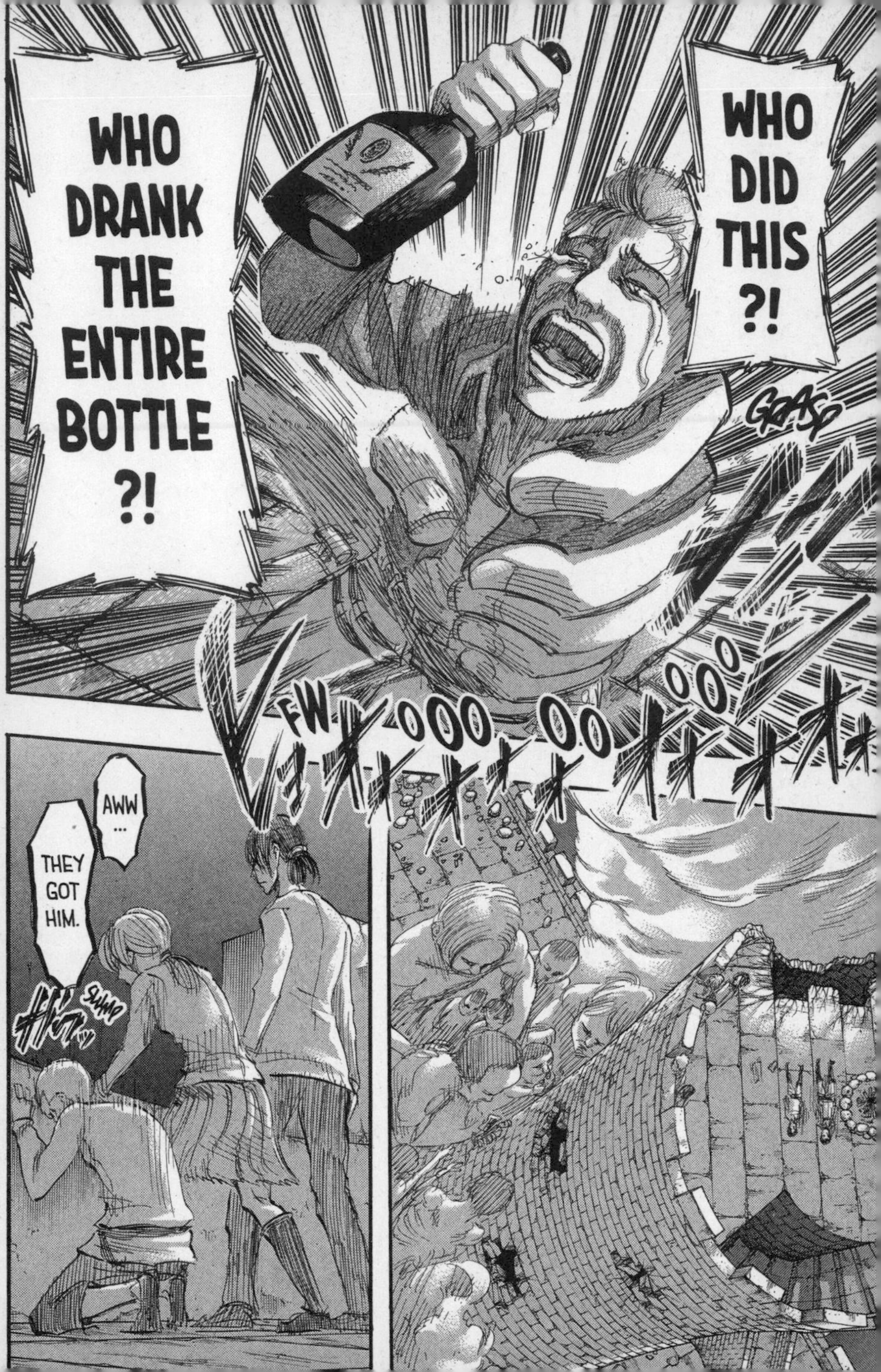
WHO DID THIS ?!
WHO DRANK THE ENTIRE BOTTLE ?!
GRASP
FWOOO OO OOO
AWW ...
THEY GOT HIM.
SLUMP

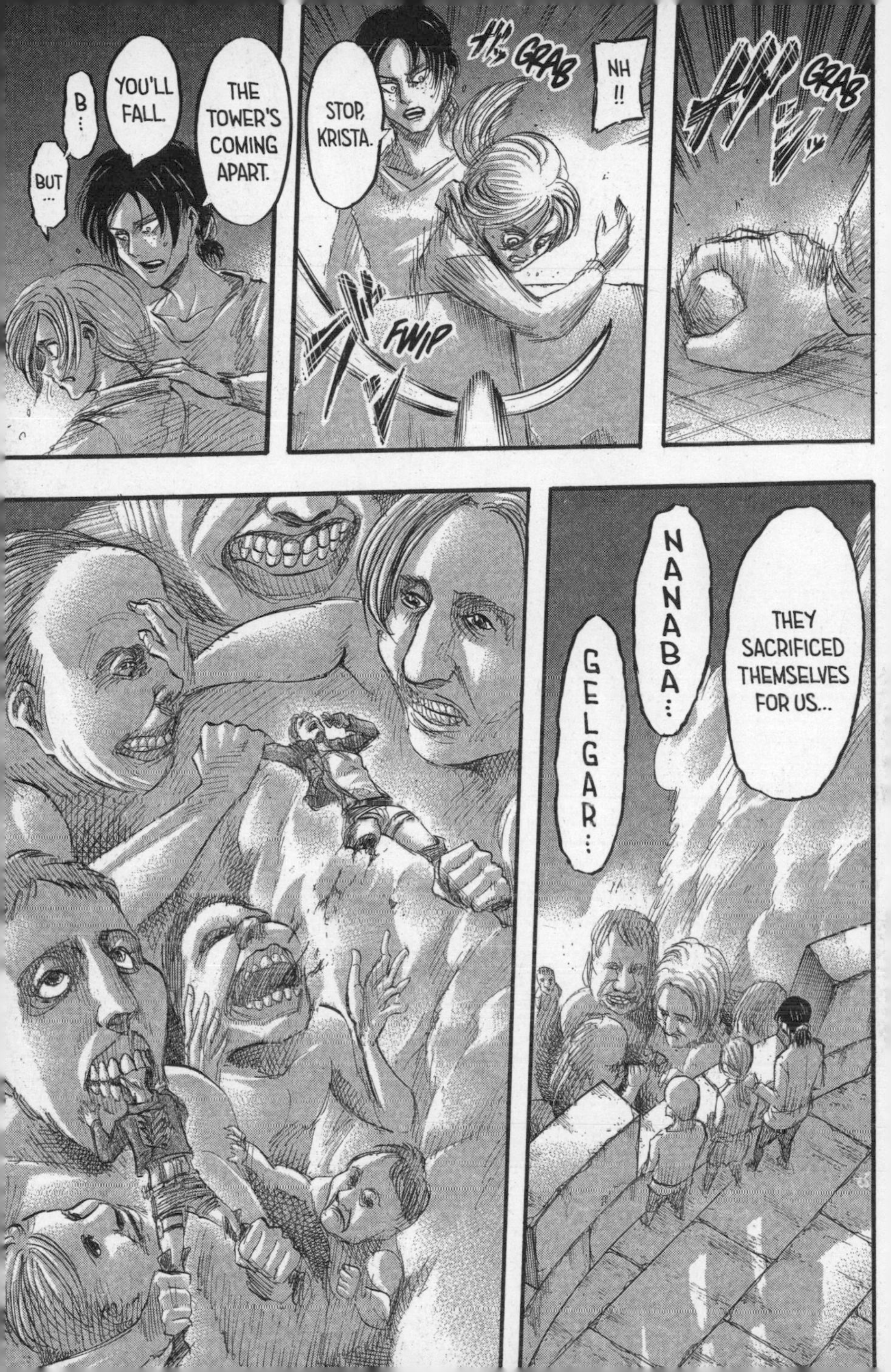
GRAB
NH!!
GRAB
STOP, KRISTA.
FWIP
THE TOWER'S COMING APART.
YOU'LL FALL.
B...
BUT...
THEY SACRIFICED THEMSELVES FOR US...
NANABA...
GELGAR...

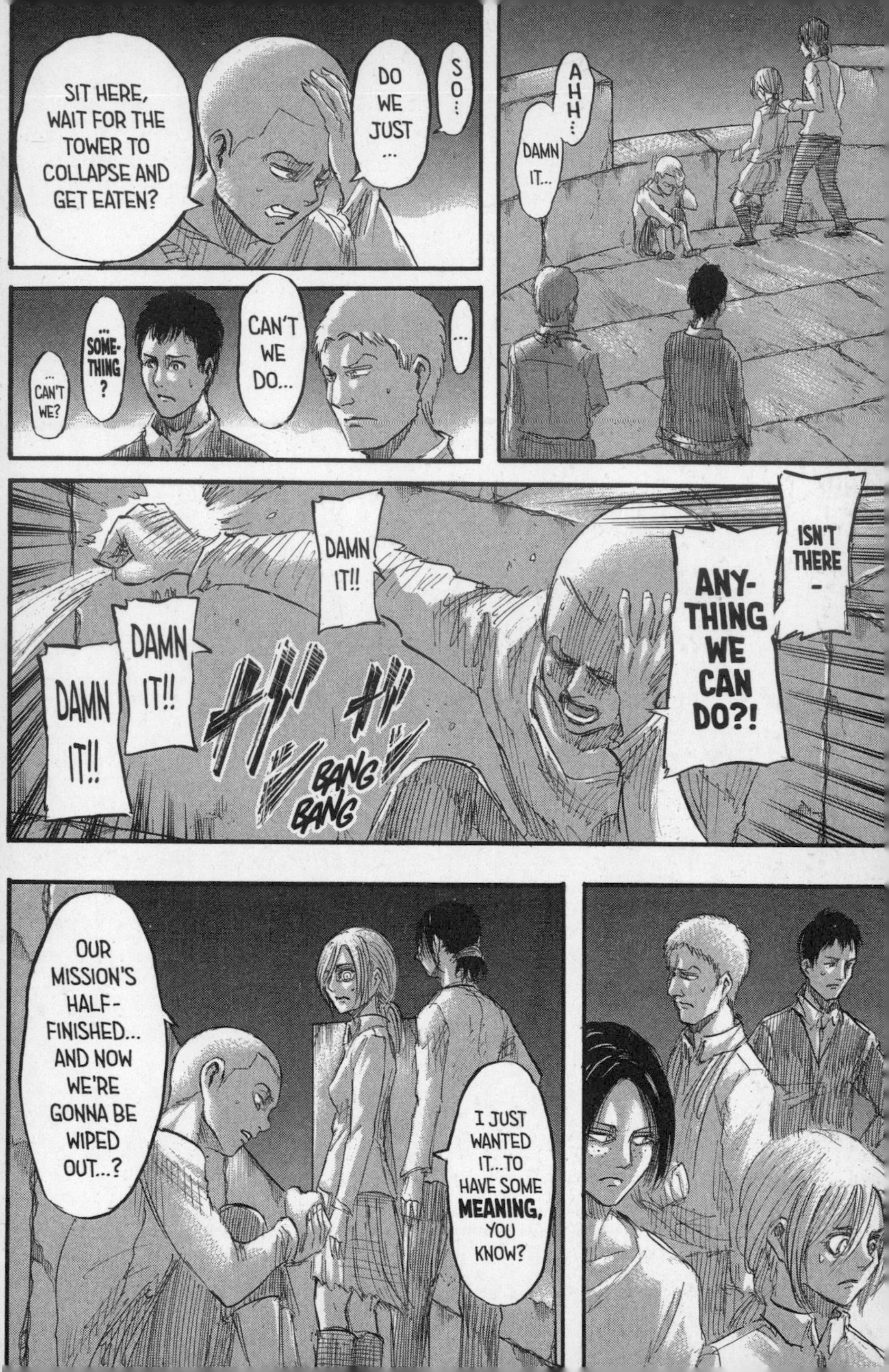

AHH...
DAMN IT...
SO...
DO WE JUST ...
SIT HERE, WAIT FOR THE TOWER TO COLLAPSE AND GET EATEN?
...
CAN'T WE DO...
...SOMETHING?
...CAN'T WE?
ISN'T THERE - ANYTHING WE CAN DO?!
DAMN IT!!
DAMN IT!!
DAMN IT!!
BANG BANG
OUR MISSION'S HALF-FINISHED... AND NOW WE'RE GONNA BE WIPED OUT...?
I JUST WANTED IT...TO HAVE SOME MEANING, YOU KNOW?

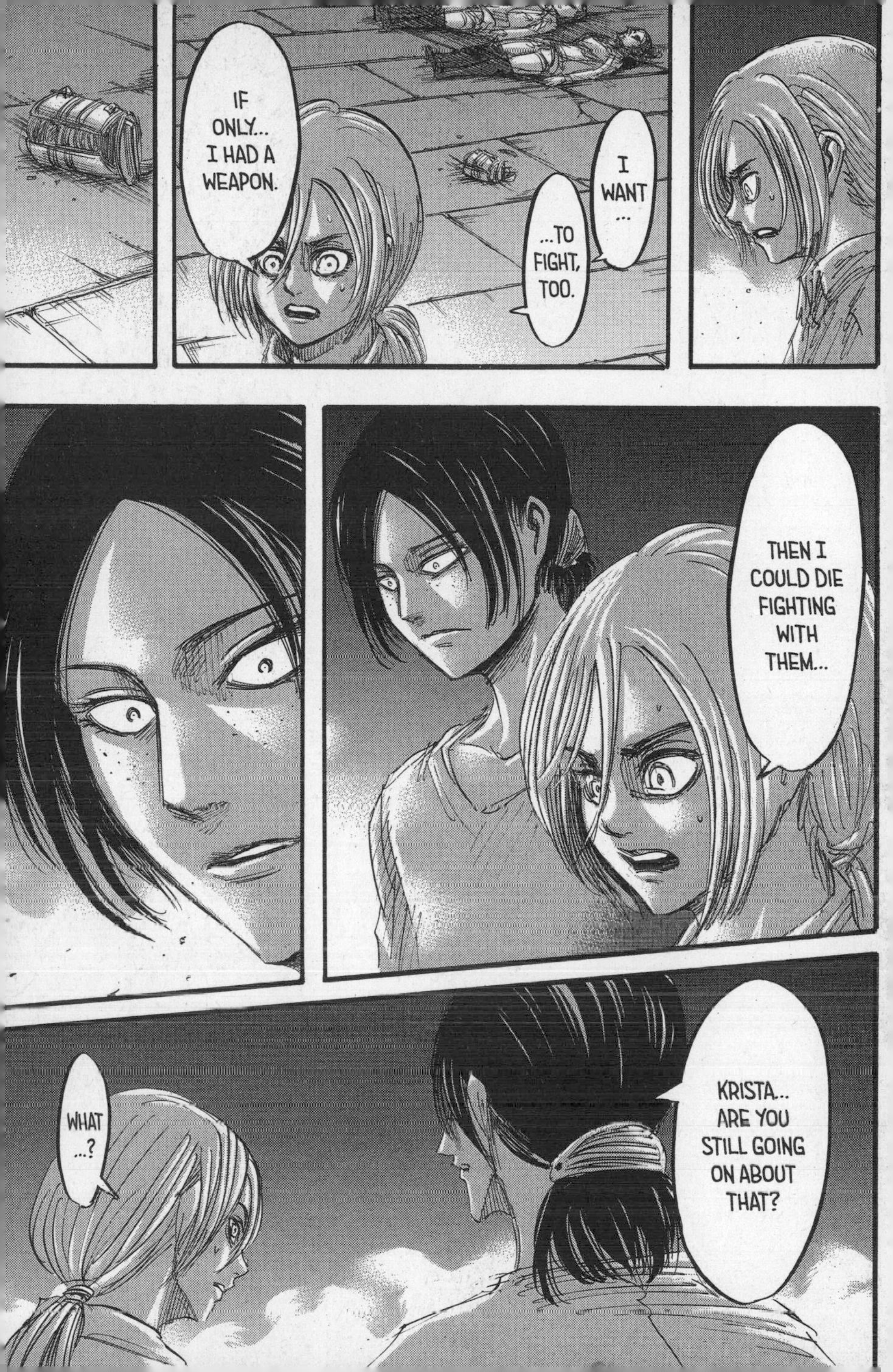

I WANT...
...TO FIGHT, TOO.
IF ONLY... I HAD A WEAPON.
THEN I COULD DIE FIGHTING WITH THEM...
KRISTA... ARE YOU STILL GOING ON ABOUT THAT?
WHAT...?

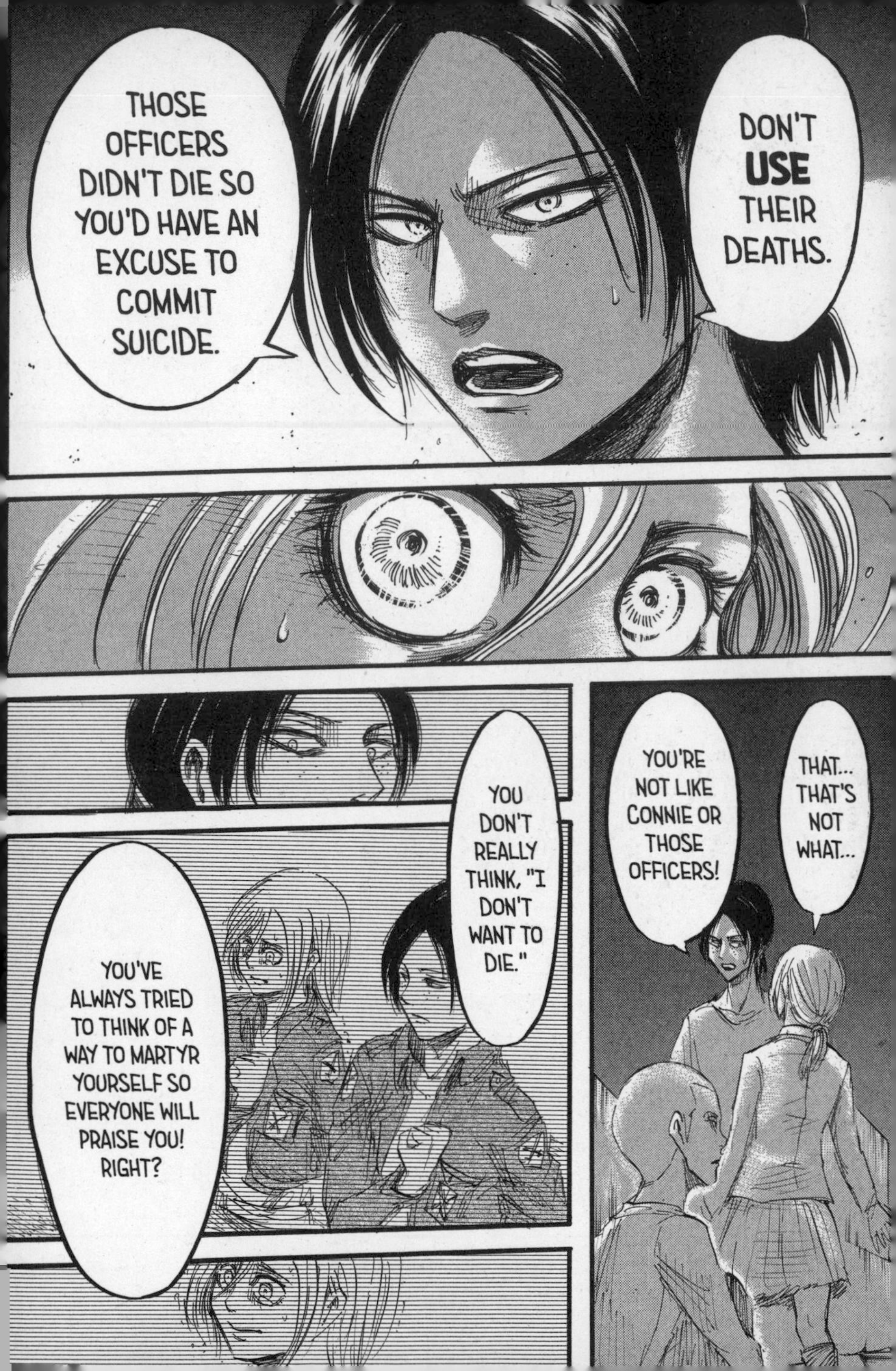
DON'T **USE** THEIR DEATHS.
THOSE OFFICERS DIDN'T DIE SO YOU'D HAVE AN EXCUSE TO COMMIT SUICIDE.
THAT... THAT'S NOT WHAT...
YOU'RE NOT LIKE CONNIE OR THOSE OFFICERS!
YOU DON'T REALLY THINK, "I DON'T WANT TO DIE."
YOU'VE ALWAYS TRIED TO THINK OF A WAY TO MARTYR YOURSELF SO EVERYONE WILL PRAISE YOU! RIGHT?

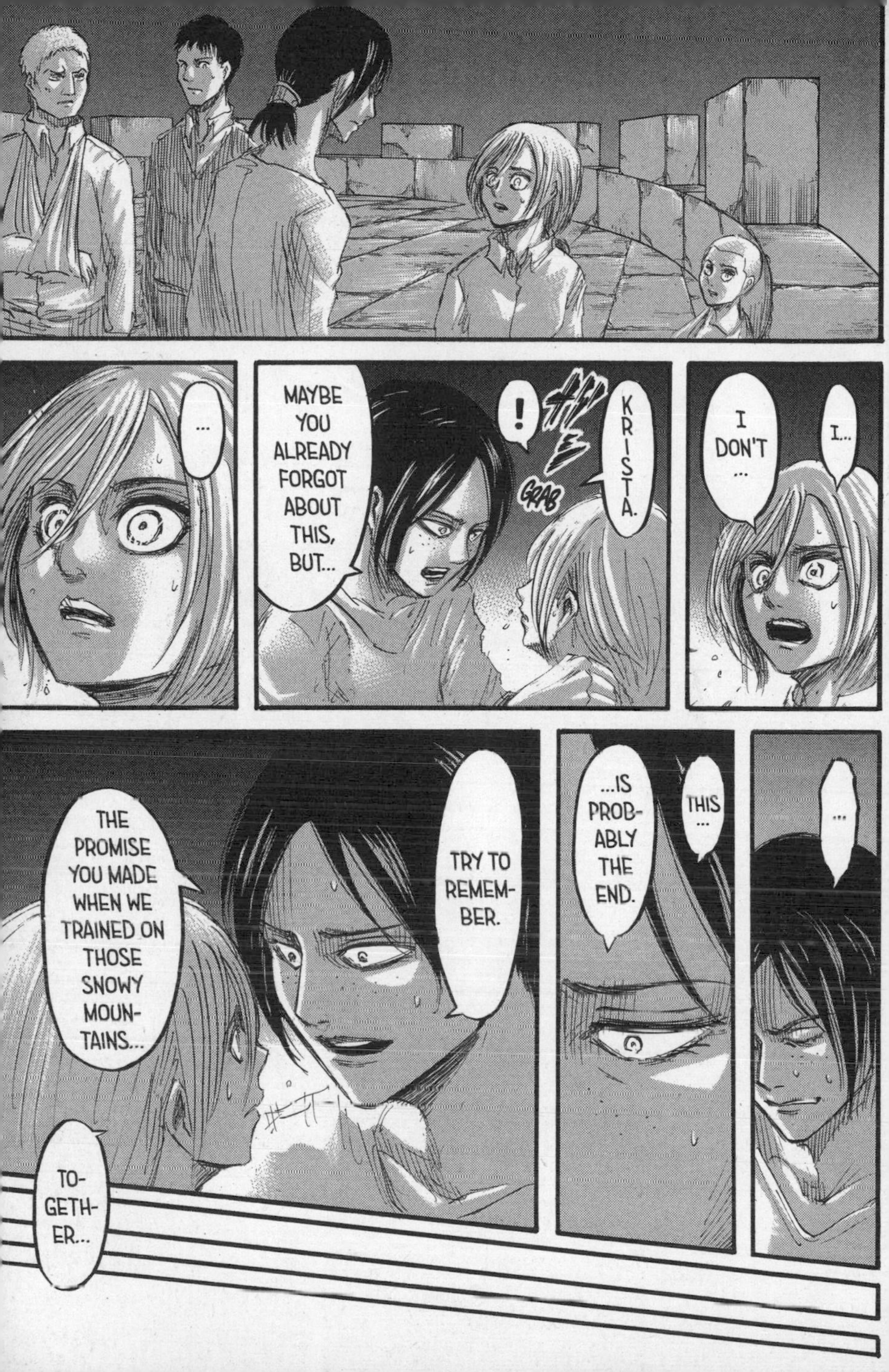
I...
I DON'T ...
KRISTA.
GRAB
!
MAYBE YOU ALREADY FORGOT ABOUT THIS, BUT...
...
...
THIS ...
...IS PROBABLY THE END.
TRY TO REMEMBER.
THE PROMISE YOU MADE WHEN WE TRAINED ON THOSE SNOWY MOUNTAINS...
TOGETHER...

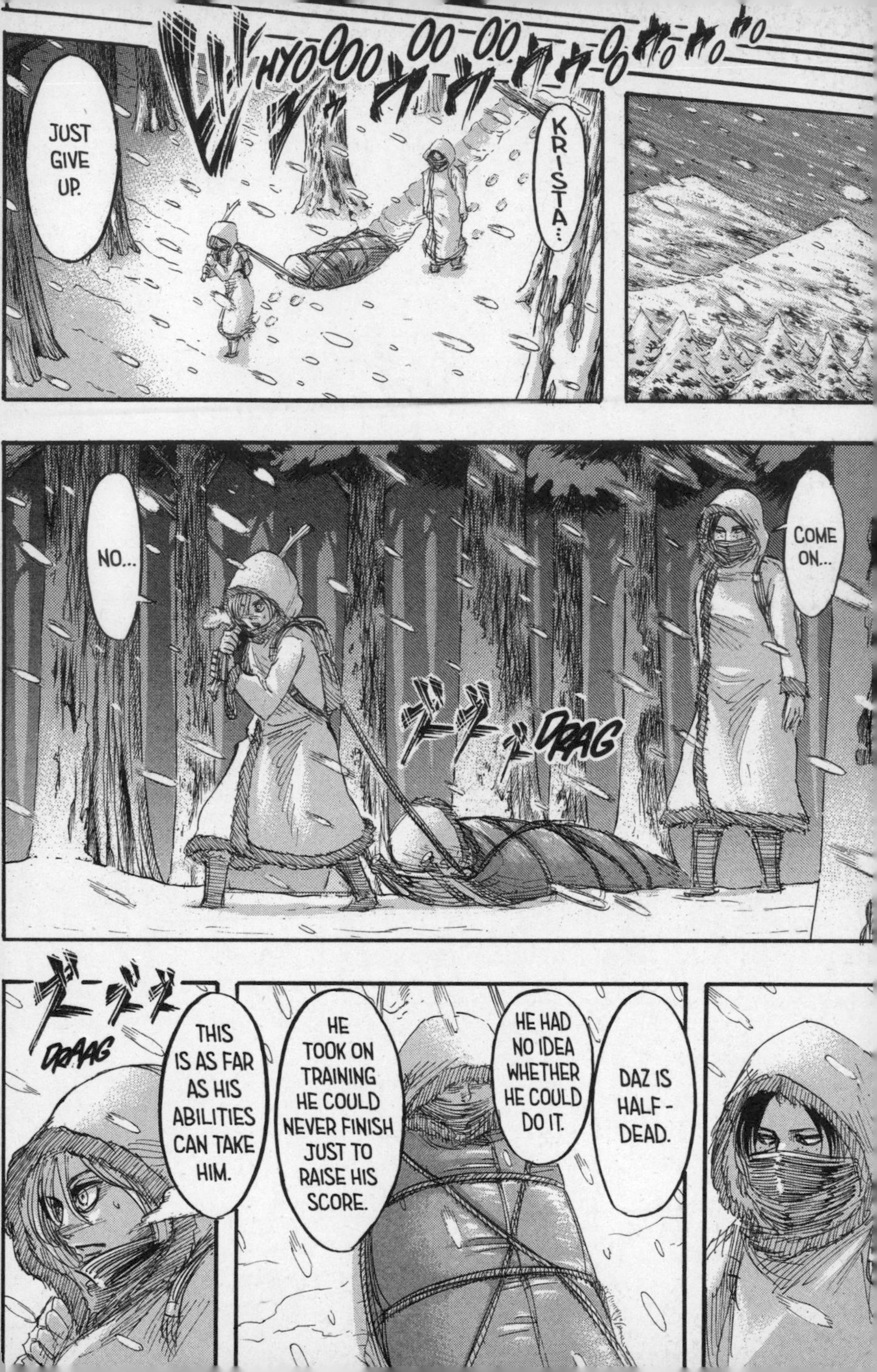

WHYOOOO OO OO
KRISTA...
JUST GIVE UP.
COME ON...
DRAG
NO...
DAZ IS HALF-DEAD.
HE HAD NO IDEA WHETHER HE COULD DO IT.
HE TOOK ON TRAINING HE COULD NEVER FINISH JUST TO RAISE HIS SCORE.
THIS IS AS FAR AS HIS ABILITIES CAN TAKE HIM.
DRAAG

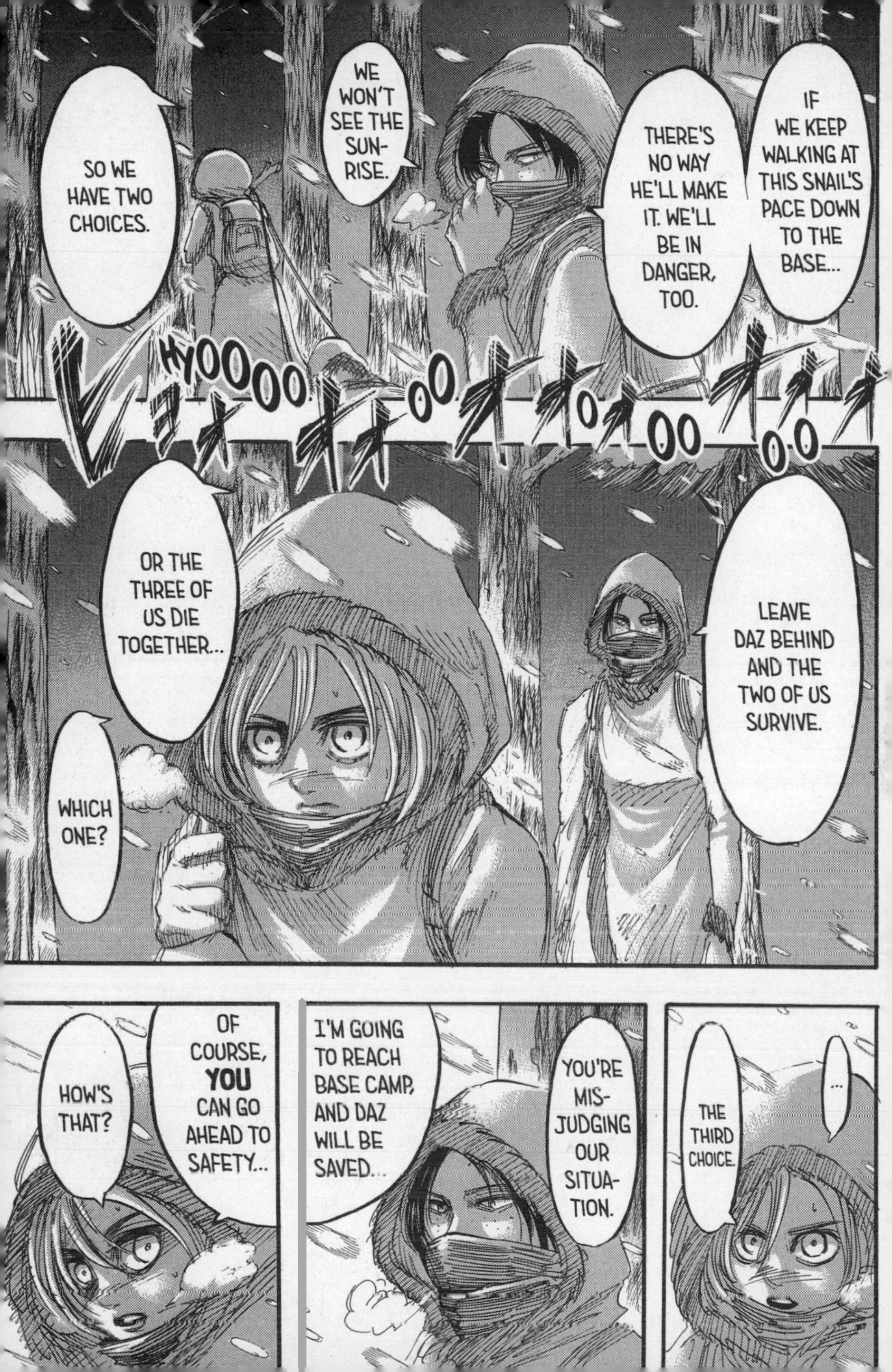
IF WE KEEP WALKING AT THIS SNAIL'S PACE DOWN TO THE BASE...
THERE'S NO WAY HE'LL MAKE IT. WE'LL BE IN DANGER, TOO.
WE WON'T SEE THE SUN-RISE.
SO WE HAVE TWO CHOICES.
HYOOOOOOOOOOOOOO
LEAVE DAZ BEHIND AND THE TWO OF US SURVIVE.
OR THE THREE OF US DIE TOGETHER...
WHICH ONE?
...
THE THIRD CHOICE.
YOU'RE MIS-JUDGING OUR SITUA-TION.
I'M GOING TO REACH BASE CAMP, AND DAZ WILL BE SAVED...
OF COURSE, **YOU** CAN GO AHEAD TO SAFETY...
HOW'S THAT?

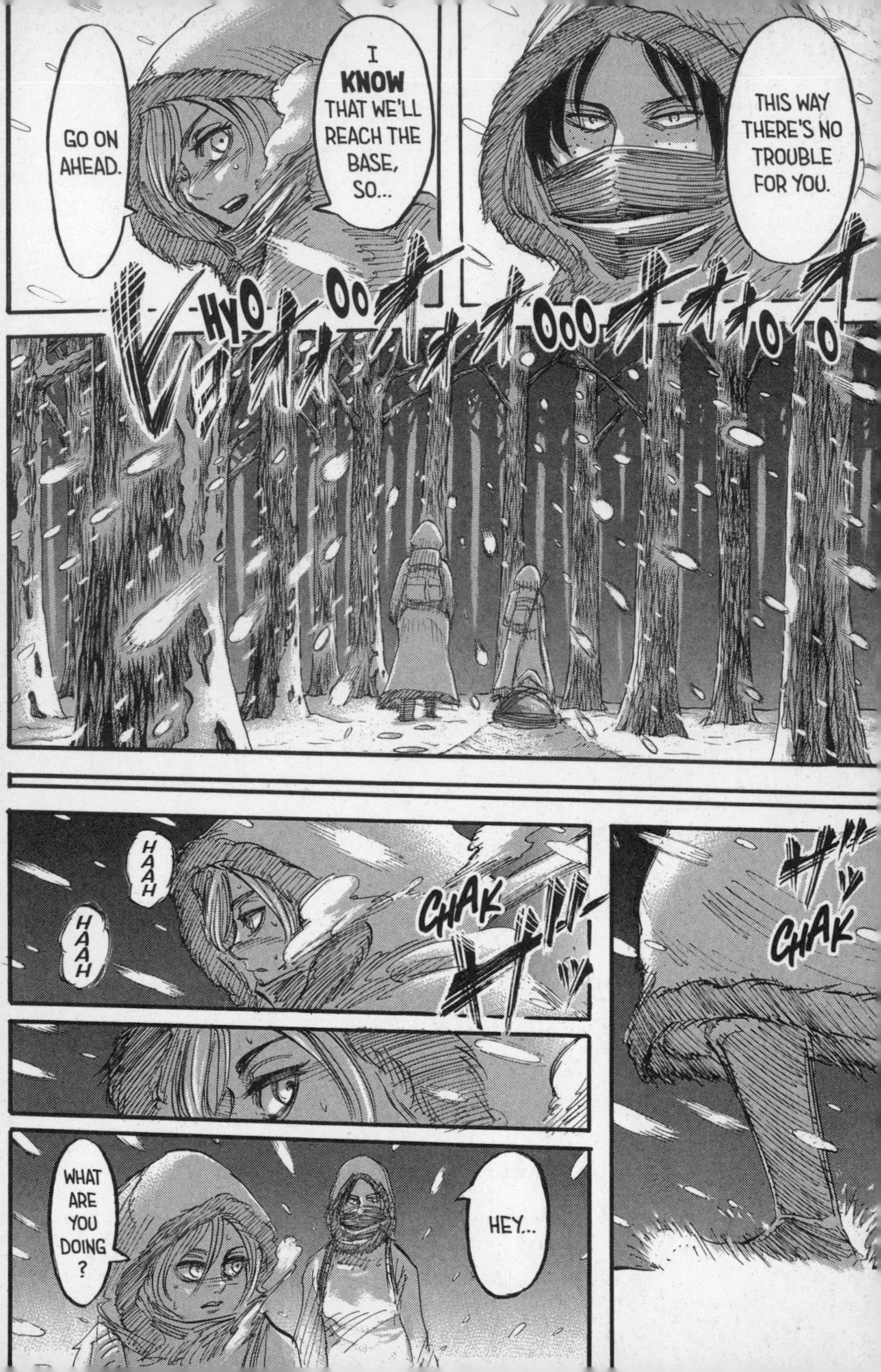

THIS WAY THERE'S NO TROUBLE FOR YOU.
I KNOW THAT WE'LL REACH THE BASE, SO...
GO ON AHEAD.
HYO OO OOO O
CHAK
HAAH
HAAAH
CHAK
HEY...
WHAT ARE YOU DOING?

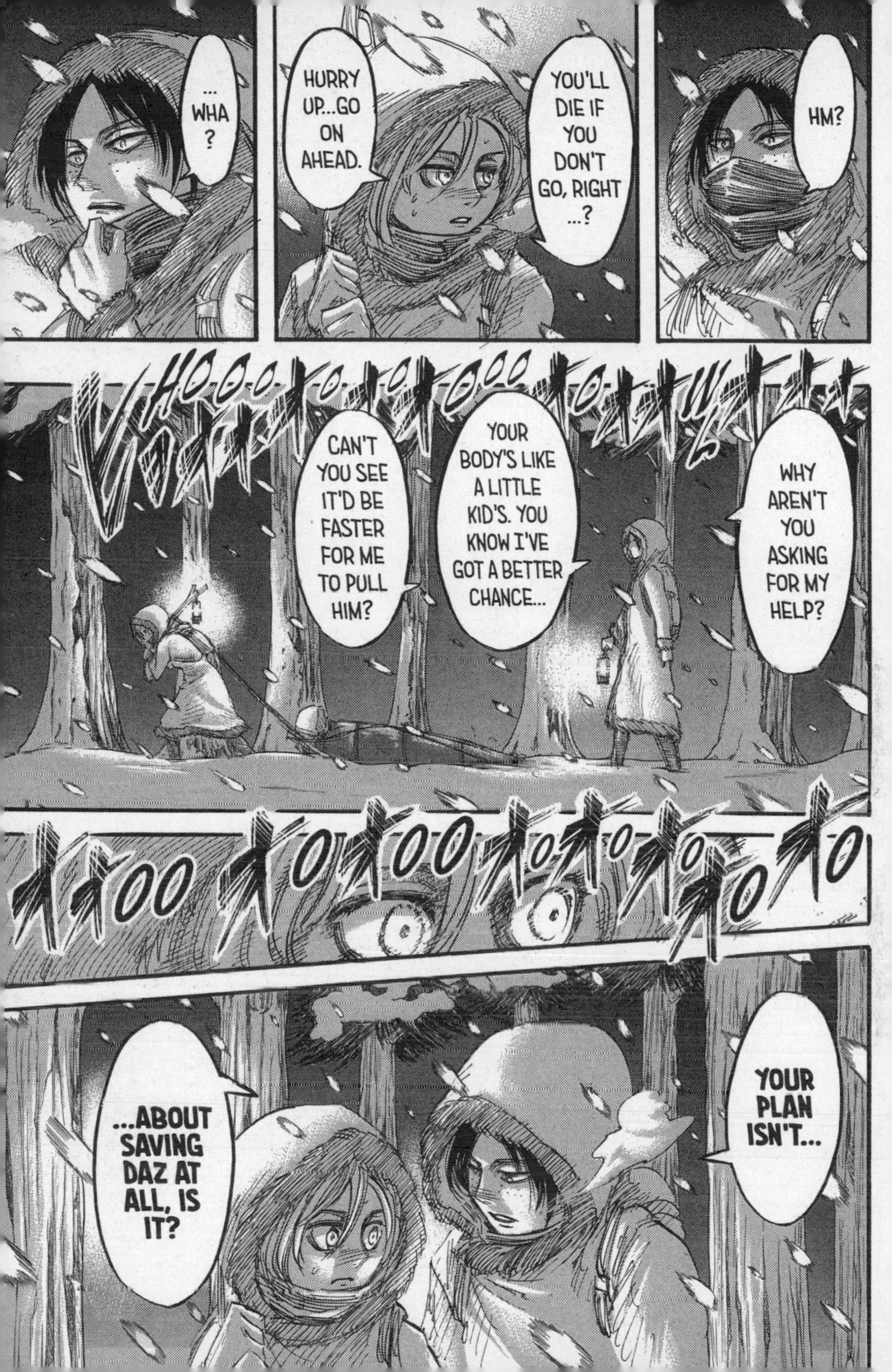
HM?
YOU'LL DIE IF YOU DON'T GO, RIGHT ...?
HURRY UP...GO ON AHEAD.
... WHA ?
WHY AREN'T YOU ASKING FOR MY HELP?
YOUR BODY'S LIKE A LITTLE KID'S. YOU KNOW I'VE GOT A BETTER CHANCE...
CAN'T YOU SEE IT'D BE FASTER FOR ME TO PULL HIM?
YOUR PLAN ISN'T...
...ABOUT SAVING DAZ AT ALL, IS IT?

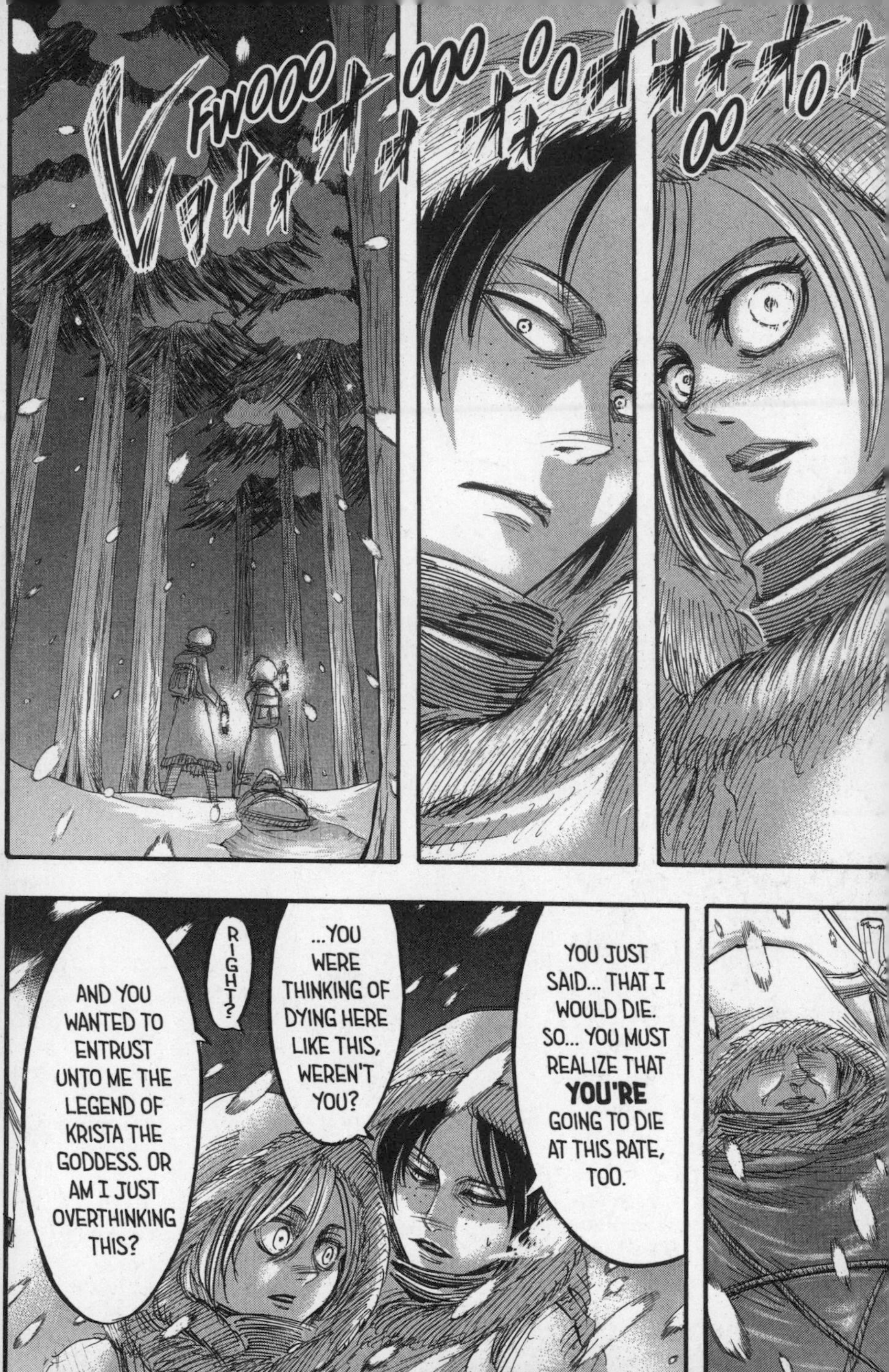

FWOOOOOOOOOOOOO
YOU JUST SAID... THAT I WOULD DIE. SO... YOU MUST REALIZE THAT YOU'RE GOING TO DIE AT THIS RATE, TOO.
...YOU WERE THINKING OF DYING HERE LIKE THIS, WEREN'T YOU?
RIGHT?
AND YOU WANTED TO ENTRUST UNTO ME THE LEGEND OF KRISTA THE GODDESS. OR AM I JUST OVERTHINKING THIS?

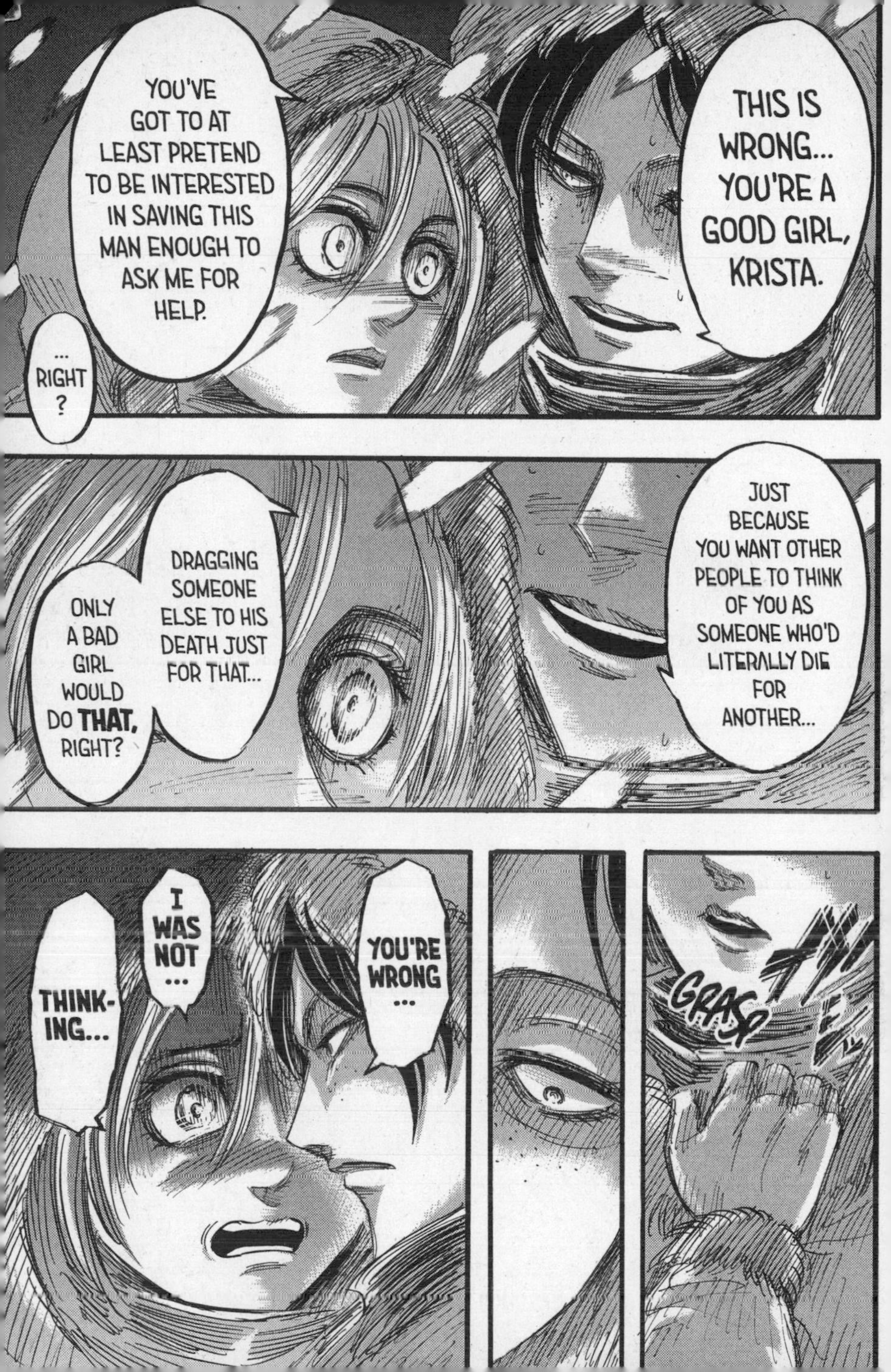
THIS IS WRONG... YOU'RE A GOOD GIRL, KRISTA.
YOU'VE GOT TO AT LEAST PRETEND TO BE INTERESTED IN SAVING THIS MAN ENOUGH TO ASK ME FOR HELP.
...RIGHT?
JUST BECAUSE YOU WANT OTHER PEOPLE TO THINK OF YOU AS SOMEONE WHO'D LITERALLY DIE FOR ANOTHER...
DRAGGING SOMEONE ELSE TO HIS DEATH JUST FOR THAT...
ONLY A BAD GIRL WOULD DO **THAT,** RIGHT?
GRASP
YOU'RE WRONG...
I WAS NOT...
THINKING...

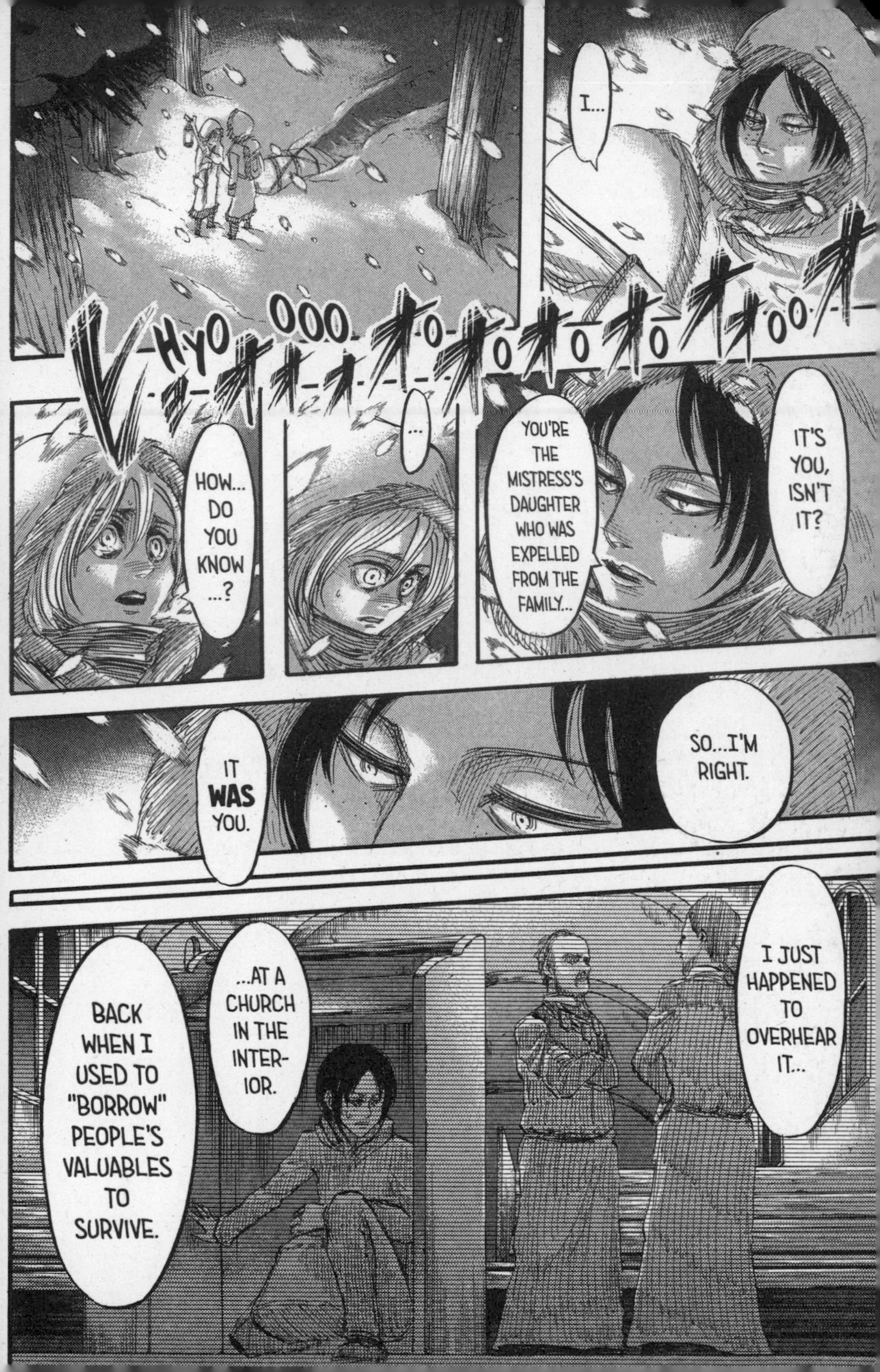
I...
VHYOOOOOOOOOOOO
IT'S YOU, ISN'T IT?
YOU'RE THE MISTRESS'S DAUGHTER WHO WAS EXPELLED FROM THE FAMILY...
...
HOW... DO YOU KNOW ...?
SO...I'M RIGHT.
IT **WAS** YOU.
I JUST HAPPENED TO OVERHEAR IT...
...AT A CHURCH IN THE INTER-IOR.
BACK WHEN I USED TO "BORROW" PEOPLE'S VALUABLES TO SURVIVE.

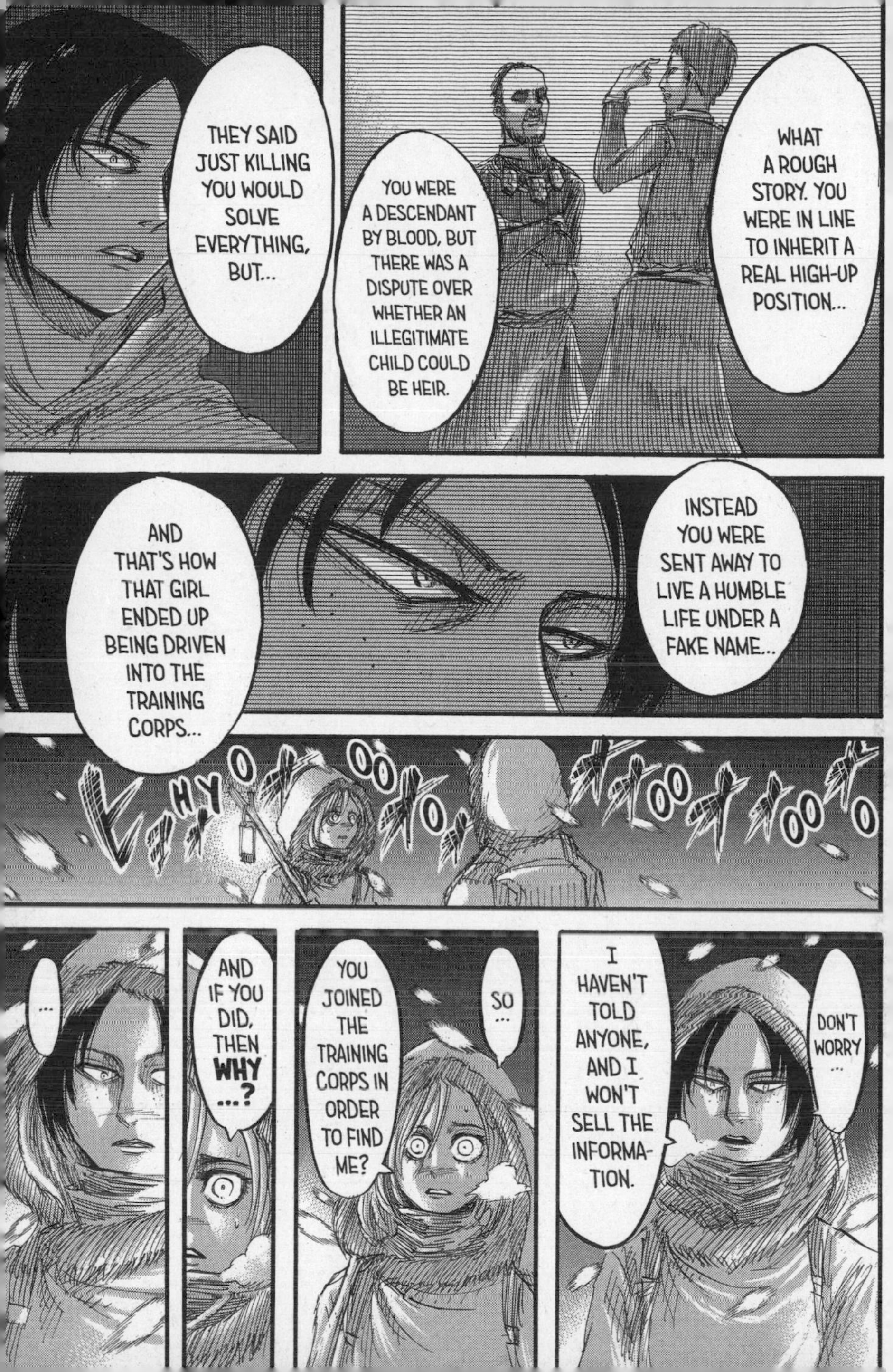
WHAT A ROUGH STORY. YOU WERE IN LINE TO INHERIT A REAL HIGH-UP POSITION...
YOU WERE A DESCENDANT BY BLOOD, BUT THERE WAS A DISPUTE OVER WHETHER AN ILLEGITIMATE CHILD COULD BE HEIR.
THEY SAID JUST KILLING YOU WOULD SOLVE EVERYTHING, BUT...
INSTEAD YOU WERE SENT AWAY TO LIVE A HUMBLE LIFE UNDER A FAKE NAME...
AND THAT'S HOW THAT GIRL ENDED UP BEING DRIVEN INTO THE TRAINING CORPS...
DON'T WORRY...
I HAVEN'T TOLD ANYONE, AND I WON'T SELL THE INFORMATION.
SO...
YOU JOINED THE TRAINING CORPS IN ORDER TO FIND ME?
AND IF YOU DID, THEN **WHY**...?
...

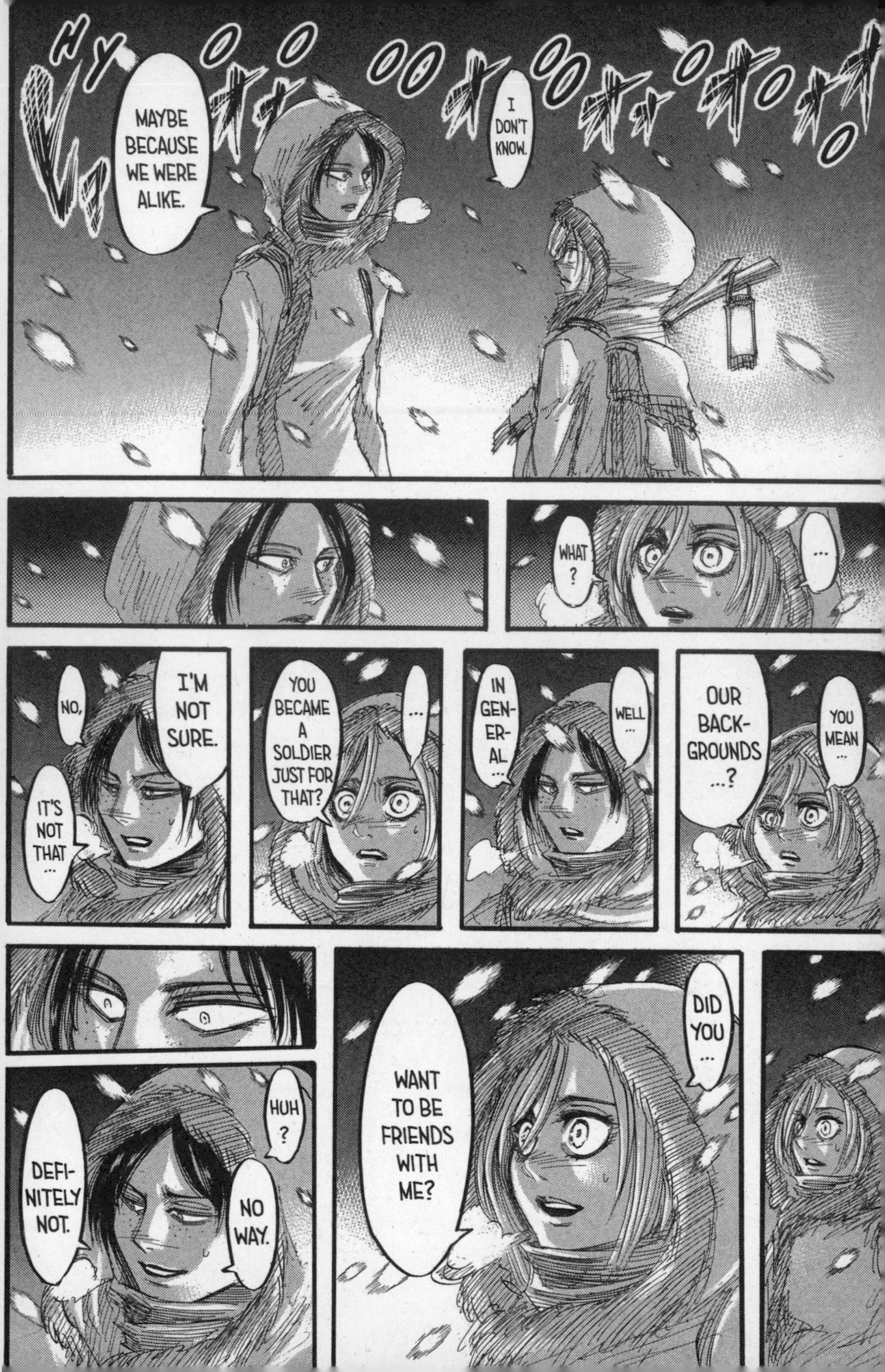
HYOOOOOOOOOO
I DON'T KNOW.
MAYBE BECAUSE WE WERE ALIKE.
...
WHAT?
YOU MEAN ...
OUR BACKGROUNDS ...?
WELL ...
IN GENERAL ...
...
YOU BECAME A SOLDIER JUST FOR THAT?
I'M NOT SURE.
NO,
IT'S NOT THAT ...
DID YOU ...
WANT TO BE FRIENDS WITH ME?
HUH?
NO WAY.
DEFINITELY NOT.

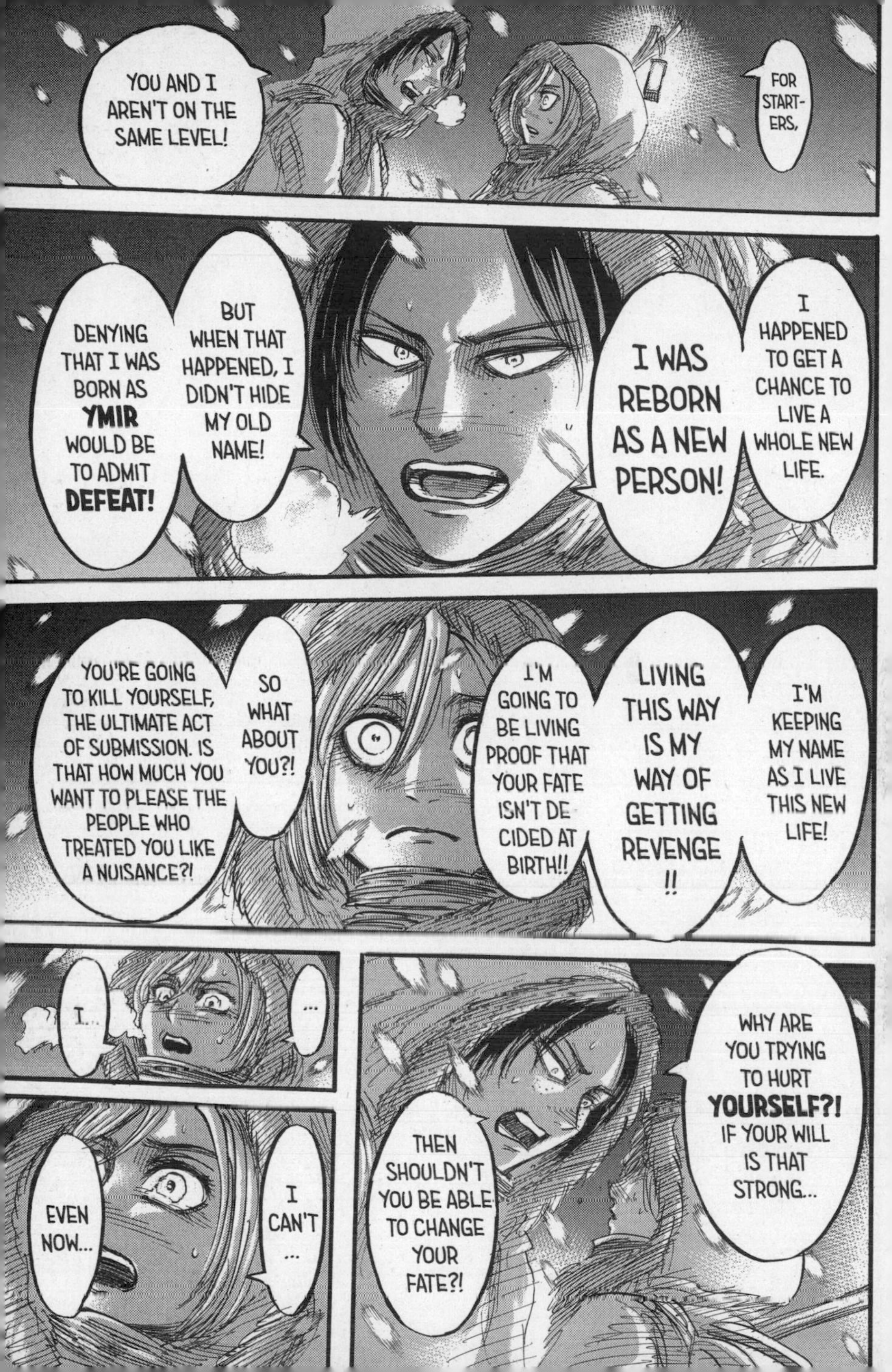
FOR STARTERS,
YOU AND I AREN'T ON THE SAME LEVEL!
I HAPPENED TO GET A CHANCE TO LIVE A WHOLE NEW LIFE.
I WAS REBORN AS A NEW PERSON!
BUT WHEN THAT HAPPENED, I DIDN'T HIDE MY OLD NAME!
DENYING THAT I WAS BORN AS **YMIR** WOULD BE TO ADMIT **DEFEAT!**
I'M KEEPING MY NAME AS I LIVE THIS NEW LIFE!
LIVING THIS WAY IS MY WAY OF GETTING REVENGE !!
I'M GOING TO BE LIVING PROOF THAT YOUR FATE ISN'T DE CIDED AT BIRTH!!
SO WHAT ABOUT YOU?!
YOU'RE GOING TO KILL YOURSELF, THE ULTIMATE ACT OF SUBMISSION. IS THAT HOW MUCH YOU WANT TO PLEASE THE PEOPLE WHO TREATED YOU LIKE A NUISANCE?!
WHY ARE YOU TRYING TO HURT **YOURSELF?!** IF YOUR WILL IS THAT STRONG...
THEN SHOULDN'T YOU BE ABLE TO CHANGE YOUR FATE?!
...
I...
I CAN'T ...
EVEN NOW...

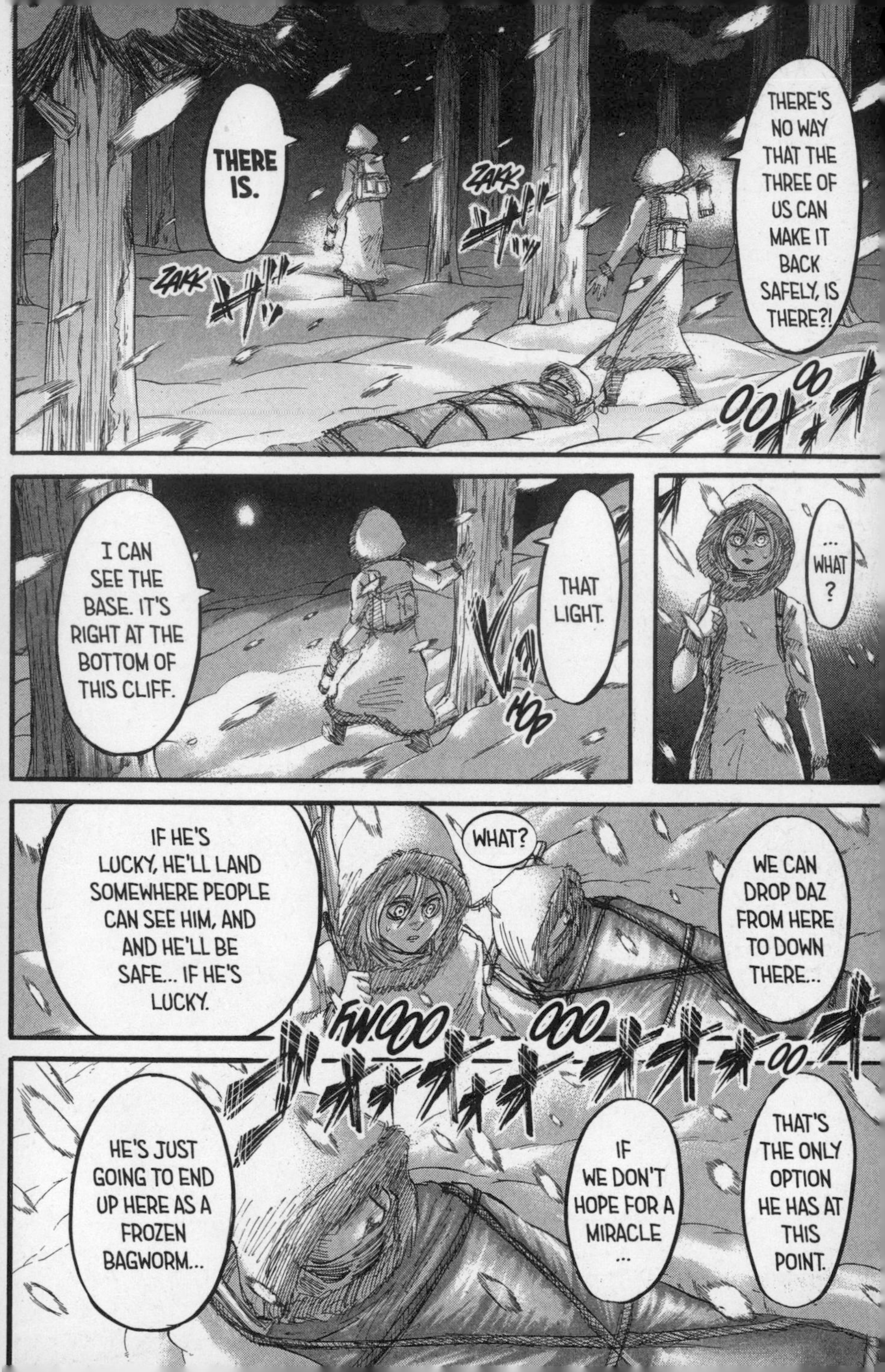
THERE'S NO WAY THAT THE THREE OF US CAN MAKE IT BACK SAFELY, IS THERE?!
ZAKK
THERE IS.
ZAKK
OOOO
... WHAT ?
THAT LIGHT.
HOP
I CAN SEE THE BASE. IT'S RIGHT AT THE BOTTOM OF THIS CLIFF.
WHAT?
WE CAN DROP DAZ FROM HERE TO DOWN THERE...
IF HE'S LUCKY, HE'LL LAND SOMEWHERE PEOPLE CAN SEE HIM, AND AND HE'LL BE SAFE... IF HE'S LUCKY.
FWOOO OOO OO
THAT'S THE ONLY OPTION HE HAS AT THIS POINT.
IF WE DON'T HOPE FOR A MIRACLE ...
HE'S JUST GOING TO END UP HERE AS A FROZEN BAGWORM...

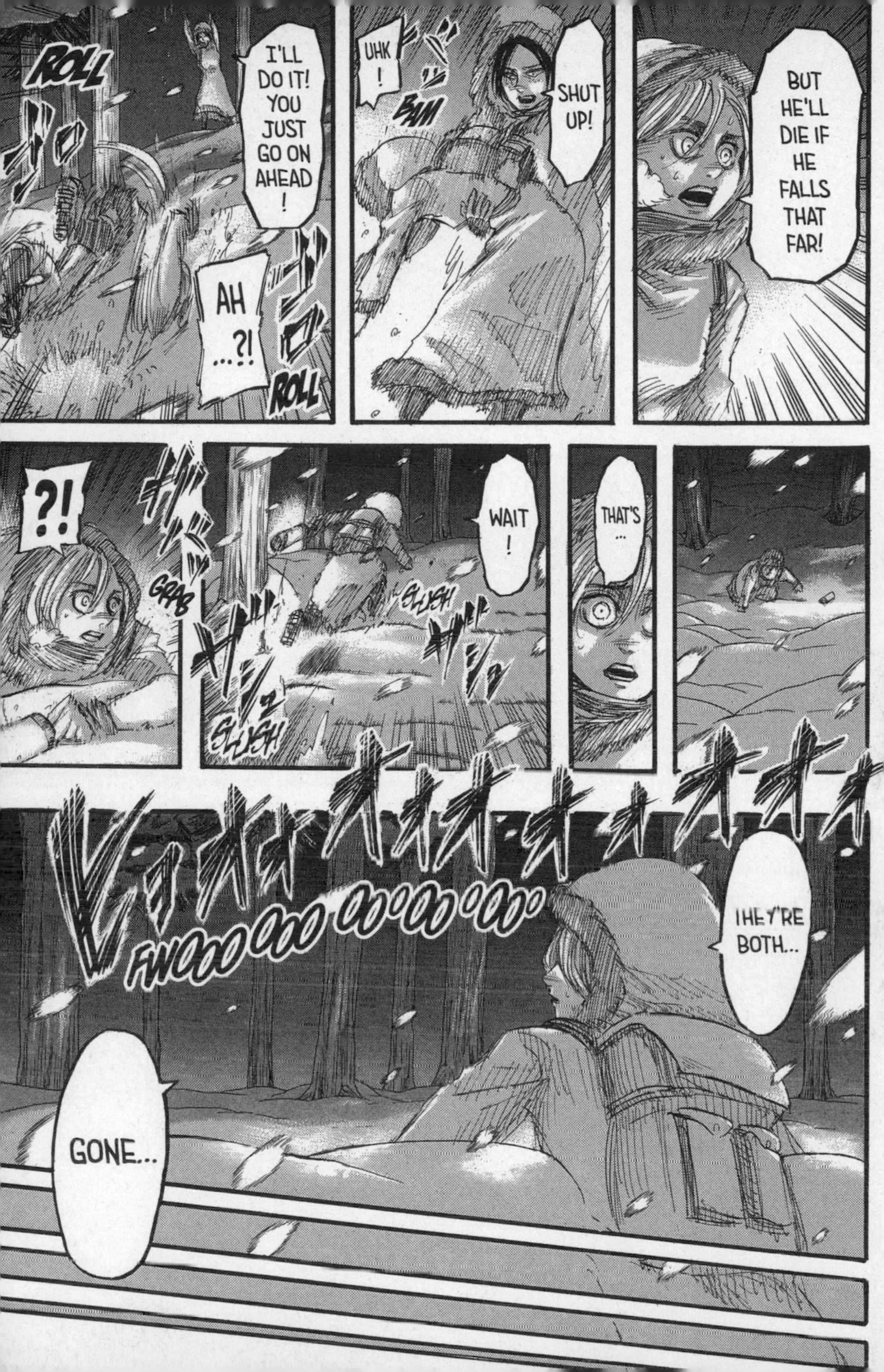
BUT HE'LL DIE IF HE FALLS THAT FAR!
UHK!
SHUT UP!
BAM
I'LL DO IT! YOU JUST GO ON AHEAD!
ROLL
AH ...?!
ROLL
THAT'S ...
WAIT!
SLUSH
SLUSH
?!
GRAB
FWOOOOOOOOOOOOOO
THEY'RE BOTH...
GONE...

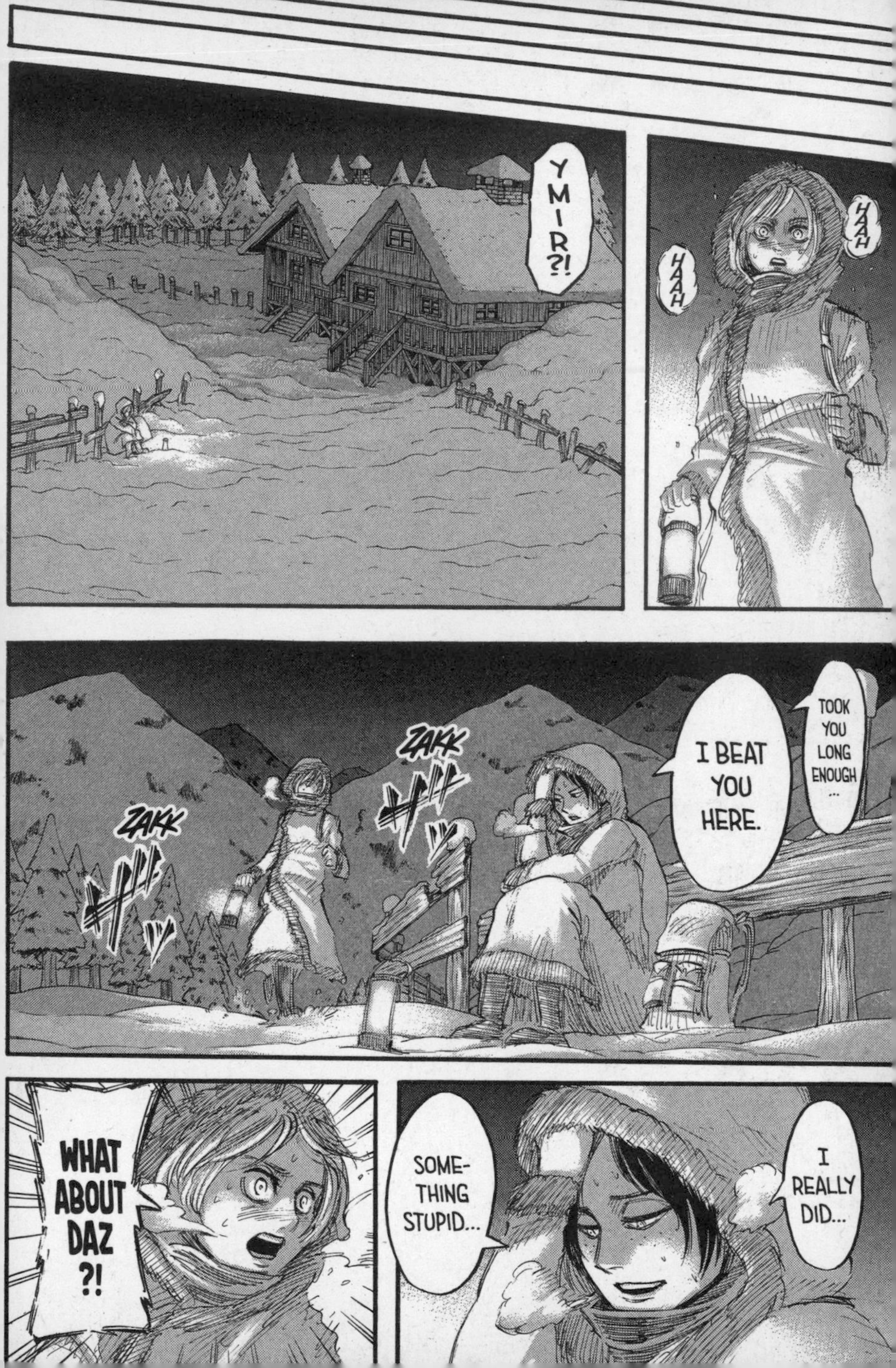
HAAH
HAAH
YMIR?!
TOOK YOU LONG ENOUGH...
I BEAT YOU HERE.
ZAKK
ZAKK
I REALLY DID...
SOME-THING STUPID...
WHAT ABOUT DAZ?!

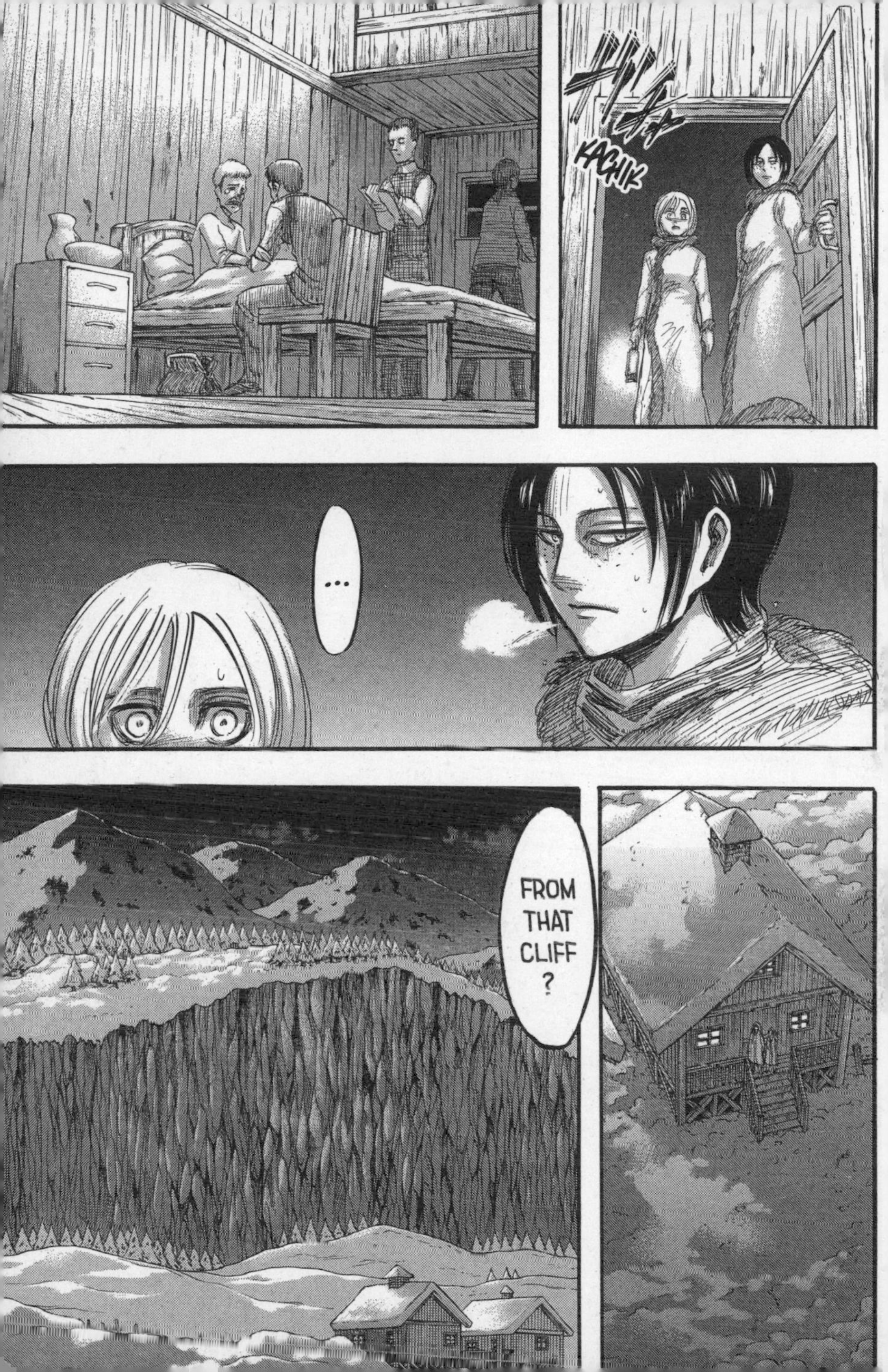
KACHIK
...
FROM THAT CLIFF ?

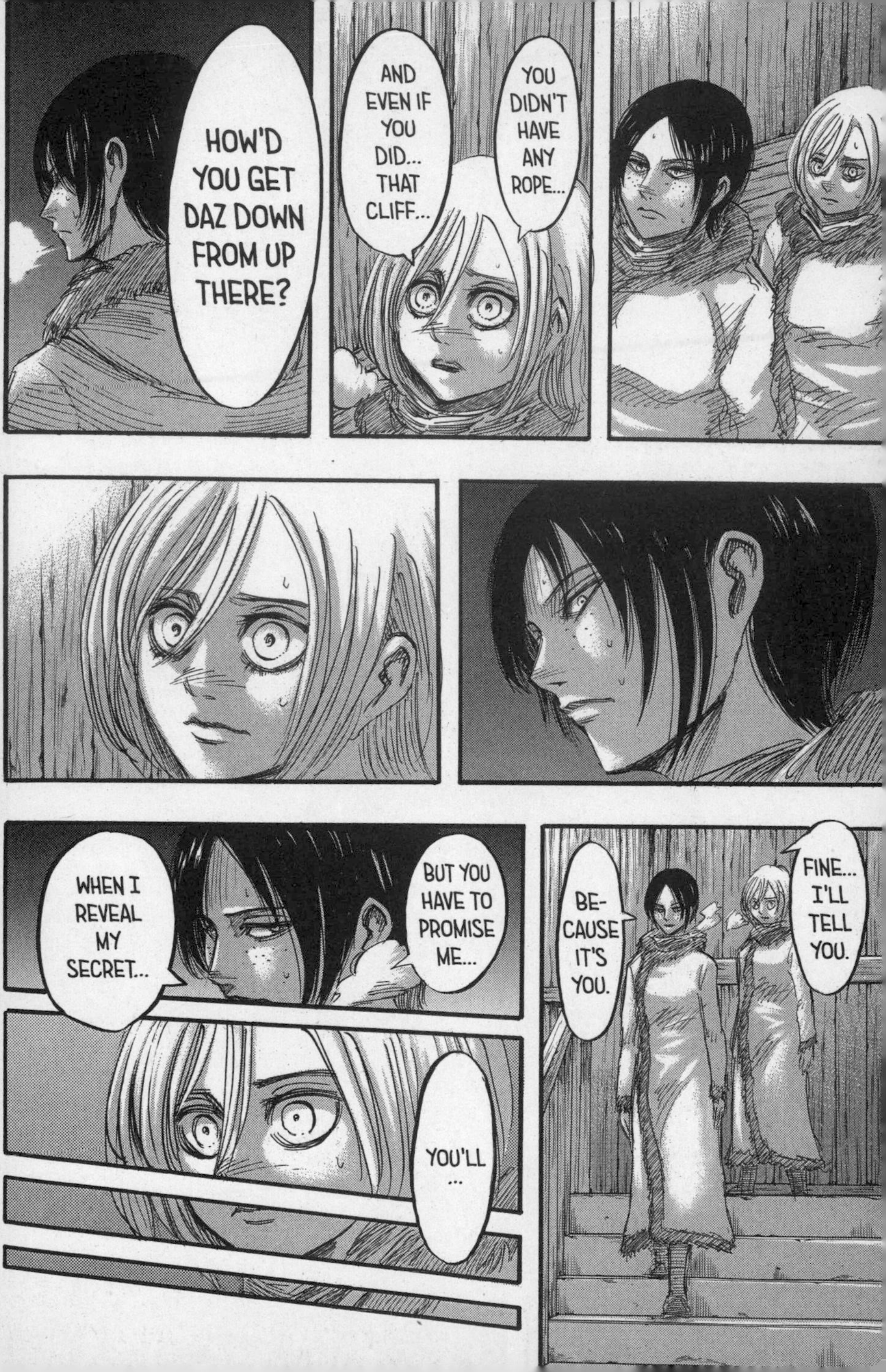
YOU DIDN'T HAVE ANY ROPE...
AND EVEN IF YOU DID... THAT CLIFF...
HOW'D YOU GET DAZ DOWN FROM UP THERE?
FINE... I'LL TELL YOU.
BE-CAUSE IT'S YOU.
BUT YOU HAVE TO PROMISE ME...
WHEN I REVEAL MY SECRET...
YOU'LL ...

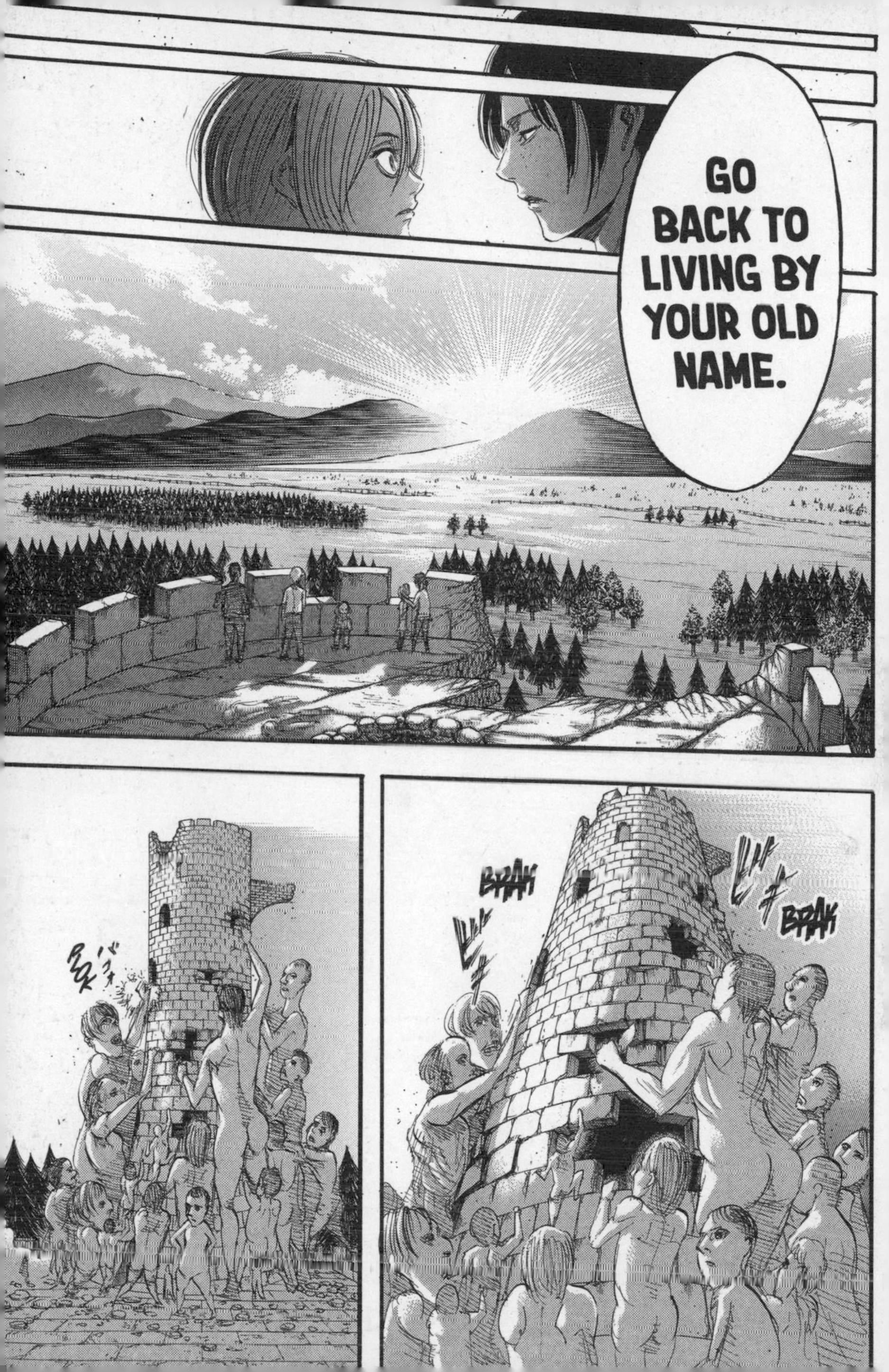
GO BACK TO LIVING BY YOUR OLD NAME.
BRAK
BRAK
BRAK

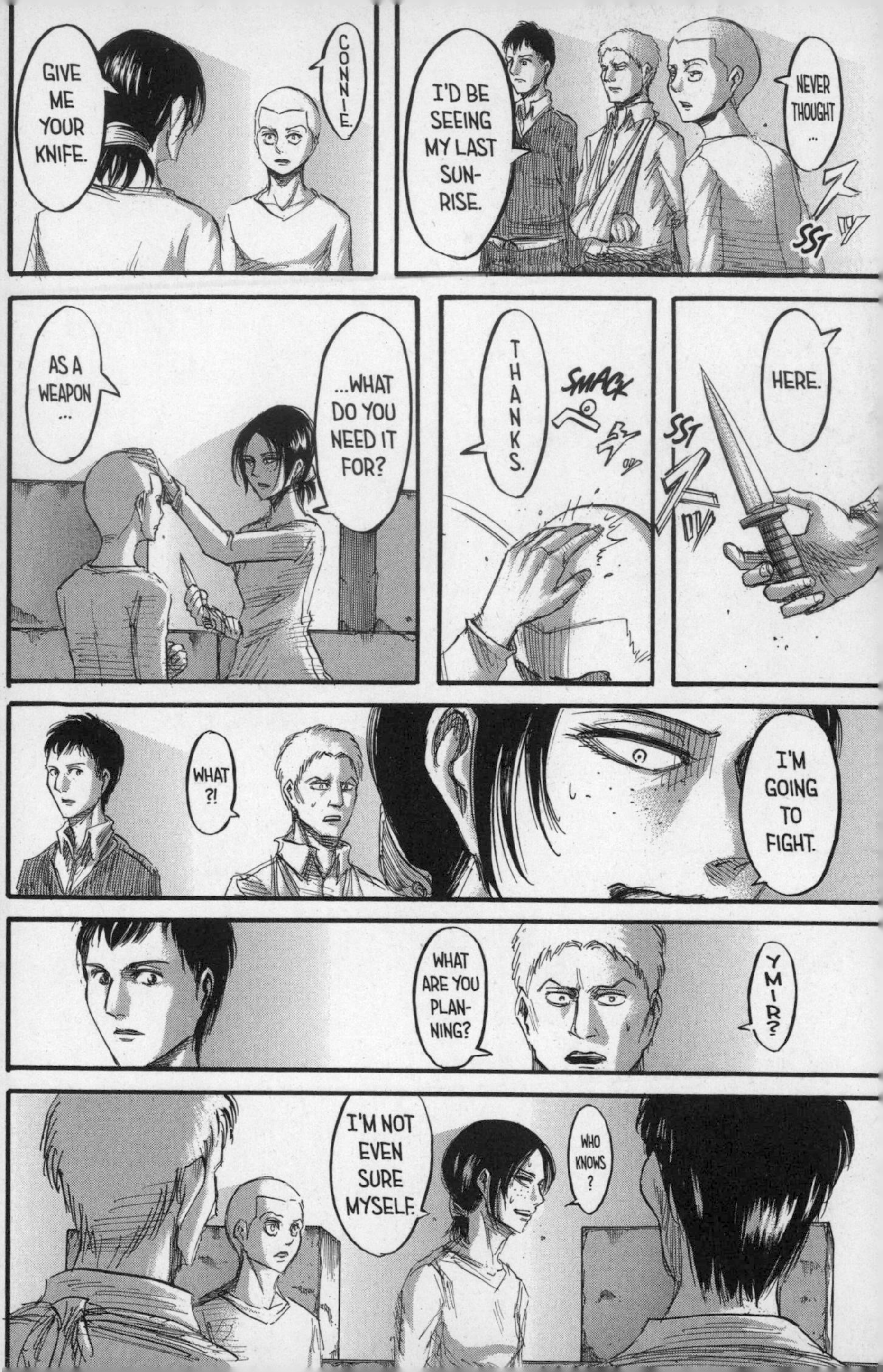
NEVER THOUGHT ...
I'D BE SEEING MY LAST SUN-RISE.
SST
CONNIE.
GIVE ME YOUR KNIFE.
HERE.
SST
THANKS.
SMACK
...WHAT DO YOU NEED IT FOR?
AS A WEAPON ...
I'M GOING TO FIGHT.
WHAT ?!
YMIR?
WHAT ARE YOU PLAN-NING?
WHO KNOWS ?
I'M NOT EVEN SURE MYSELF.

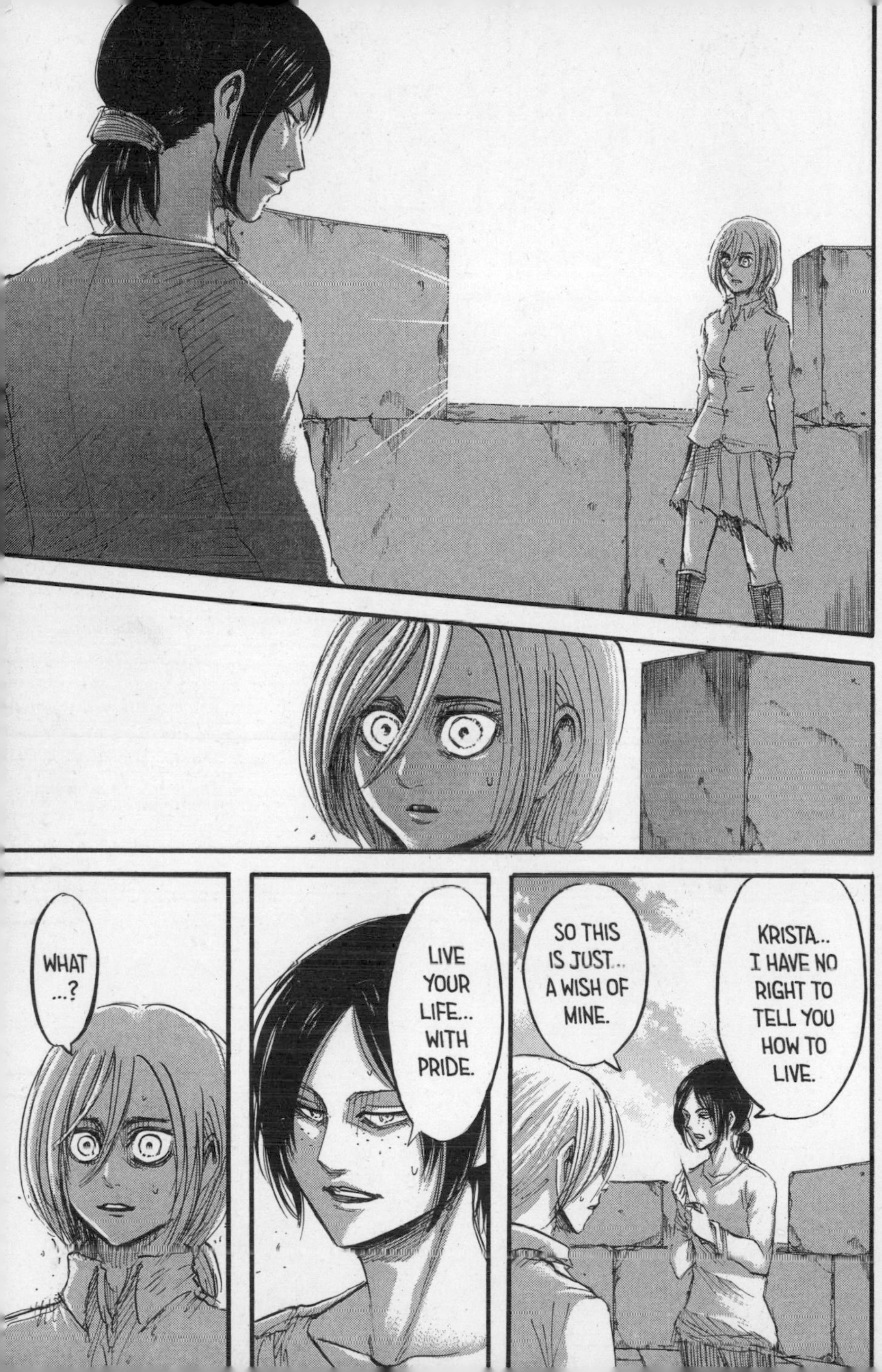
KRISTA... I HAVE NO RIGHT TO TELL YOU HOW TO LIVE.
SO THIS IS JUST... A WISH OF MINE.
LIVE YOUR LIFE... WITH PRIDE.
WHAT ...?

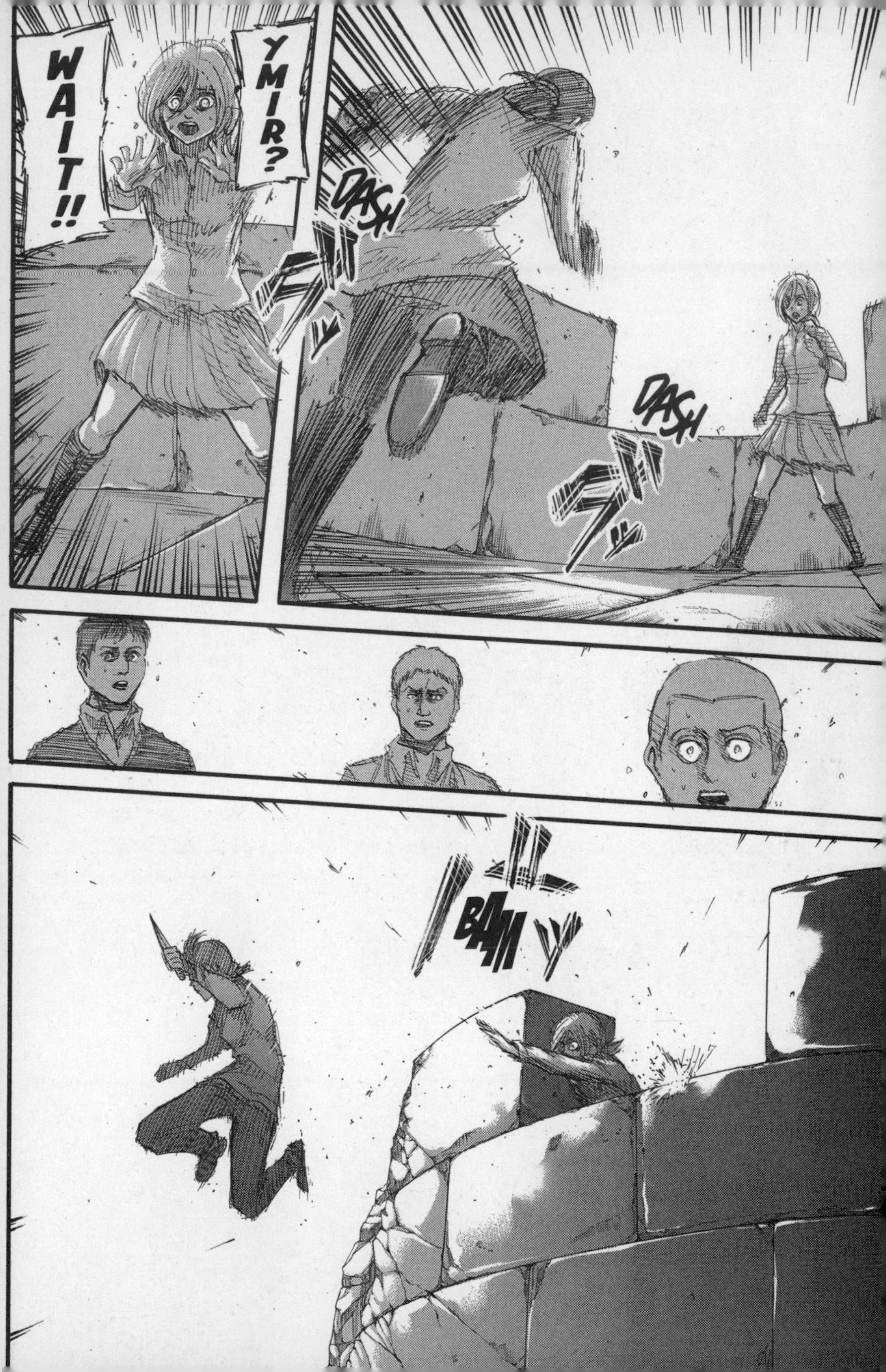
DASH
DASH
YMIR?
WAIT!!
BAM

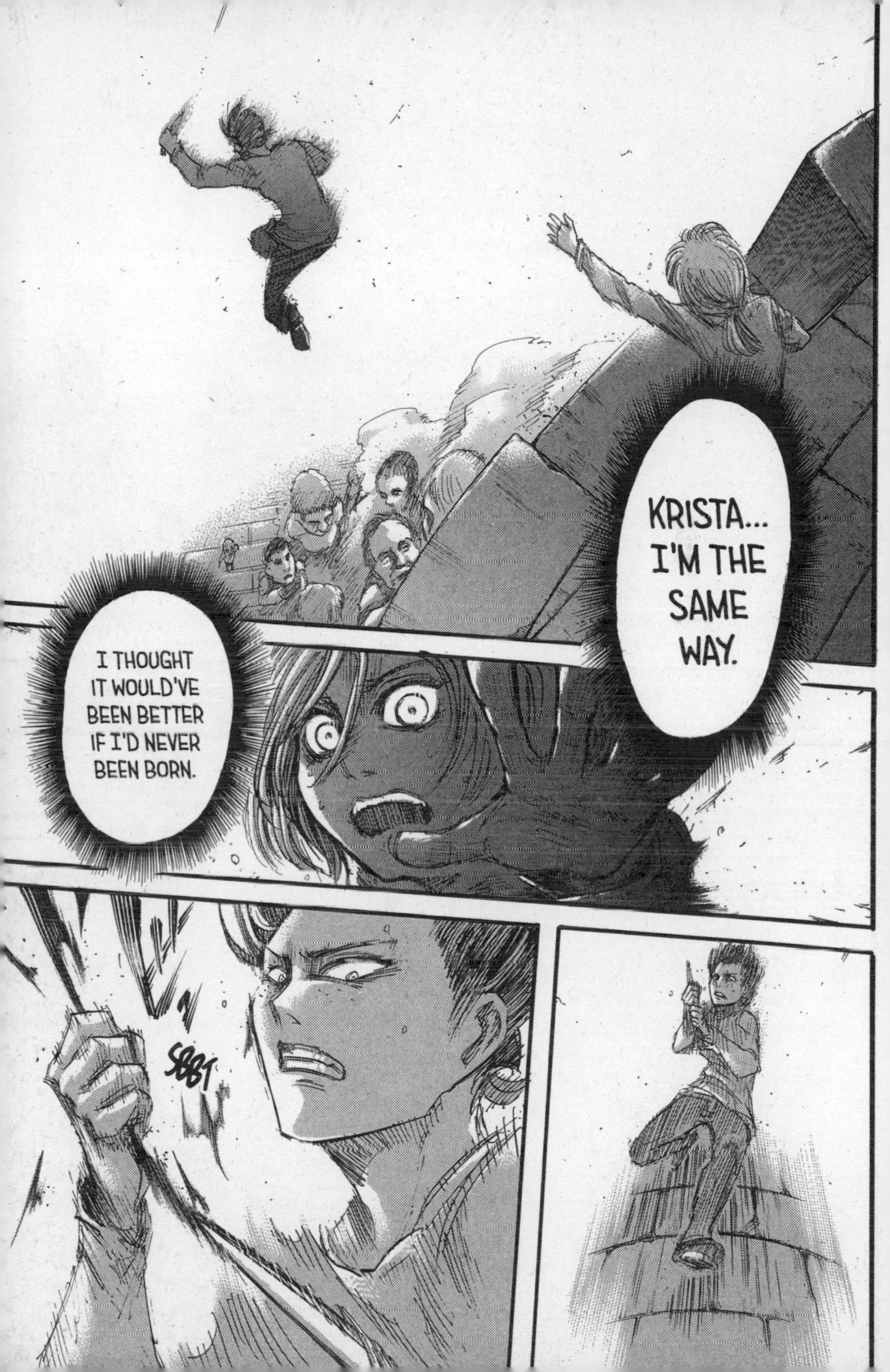
KRISTA... I'M THE SAME WAY.
I THOUGHT IT WOULD'VE BEEN BETTER IF I'D NEVER BEEN BORN.
SBBT

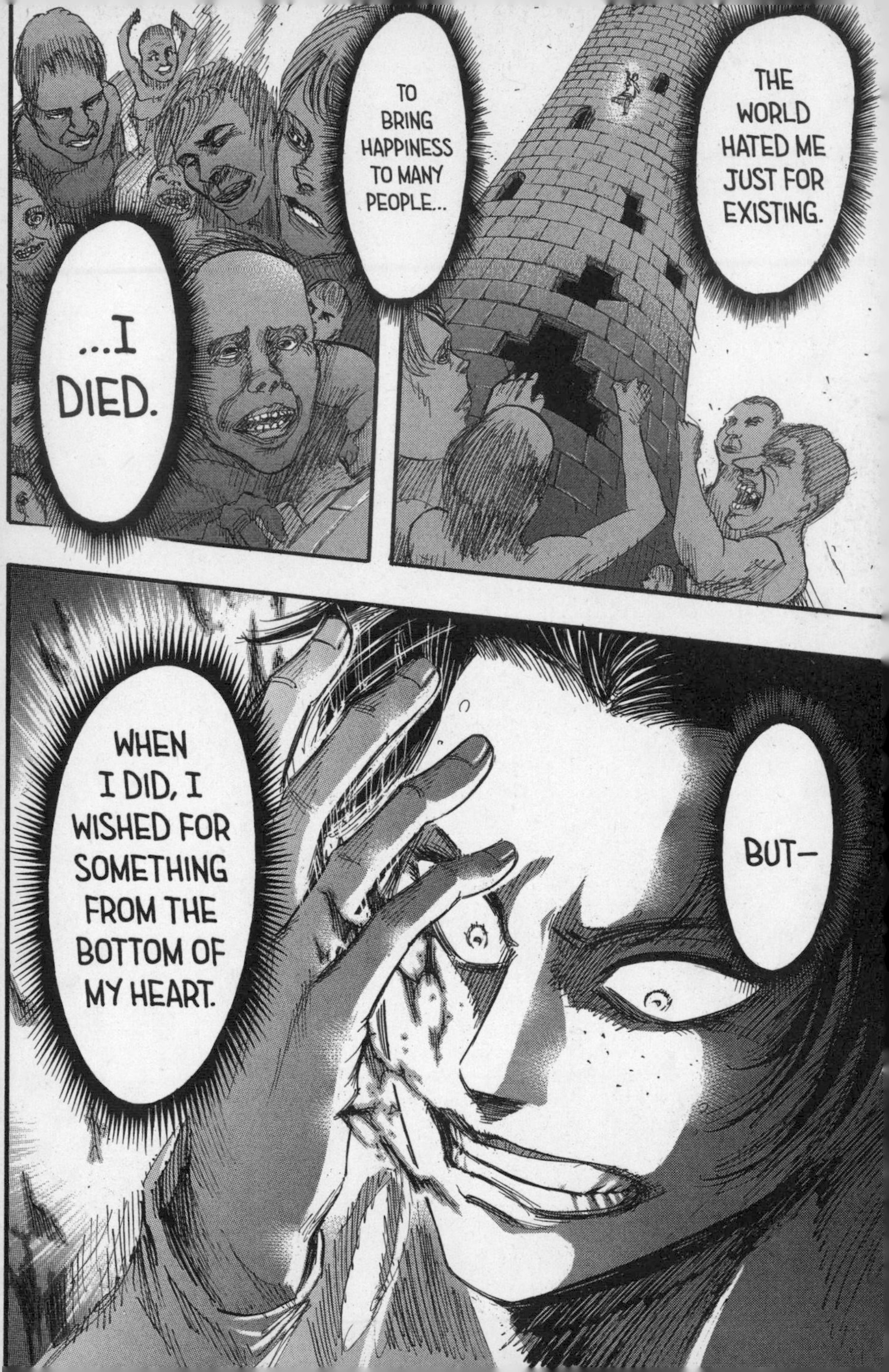
THE WORLD HATED ME JUST FOR EXISTING.
TO BRING HAPPINESS TO MANY PEOPLE...
...I DIED.
BUT—
WHEN I DID, I WISHED FOR SOMETHING FROM THE BOTTOM OF MY HEART.

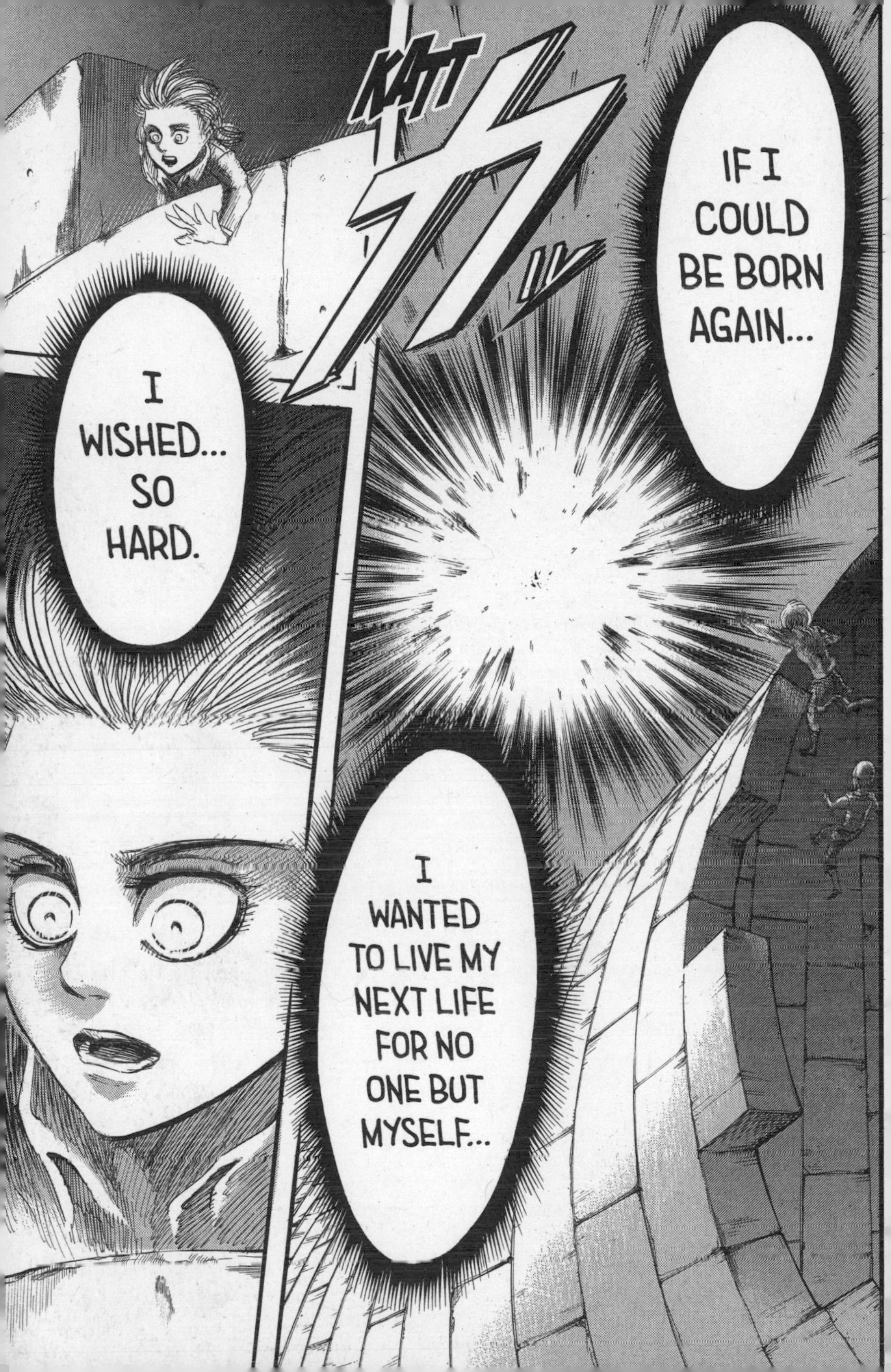
IF I COULD BE BORN AGAIN...
KATT
I WISHED... SO HARD.
I WANTED TO LIVE MY NEXT LIFE FOR NO ONE BUT MYSELF...

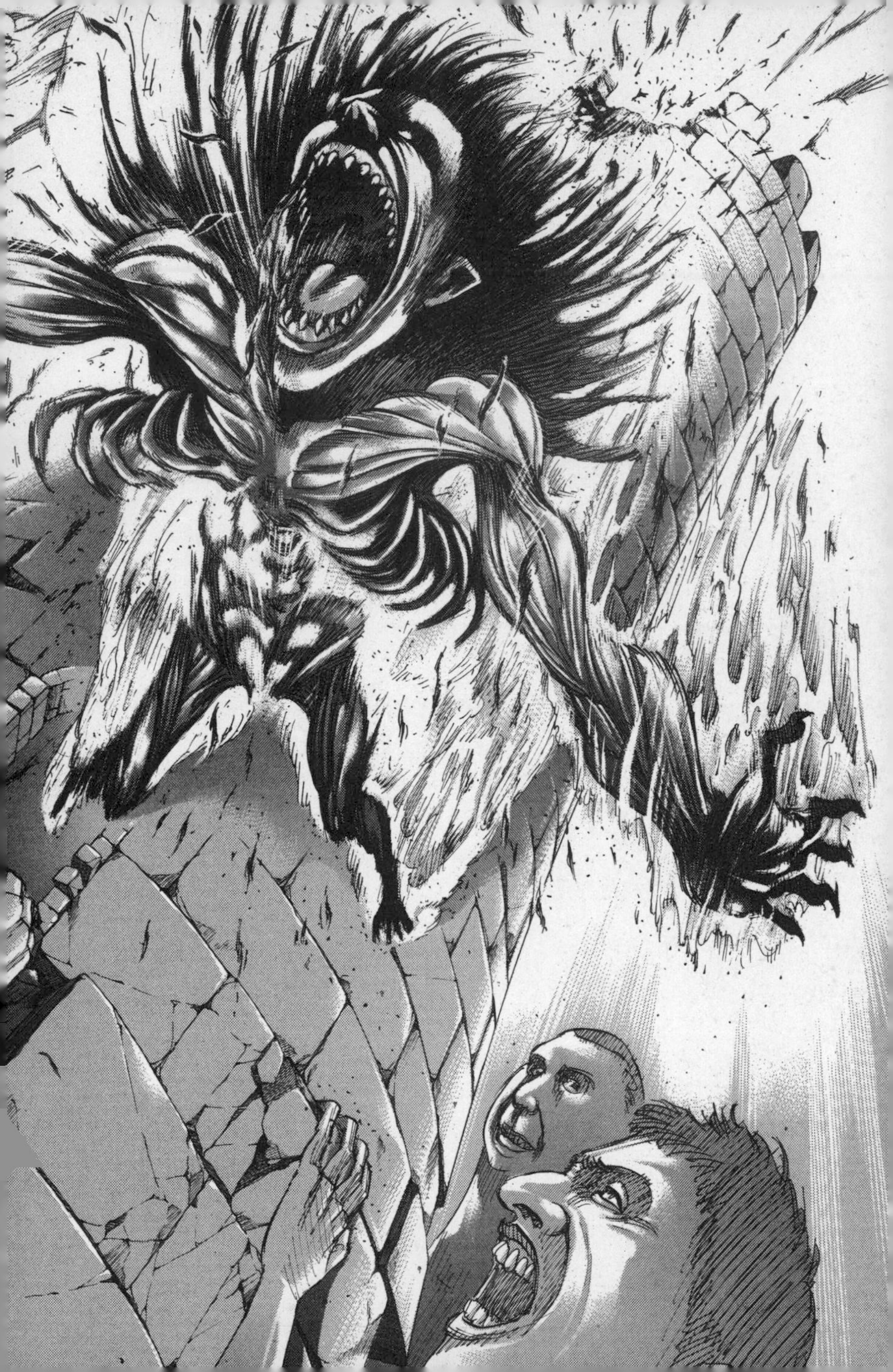

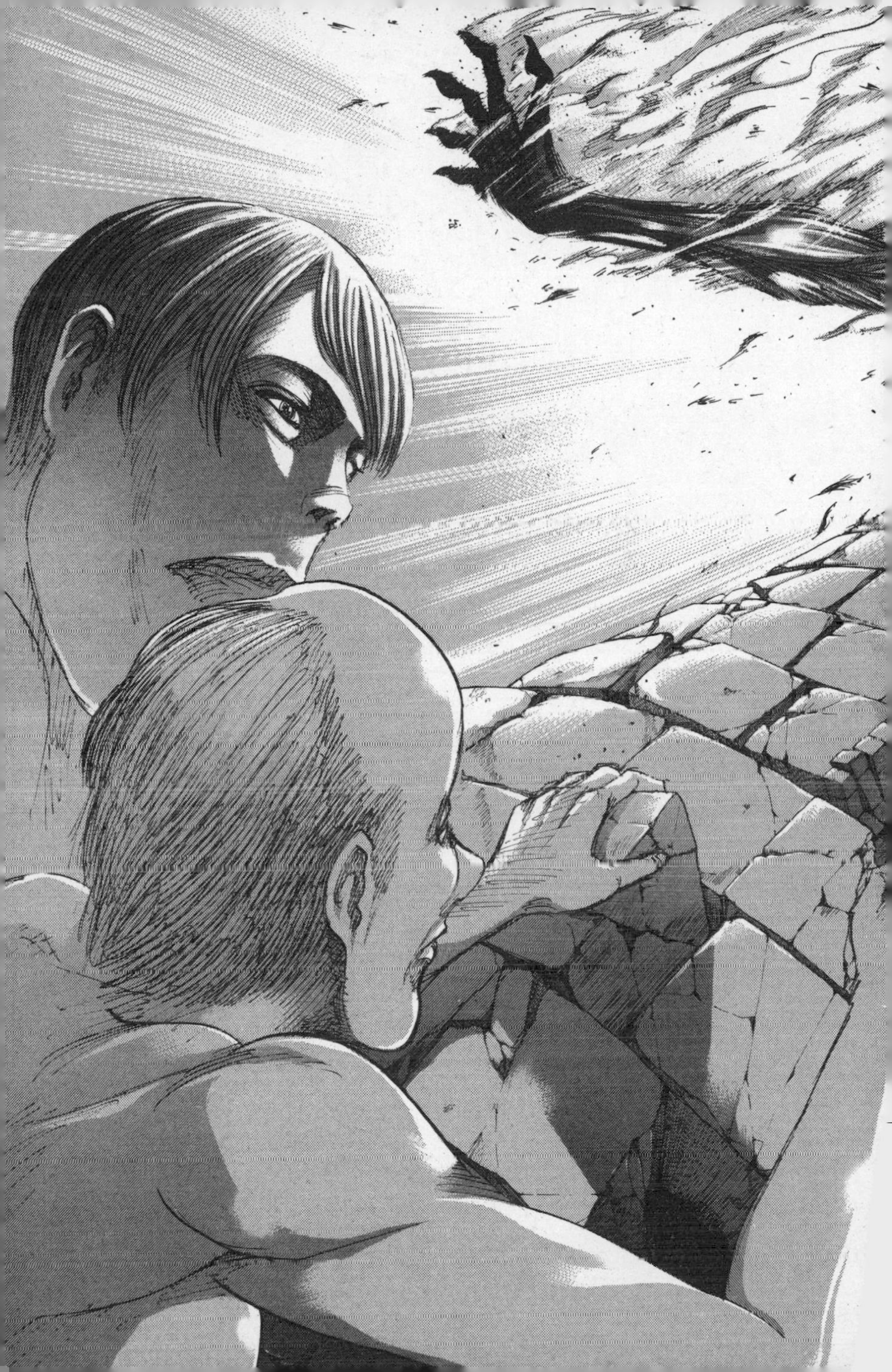

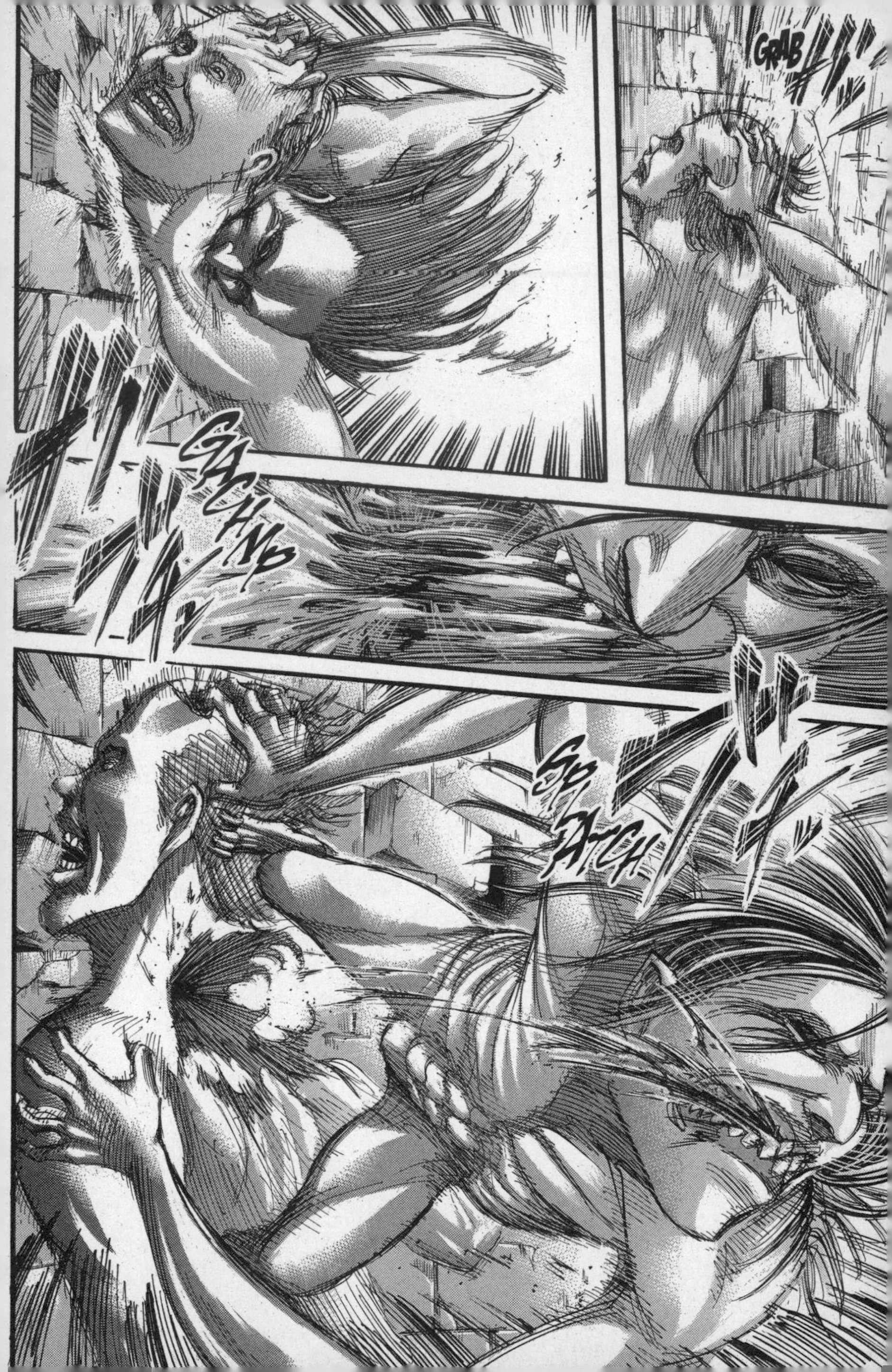
GRAB
GACHNP
SPLATCH

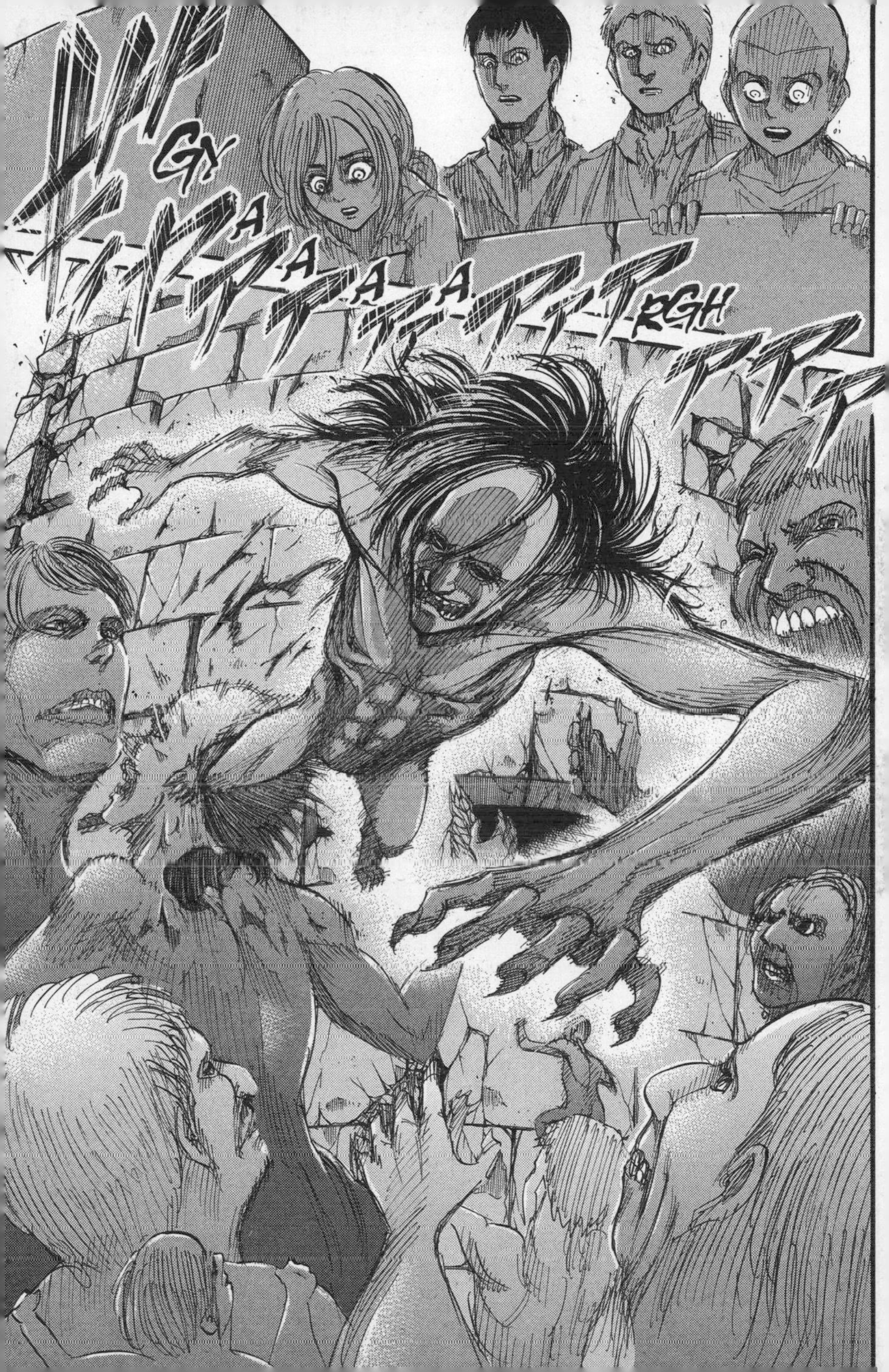
GYAAAARGH

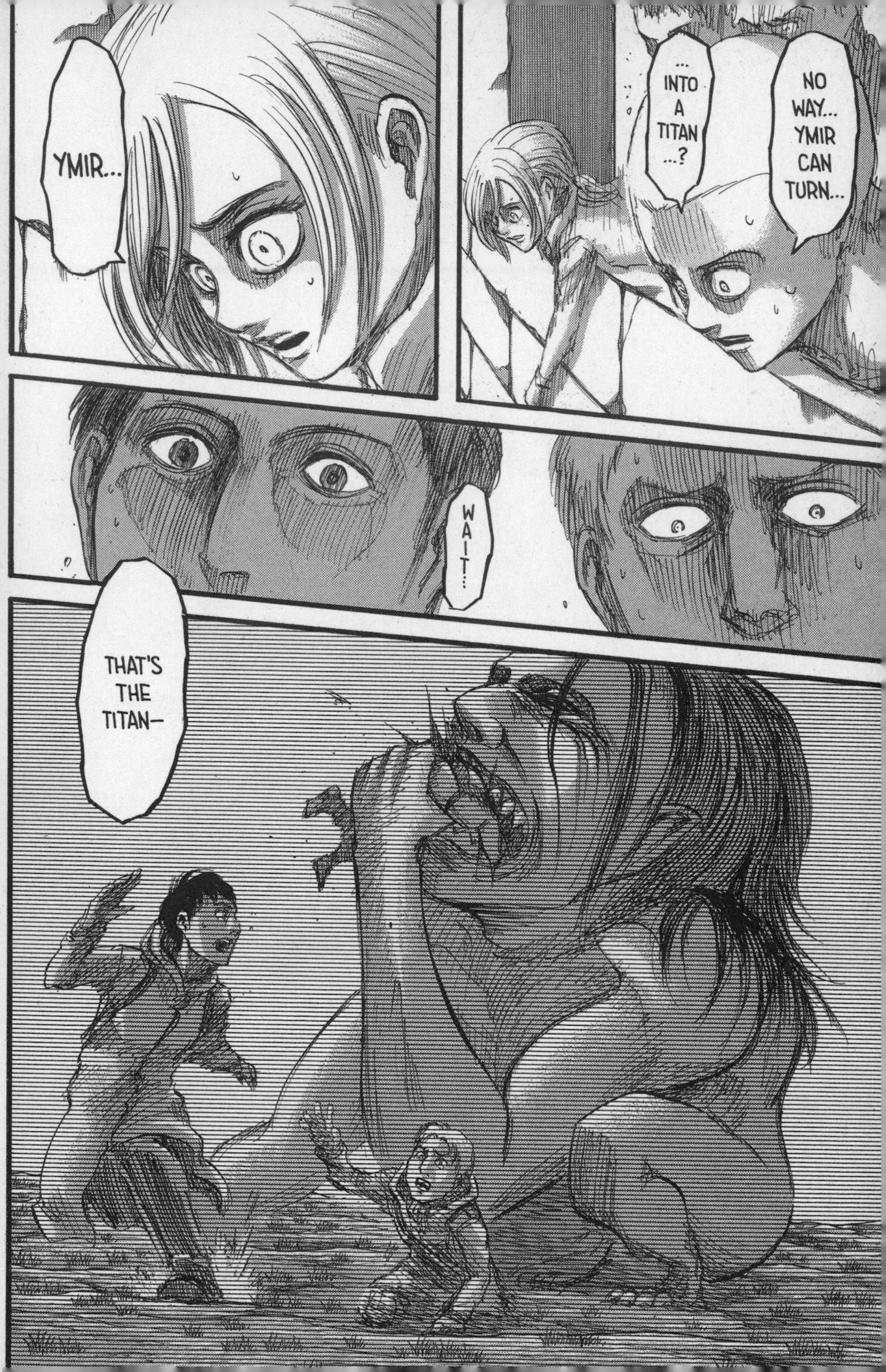
NO WAY... YMIR CAN TURN...
...INTO A TITAN ...?
YMIR...
WAIT...
THAT'S THE TITAN—

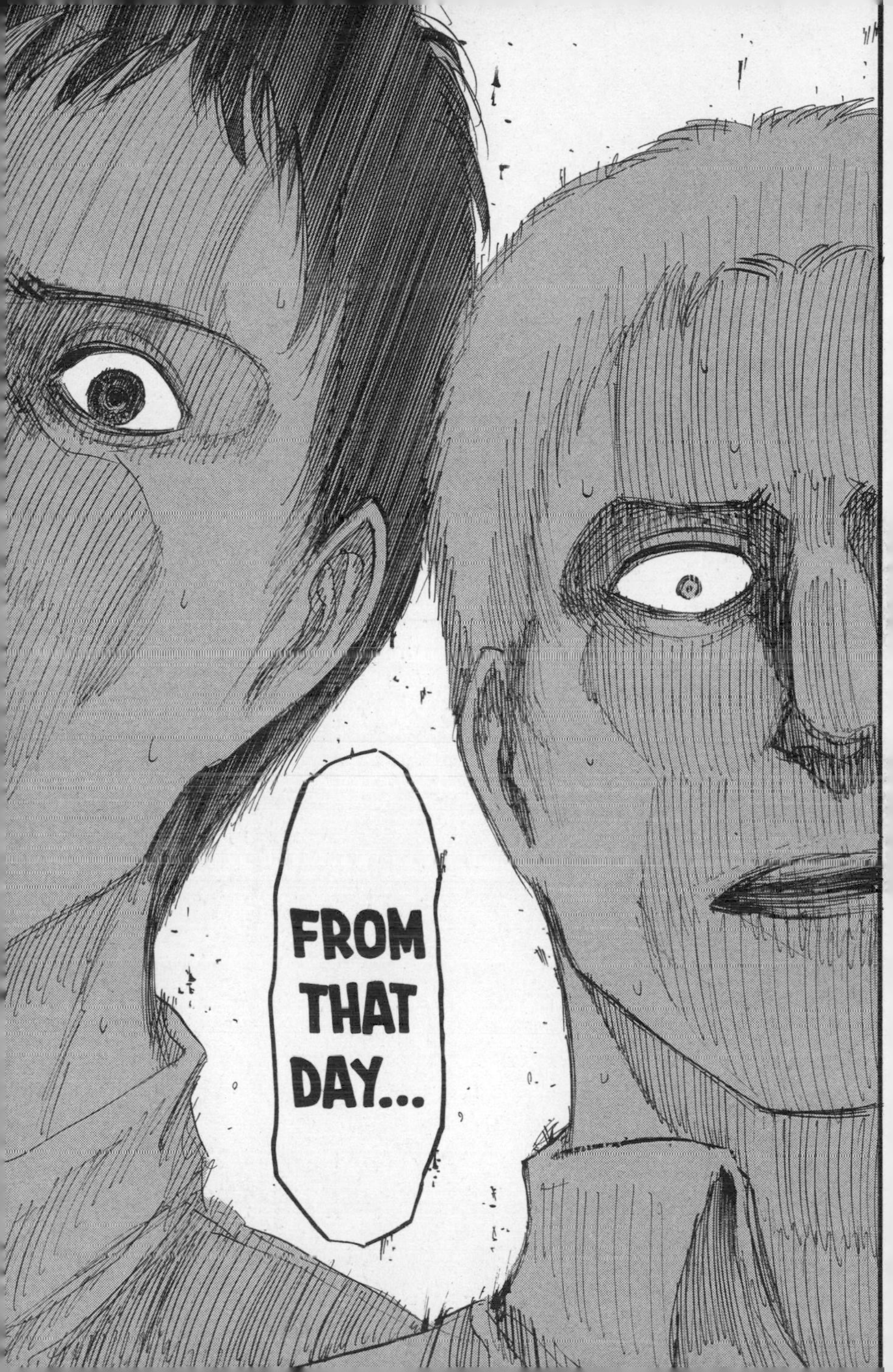
FROM THAT DAY...

ATTACK on TITAN

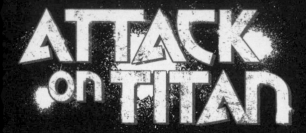

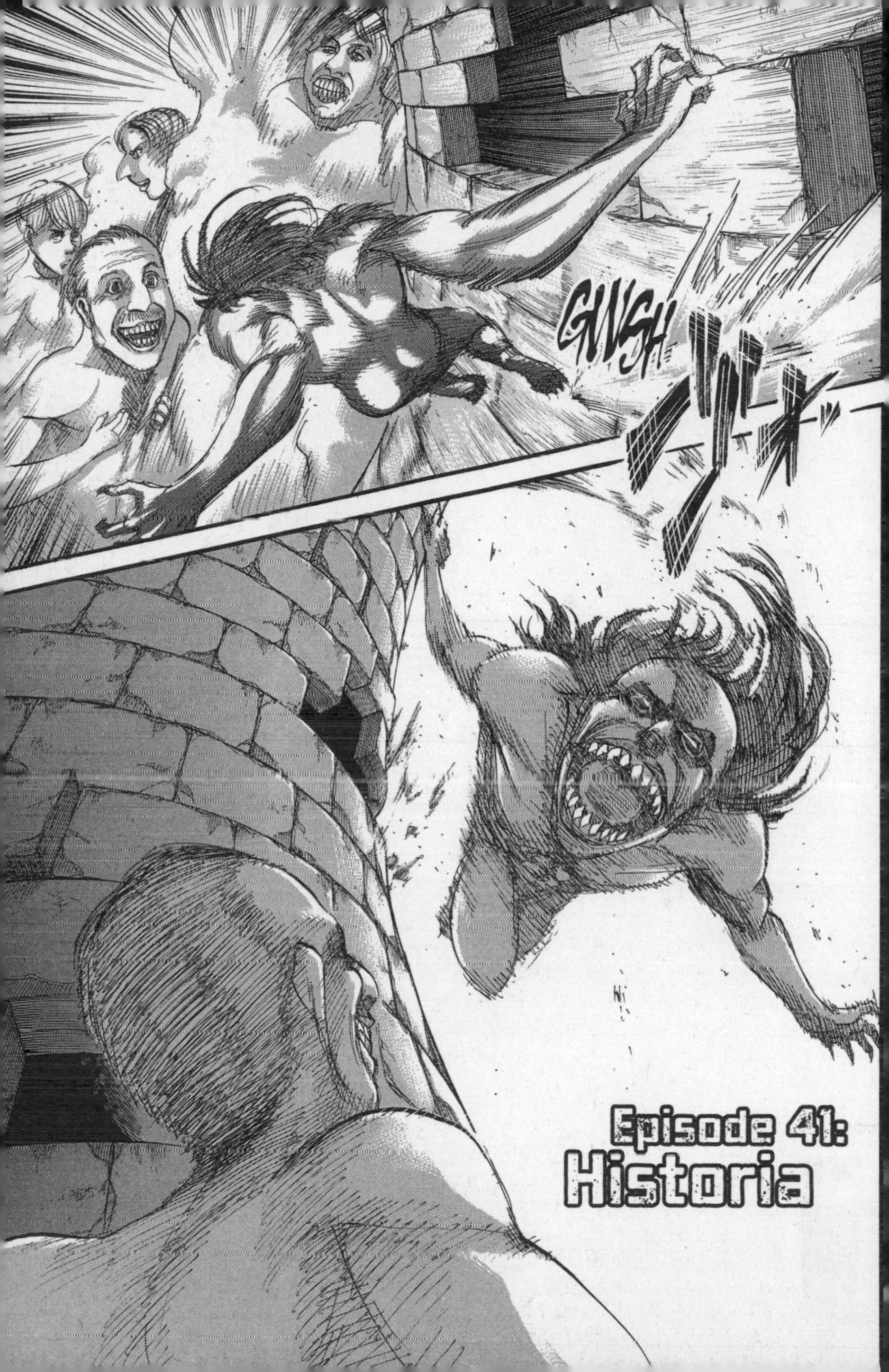
GUNSH
Episode 41:
Historia

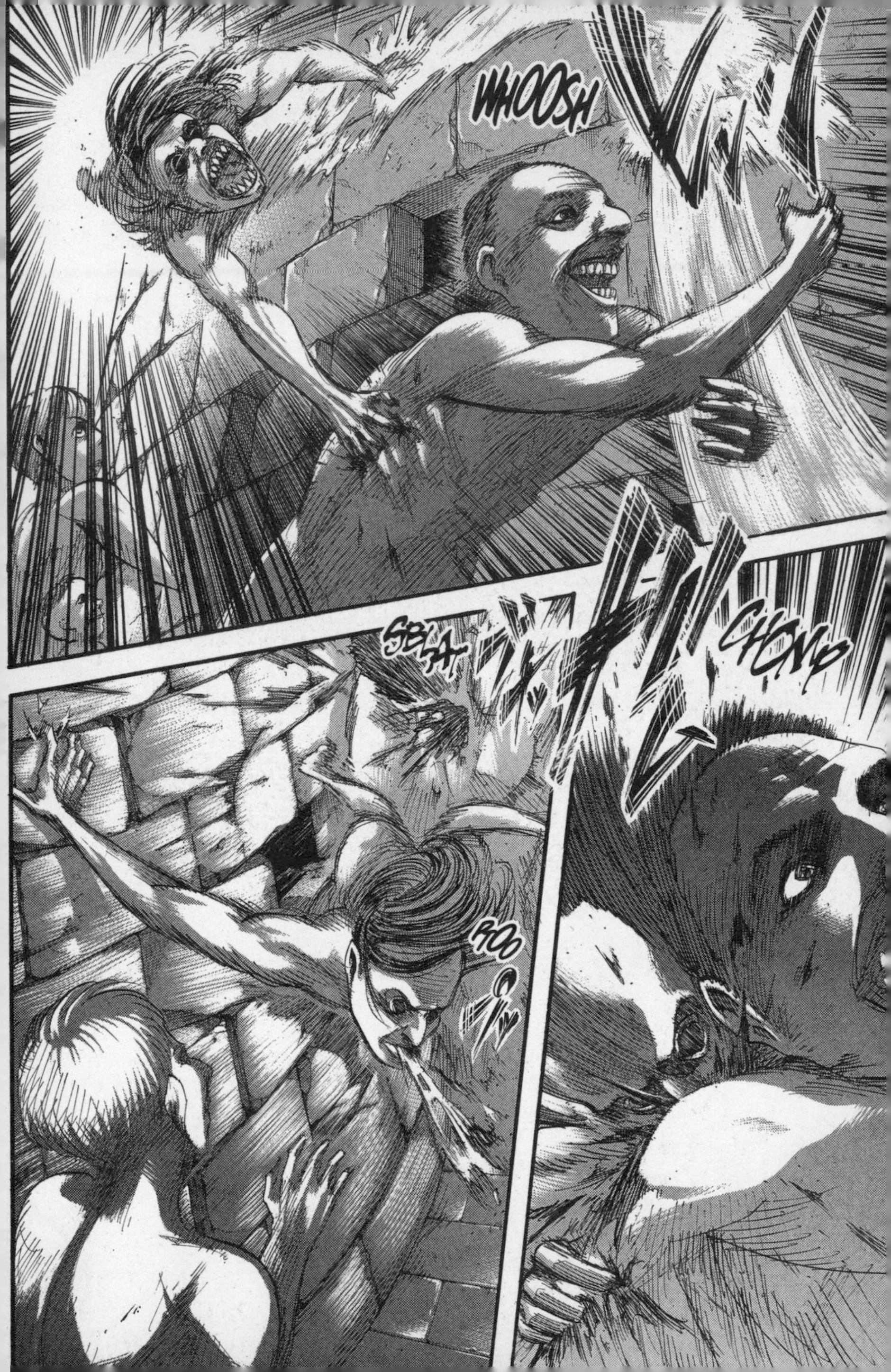
WHOOSH
CHOMP
SBLAM
ROO

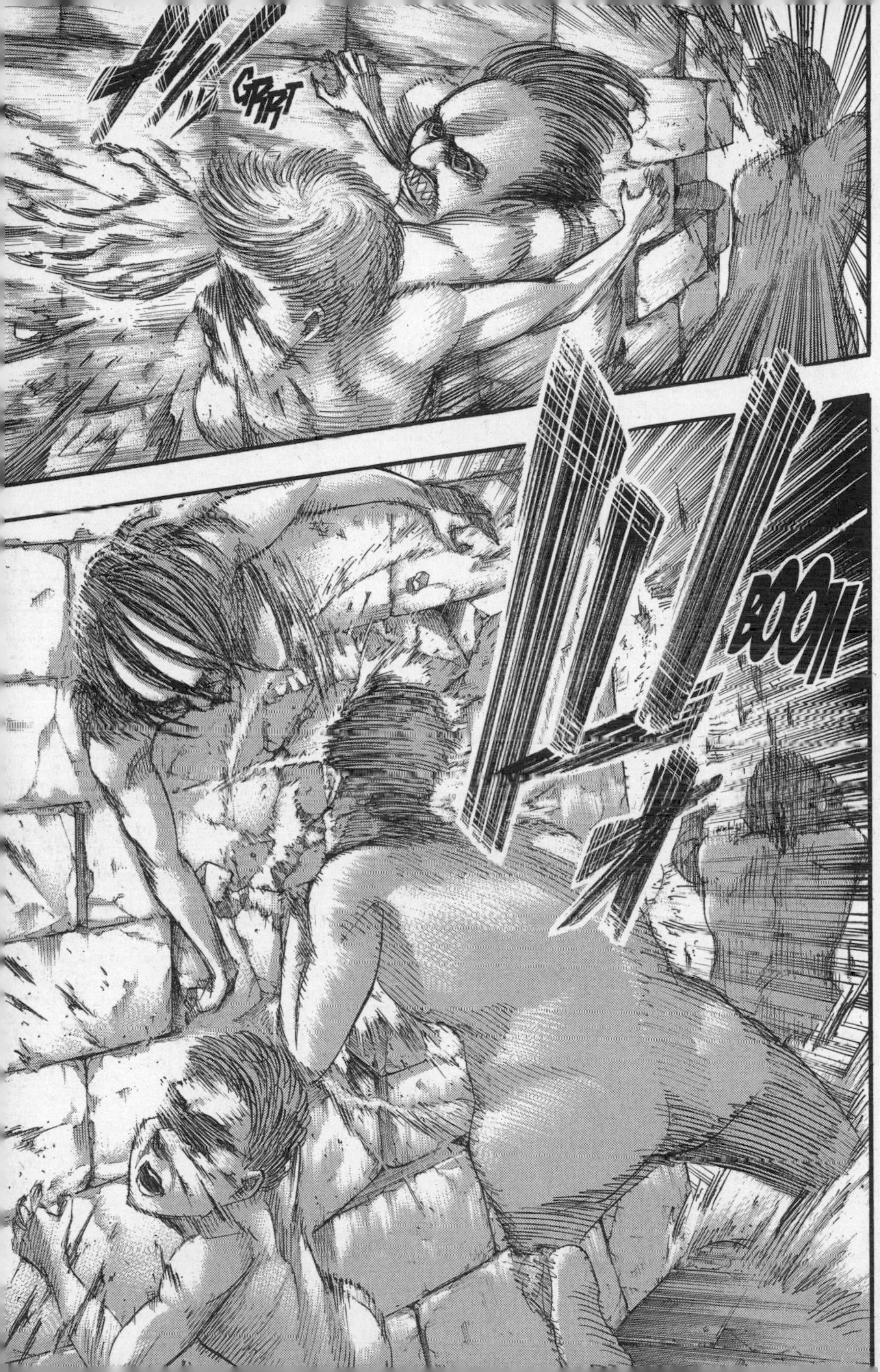
GRRRT
BOOM

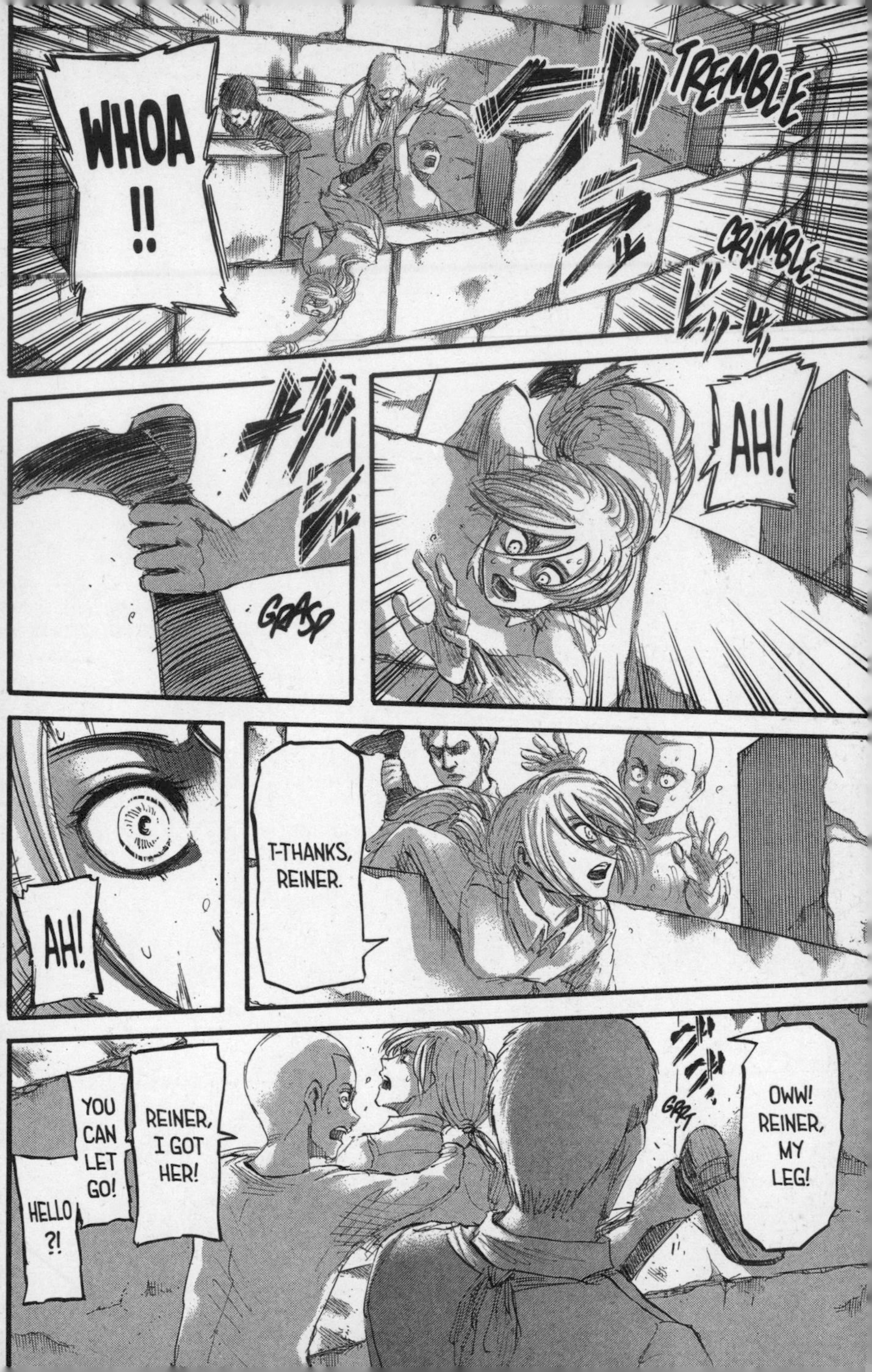
TREMBLE
CRUMBLE
WHOA!!
AH!
GRASP
T-THANKS, REINER.
AH!
OWW! REINER, MY LEG!
REINER, I GOT HER!
YOU CAN LET GO!
HELLO?!

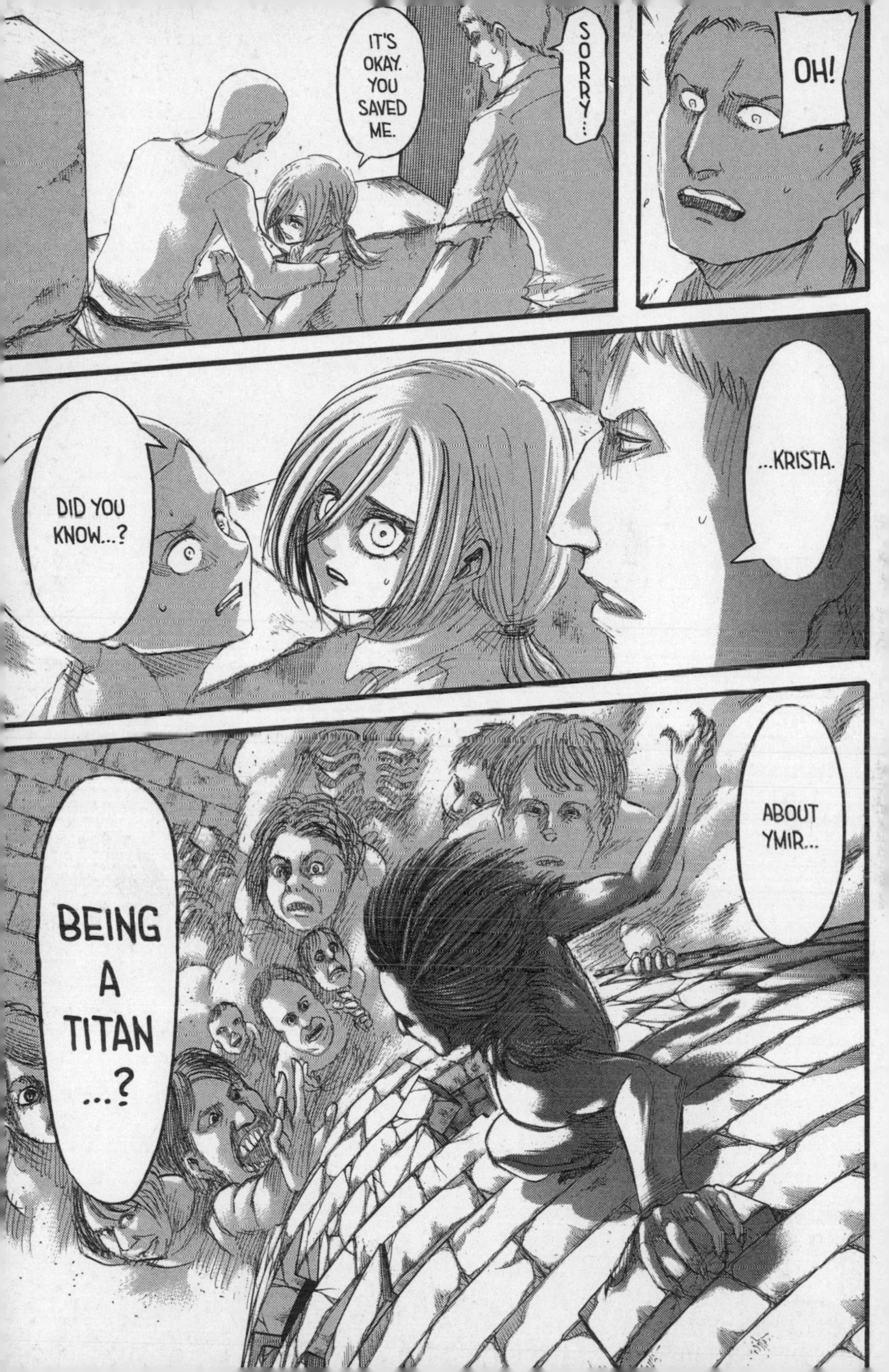
OH!
SORRY...
IT'S OKAY. YOU SAVED ME.
...KRISTA.
DID YOU KNOW...?
ABOUT YMIR...
BEING A TITAN ...?

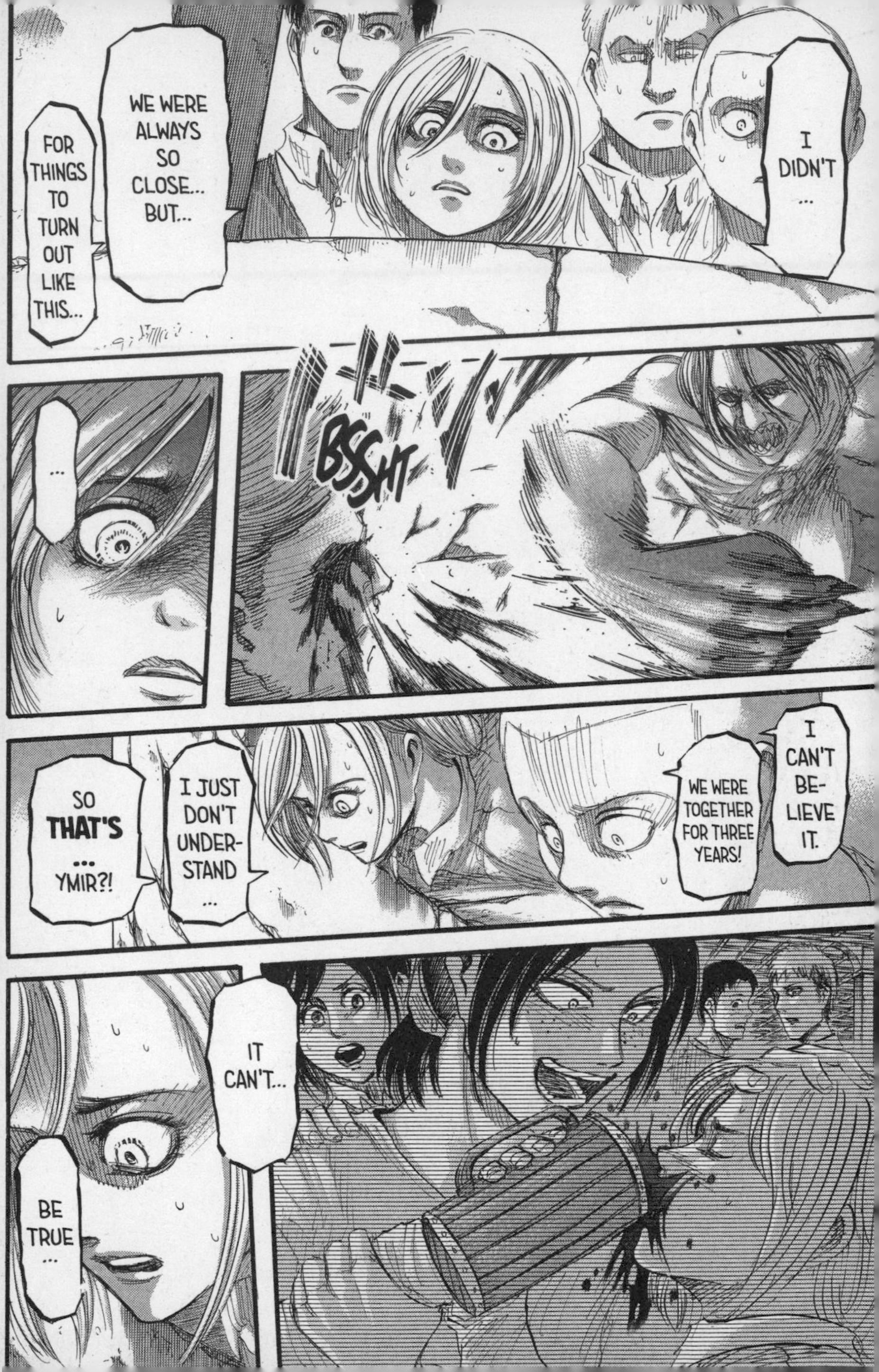
I DIDN'T ...
WE WERE ALWAYS SO CLOSE... BUT...
FOR THINGS TO TURN OUT LIKE THIS...
BSSHT
...
I CAN'T BE-LIEVE IT.
WE WERE TOGETHER FOR THREE YEARS!
I JUST DON'T UNDER-STAND ...
SO THAT'S ... YMIR?!
IT CAN'T...
BE TRUE ...

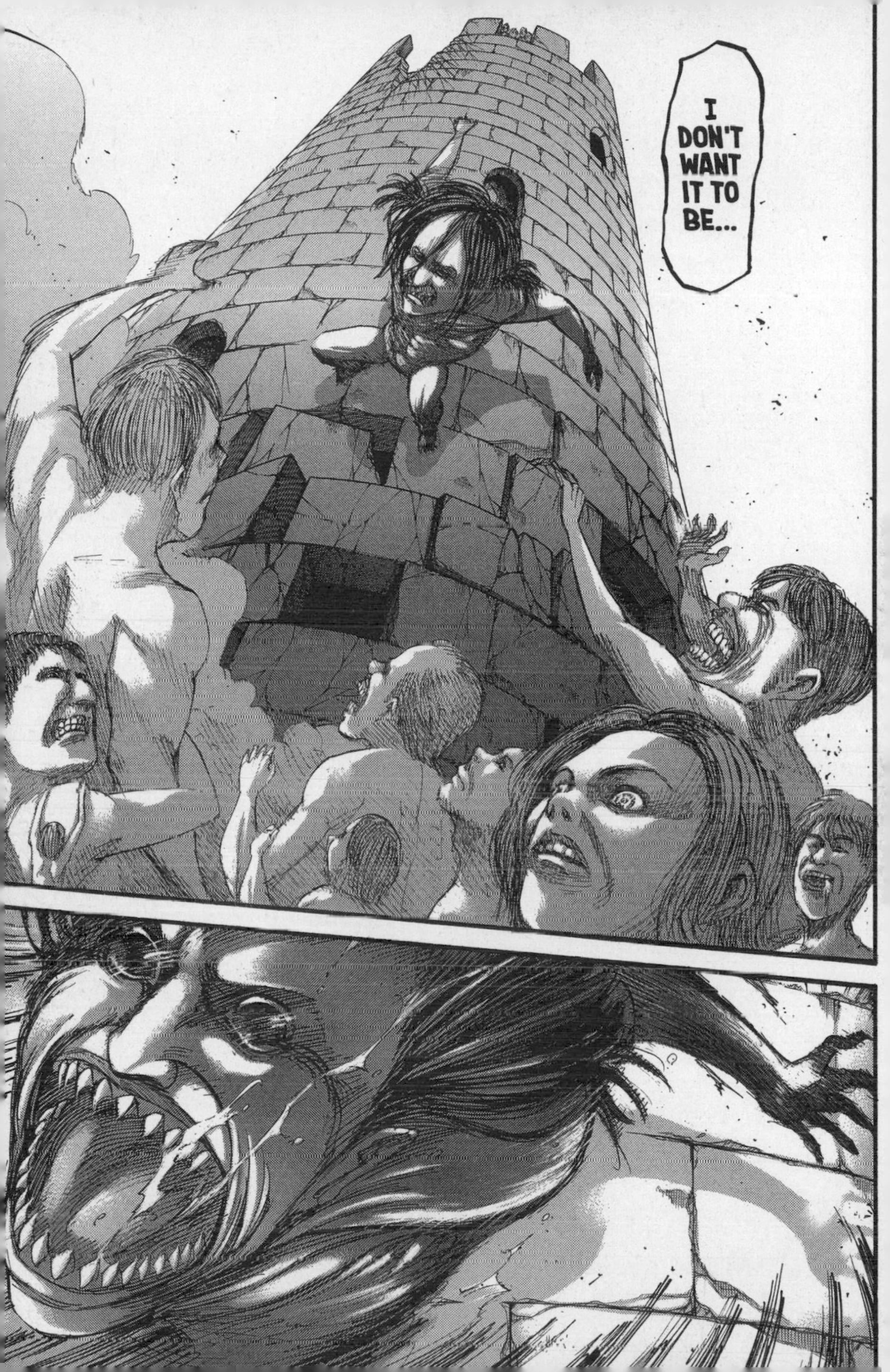
I DON'T WANT IT TO BE...

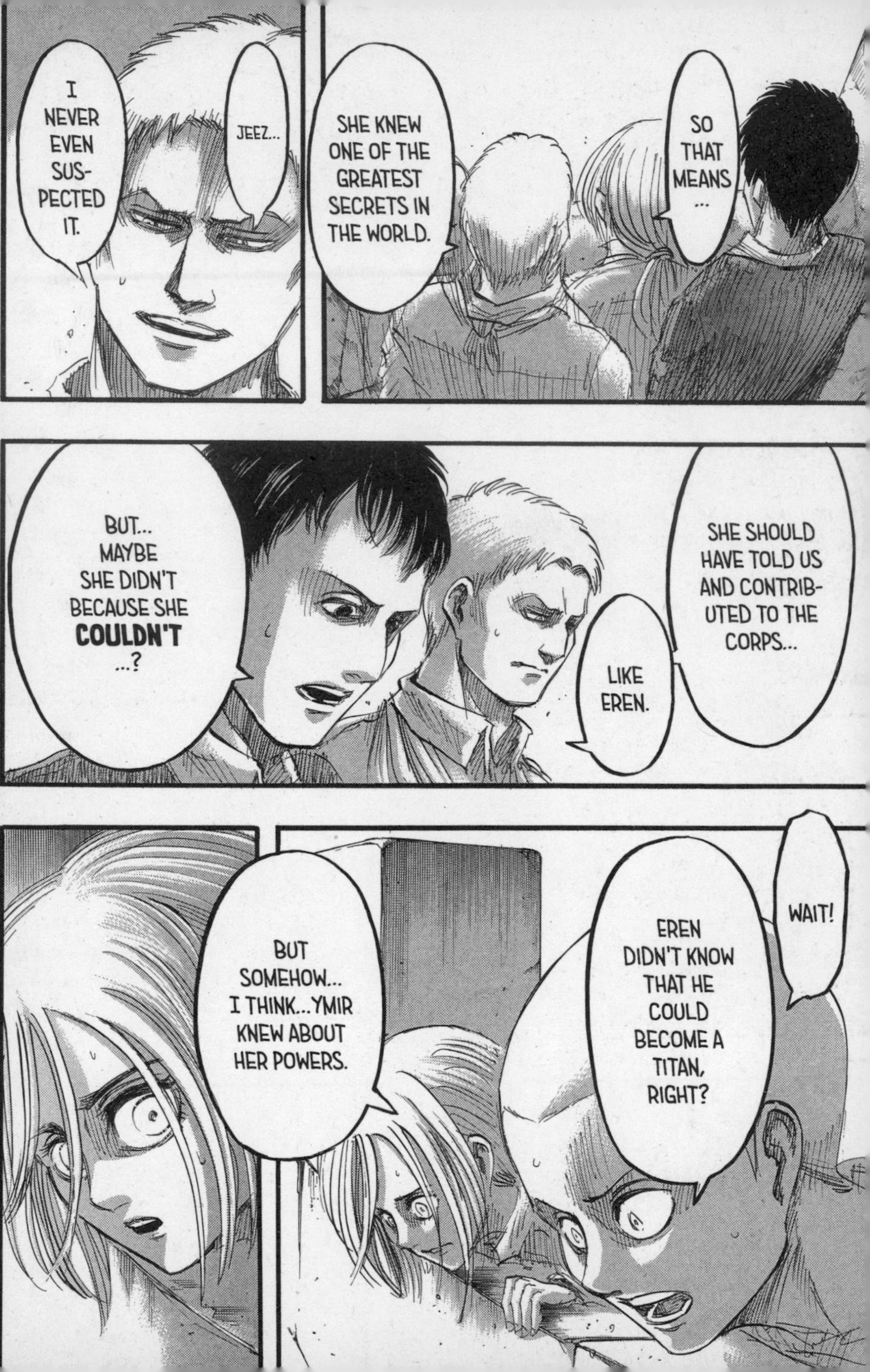
SO THAT MEANS ...
SHE KNEW ONE OF THE GREATEST SECRETS IN THE WORLD.
JEEZ...
I NEVER EVEN SUSPECTED IT.
SHE SHOULD HAVE TOLD US AND CONTRIBUTED TO THE CORPS...
LIKE EREN.
BUT... MAYBE SHE DIDN'T BECAUSE SHE **COULDN'T** ...?
WAIT!
EREN DIDN'T KNOW THAT HE COULD BECOME A TITAN, RIGHT?
BUT SOMEHOW... I THINK...YMIR KNEW ABOUT HER POWERS.

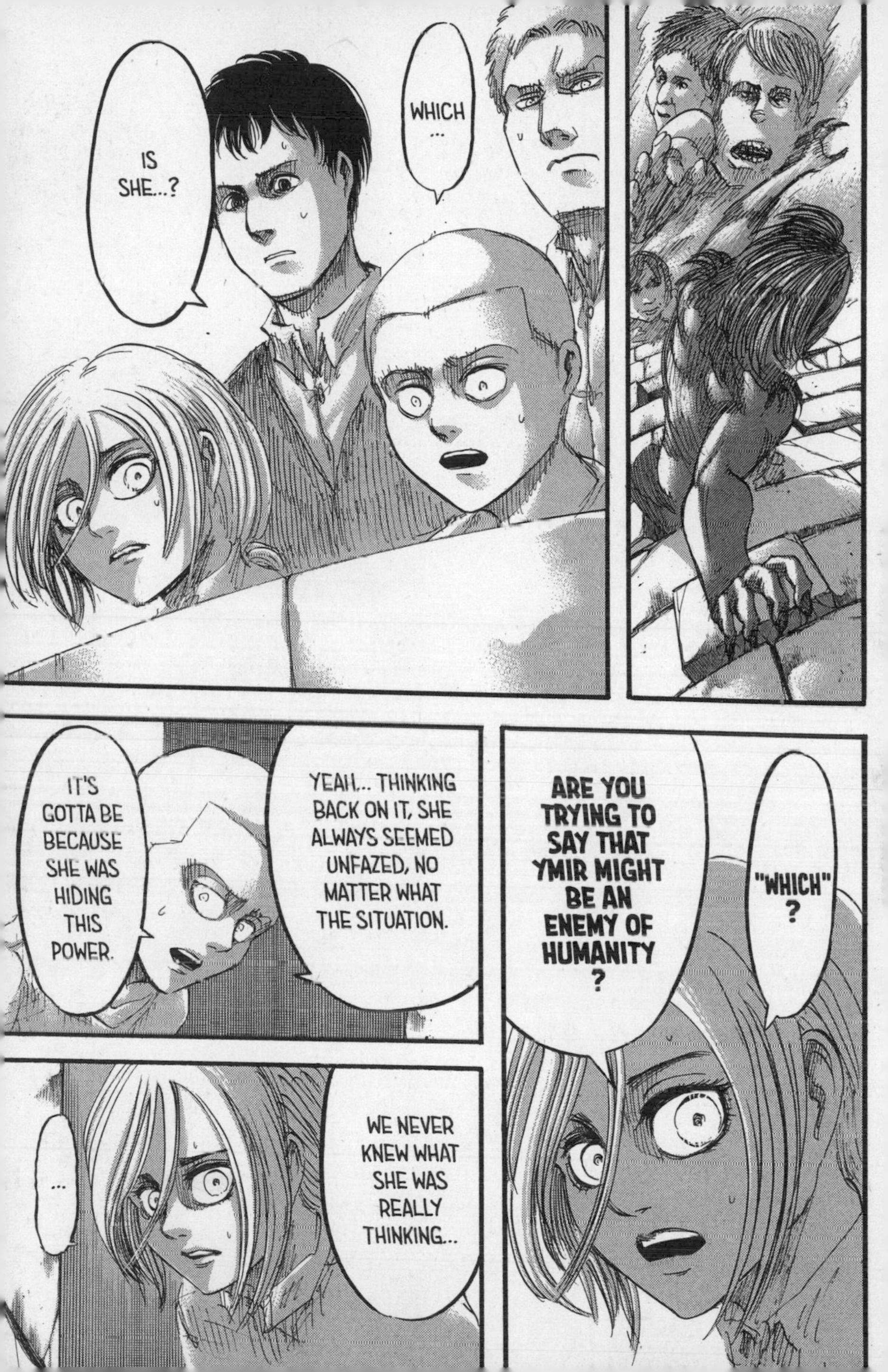
WHICH ...
IS SHE...?
"WHICH" ?
ARE YOU TRYING TO SAY THAT YMIR MIGHT BE AN ENEMY OF HUMANITY ?
YEAH... THINKING BACK ON IT, SHE ALWAYS SEEMED UNFAZED, NO MATTER WHAT THE SITUATION.
IT'S GOTTA BE BECAUSE SHE WAS HIDING THIS POWER.
WE NEVER KNEW WHAT SHE WAS REALLY THINKING...
...

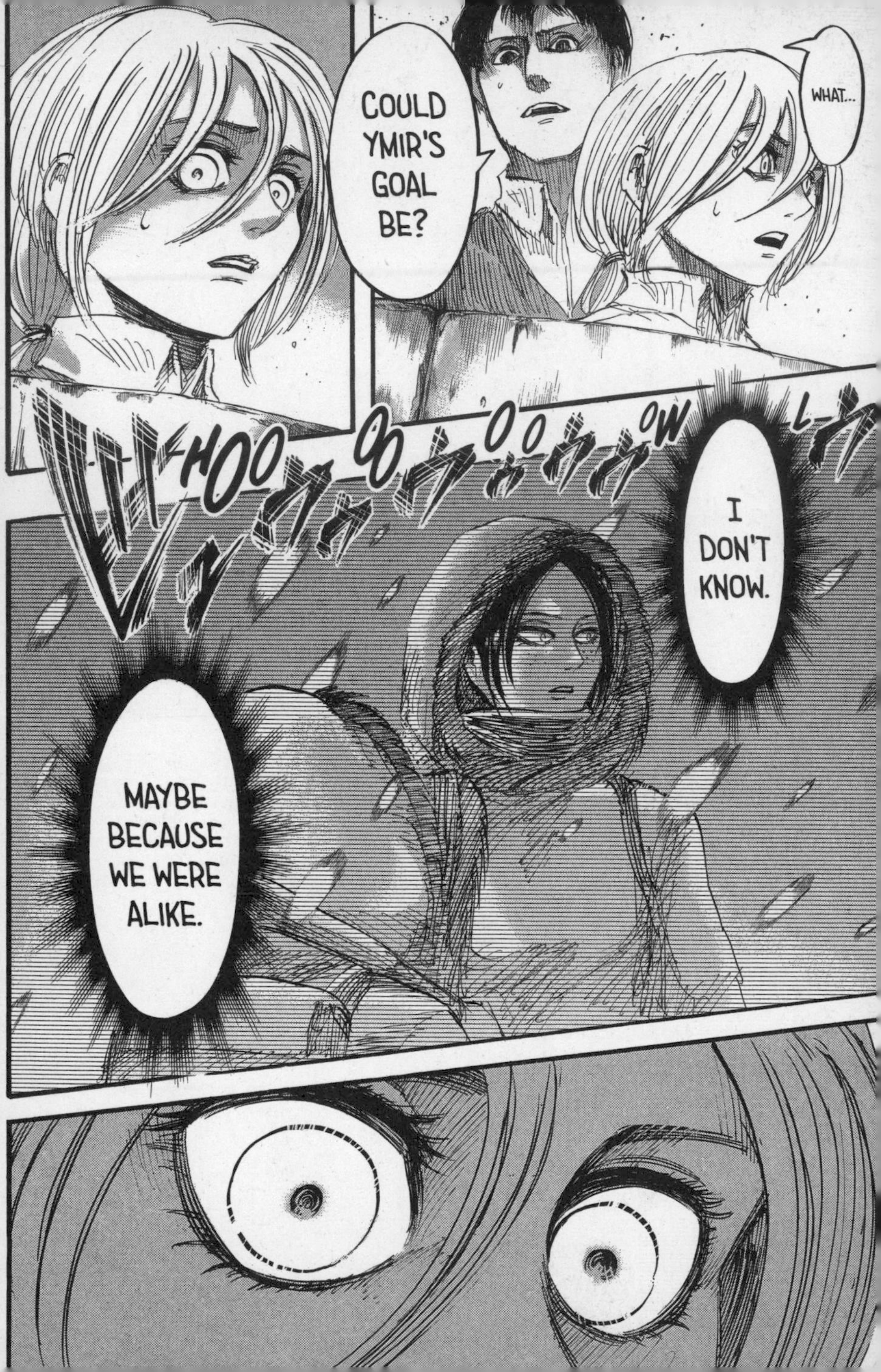
WHAT...
COULD YMIR'S GOAL BE?
WHOOOOOOOW
I DON'T KNOW.
MAYBE BECAUSE WE WERE ALIKE.

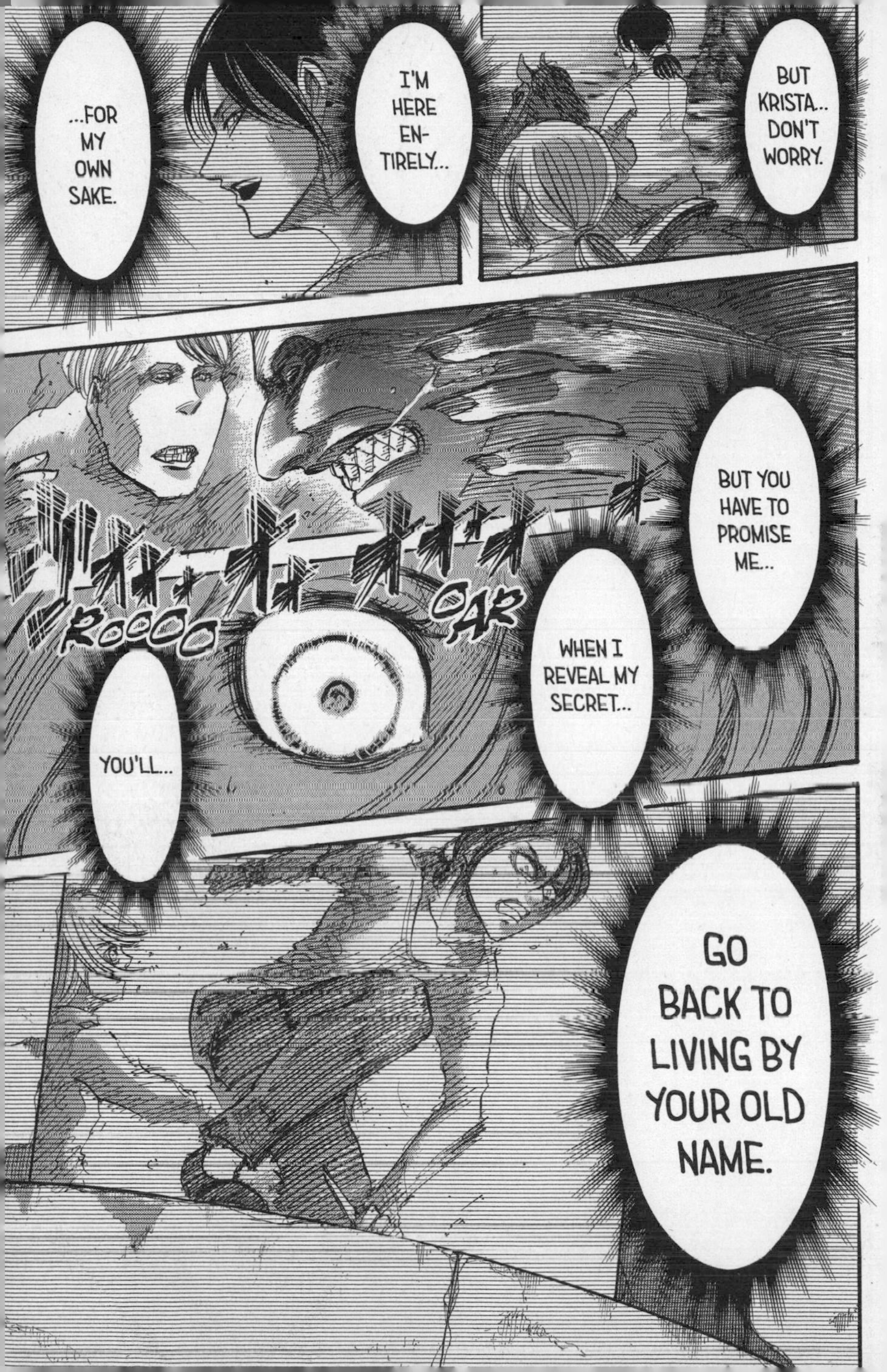
BUT KRISTA... DON'T WORRY.
I'M HERE EN-TIRELY...
...FOR MY OWN SAKE.
BUT YOU HAVE TO PROMISE ME...
WHEN I REVEAL MY SECRET...
ROOOOOAR
YOU'LL...
GO BACK TO LIVING BY YOUR OLD NAME.

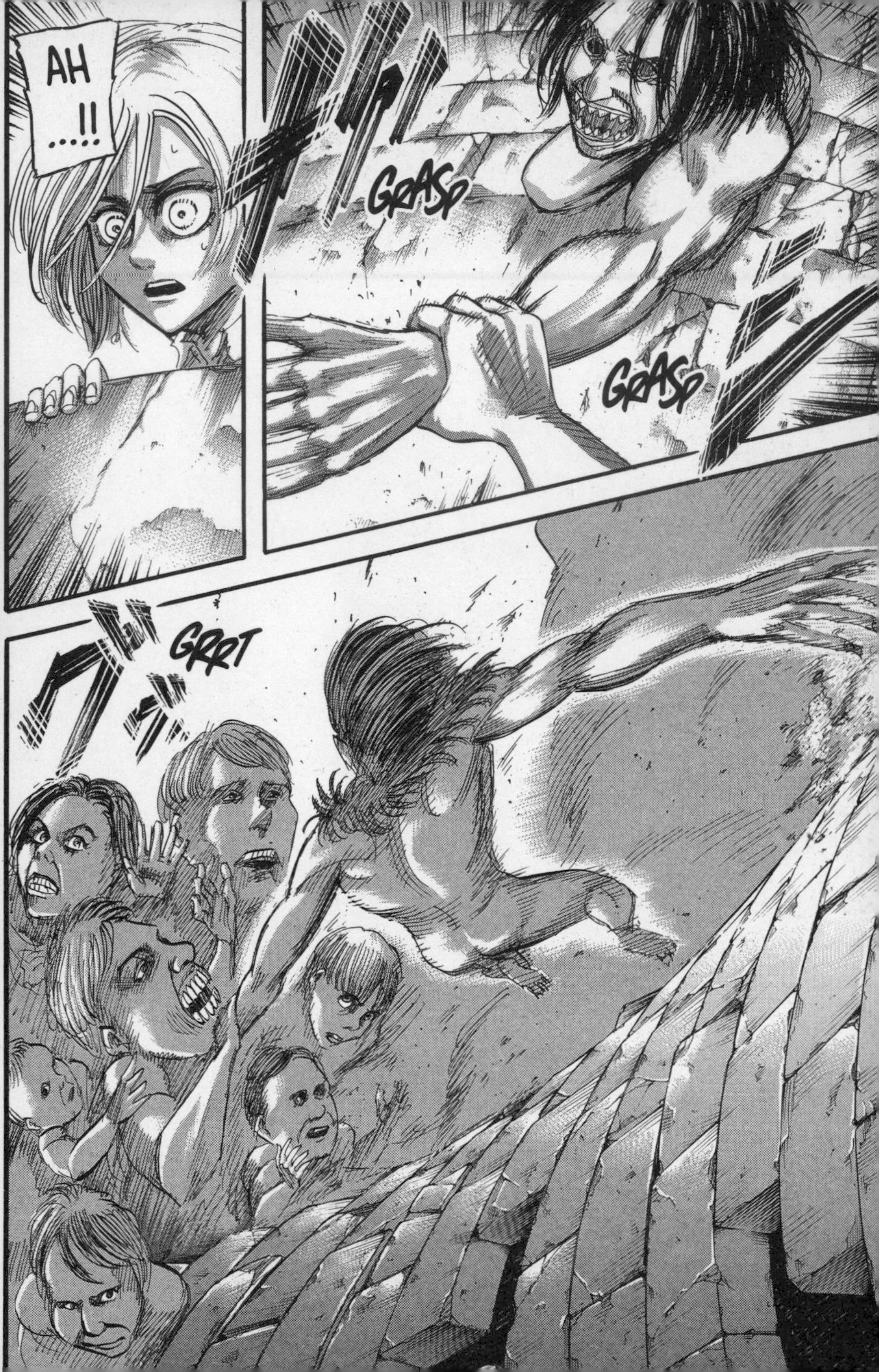
GRASP
GRASP
AH ...!!
GRRT

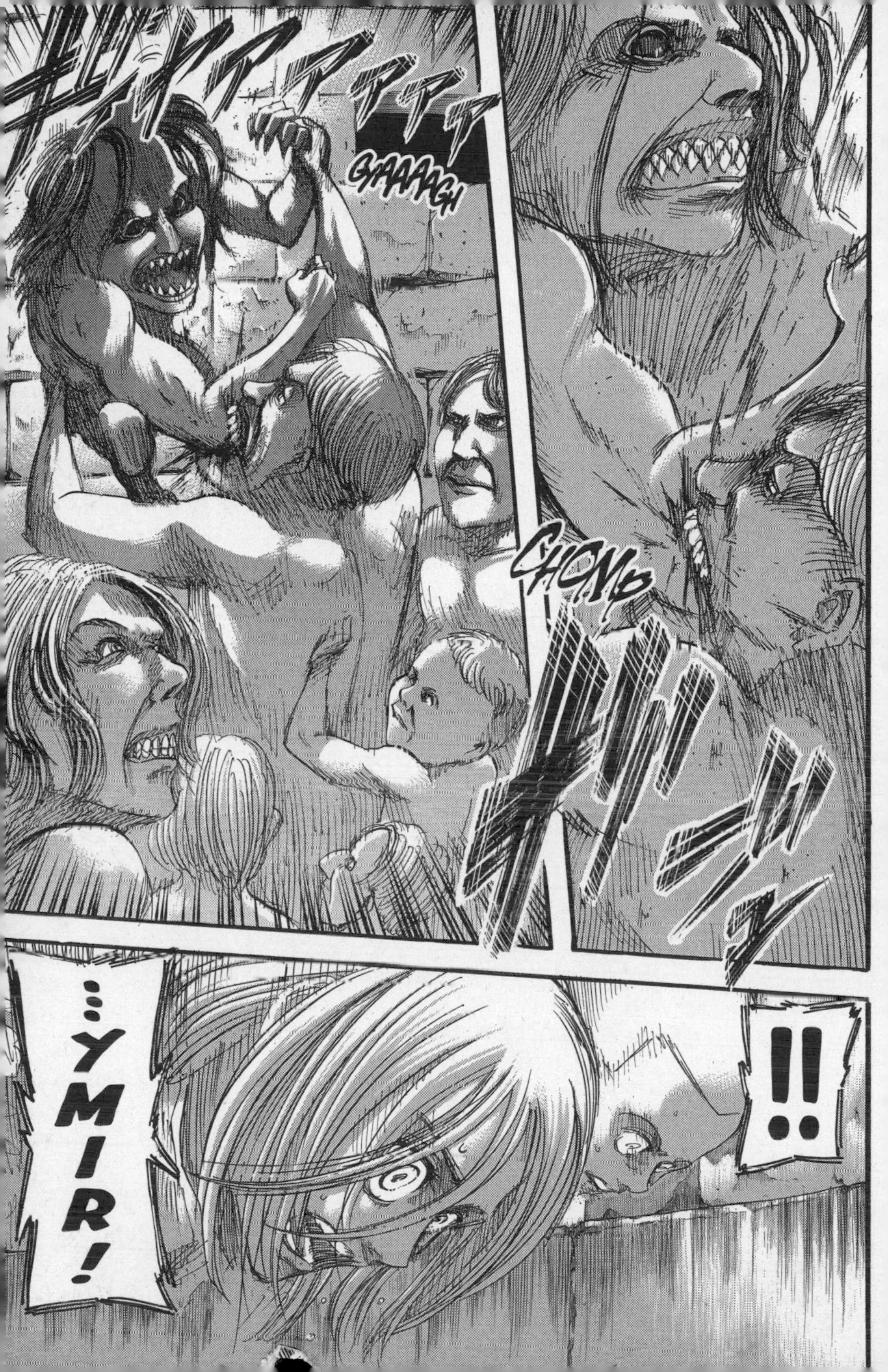
GYAAAAGH
CHOMP
!!
...YMIR!

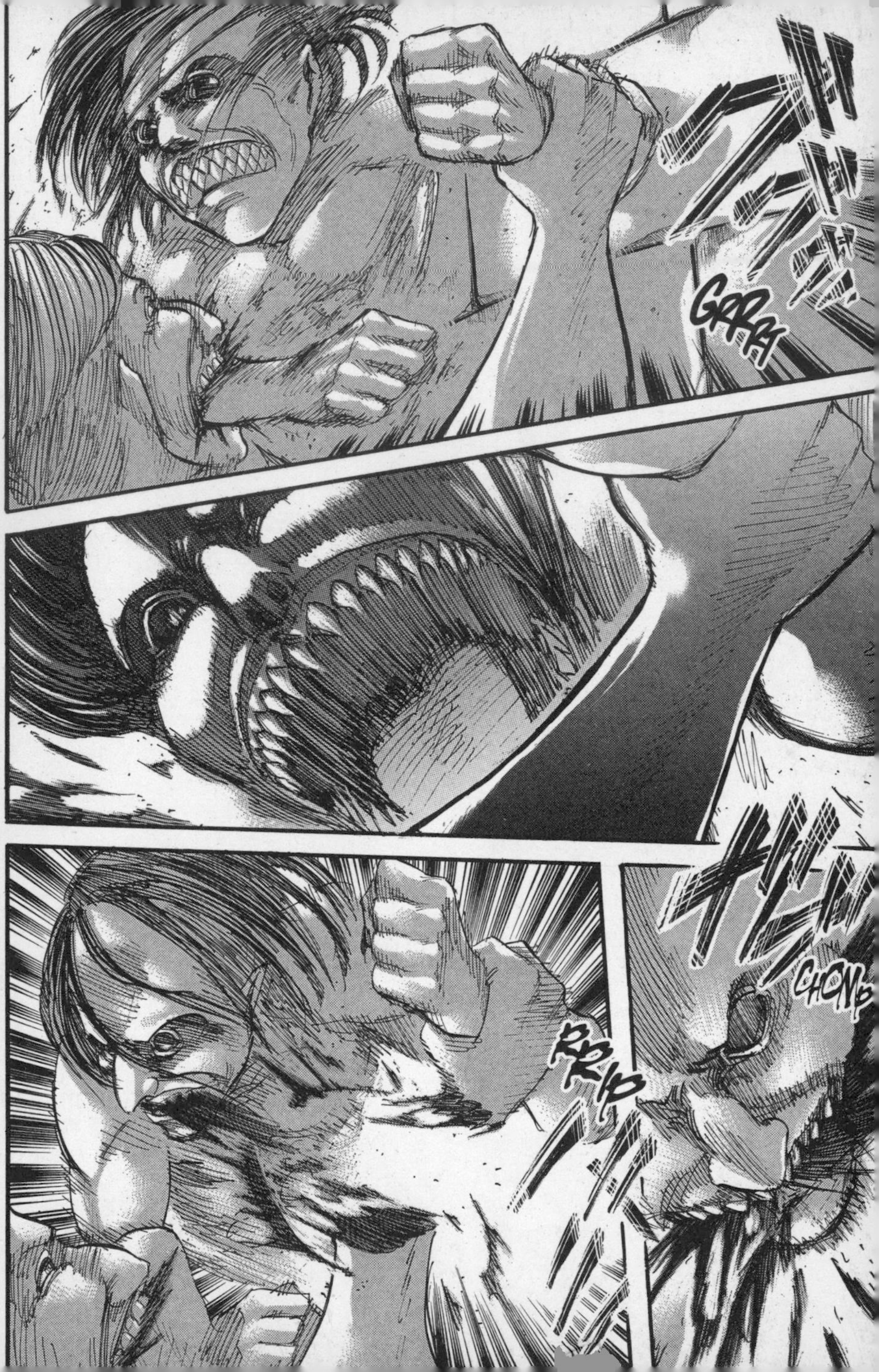
GRRR
CHOMP
RRRIP

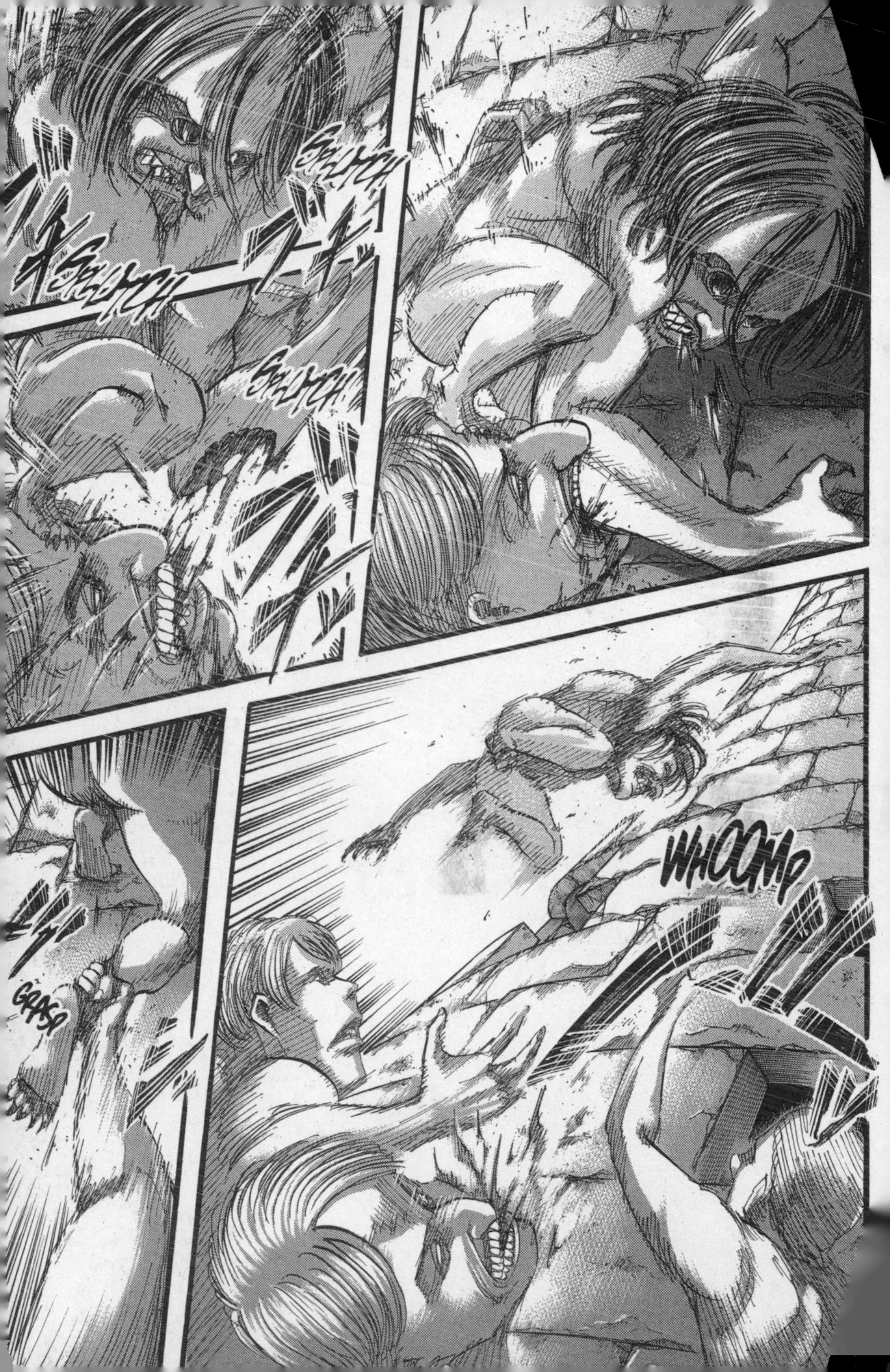
GSHLUTCH
GSHLUTCH
GSHLUTCH
WHOOMP
GRASP

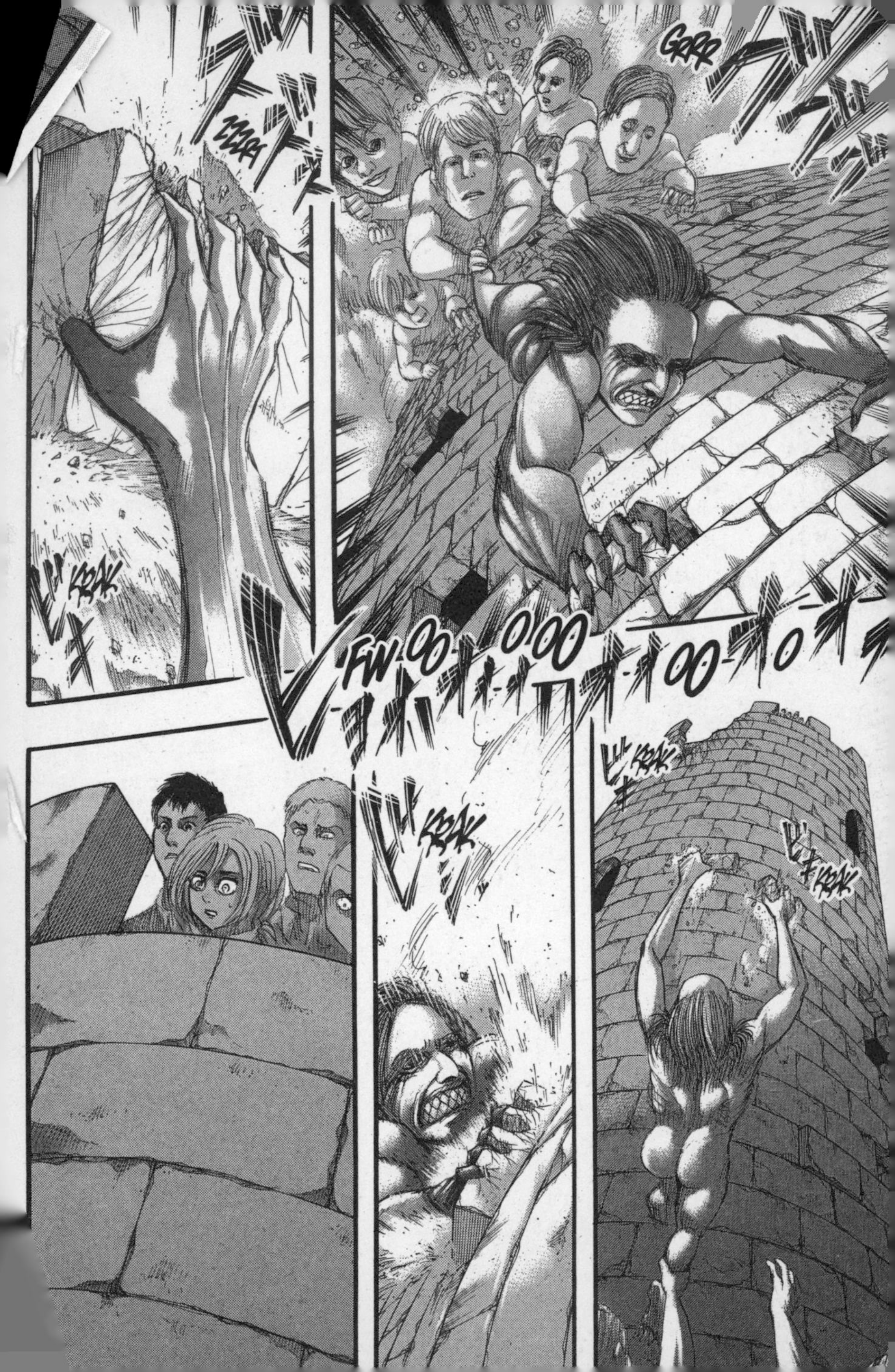

GRRR
ZZZRT
KRAK
FWOOOOOOOOO
KRAK
KRAK
KRAK

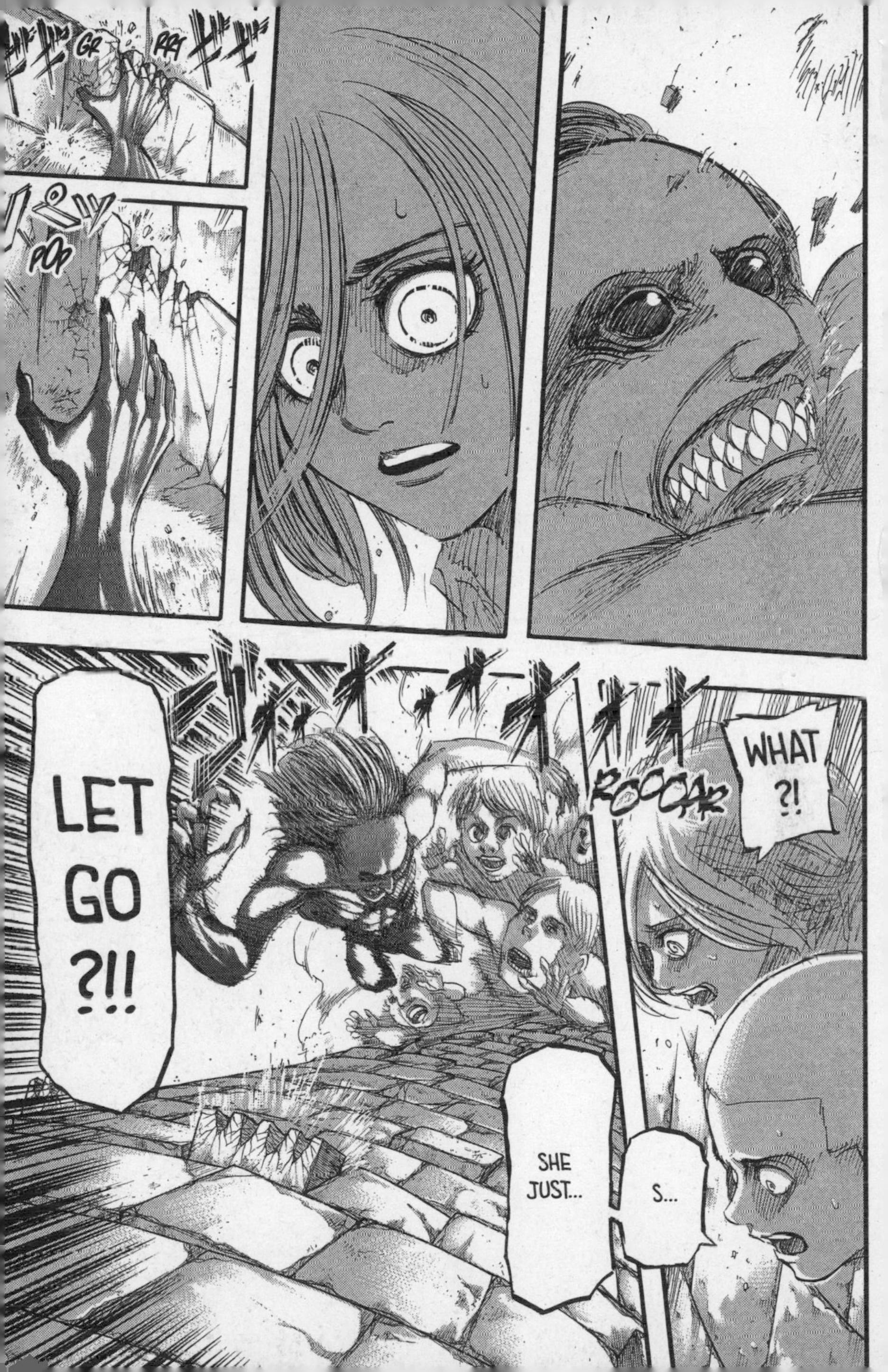

GR
RRT
POP
WHAT ?!
S...
ROOOAR
LET GO ?!!
SHE JUST...

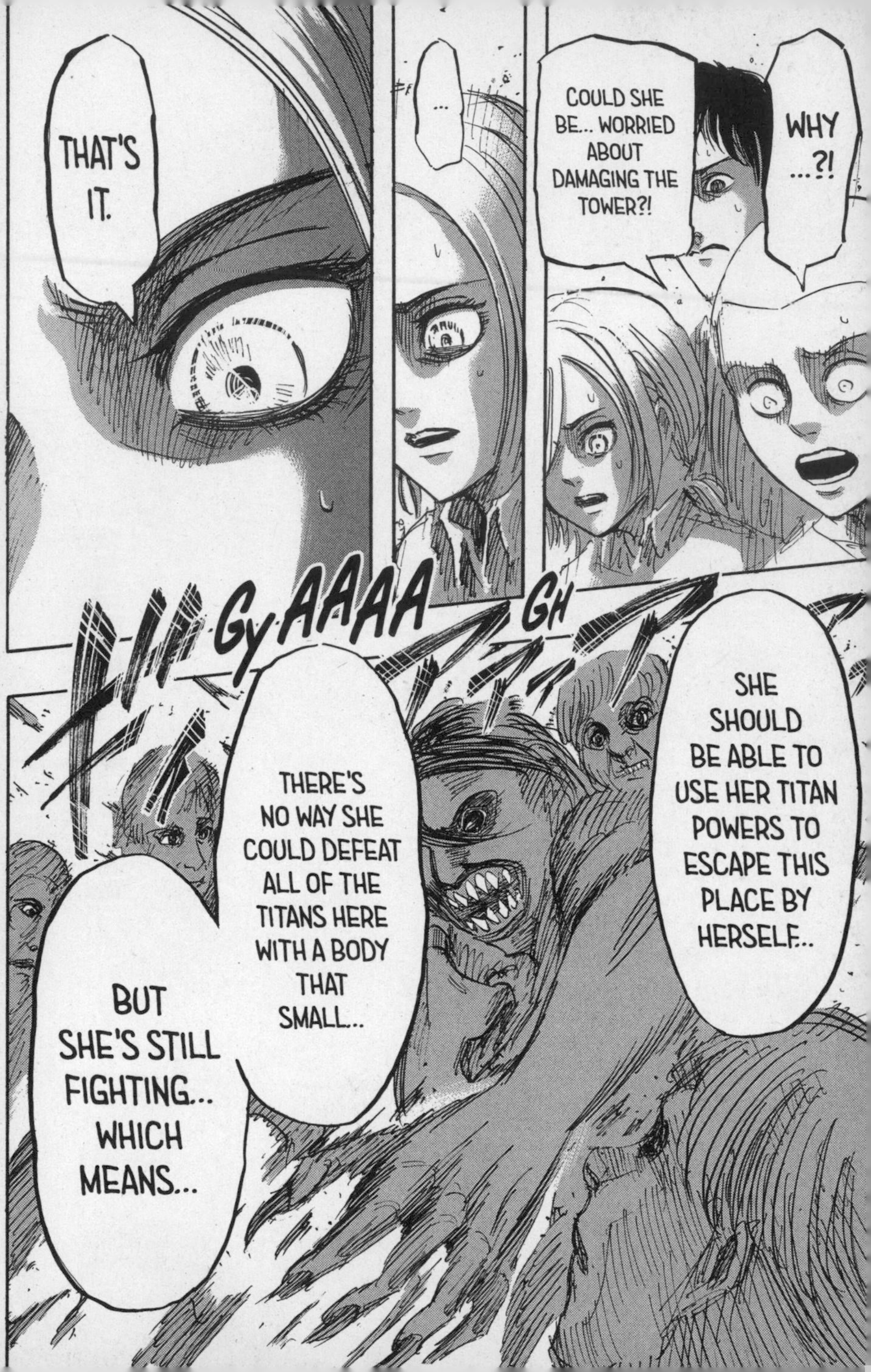
WHY ...?!
COULD SHE BE... WORRIED ABOUT DAMAGING THE TOWER?!
...
THAT'S IT.
GYAAAAGH
SHE SHOULD BE ABLE TO USE HER TITAN POWERS TO ESCAPE THIS PLACE BY HERSELF...
THERE'S NO WAY SHE COULD DEFEAT ALL OF THE TITANS HERE WITH A BODY THAT SMALL...
BUT SHE'S STILL FIGHTING... WHICH MEANS...

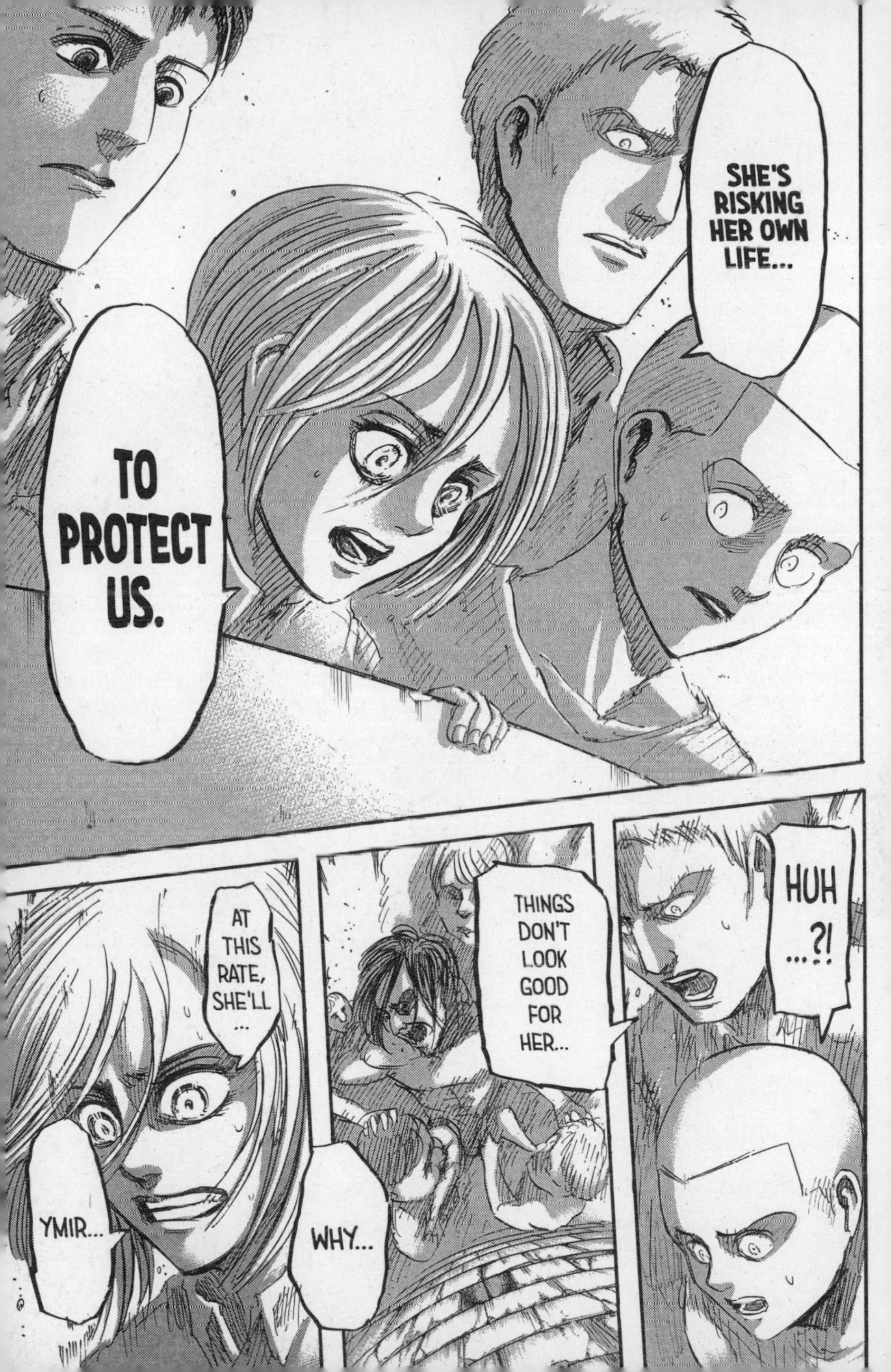
SHE'S RISKING HER OWN LIFE...
TO PROTECT US.
HUH ...?!
THINGS DON'T LOOK GOOD FOR HER...
AT THIS RATE, SHE'LL ...
WHY...
YMIR...

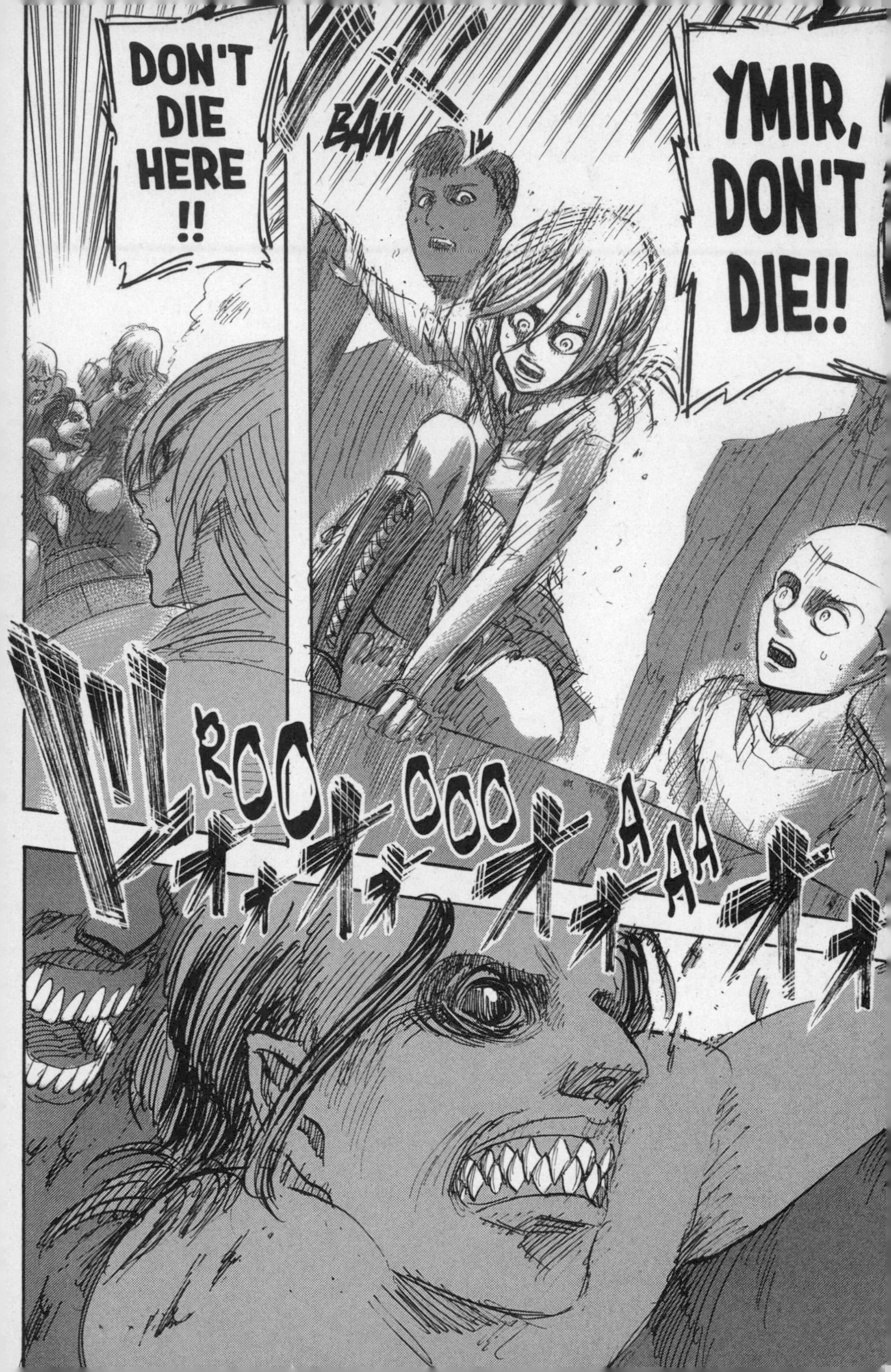
YMIR, DON'T DIE!!
BAM
DON'T DIE HERE!!
ROOOOOOAAA

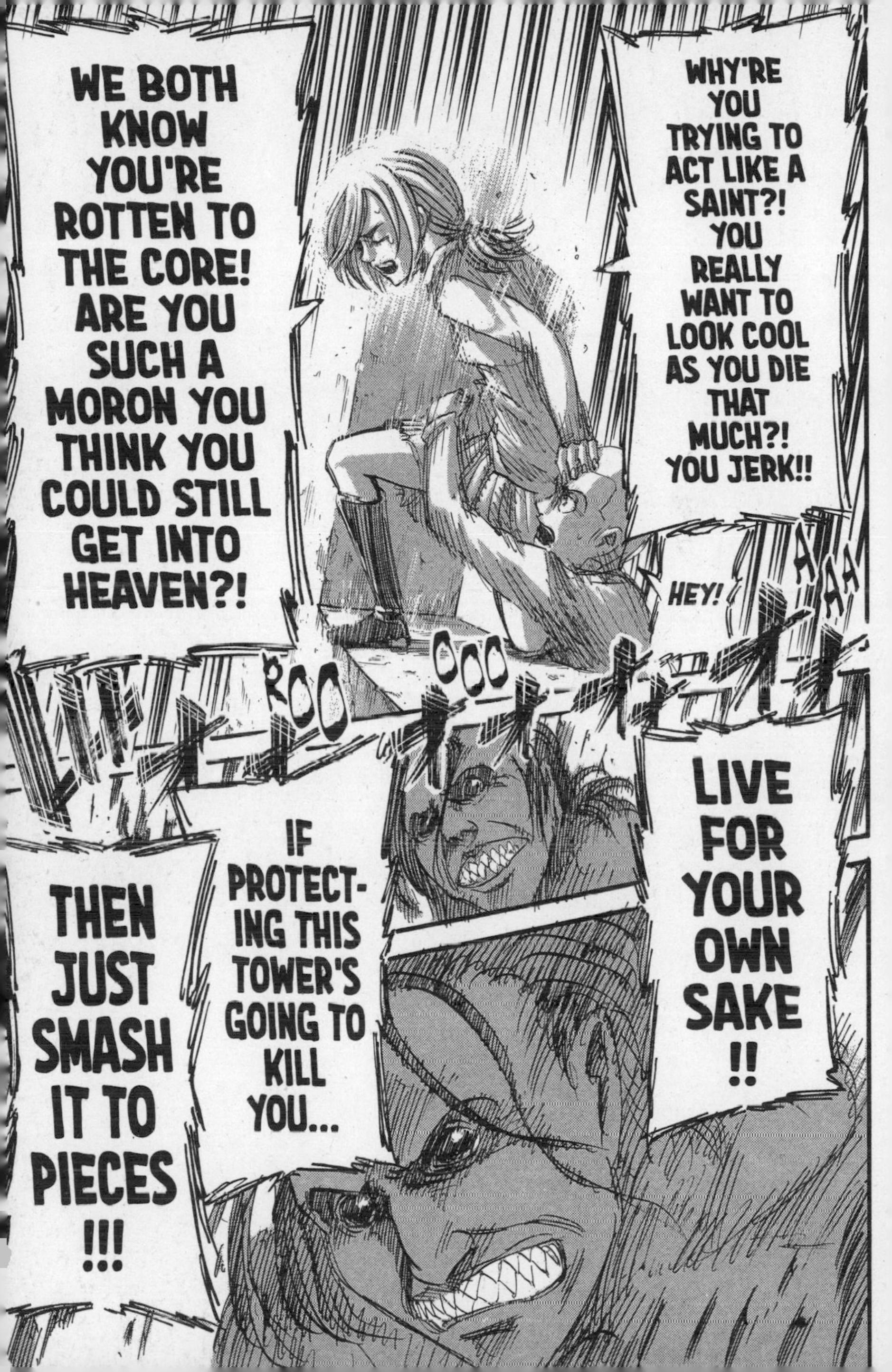
WHY'RE YOU TRYING TO ACT LIKE A SAINT?! YOU REALLY WANT TO LOOK COOL AS YOU DIE THAT MUCH?! YOU JERK!!
WE BOTH KNOW YOU'RE ROTTEN TO THE CORE! ARE YOU SUCH A MORON YOU THINK YOU COULD STILL GET INTO HEAVEN?!
HEY!
ROOOOOO
LIVE FOR YOUR OWN SAKE!!
IF PROTECT-ING THIS TOWER'S GOING TO KILL YOU...
THEN JUST SMASH IT TO PIECES!!!

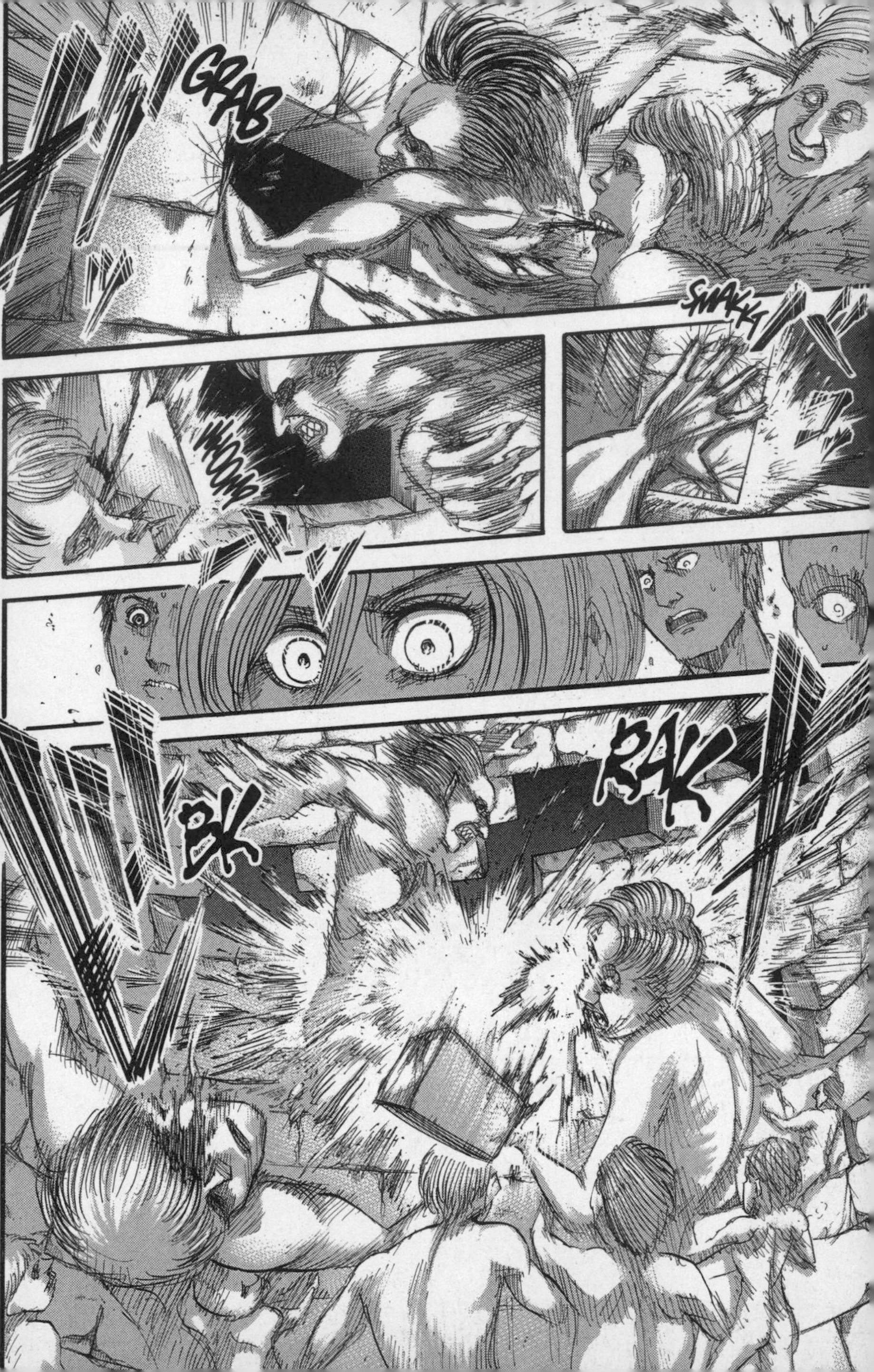
GRAB
SMAKK
WHOOMP
RAK
BK

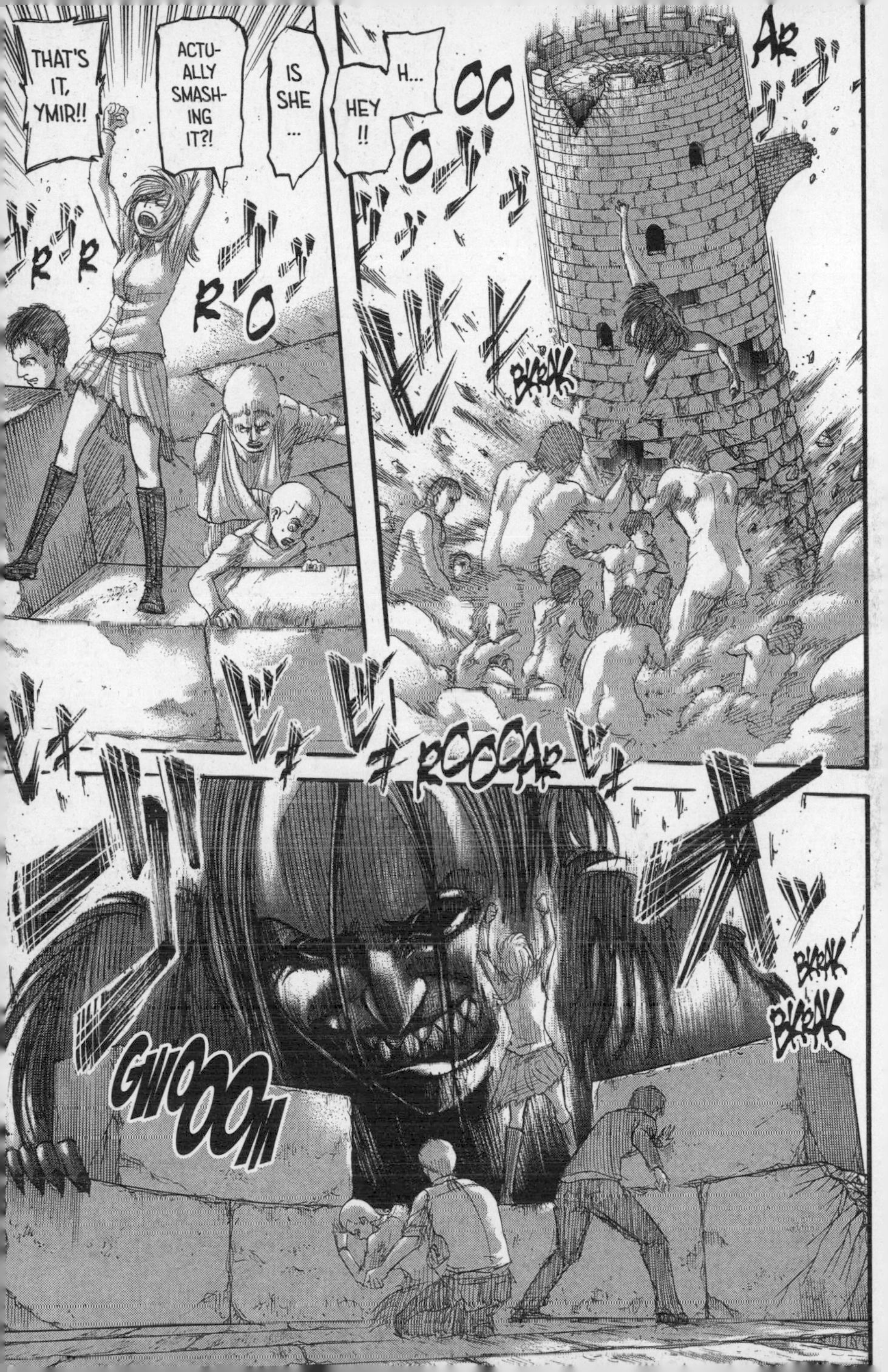
AR
H... HEY!!
OO
O
BKRAK
IS SHE ...
ACTU-ALLY SMASH-ING IT?!
THAT'S IT, YMIR!!
RR
RO
ROOOAR
BKRAK
BKRAK
GWOOOM

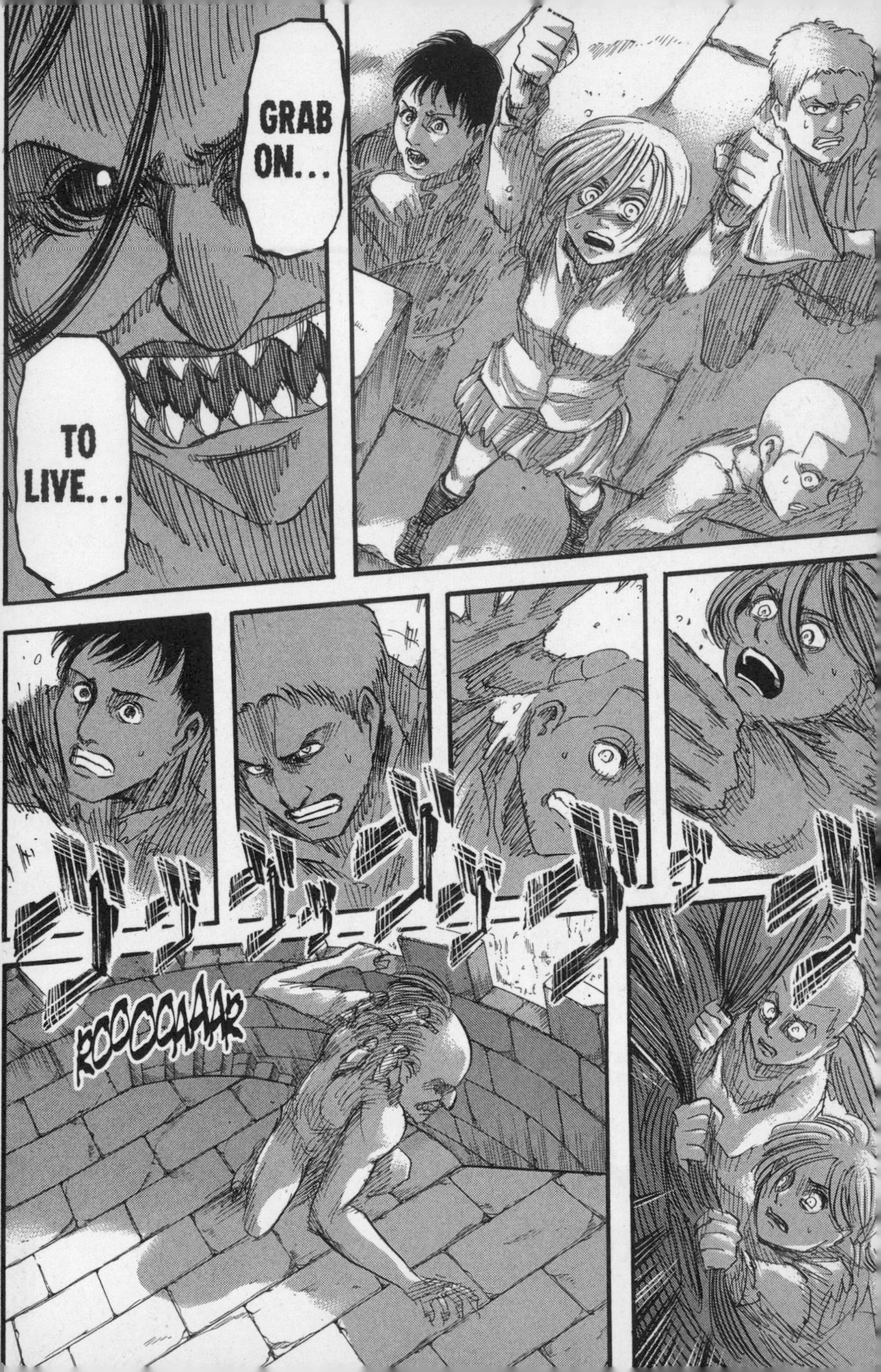
GRAB ON...
TO LIVE...
ROOOOAAAR

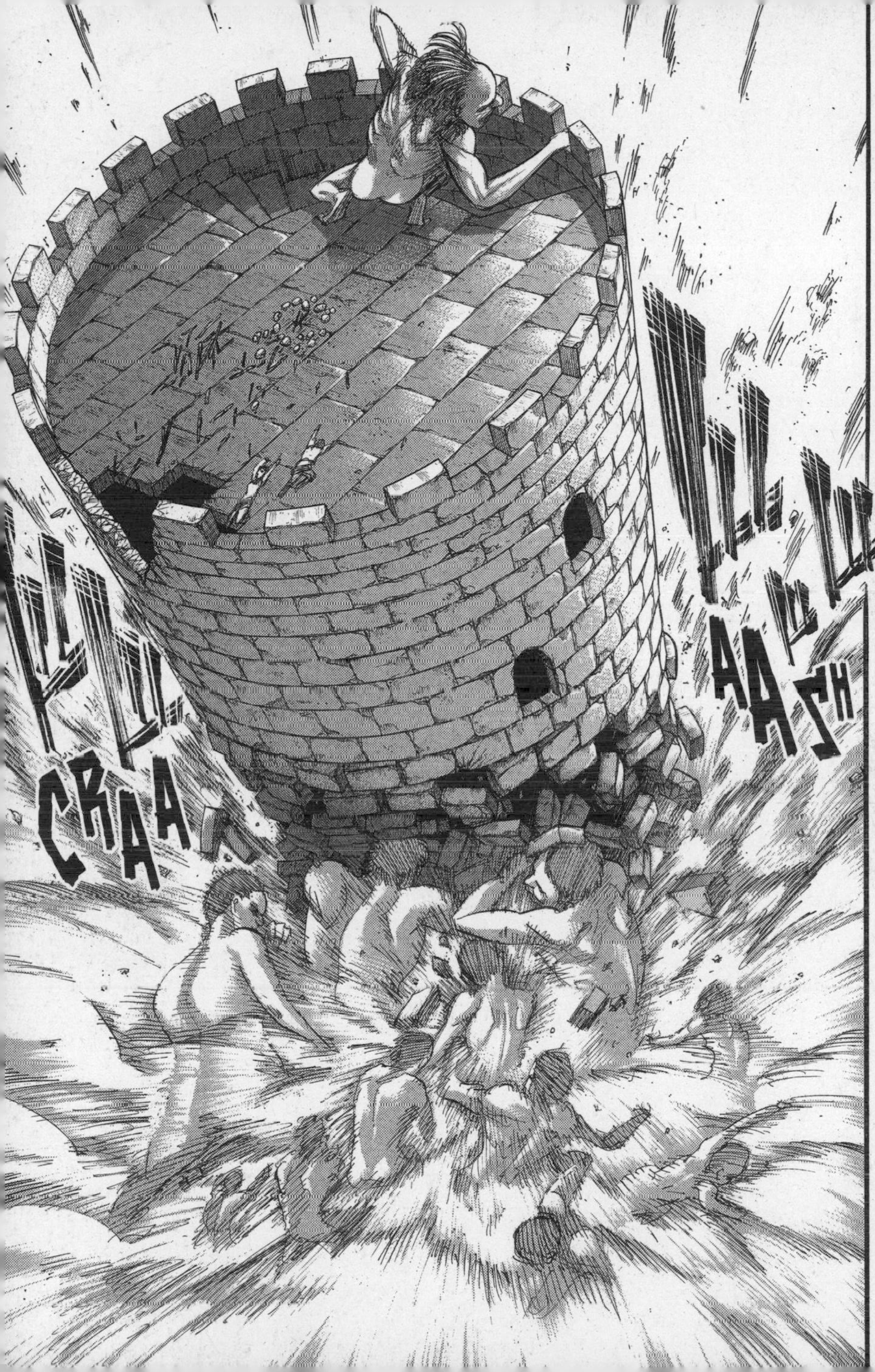
CRAA
AASH

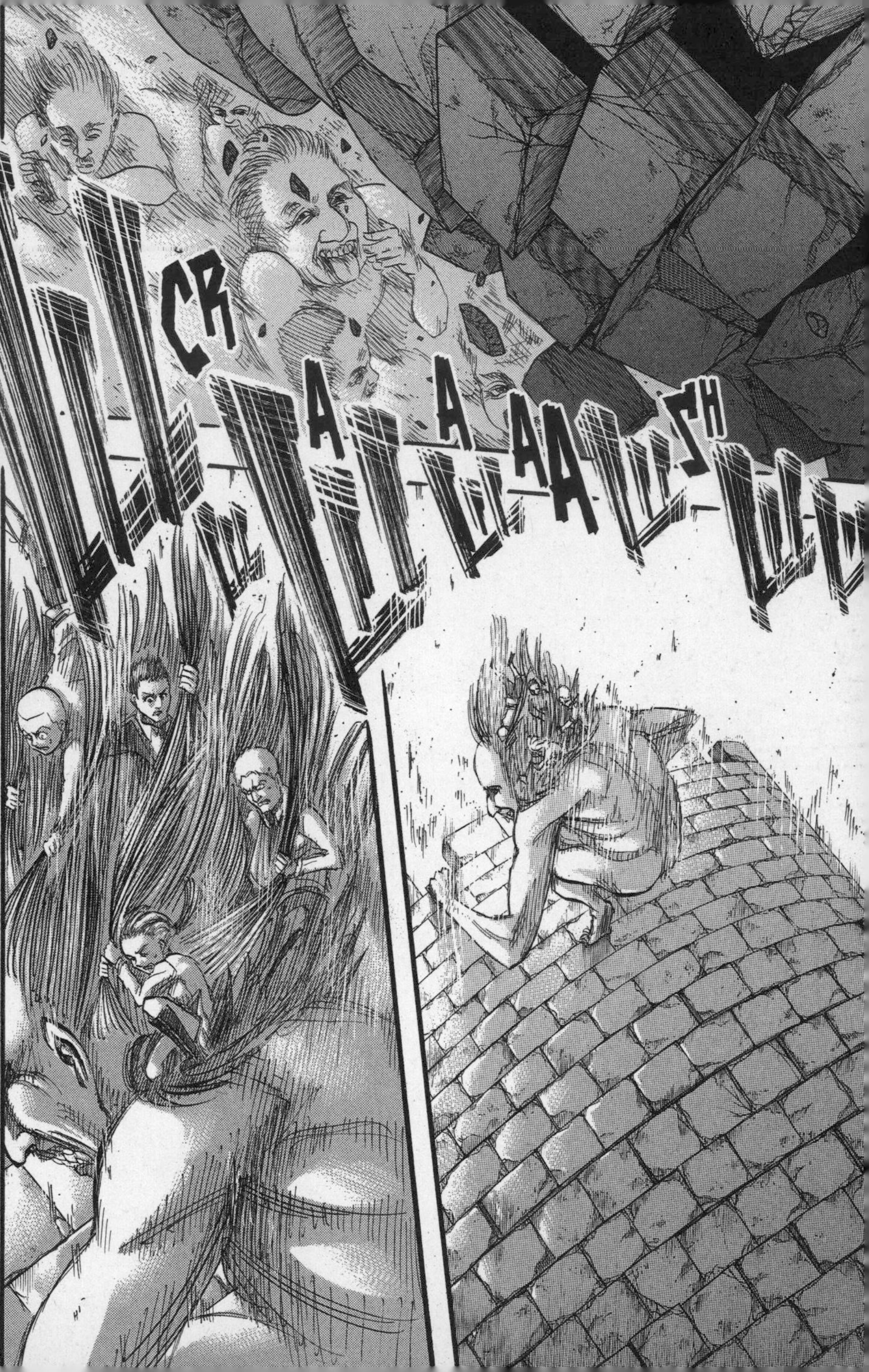
CRAAAASH

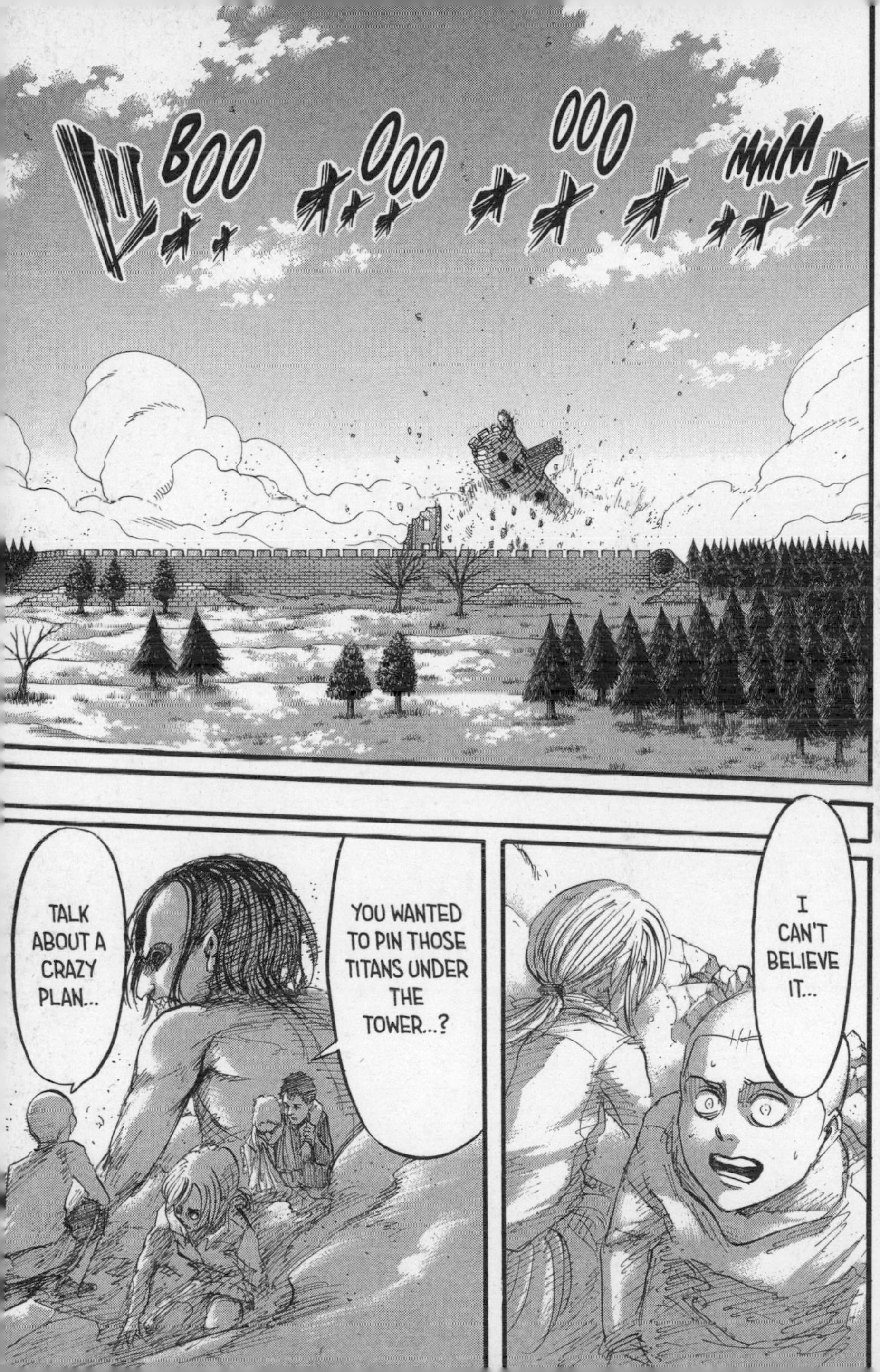
BOOOOOOOOOMMM
I CAN'T BELIEVE IT...
YOU WANTED TO PIN THOSE TITANS UNDER THE TOWER...?
TALK ABOUT A CRAZY PLAN...

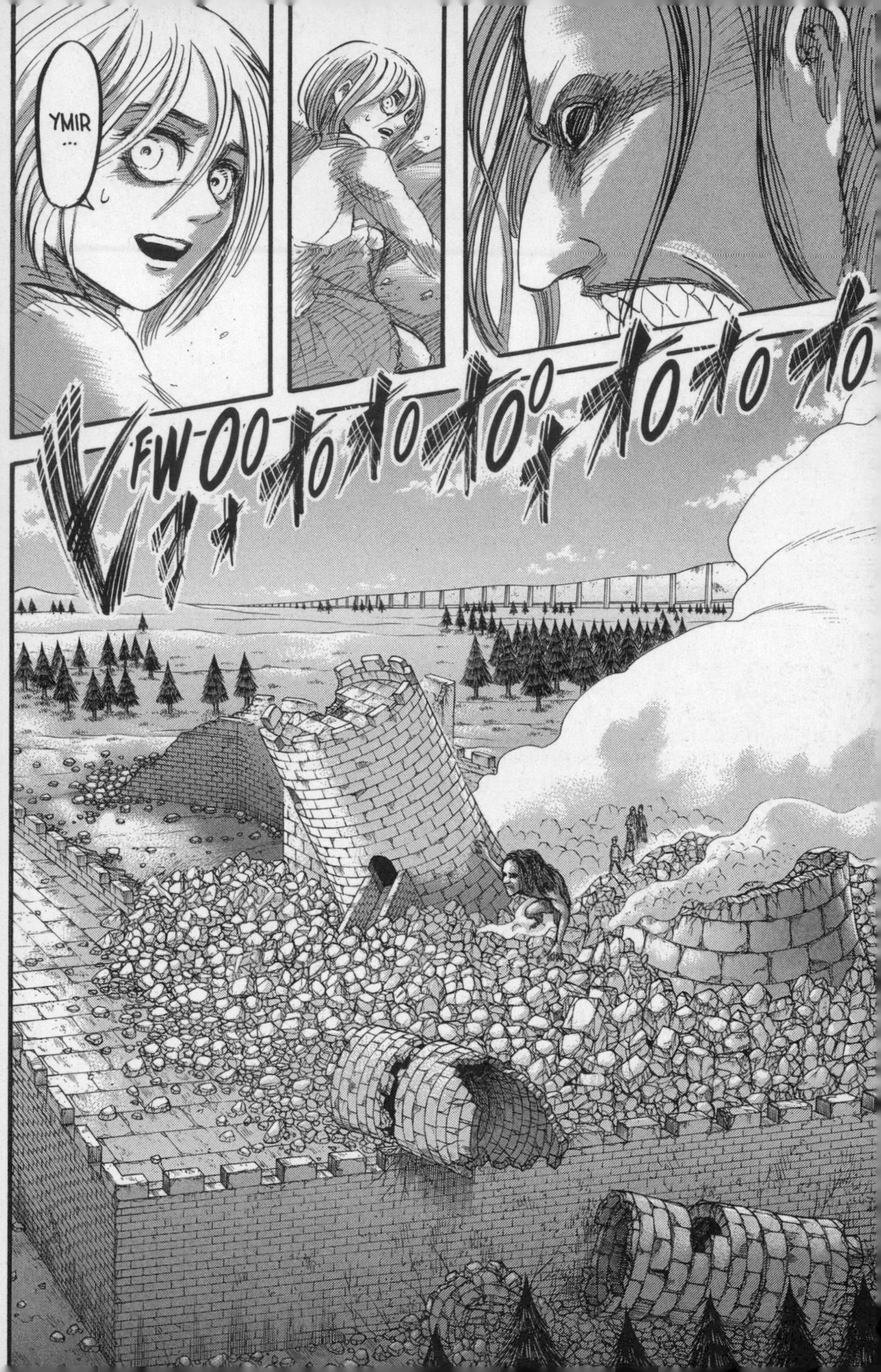
YMIR
...
VFWOOOOOOOOOO

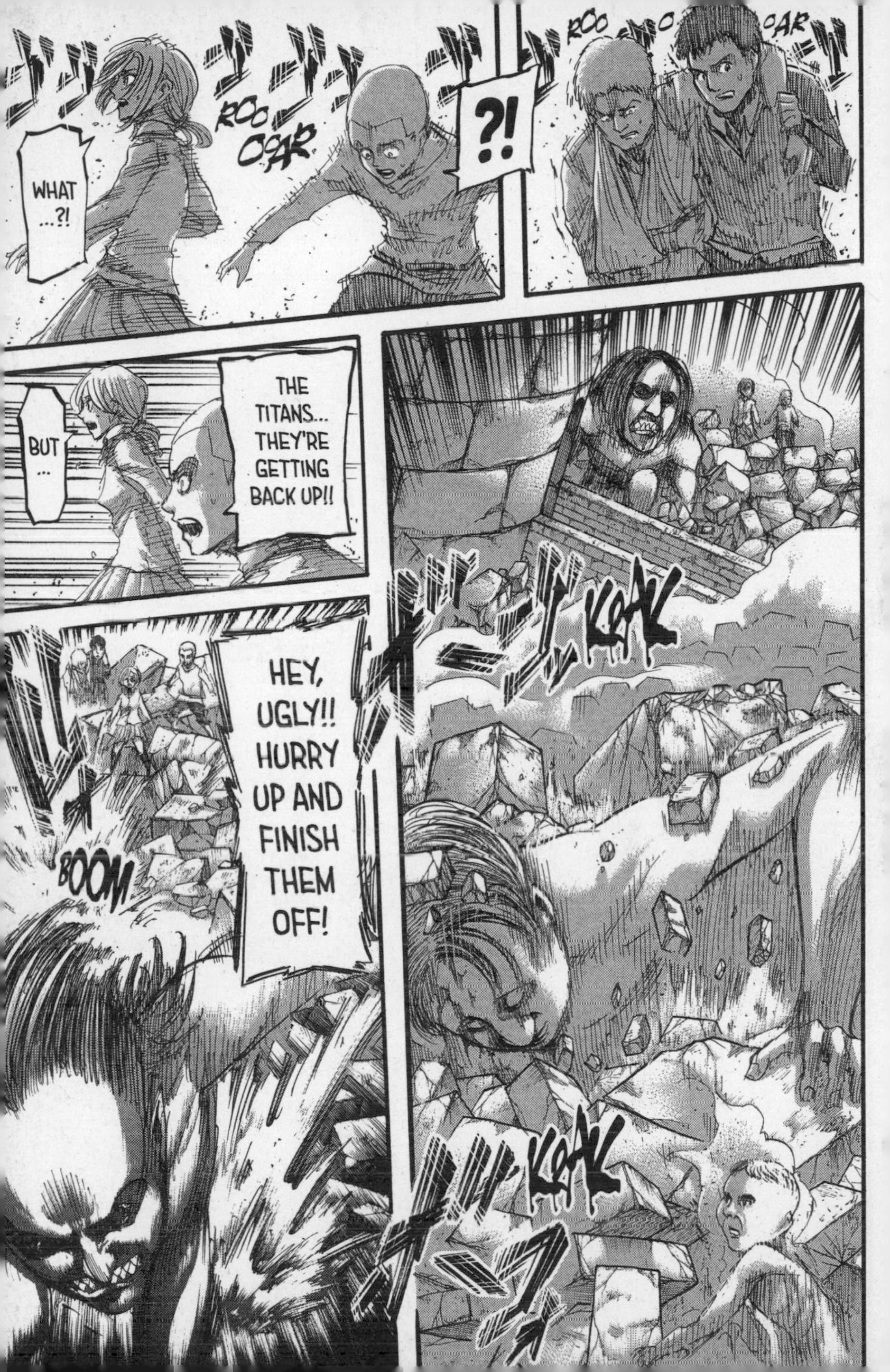

ROO
OAR
?!
ROO OOAR
WHAT ...?!
KRAK
KRAK
THE TITANS... THEY'RE GETTING BACK UP!!
BUT ...
HEY, UGLY!! HURRY UP AND FINISH THEM OFF!
BOOM

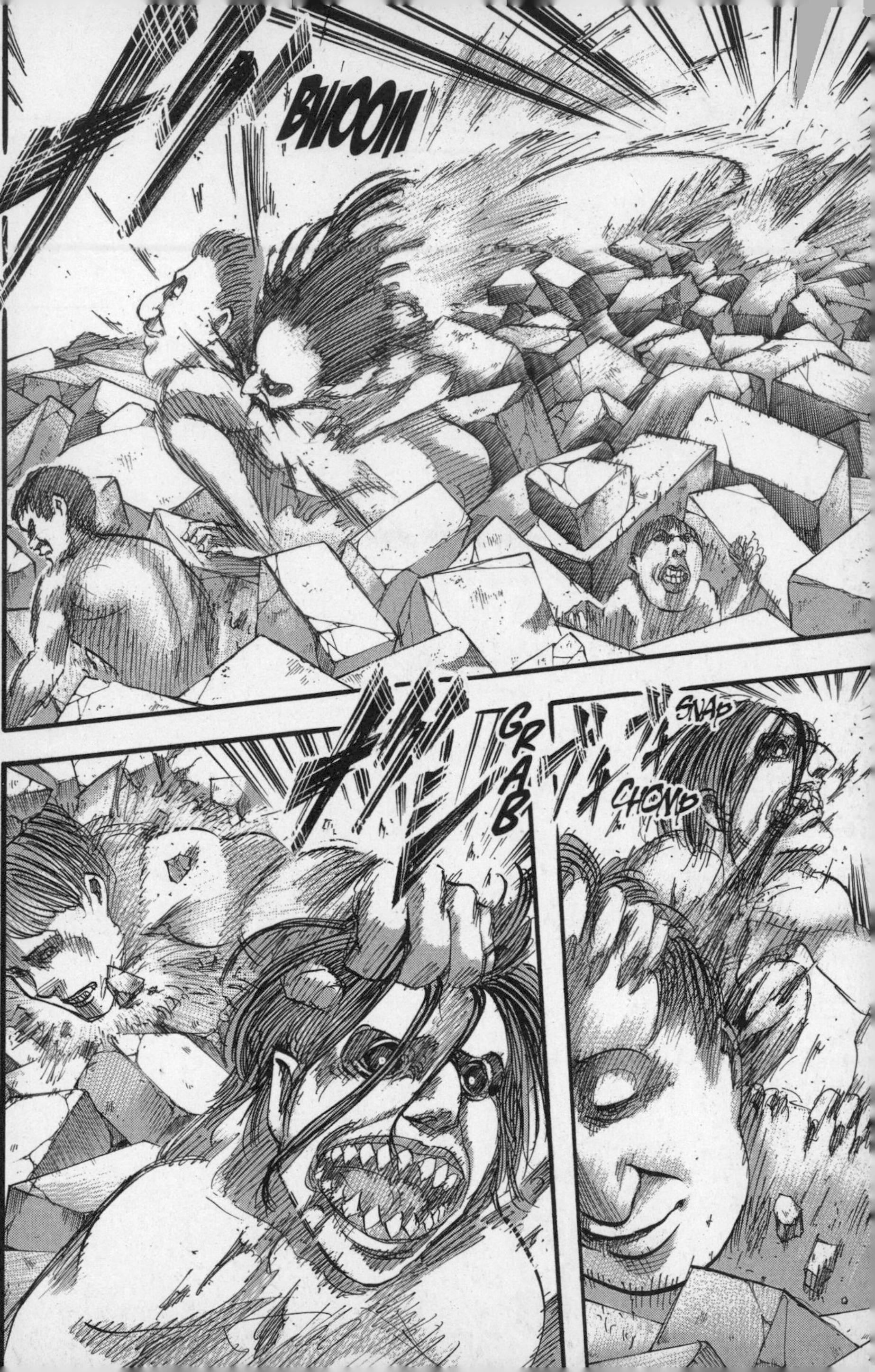
BWOOM
SNAP
CHOMP
GRAB

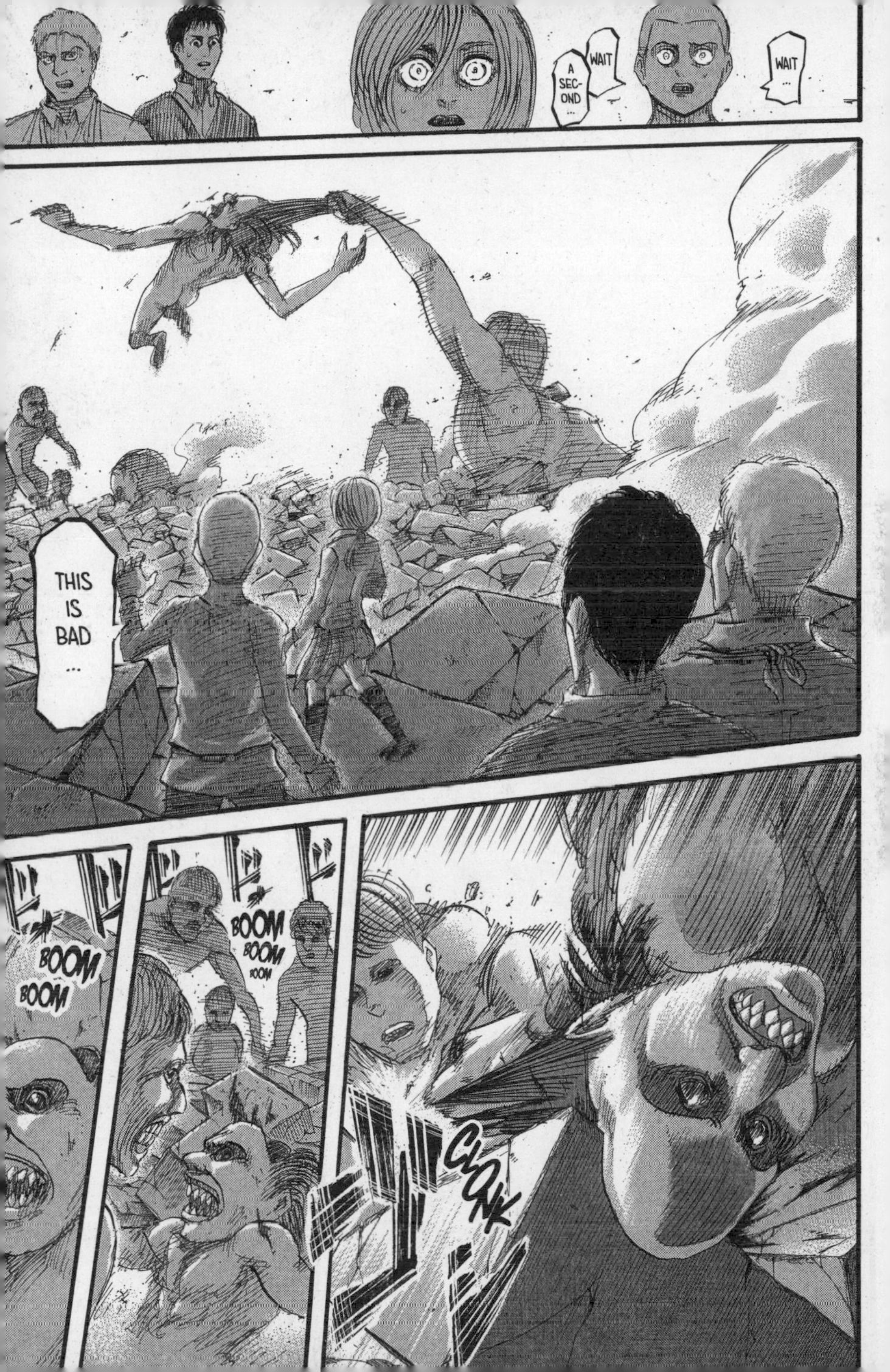
WAIT ...
WAIT
A SEC-OND ...
THIS IS BAD ...
CLONK
BOOM BOOM BOOM
BOOM BOOM

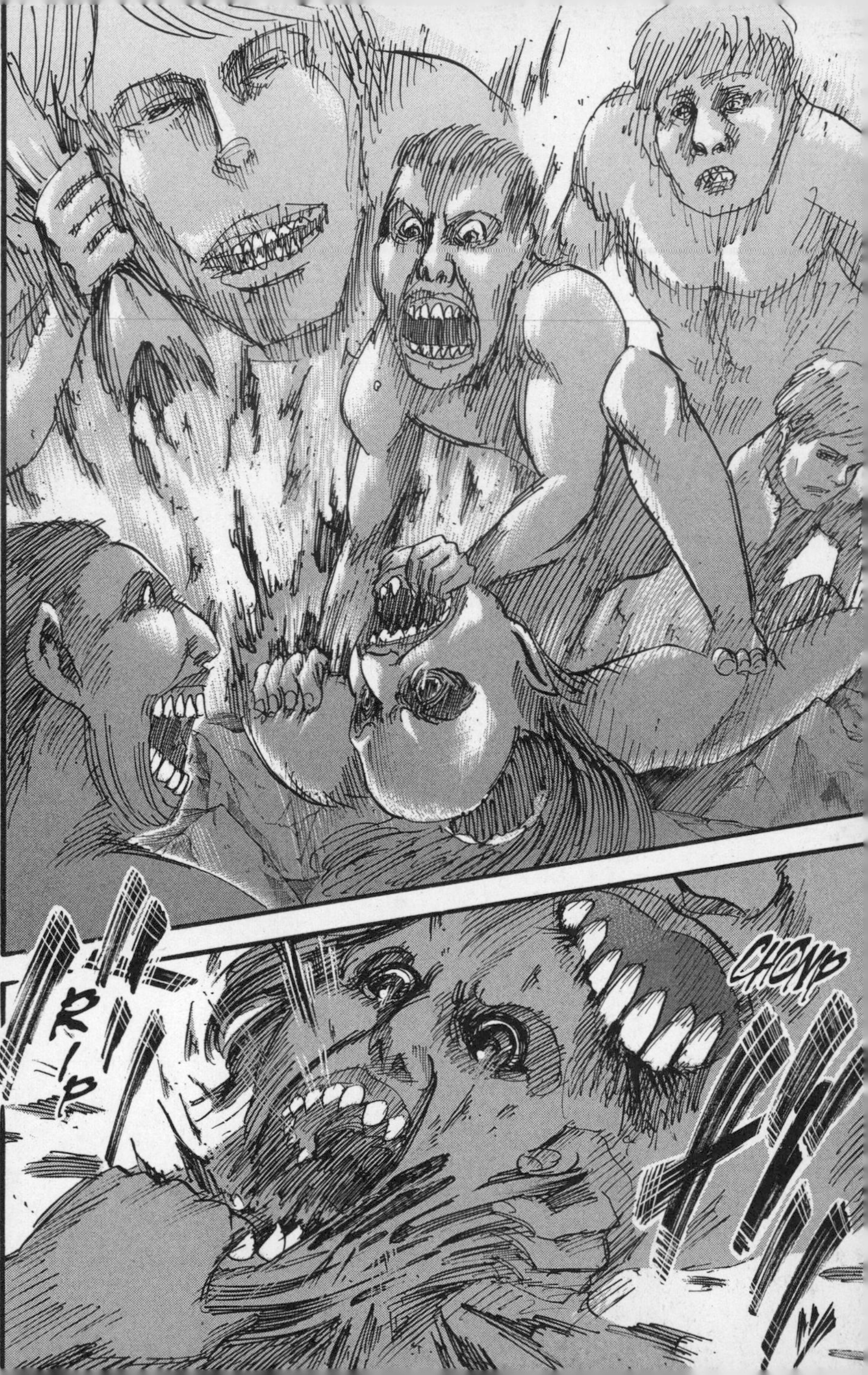
CHOMP
R-I-I-P

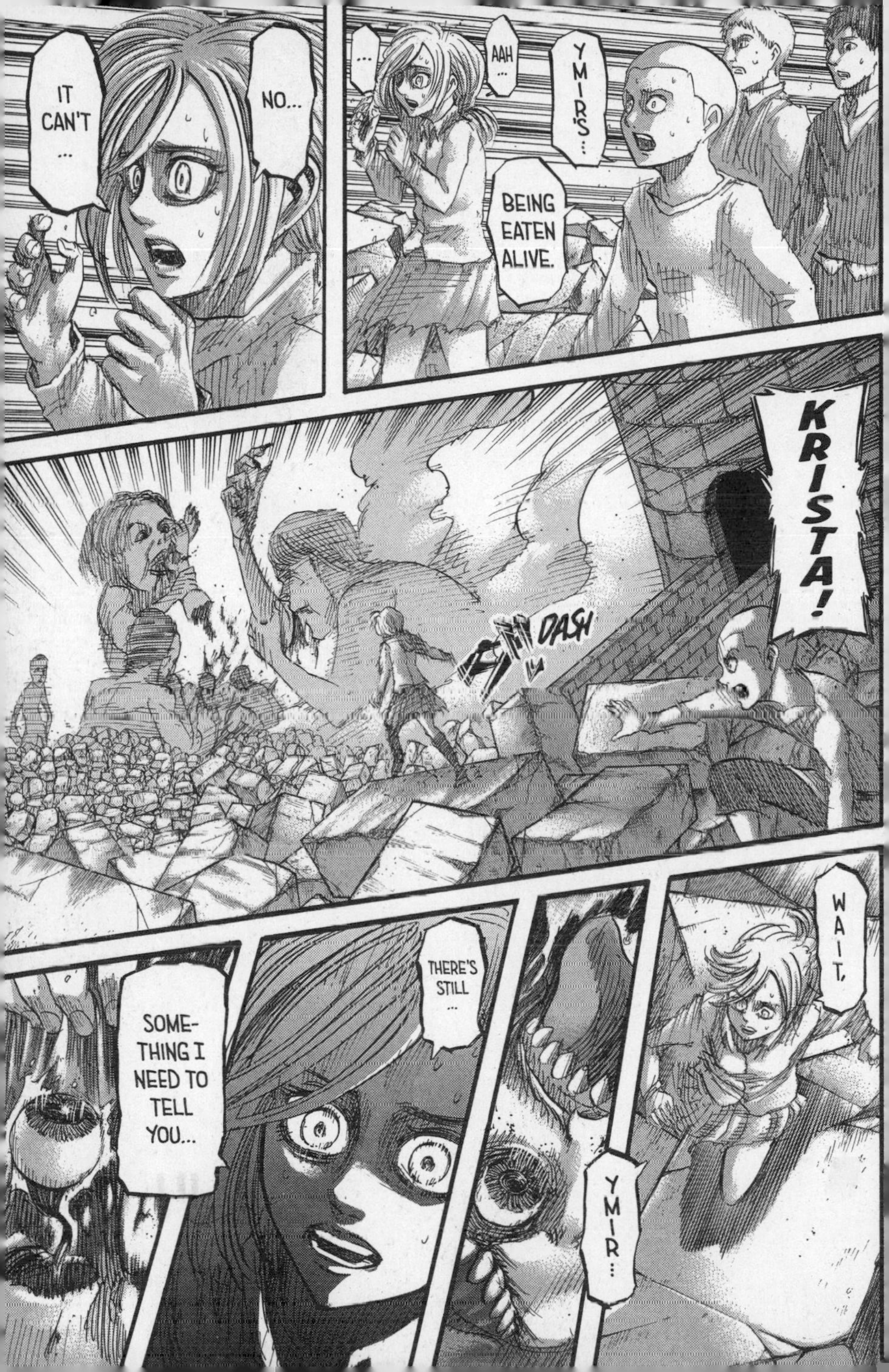
YMIR'S...
BEING EATEN ALIVE.
AAH ...
...
NO...
IT CAN'T ...
KRISTA!
DASH
WAIT,
YMIR...
THERE'S STILL ...
SOME-THING I NEED TO TELL YOU...

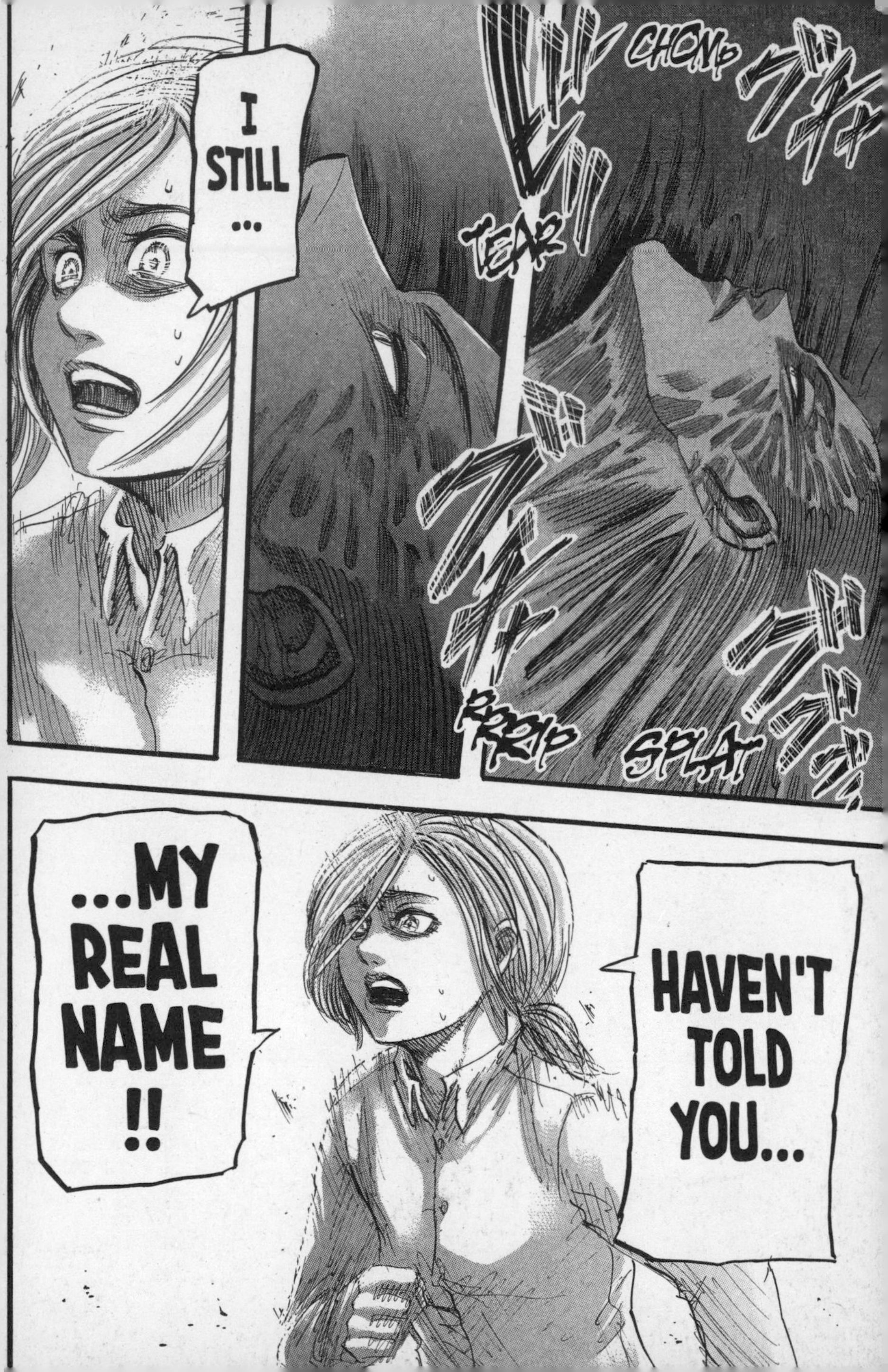
CHOMP
TEAR
RRRIP
SPLAT
I STILL ...
HAVEN'T TOLD YOU...
...MY REAL NAME !!

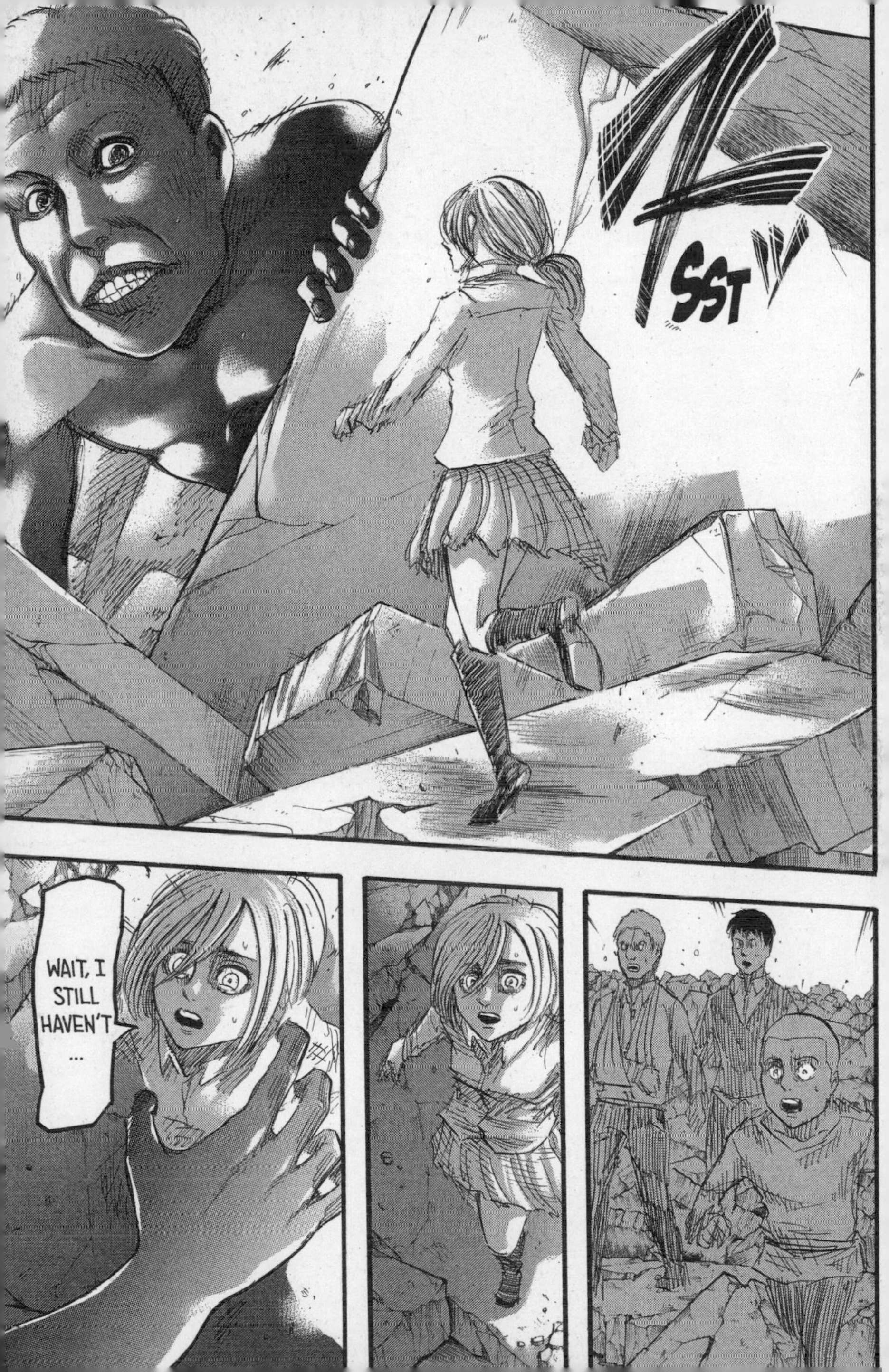
SSST
WAIT, I STILL HAVEN'T ...

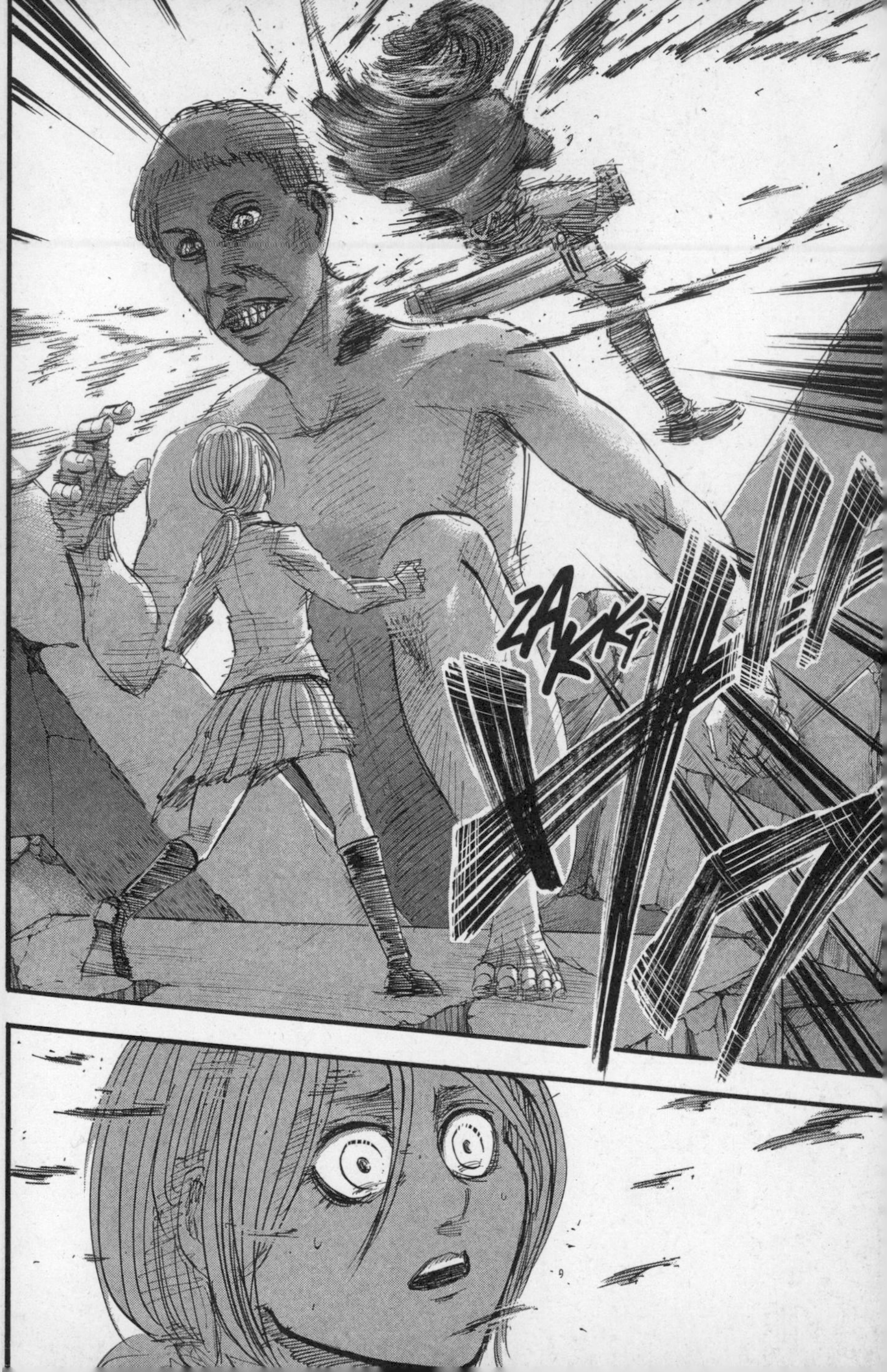
ZAKK!

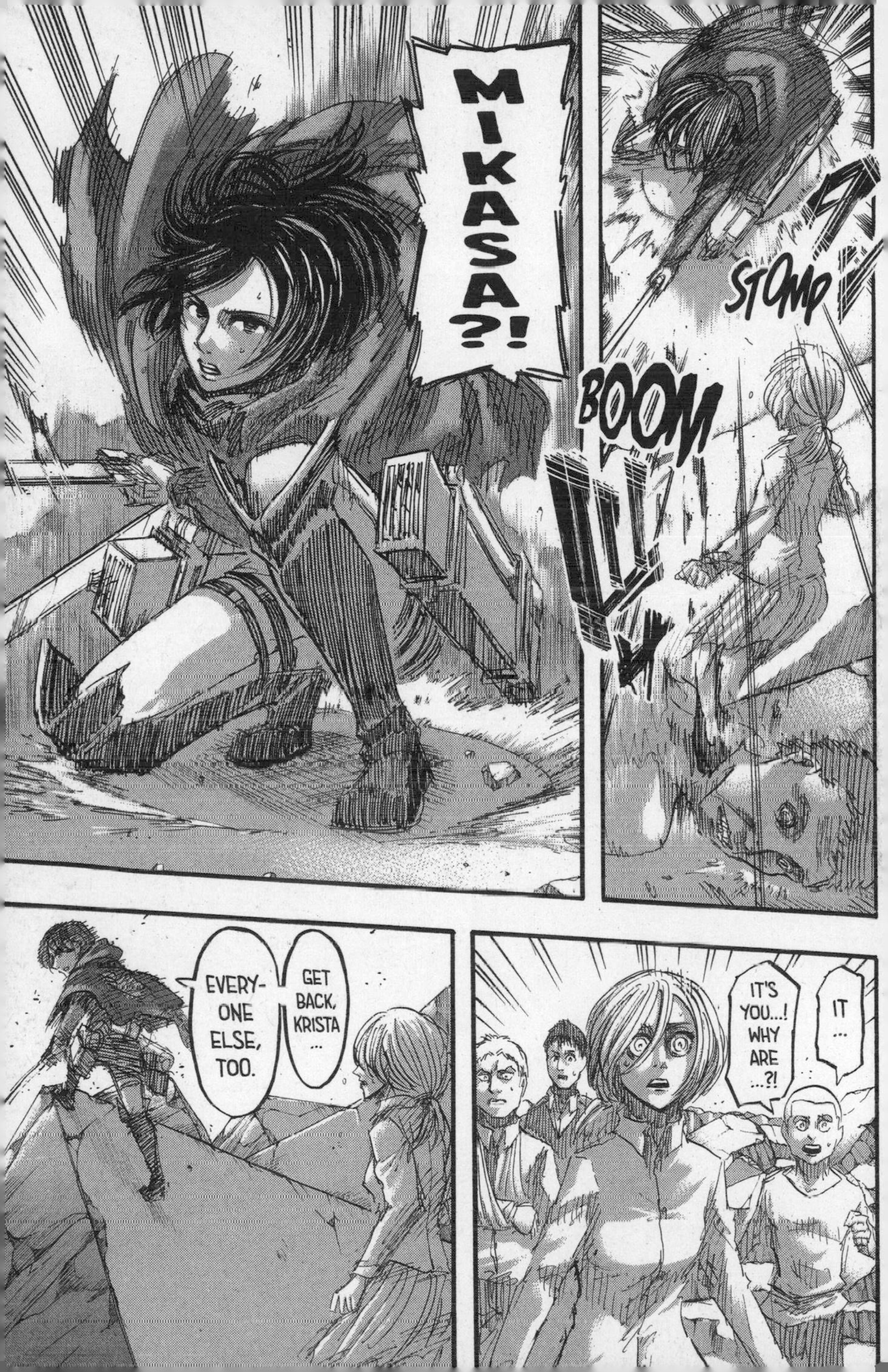
STOMP
BOOM
MIKASA?!
IT ...
IT'S YOU...! WHY ARE ...?!
GET BACK, KRISTA ...
EVERY-ONE ELSE, TOO.

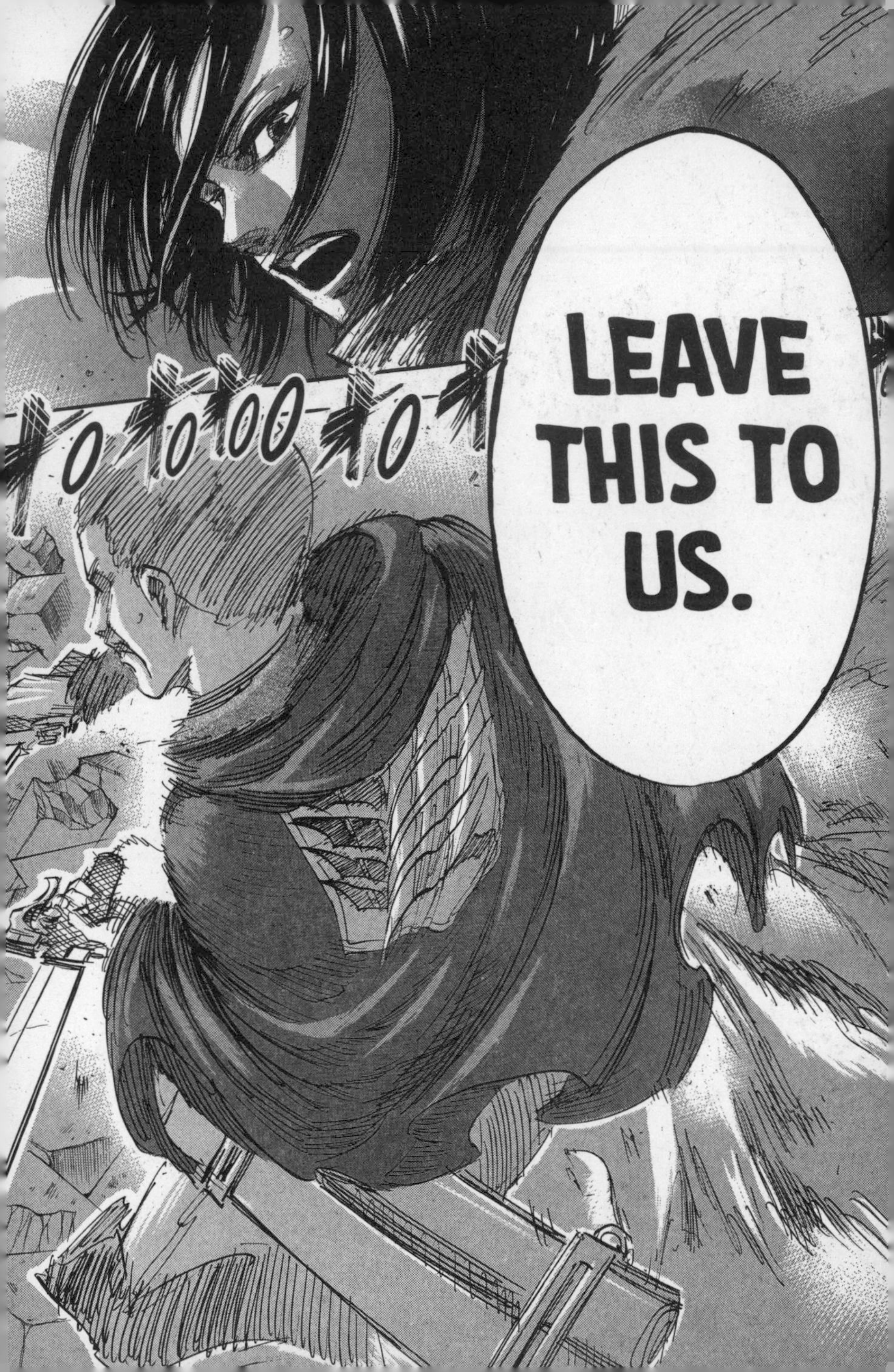
LEAVE THIS TO US.

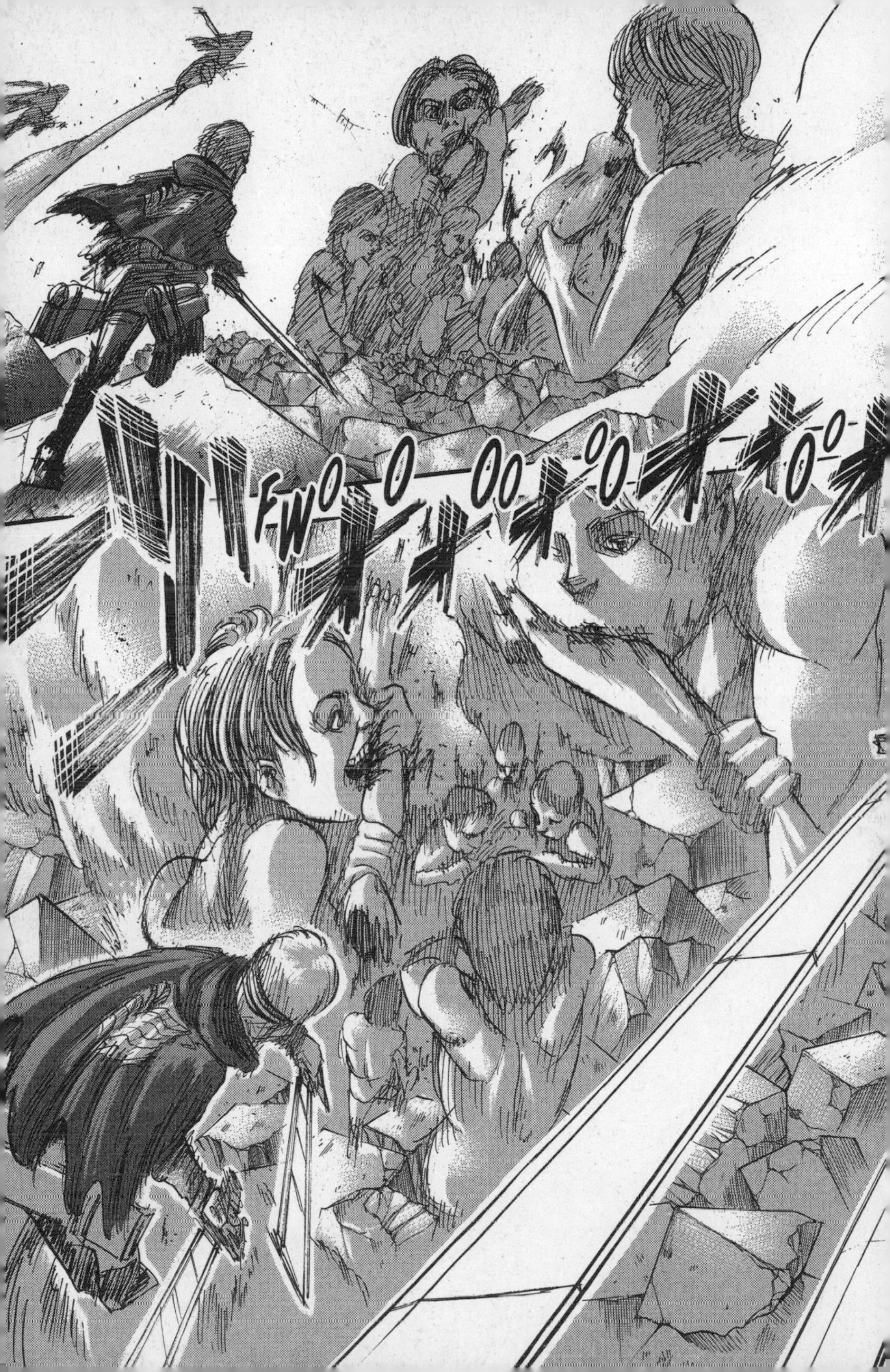
FWO-O—OO-OO-OO

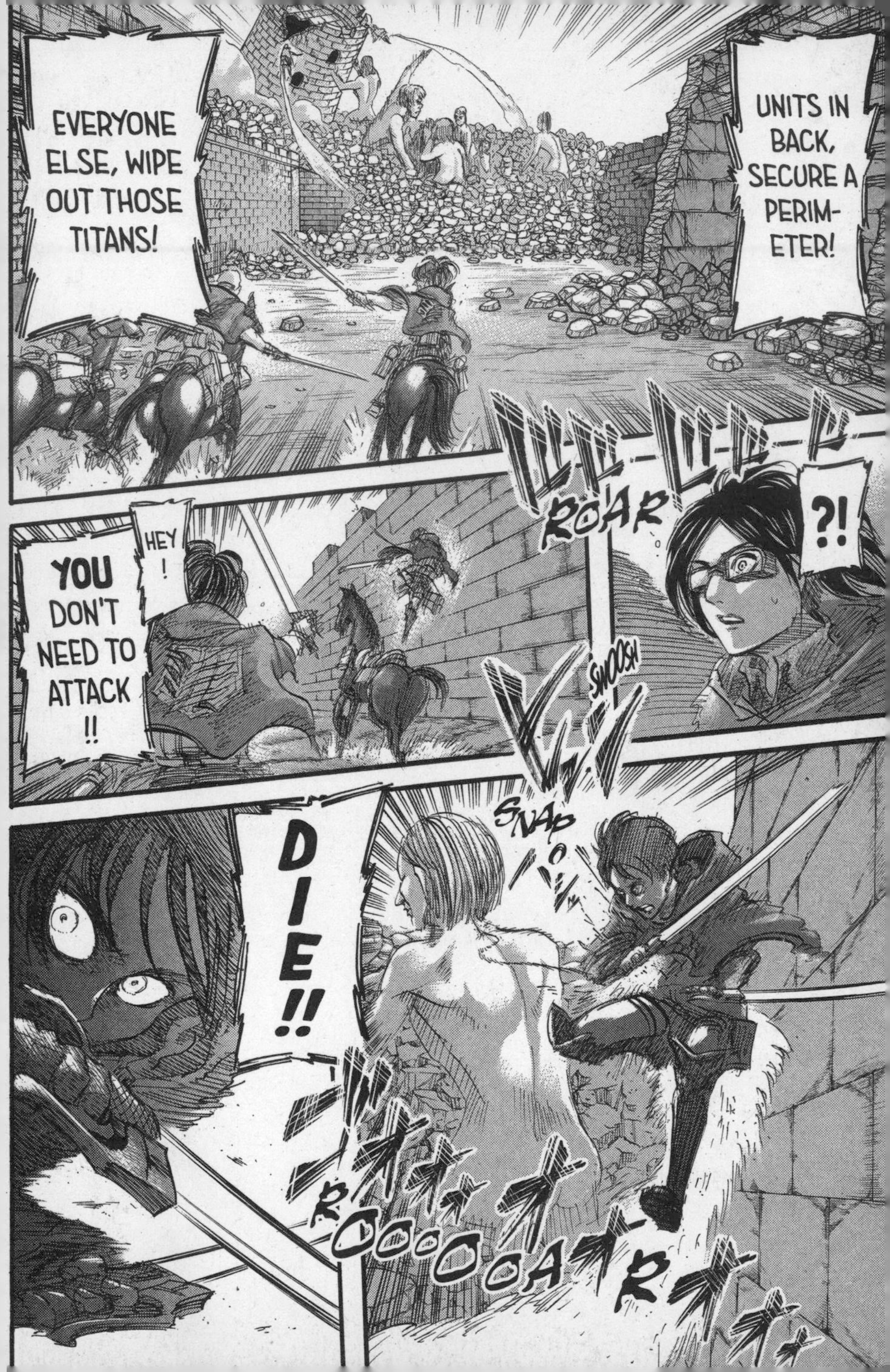
UNITS IN BACK, SECURE A PERIMETER!
EVERYONE ELSE, WIPE OUT THOSE TITANS!
ROAR
?!
HEY!
YOU DON'T NEED TO ATTACK!!
SWOOSH
SNAP
DIE!!
ROOOOOAR

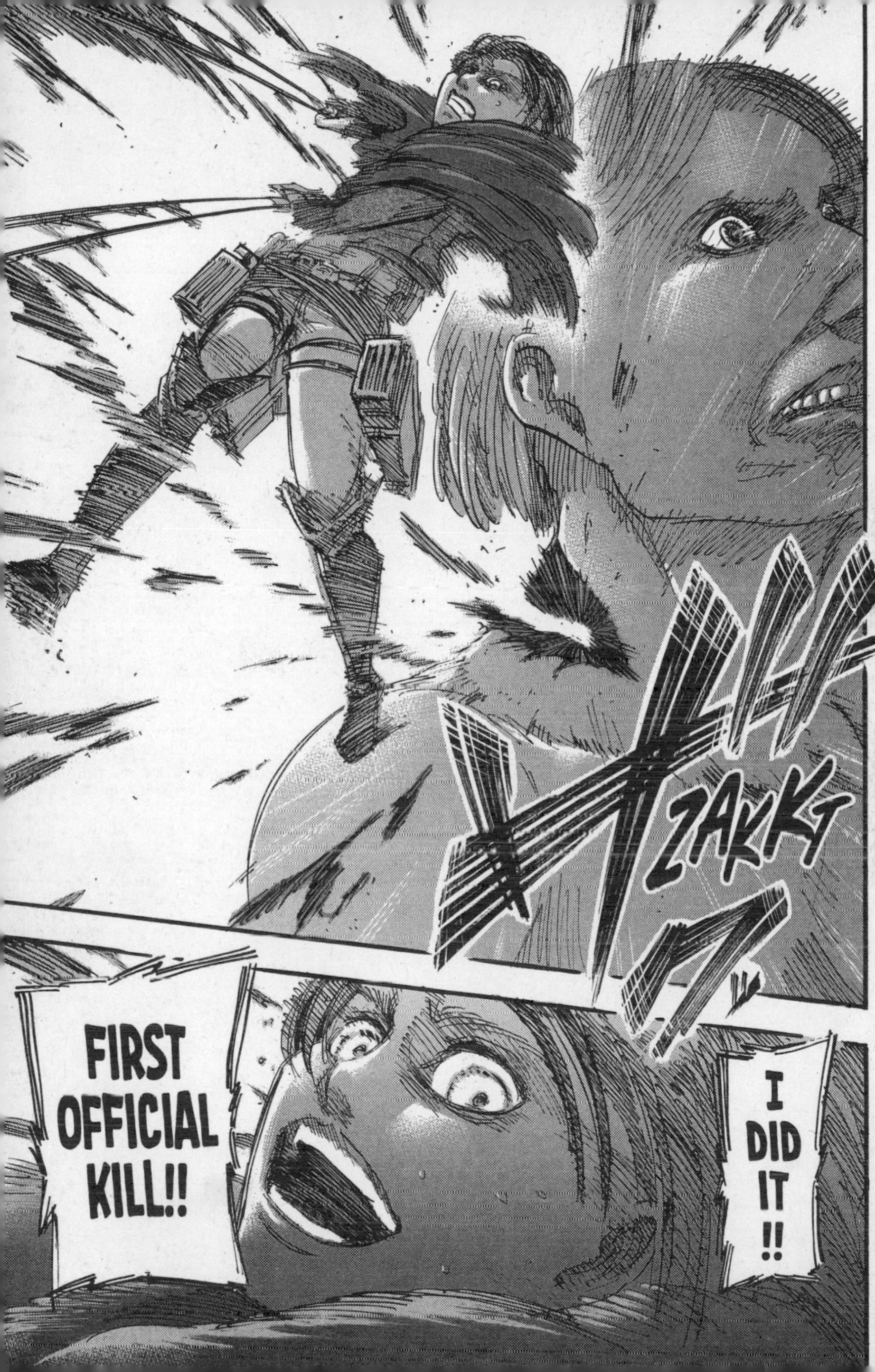
ZAKKT
I DID IT!!
FIRST OFFICIAL KILL!!

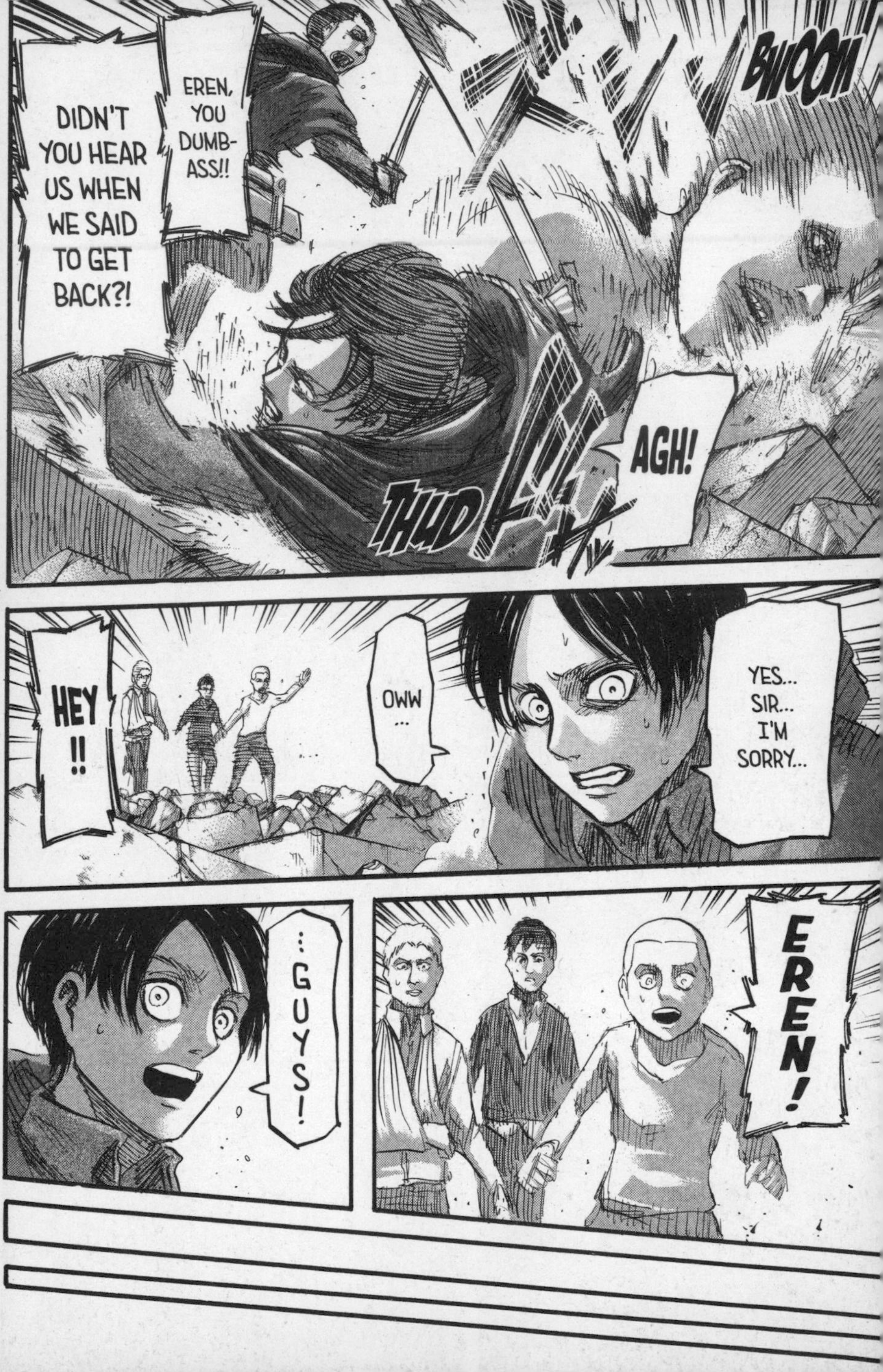
BWOOM
EREN, YOU DUMB-ASS!!
DIDN'T YOU HEAR US WHEN WE SAID TO GET BACK?!
AGH!
THUD
YES... SIR... I'M SORRY...
OWW...
HEY!!
EREN!
...GUYS!

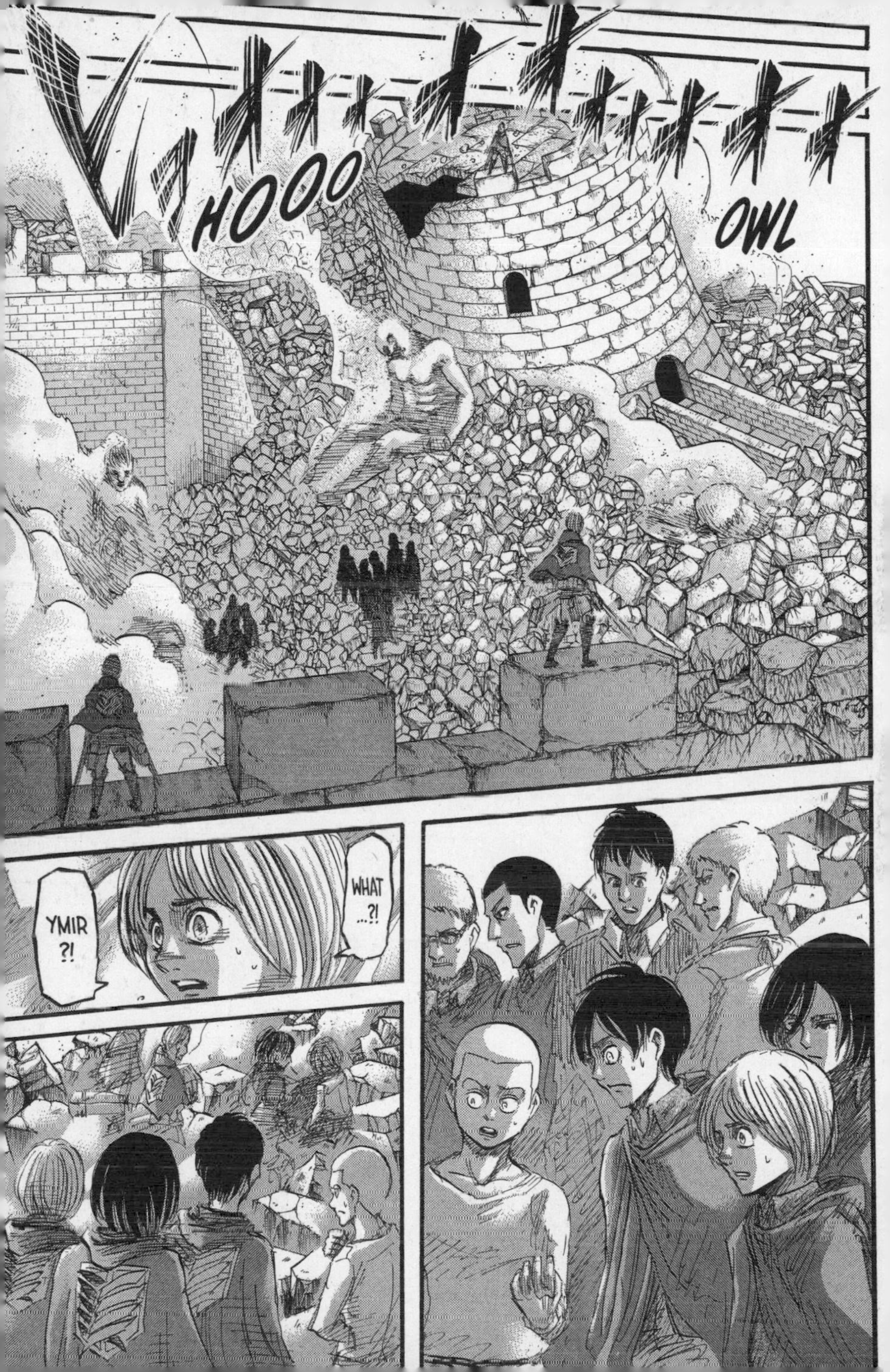
HOOO
OWL
WHAT ...?!
YMIR ?!

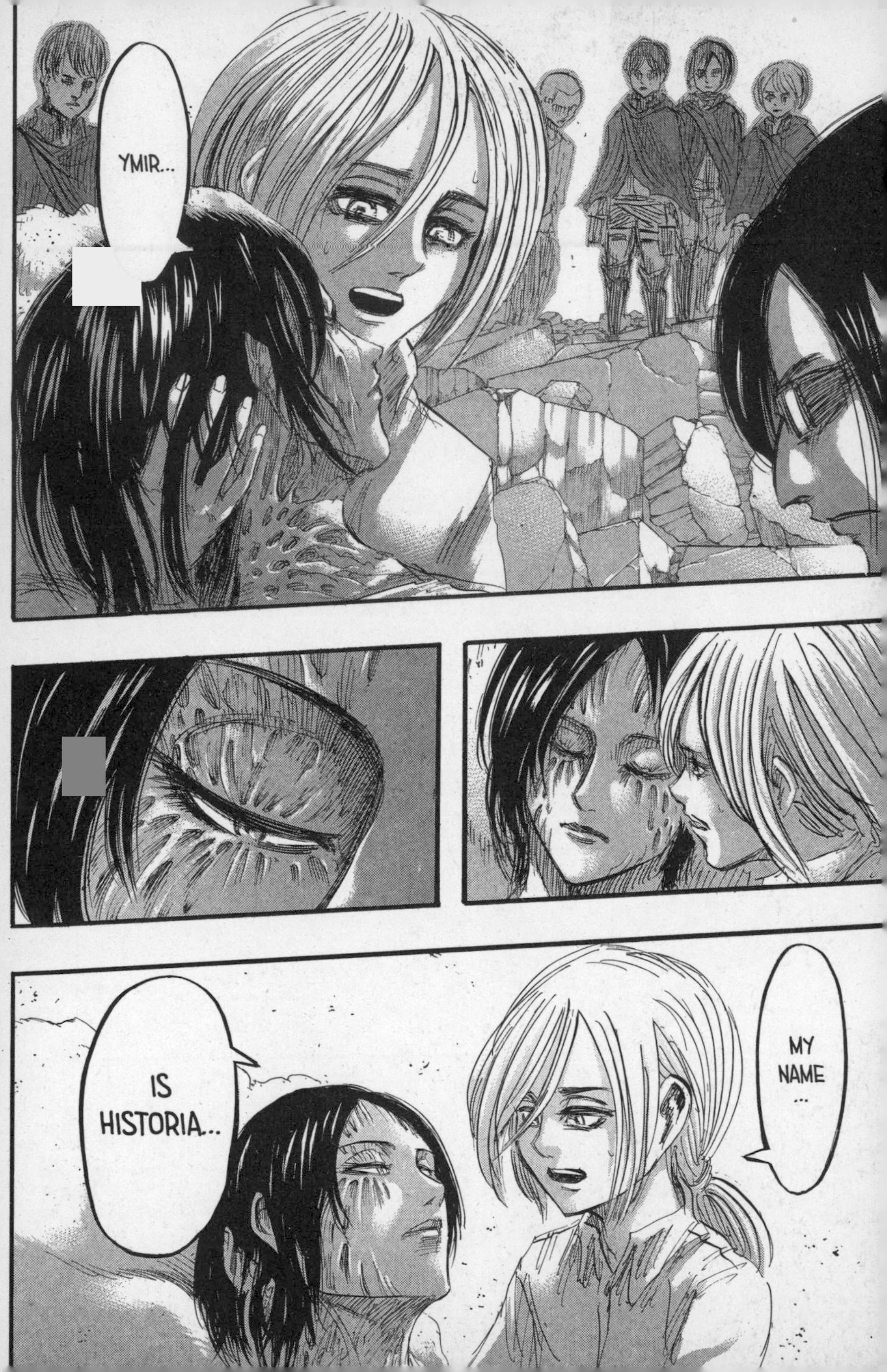
YMIR...
MY NAME ...
IS HISTORIA...

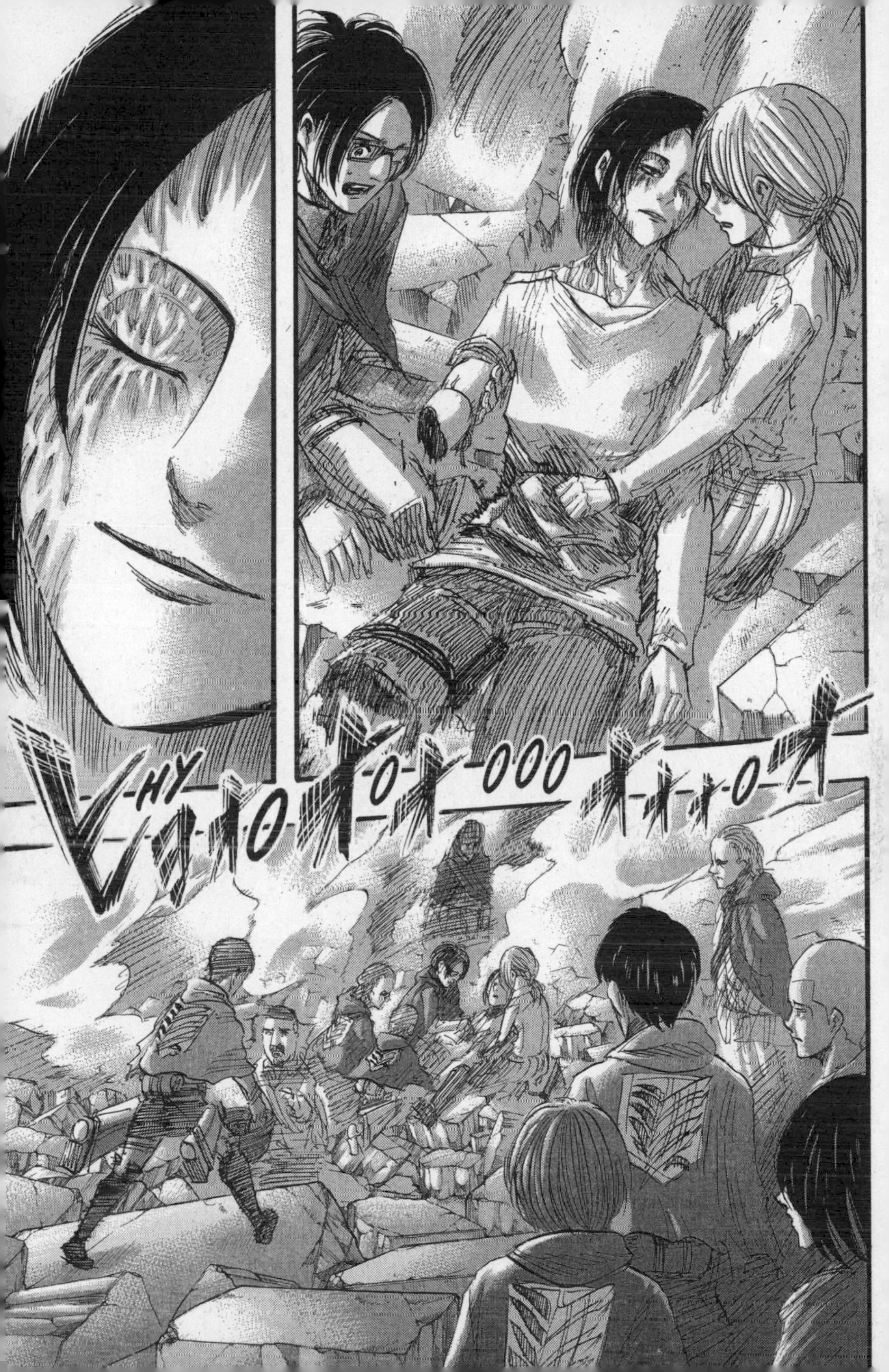

ATTACK ON TITAN

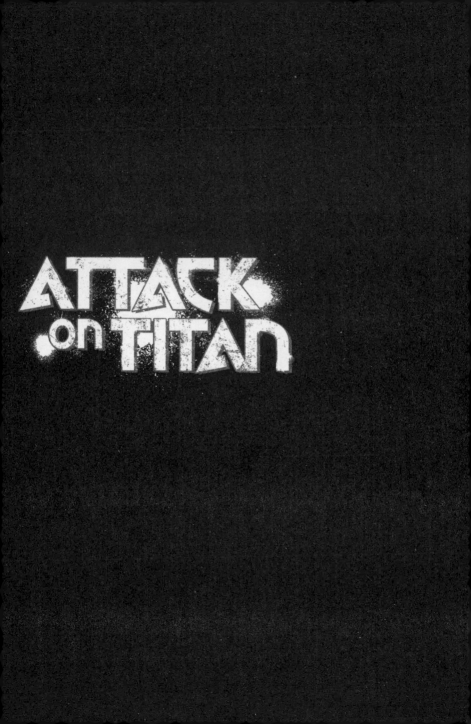

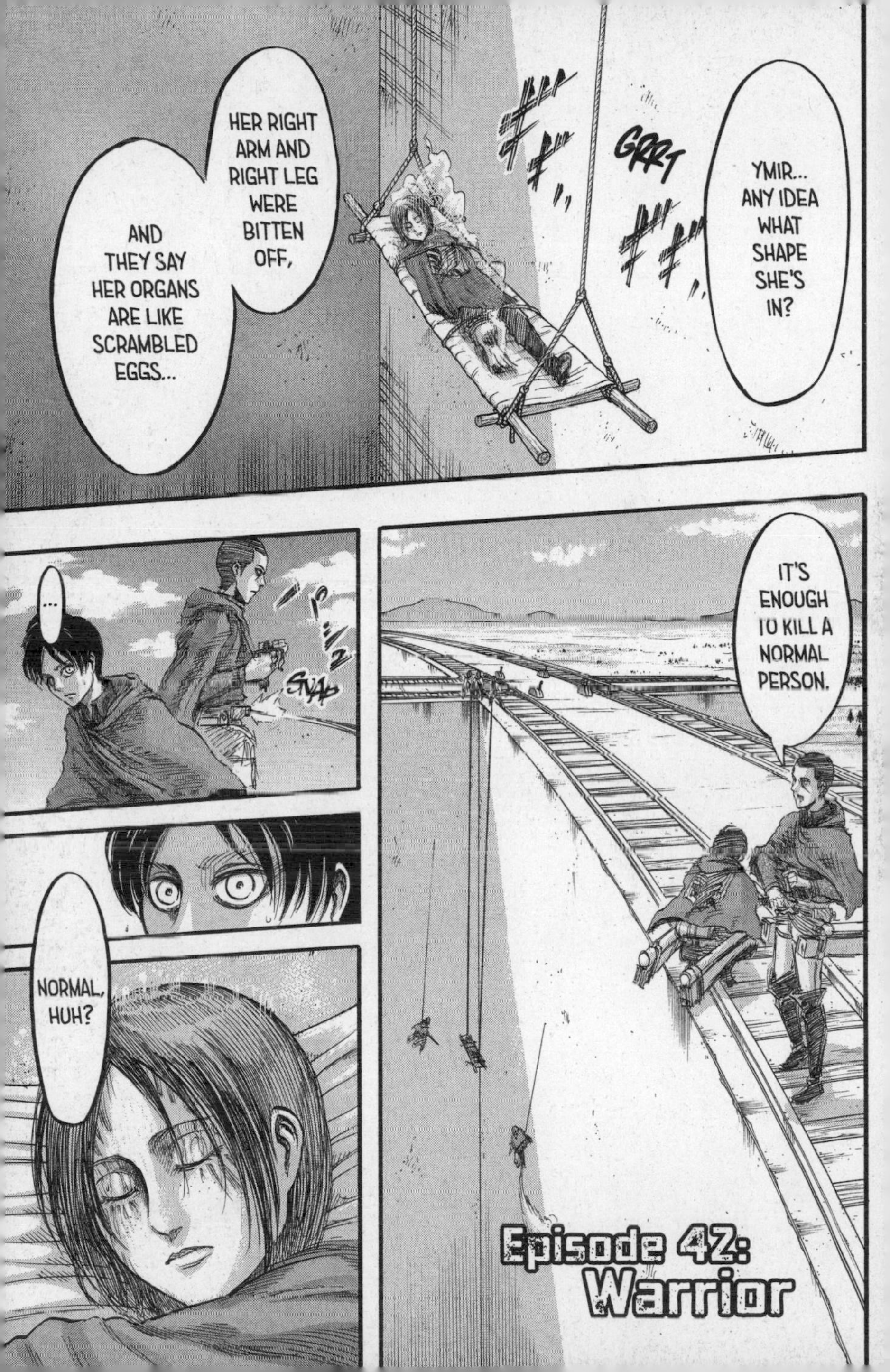

YMIR... ANY IDEA WHAT SHAPE SHE'S IN?
GRRT
HER RIGHT ARM AND RIGHT LEG WERE BITTEN OFF,
AND THEY SAY HER ORGANS ARE LIKE SCRAMBLED EGGS...
IT'S ENOUGH TO KILL A NORMAL PERSON.
SNAP
...
NORMAL, HUH?
Episode 42: Warrior

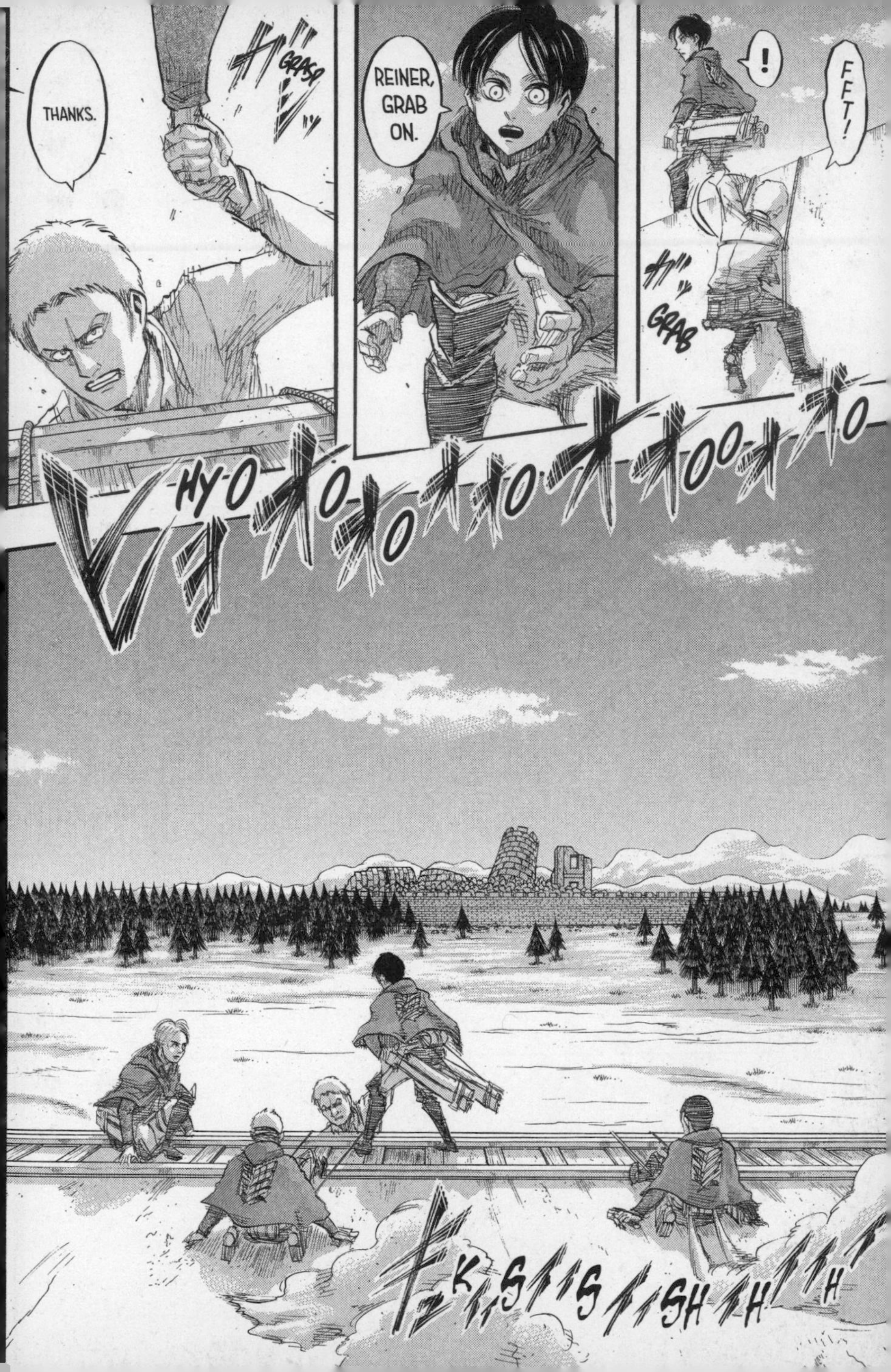
FFT!
!
GRAB
REINER, GRAB ON.
GRASP
THANKS.
HY-O-O-O-O-O-OO-O
KSSSHHH

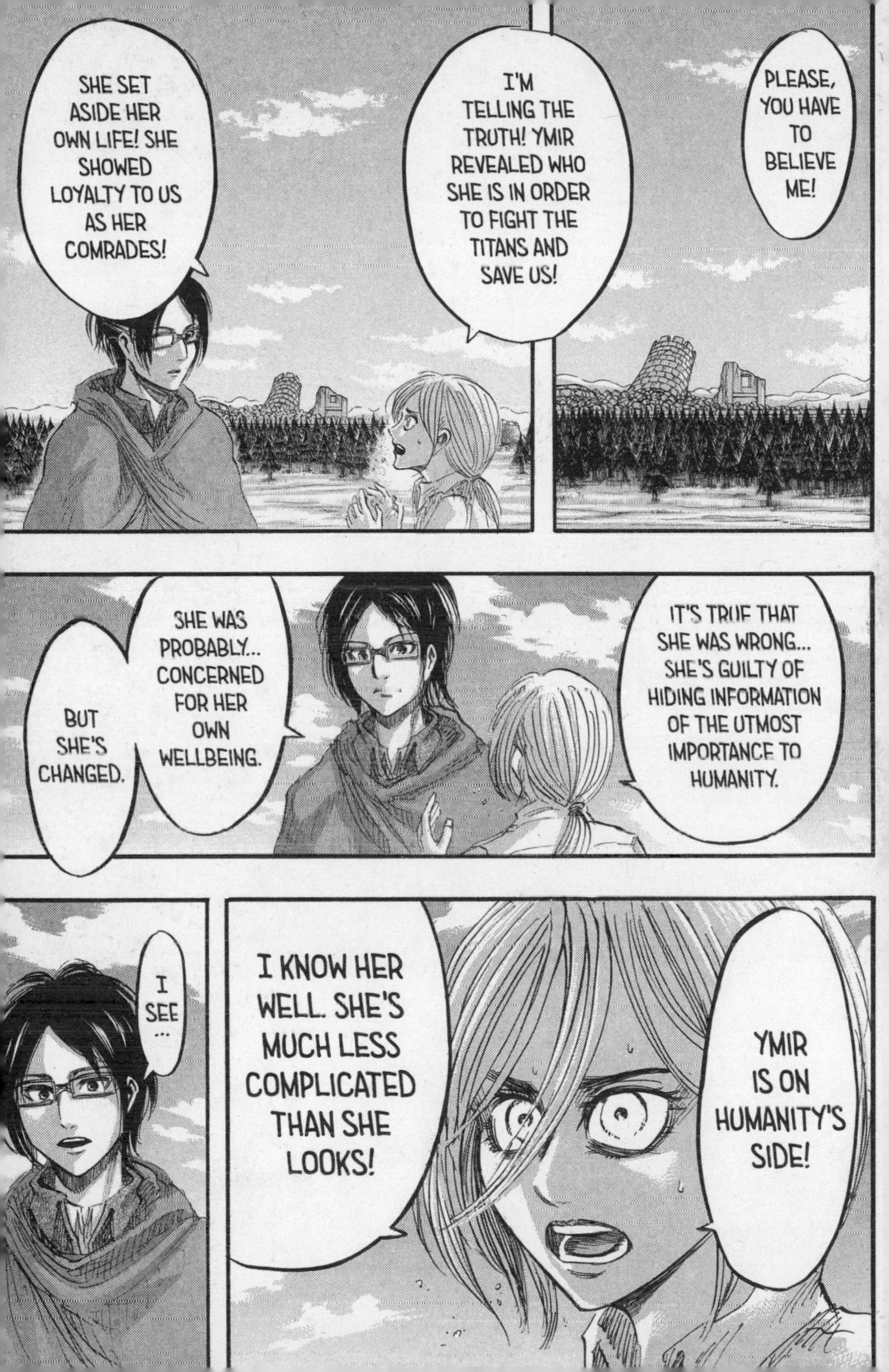
PLEASE, YOU HAVE TO BELIEVE ME!
I'M TELLING THE TRUTH! YMIR REVEALED WHO SHE IS IN ORDER TO FIGHT THE TITANS AND SAVE US!
SHE SET ASIDE HER OWN LIFE! SHE SHOWED LOYALTY TO US AS HER COMRADES!
IT'S TRUE THAT SHE WAS WRONG... SHE'S GUILTY OF HIDING INFORMATION OF THE UTMOST IMPORTANCE TO HUMANITY.
SHE WAS PROBABLY... CONCERNED FOR HER OWN WELLBEING.
BUT SHE'S CHANGED.
YMIR IS ON HUMANITY'S SIDE!
I KNOW HER WELL. SHE'S MUCH LESS COMPLICATED THAN SHE LOOKS!
I SEE ...

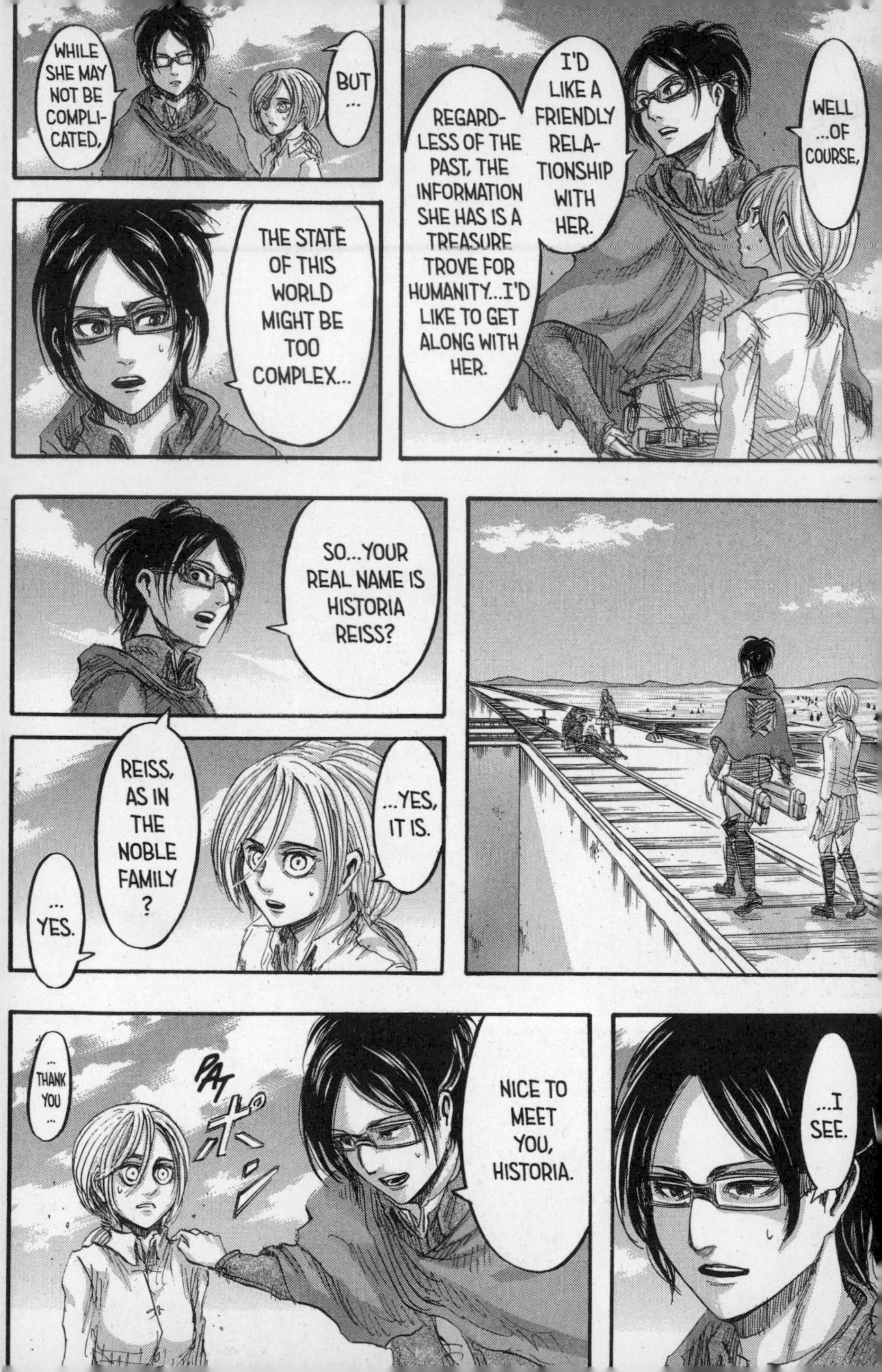
WELL ...OF COURSE,
I'D LIKE A FRIENDLY RELA-TIONSHIP WITH HER.
REGARD-LESS OF THE PAST, THE INFORMATION SHE HAS IS A TREASURE TROVE FOR HUMANITY...I'D LIKE TO GET ALONG WITH HER.
BUT ...
WHILE SHE MAY NOT BE COMPLI-CATED,
THE STATE OF THIS WORLD MIGHT BE TOO COMPLEX...
SO...YOUR REAL NAME IS HISTORIA REISS?
...YES, IT IS.
REISS, AS IN THE NOBLE FAMILY ?
... YES.
...I SEE.
NICE TO MEET YOU, HISTORIA.
PAT
ポン
... THANK YOU ...

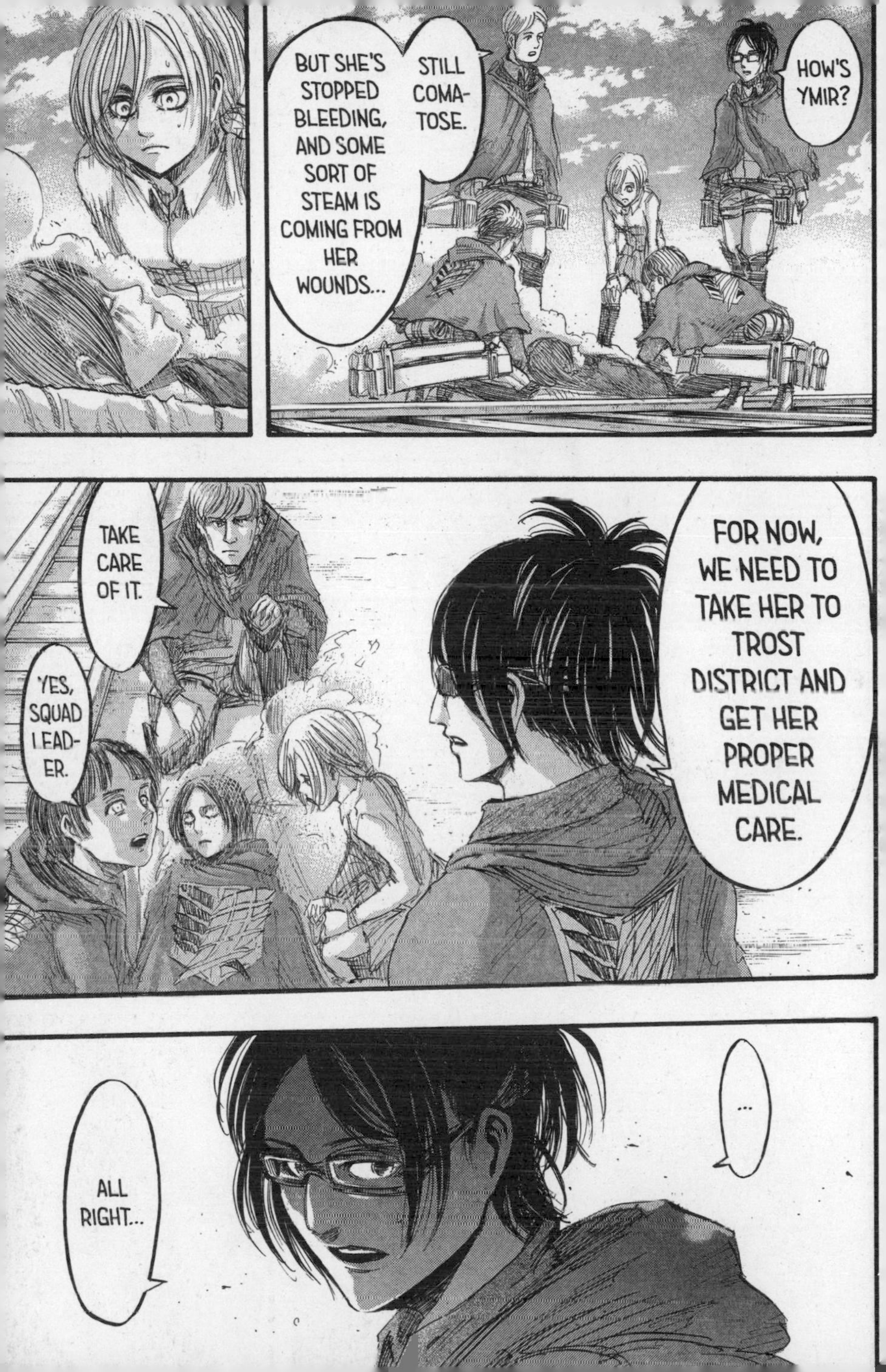
HOW'S YMIR?
STILL COMA-TOSE.
BUT SHE'S STOPPED BLEEDING, AND SOME SORT OF STEAM IS COMING FROM HER WOUNDS...
FOR NOW, WE NEED TO TAKE HER TO TROST DISTRICT AND GET HER PROPER MEDICAL CARE.
TAKE CARE OF IT.
YES, SQUAD LEAD-ER.
...
ALL RIGHT...

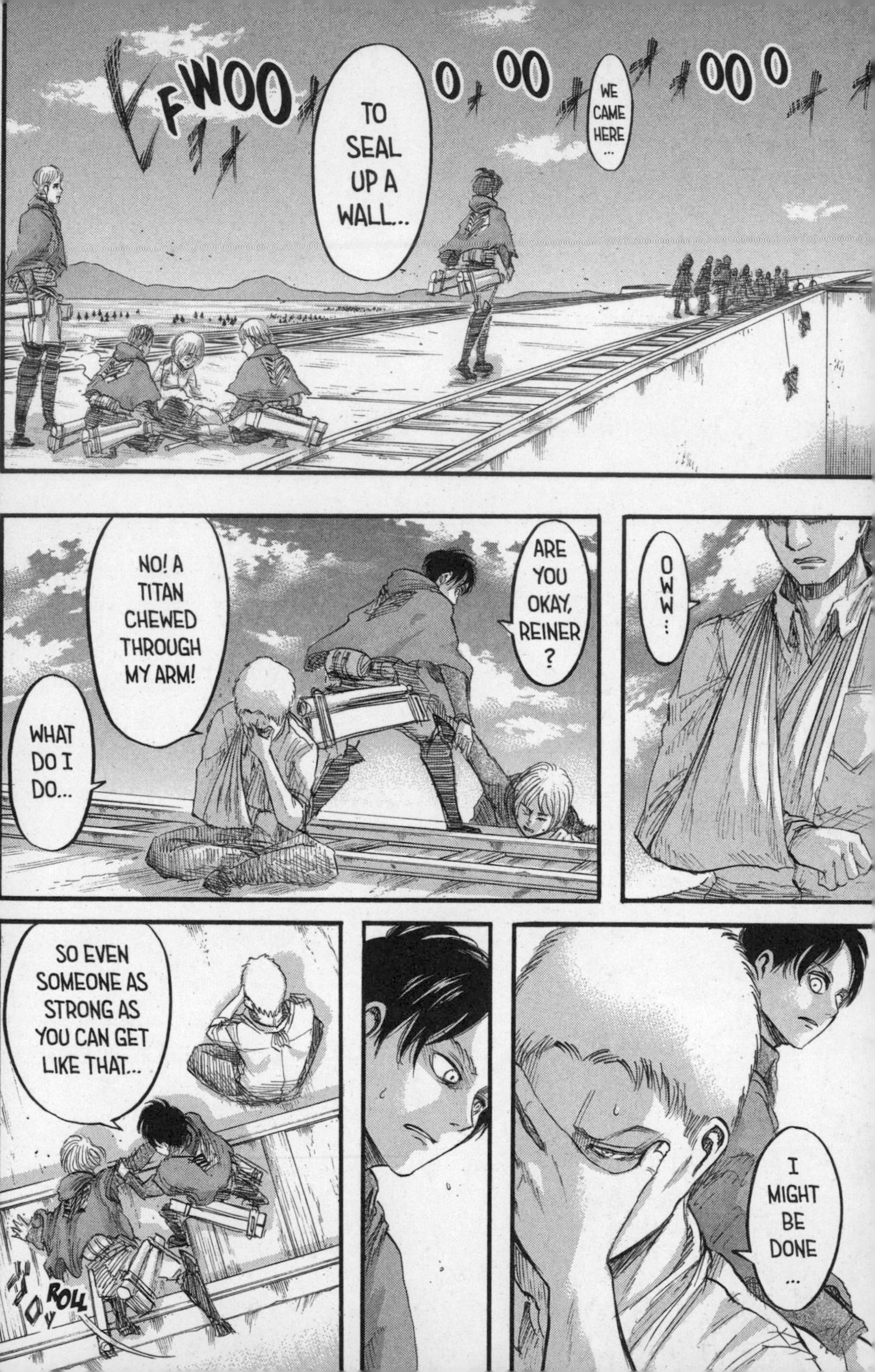
FWOOOOOOOOO
WE CAME HERE ...
TO SEAL UP A WALL...
OWW...
ARE YOU OKAY, REINER?
NO! A TITAN CHEWED THROUGH MY ARM!
WHAT DO I DO...
I MIGHT BE DONE ...
SO EVEN SOMEONE AS STRONG AS YOU CAN GET LIKE THAT...
ROLL

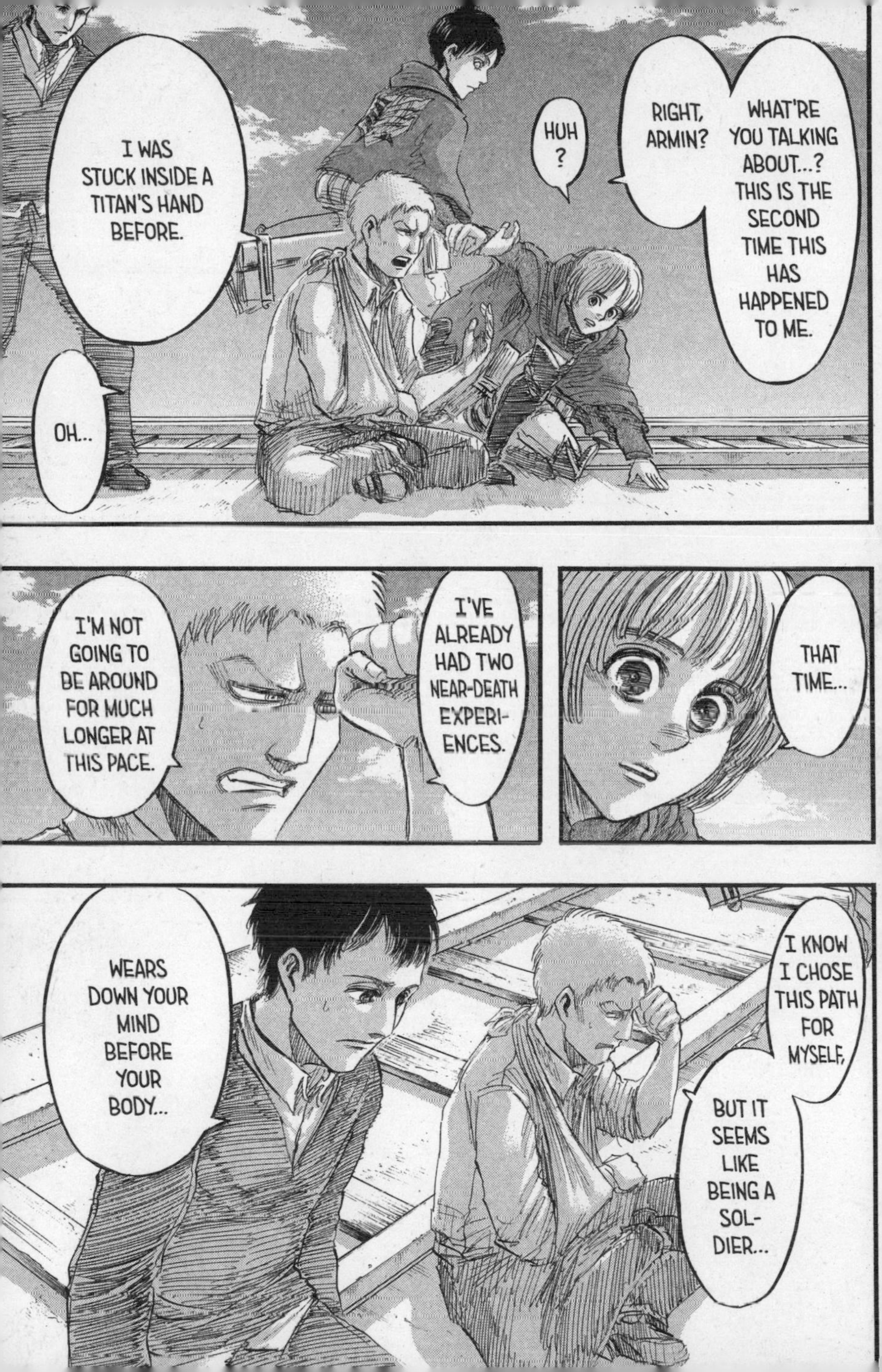
WHAT'RE YOU TALKING ABOUT...? THIS IS THE SECOND TIME THIS HAS HAPPENED TO ME.
RIGHT, ARMIN?
HUH ?
I WAS STUCK INSIDE A TITAN'S HAND BEFORE.
OH...
THAT TIME...
I'VE ALREADY HAD TWO NEAR-DEATH EXPERI-ENCES.
I'M NOT GOING TO BE AROUND FOR MUCH LONGER AT THIS PACE.
I KNOW I CHOSE THIS PATH FOR MYSELF,
BUT IT SEEMS LIKE BEING A SOL-DIER...
WEARS DOWN YOUR MIND BEFORE YOUR BODY...

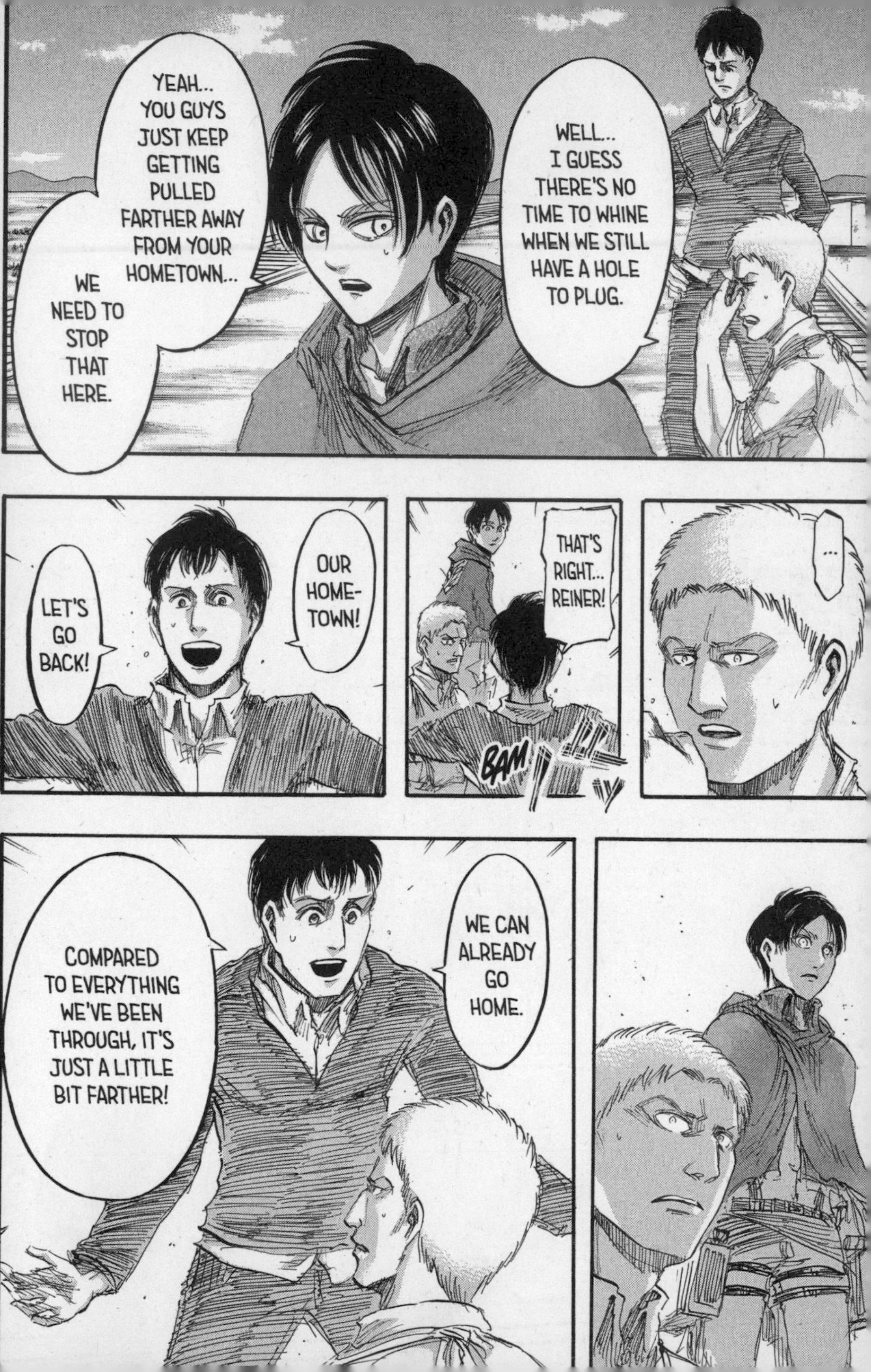

WELL... I GUESS THERE'S NO TIME TO WHINE WHEN WE STILL HAVE A HOLE TO PLUG.
YEAH... YOU GUYS JUST KEEP GETTING PULLED FARTHER AWAY FROM YOUR HOMETOWN...
WE NEED TO STOP THAT HERE.
...
THAT'S RIGHT... REINER!
BAM
OUR HOME-TOWN!
LET'S GO BACK!
WE CAN ALREADY GO HOME.
COMPARED TO EVERYTHING WE'VE BEEN THROUGH, IT'S JUST A LITTLE BIT FARTHER!

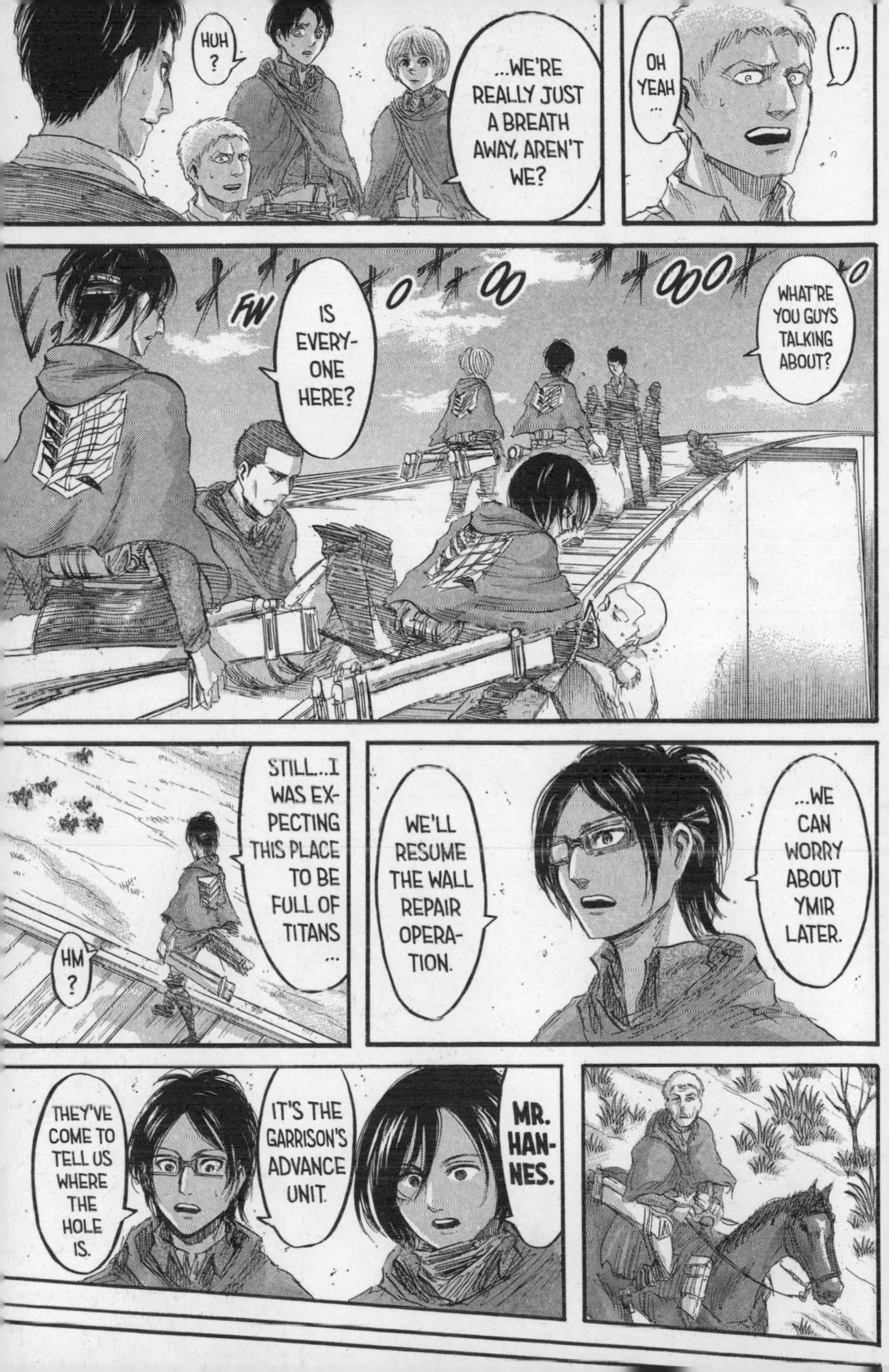
...
OH YEAH ...
...WE'RE REALLY JUST A BREATH AWAY, AREN'T WE?
HUH ?
WHAT'RE YOU GUYS TALKING ABOUT?
FW O OO OOOO O
IS EVERY-ONE HERE?
...WE CAN WORRY ABOUT YMIR LATER.
WE'LL RESUME THE WALL REPAIR OPERA-TION.
STILL...I WAS EX-PECTING THIS PLACE TO BE FULL OF TITANS ...
HM ?
MR. HAN-NES.
IT'S THE GARRISON'S ADVANCE UNIT.
THEY'VE COME TO TELL US WHERE THE HOLE IS.

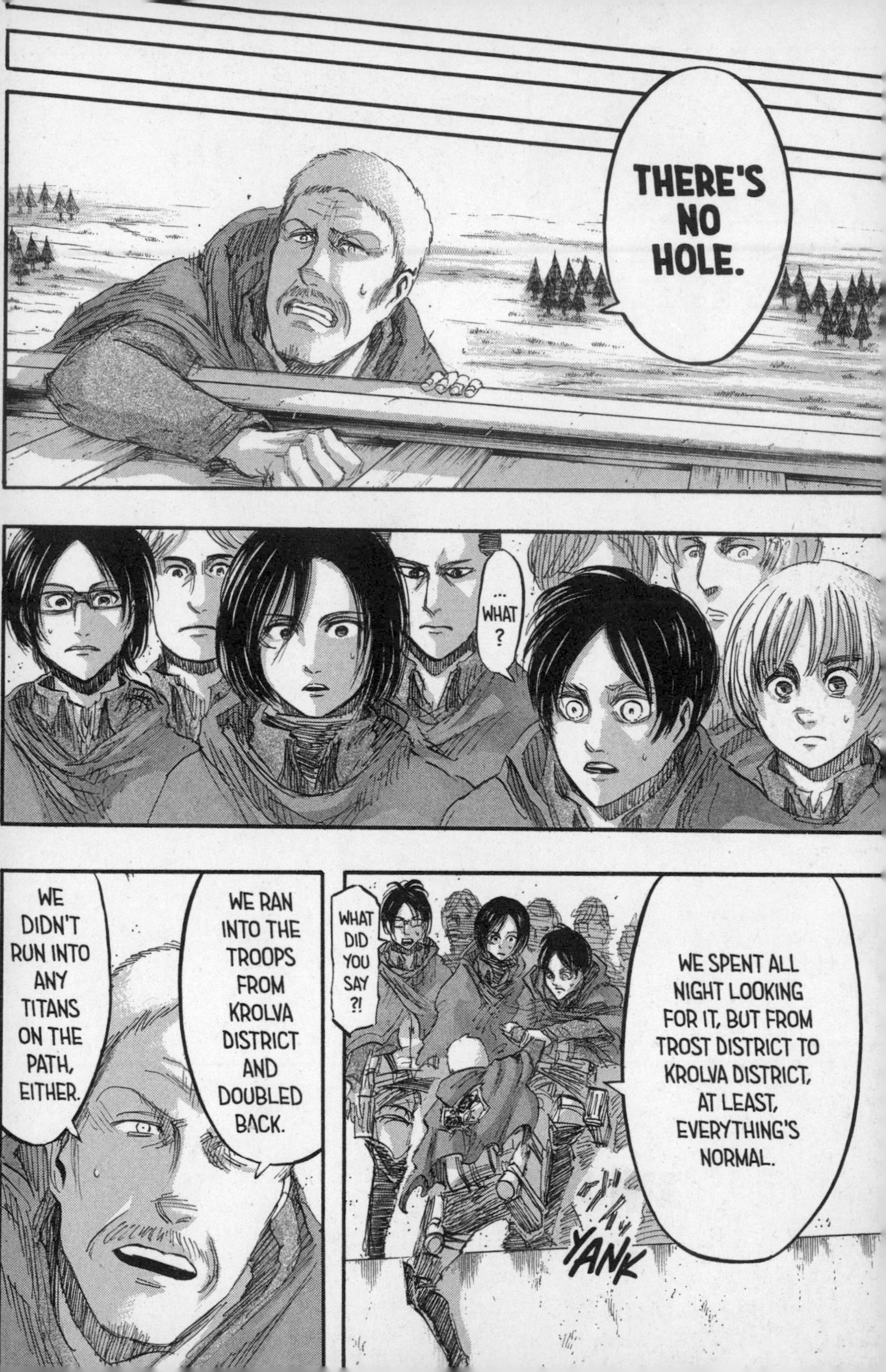
THERE'S NO HOLE.
...WHAT?
WE SPENT ALL NIGHT LOOKING FOR IT, BUT FROM TROST DISTRICT TO KROLVA DISTRICT, AT LEAST, EVERYTHING'S NORMAL.
WHAT DID YOU SAY?!
YANK
WE RAN INTO THE TROOPS FROM KROLVA DISTRICT AND DOUBLED BACK.
WE DIDN'T RUN INTO ANY TITANS ON THE PATH, EITHER.

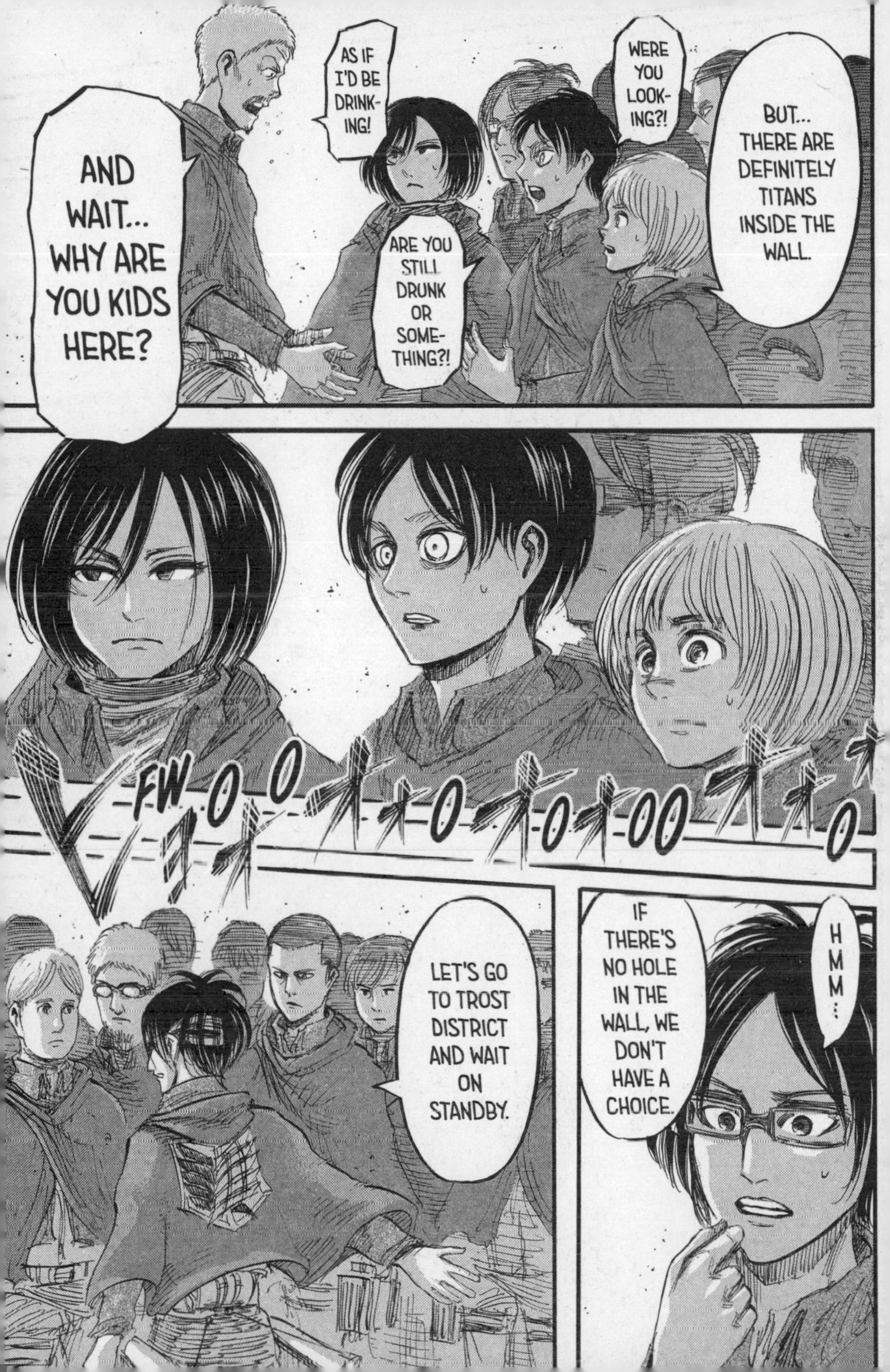
BUT... THERE ARE DEFINITELY TITANS INSIDE THE WALL.
WERE YOU LOOKING?!
ARE YOU STILL DRUNK OR SOMETHING?!
AS IF I'D BE DRINKING!
AND WAIT... WHY ARE YOU KIDS HERE?
FWOOOOOOOOOO
HMM...
IF THERE'S NO HOLE IN THE WALL, WE DON'T HAVE A CHOICE.
LET'S GO TO TROST DISTRICT AND WAIT ON STANDBY.

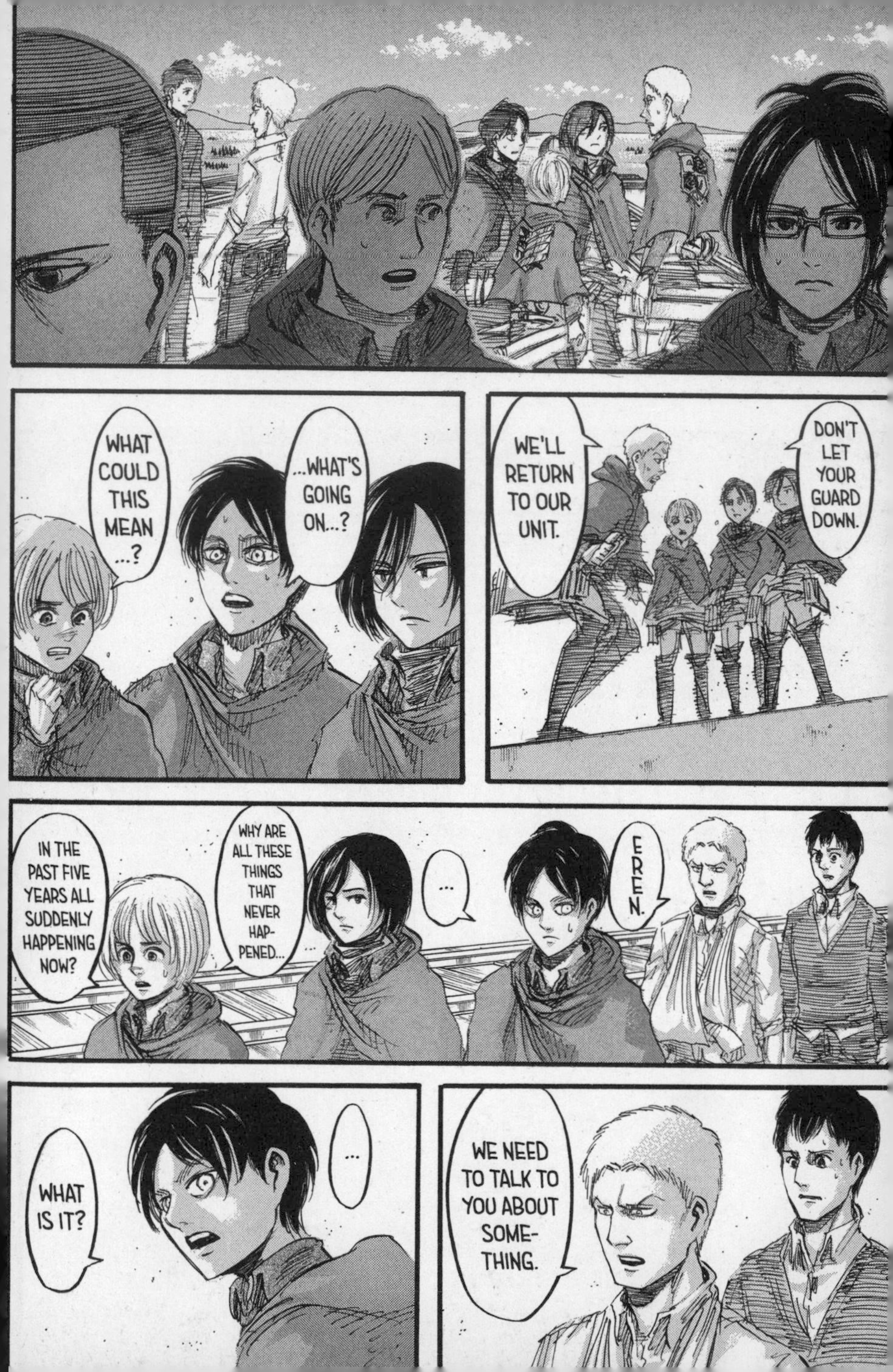
DON'T LET YOUR GUARD DOWN.
WE'LL RETURN TO OUR UNIT.
...WHAT'S GOING ON...?
WHAT COULD THIS MEAN ...?
EREN.
...
WHY ARE ALL THESE THINGS THAT NEVER HAP-PENED...
IN THE PAST FIVE YEARS ALL SUDDENLY HAPPENING NOW?
WE NEED TO TALK TO YOU ABOUT SOME-THING.
...
WHAT IS IT?

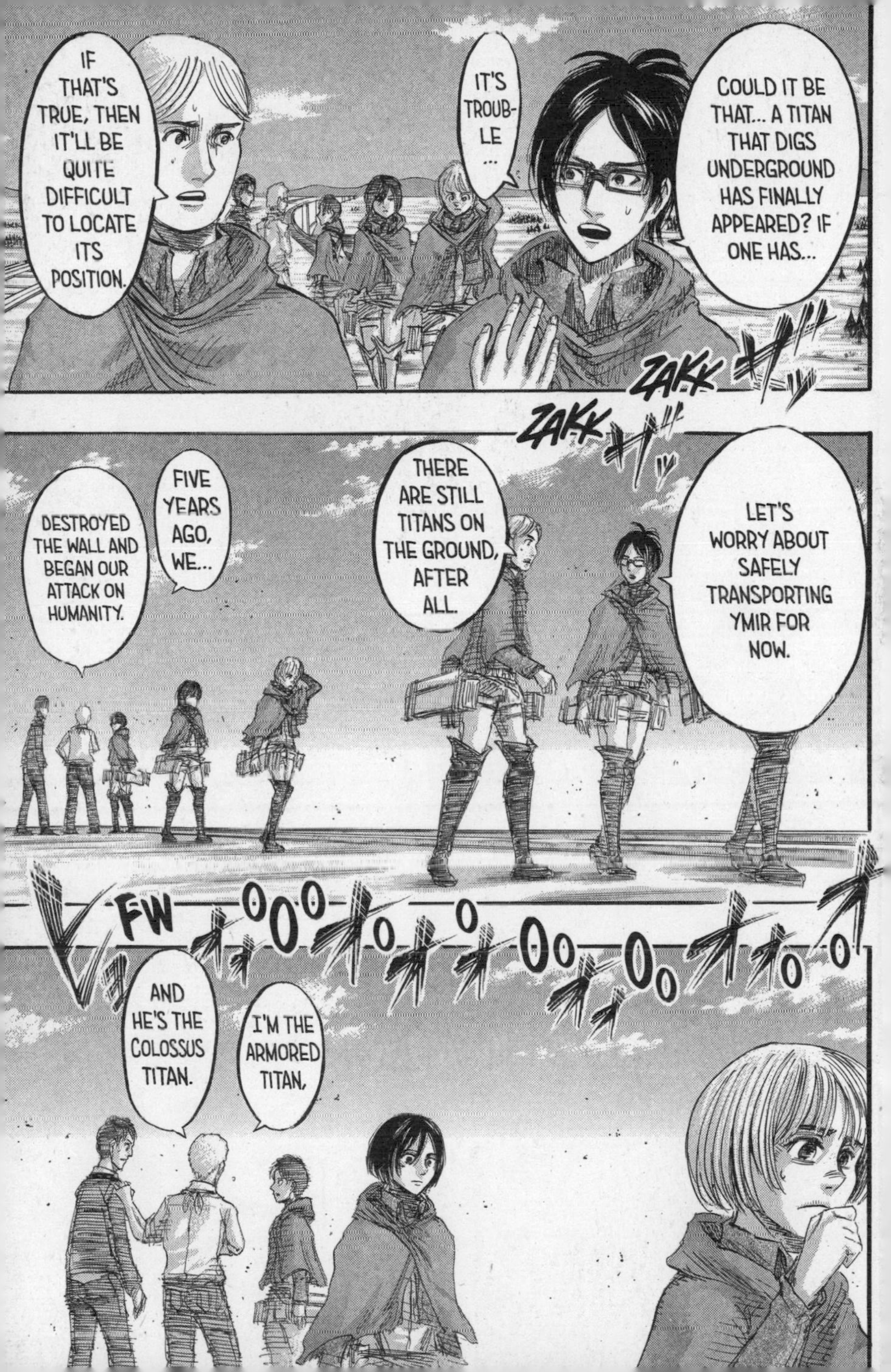
COULD IT BE THAT... A TITAN THAT DIGS UNDERGROUND HAS FINALLY APPEARED? IF ONE HAS...
IT'S TROUBLE-LE...
IF THAT'S TRUE, THEN IT'LL BE QUITE DIFFICULT TO LOCATE ITS POSITION.
ZAKK
ZAKK
LET'S WORRY ABOUT SAFELY TRANSPORTING YMIR FOR NOW.
THERE ARE STILL TITANS ON THE GROUND, AFTER ALL.
FIVE YEARS AGO, WE...
DESTROYED THE WALL AND BEGAN OUR ATTACK ON HUMANITY.
FWOOOOOOOOOOO!
I'M THE ARMORED TITAN,
AND HE'S THE COLOSSUS TITAN.

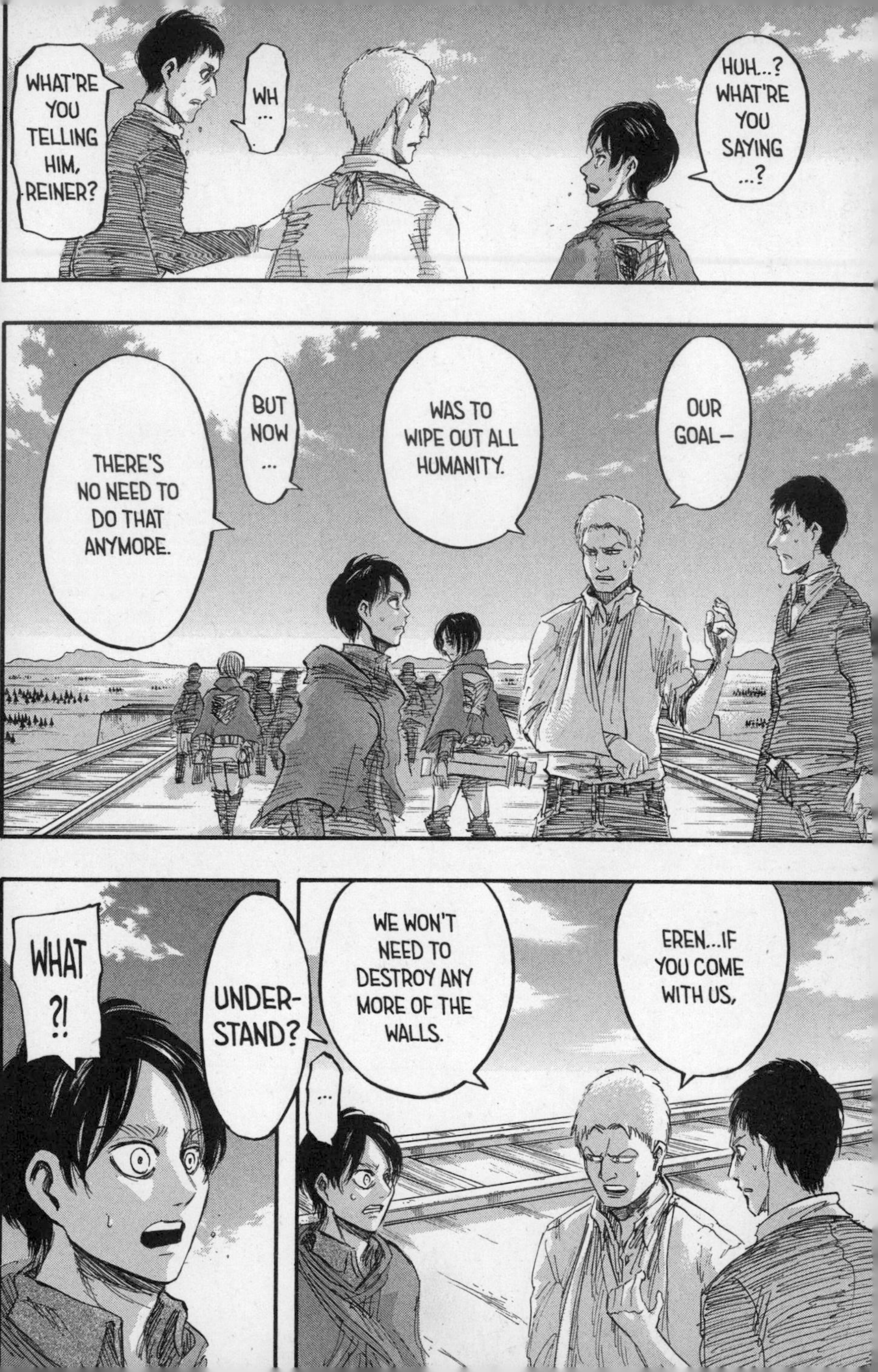
HUH...? WHAT'RE YOU SAYING ...?
WH ...
WHAT'RE YOU TELLING HIM, REINER?
OUR GOAL—
WAS TO WIPE OUT ALL HUMANITY.
BUT NOW ...
THERE'S NO NEED TO DO THAT ANYMORE.
EREN...IF YOU COME WITH US,
WE WON'T NEED TO DESTROY ANY MORE OF THE WALLS.
UNDER-STAND?
...
WHAT ?!

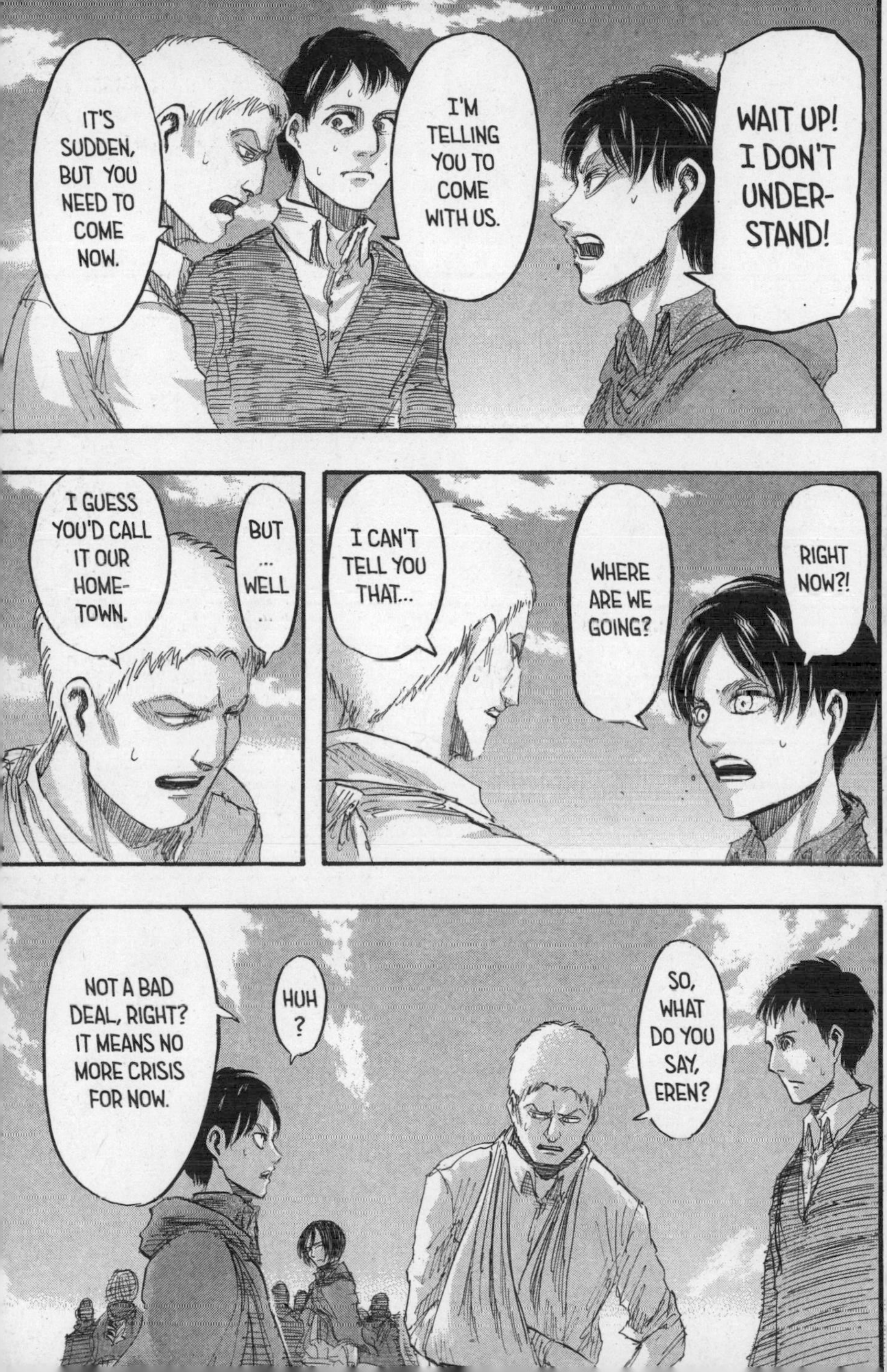
WAIT UP! I DON'T UNDER-STAND!
I'M TELLING YOU TO COME WITH US.
IT'S SUDDEN, BUT YOU NEED TO COME NOW.
RIGHT NOW?!
WHERE ARE WE GOING?
I CAN'T TELL YOU THAT...
BUT ... WELL ...
I GUESS YOU'D CALL IT OUR HOME-TOWN.
SO, WHAT DO YOU SAY, EREN?
HUH?
NOT A BAD DEAL, RIGHT? IT MEANS NO MORE CRISIS FOR NOW.

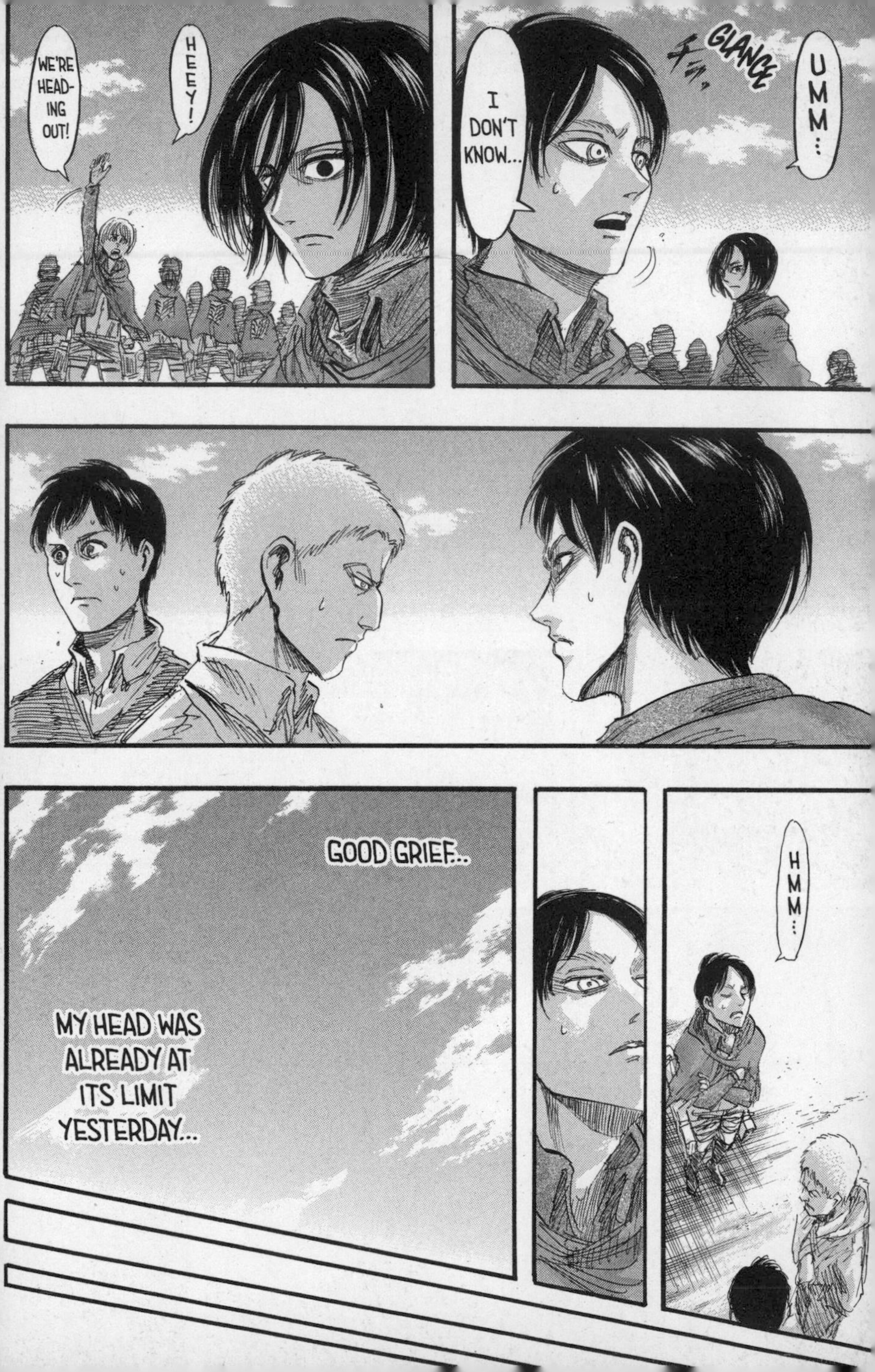
UMM...
GLANCE
I DON'T KNOW...
HEEY!
WE'RE HEAD-ING OUT!
HMM...
GOOD GRIEF..
MY HEAD WAS ALREADY AT ITS LIMIT YESTERDAY...

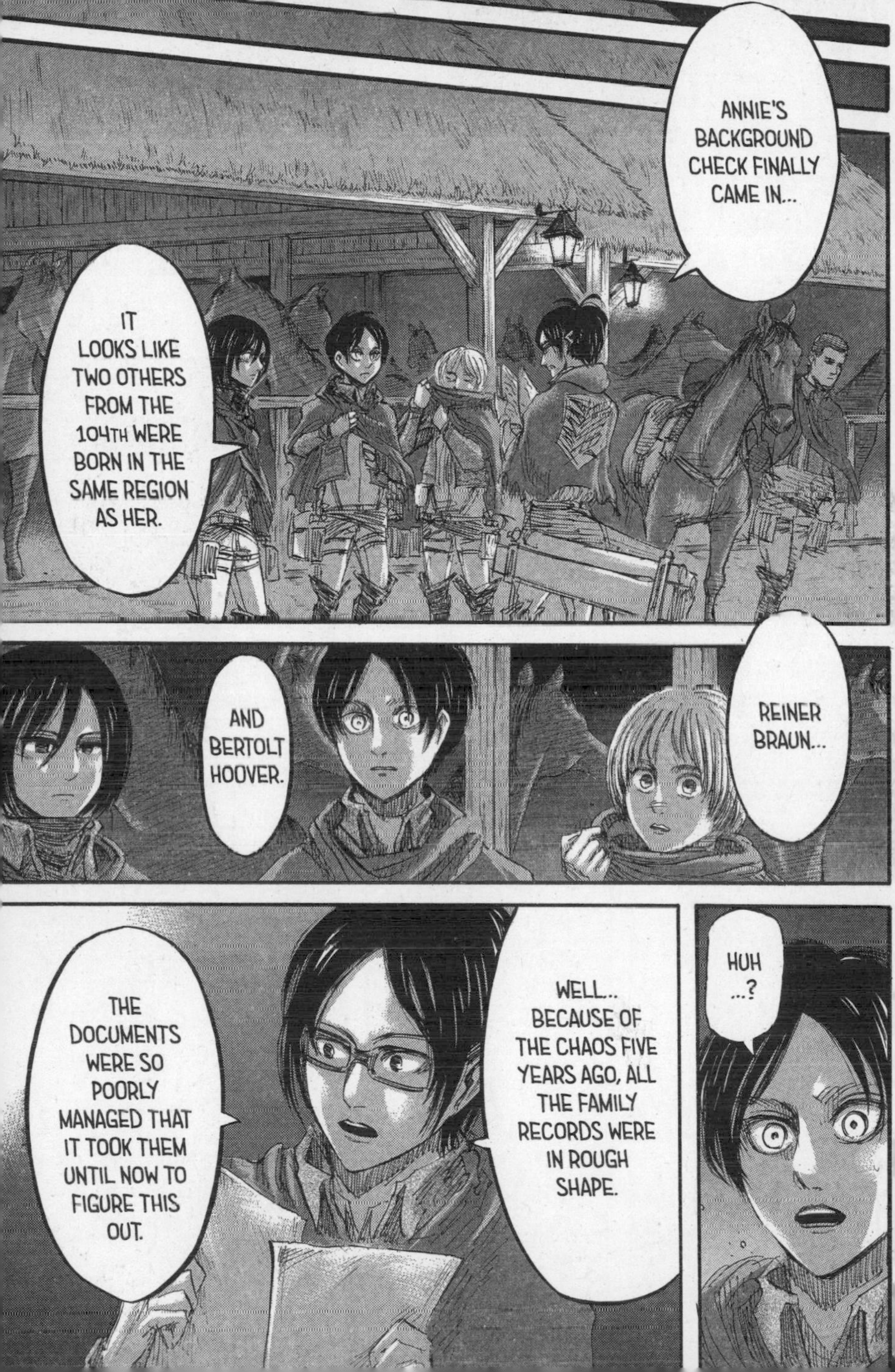
ANNIE'S BACKGROUND CHECK FINALLY CAME IN...
IT LOOKS LIKE TWO OTHERS FROM THE 104TH WERE BORN IN THE SAME REGION AS HER.
REINER BRAUN...
AND BERTOLT HOOVER.
HUH ...?
WELL... BECAUSE OF THE CHAOS FIVE YEARS AGO, ALL THE FAMILY RECORDS WERE IN ROUGH SHAPE.
THE DOCUMENTS WERE SO POORLY MANAGED THAT IT TOOK THEM UNTIL NOW TO FIGURE THIS OUT.

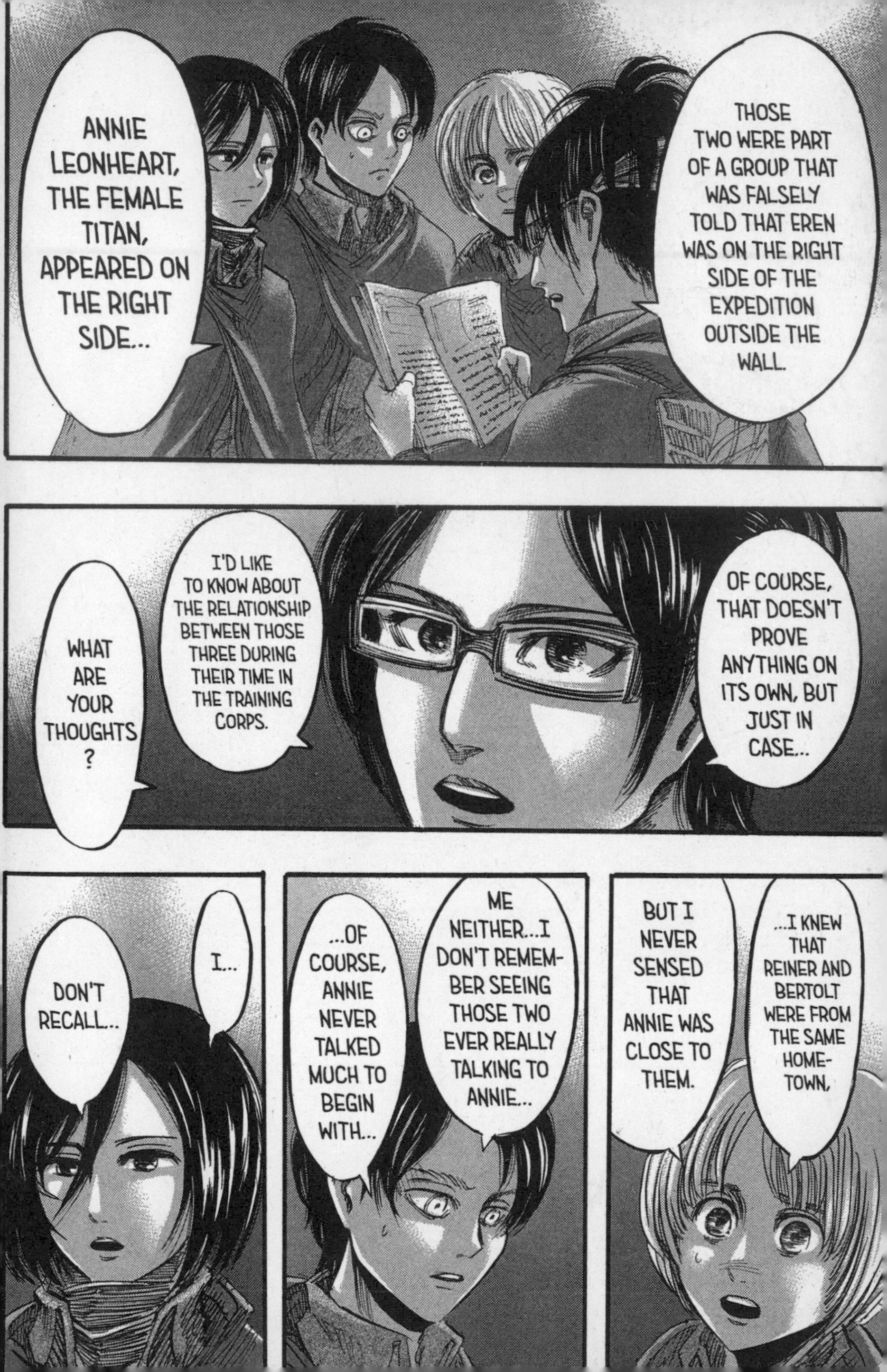
THOSE TWO WERE PART OF A GROUP THAT WAS FALSELY TOLD THAT EREN WAS ON THE RIGHT SIDE OF THE EXPEDITION OUTSIDE THE WALL.
ANNIE LEONHEART, THE FEMALE TITAN, APPEARED ON THE RIGHT SIDE...
OF COURSE, THAT DOESN'T PROVE ANYTHING ON ITS OWN, BUT JUST IN CASE...
I'D LIKE TO KNOW ABOUT THE RELATIONSHIP BETWEEN THOSE THREE DURING THEIR TIME IN THE TRAINING CORPS.
WHAT ARE YOUR THOUGHTS?
...I KNEW THAT REINER AND BERTOLT WERE FROM THE SAME HOME-TOWN,
BUT I NEVER SENSED THAT ANNIE WAS CLOSE TO THEM.
ME NEITHER...I DON'T REMEMBER SEEING THOSE TWO EVER REALLY TALKING TO ANNIE...
...OF COURSE, ANNIE NEVER TALKED MUCH TO BEGIN WITH...
I...
DON'T RECALL...

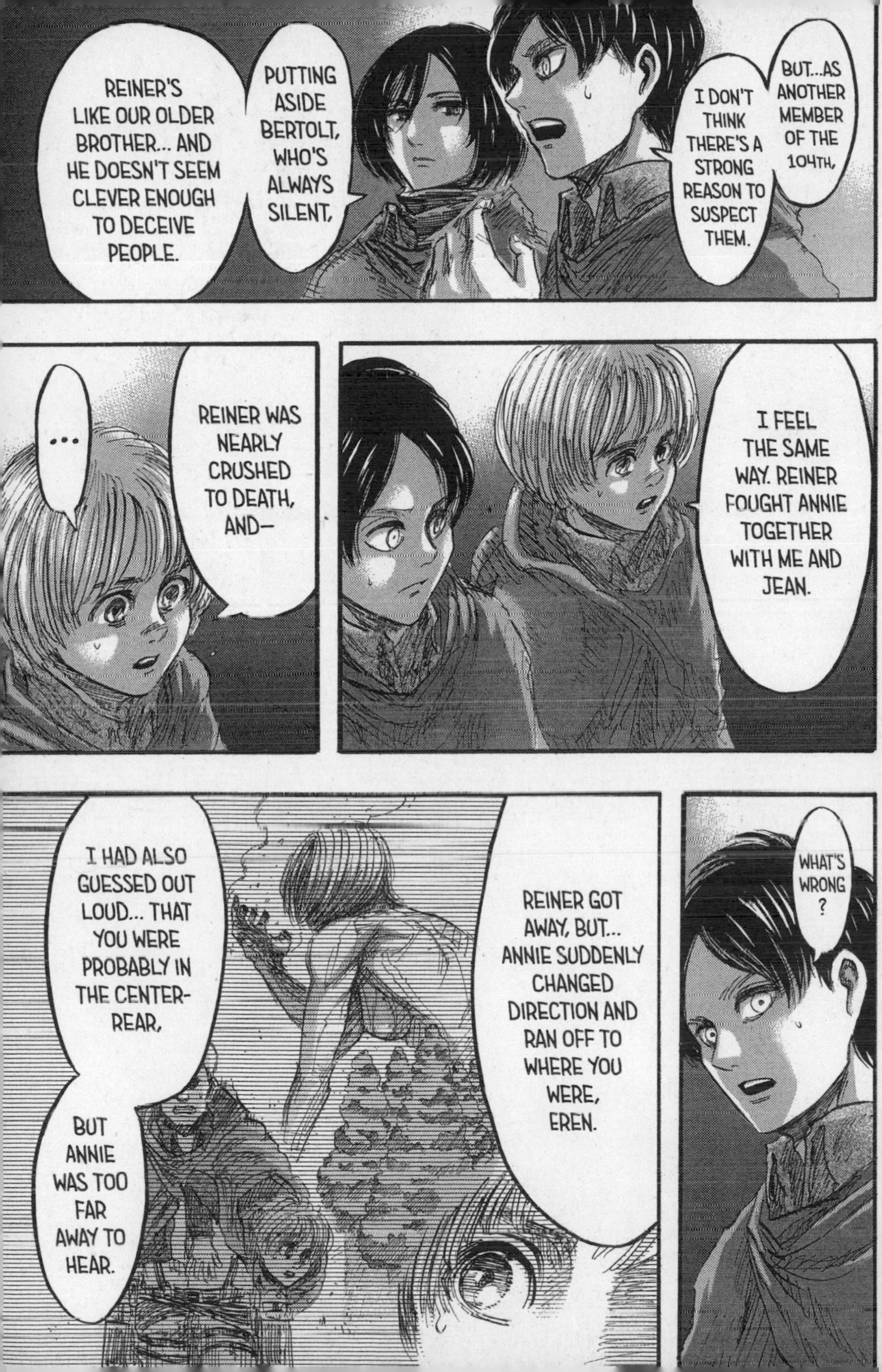
BUT...AS ANOTHER MEMBER OF THE 104TH,
I DON'T THINK THERE'S A STRONG REASON TO SUSPECT THEM.
PUTTING ASIDE BERTOLT, WHO'S ALWAYS SILENT,
REINER'S LIKE OUR OLDER BROTHER... AND HE DOESN'T SEEM CLEVER ENOUGH TO DECEIVE PEOPLE.
I FEEL THE SAME WAY. REINER FOUGHT ANNIE TOGETHER WITH ME AND JEAN.
REINER WAS NEARLY CRUSHED TO DEATH, AND—
...
WHAT'S WRONG ?
REINER GOT AWAY, BUT... ANNIE SUDDENLY CHANGED DIRECTION AND RAN OFF TO WHERE YOU WERE, EREN.
I HAD ALSO GUESSED OUT LOUD... THAT YOU WERE PROBABLY IN THE CENTER-REAR,
BUT ANNIE WAS TOO FAR AWAY TO HEAR.

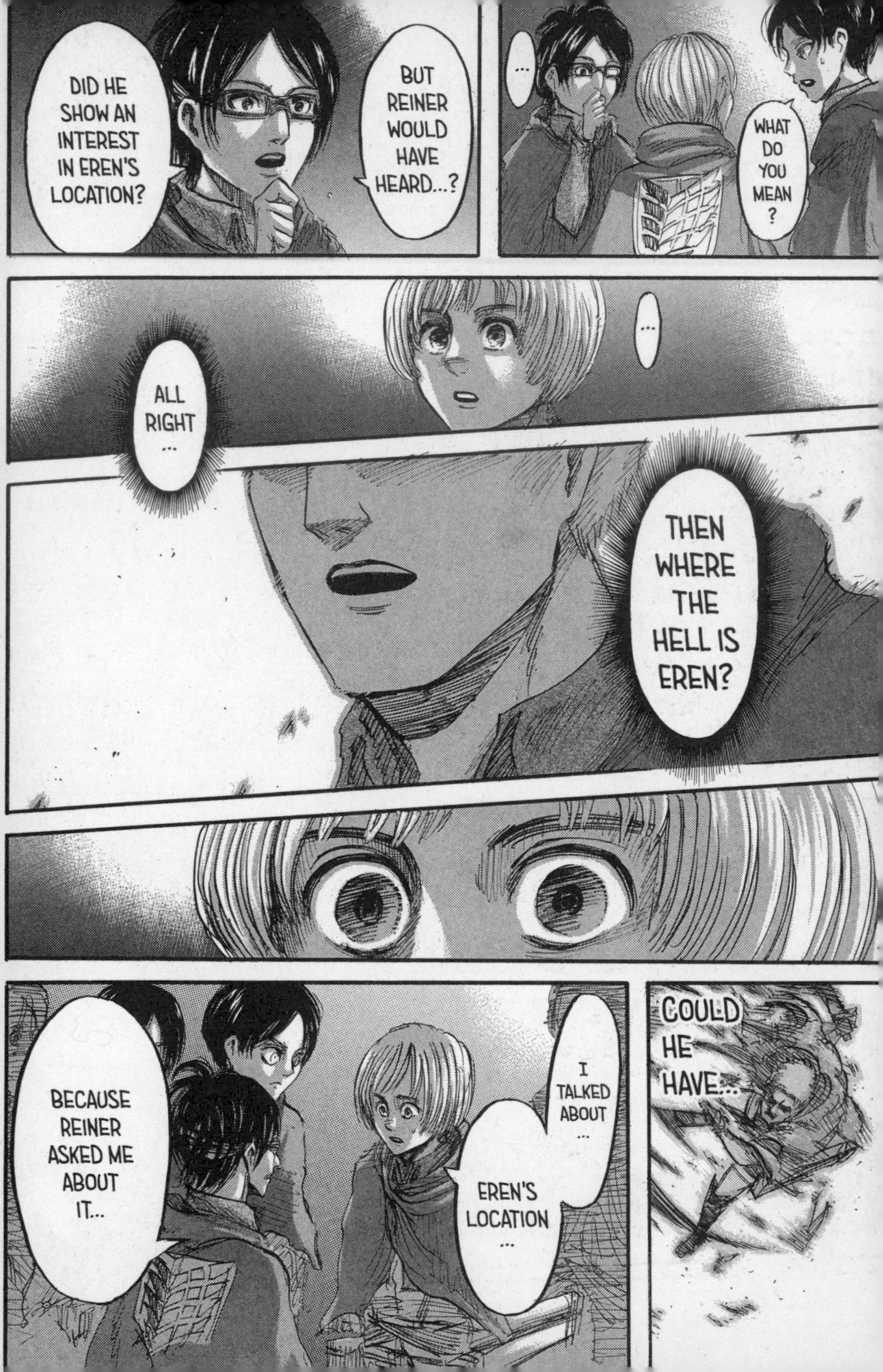
WHAT DO YOU MEAN ?
...
BUT REINER WOULD HAVE HEARD...?
DID HE SHOW AN INTEREST IN EREN'S LOCATION?
...
ALL RIGHT ...
THEN WHERE THE HELL IS EREN?
COULD HE HAVE...
I TALKED ABOUT ...
EREN'S LOCATION ...
BECAUSE REINER ASKED ME ABOUT IT...

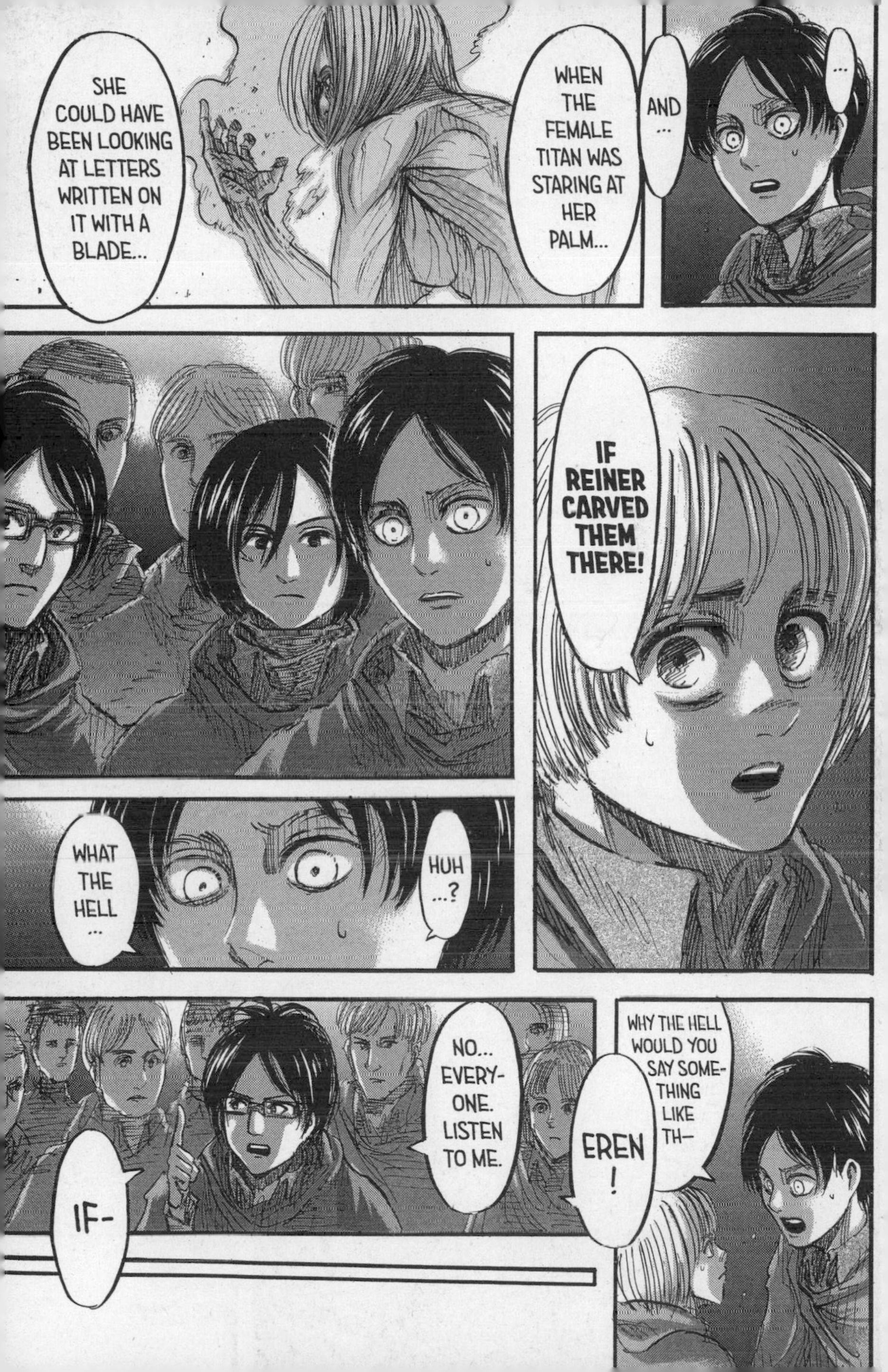
...
AND ...
WHEN THE FEMALE TITAN WAS STARING AT HER PALM...
SHE COULD HAVE BEEN LOOKING AT LETTERS WRITTEN ON IT WITH A BLADE...
IF REINER CARVED THEM THERE!
HUH ...?
WHAT THE HELL ...
WHY THE HELL WOULD YOU SAY SOME-THING LIKE TH—
EREN !
NO... EVERY-ONE. LISTEN TO ME.
IF-

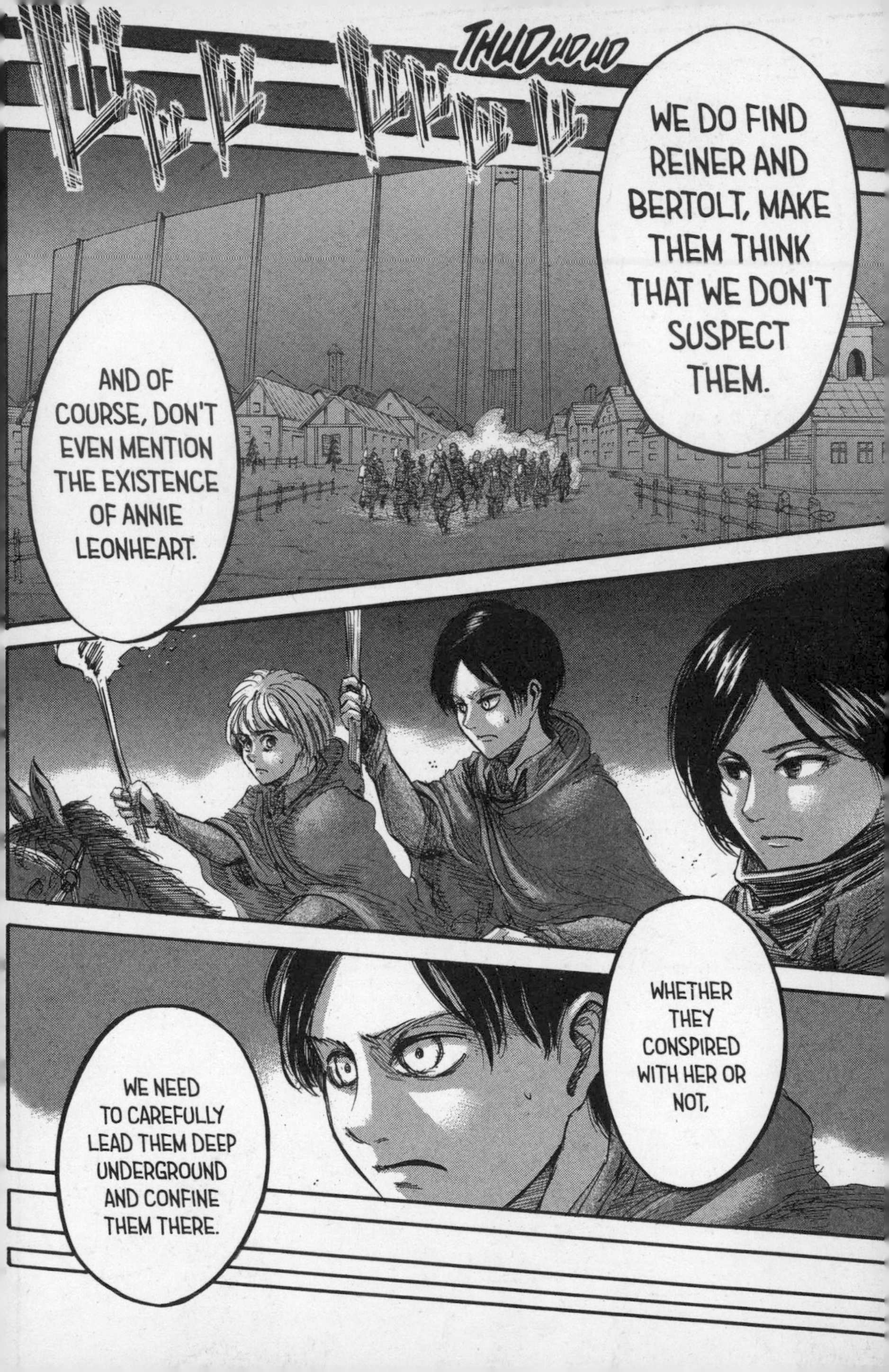
THUDUDUD
WE DO FIND REINER AND BERTOLT, MAKE THEM THINK THAT WE DON'T SUSPECT THEM.
AND OF COURSE, DON'T EVEN MENTION THE EXISTENCE OF ANNIE LEONHEART.
WHETHER THEY CONSPIRED WITH HER OR NOT,
WE NEED TO CAREFULLY LEAD THEM DEEP UNDERGROUND AND CONFINE THEM THERE.

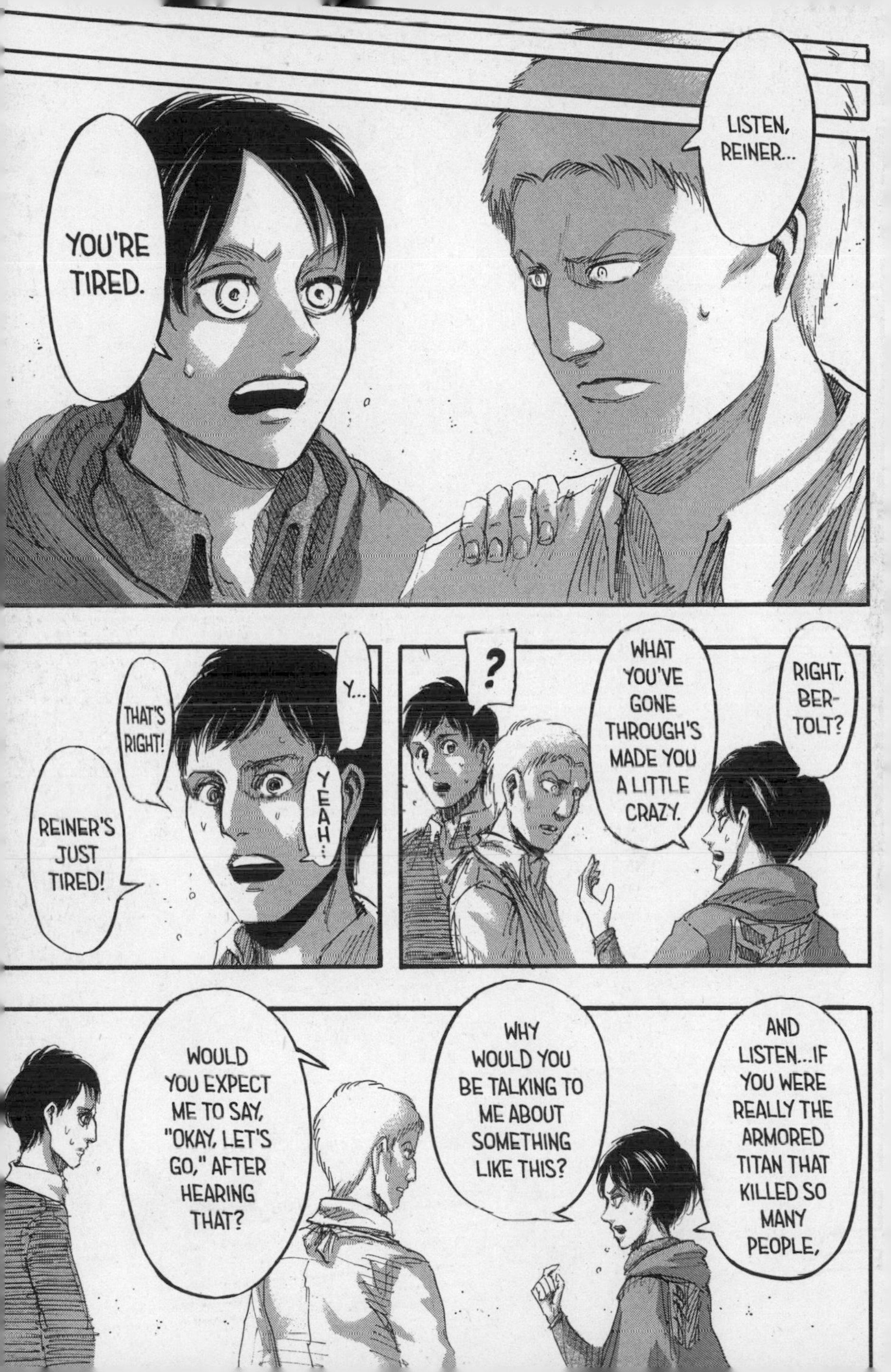
LISTEN, REINER...
YOU'RE TIRED.
RIGHT, BERTOLT?
WHAT YOU'VE GONE THROUGH'S MADE YOU A LITTLE CRAZY.
?
Y...
YEAH...
THAT'S RIGHT!
REINER'S JUST TIRED!
AND LISTEN...IF YOU WERE REALLY THE ARMORED TITAN THAT KILLED SO MANY PEOPLE,
WHY WOULD YOU BE TALKING TO ME ABOUT SOMETHING LIKE THIS?
WOULD YOU EXPECT ME TO SAY, "OKAY, LET'S GO," AFTER HEARING THAT?

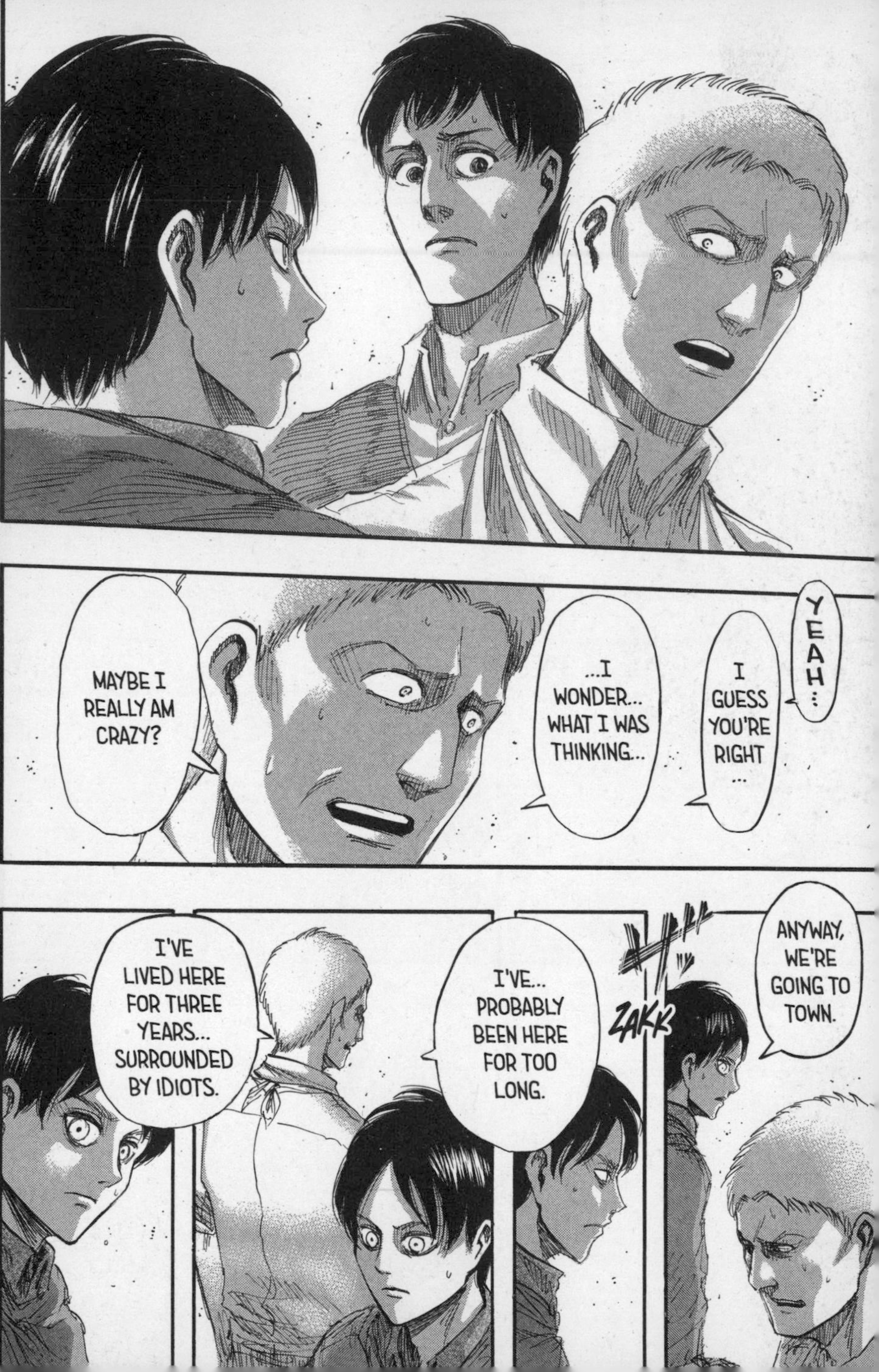
YEAH...
I GUESS YOU'RE RIGHT ...
...I WONDER... WHAT I WAS THINKING...
MAYBE I REALLY AM CRAZY?
ANYWAY, WE'RE GOING TO TOWN.
ZAKK
I'VE... PROBABLY BEEN HERE FOR TOO LONG.
I'VE LIVED HERE FOR THREE YEARS... SURROUNDED BY IDIOTS.

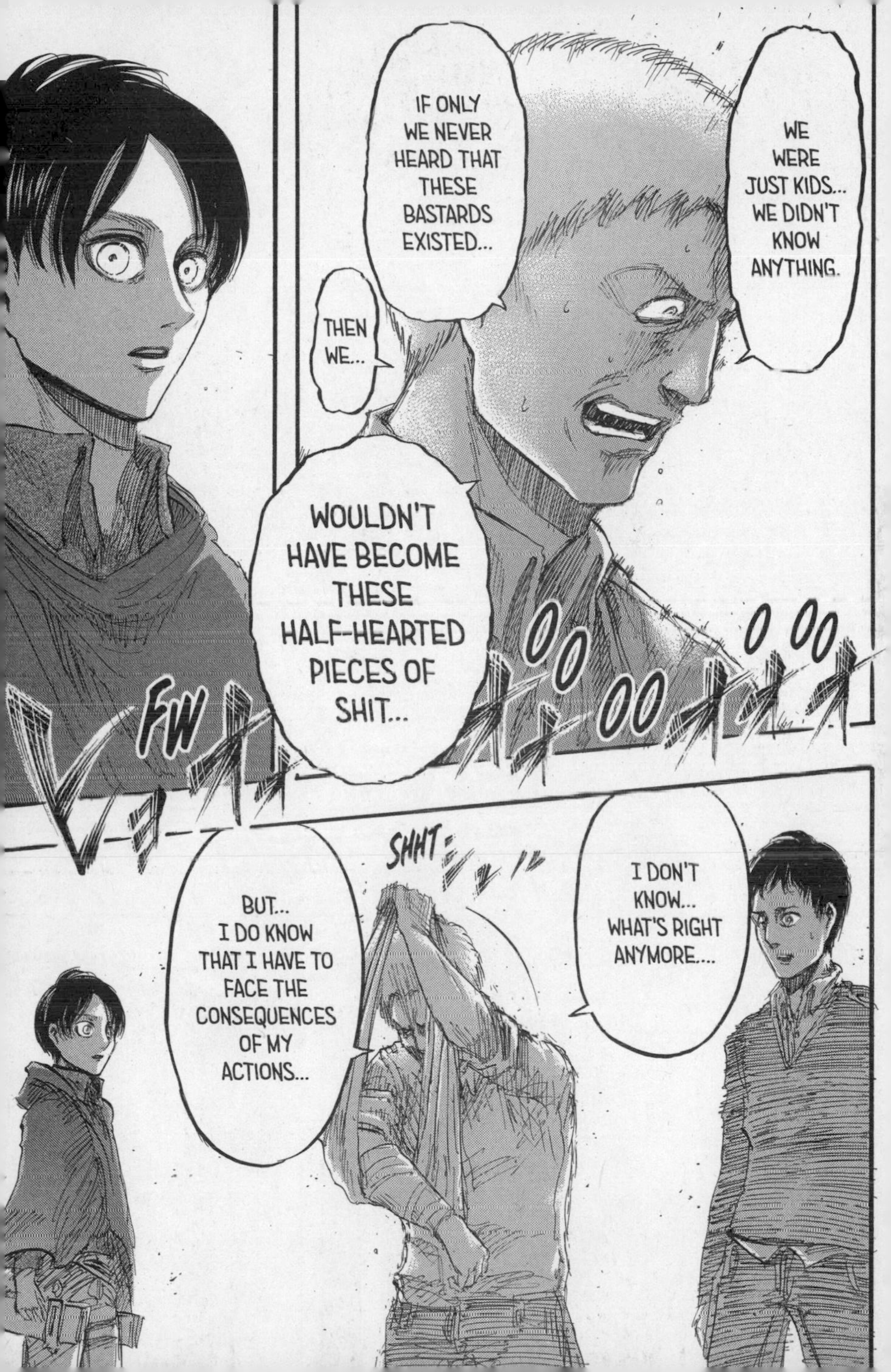
WE WERE JUST KIDS... WE DIDN'T KNOW ANYTHING.
IF ONLY WE NEVER HEARD THAT THESE BASTARDS EXISTED...
THEN WE...
WOULDN'T HAVE BECOME THESE HALF-HEARTED PIECES OF SHIT...
OO OO OO OO OO
FW
I DON'T KNOW... WHAT'S RIGHT ANYMORE....
SHHT
BUT... I DO KNOW THAT I HAVE TO FACE THE CONSEQUENCES OF MY ACTIONS...

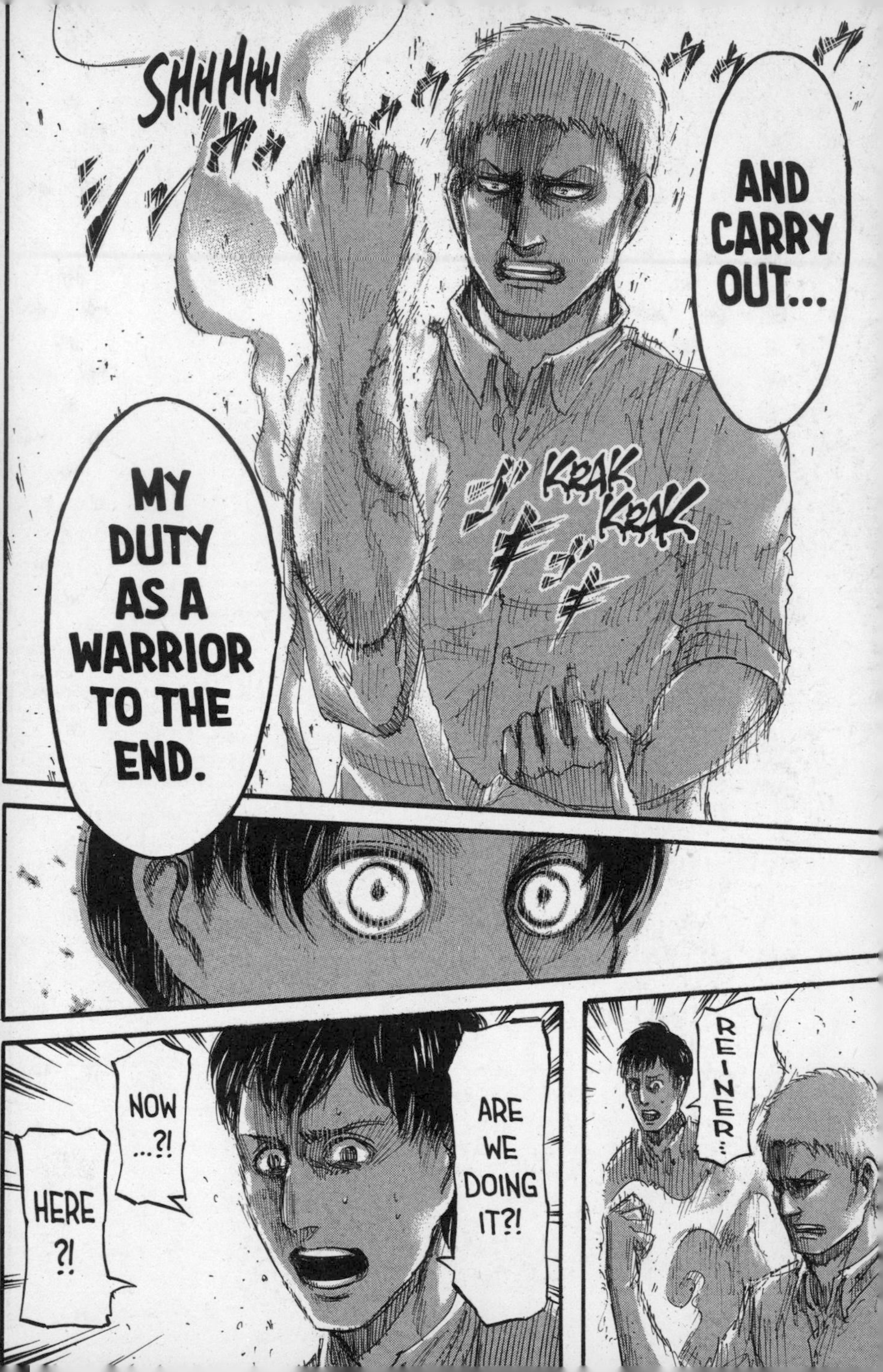
AND CARRY OUT...
SHHHHH
MY DUTY AS A WARRIOR TO THE END.
KRAK KRAK
REINER...
ARE WE DOING IT?!
NOW ...?!
HERE ?!

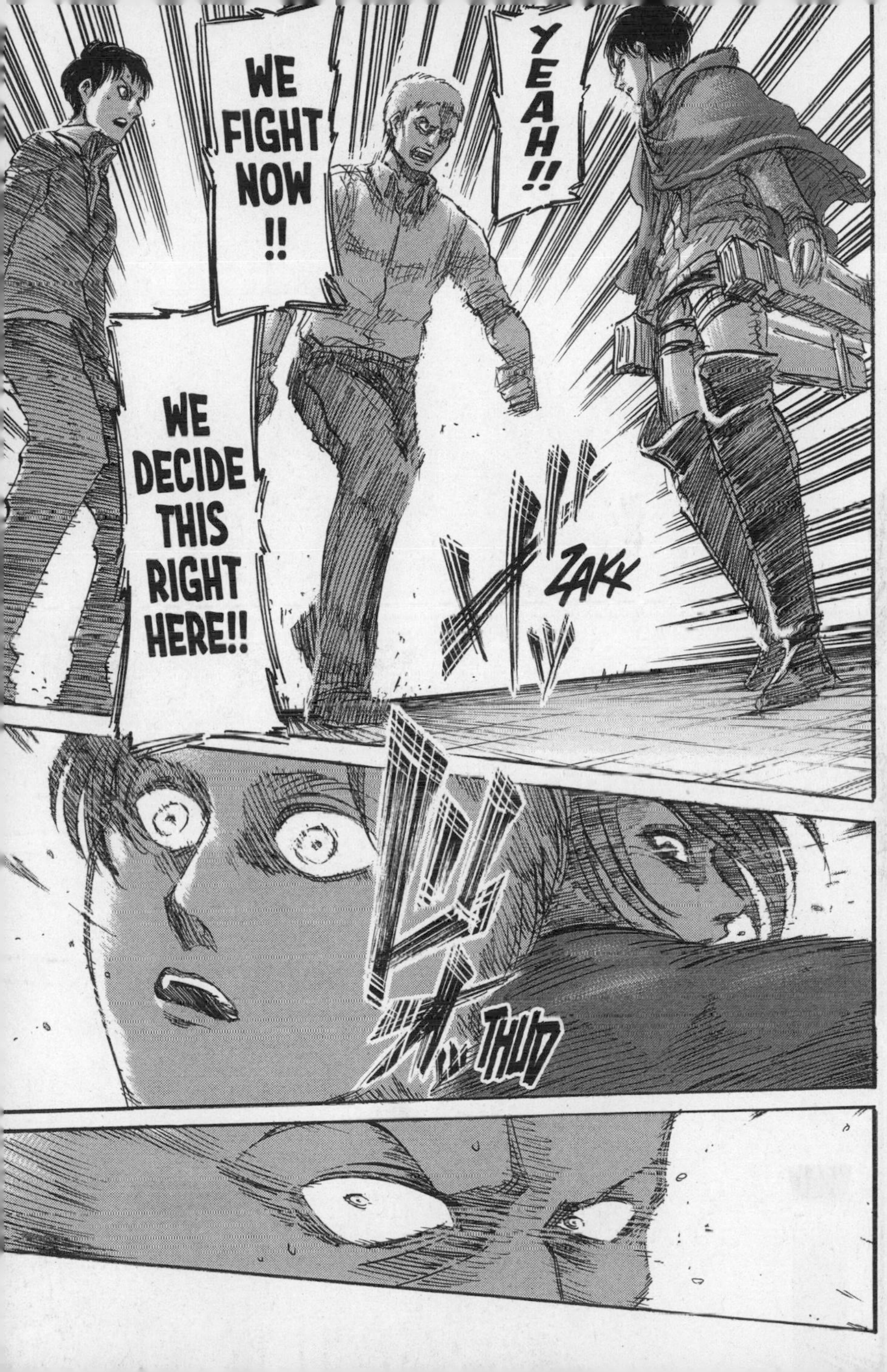
YEAH!!
WE FIGHT NOW !!
WE DECIDE THIS RIGHT HERE!!
ZAKK
THUD

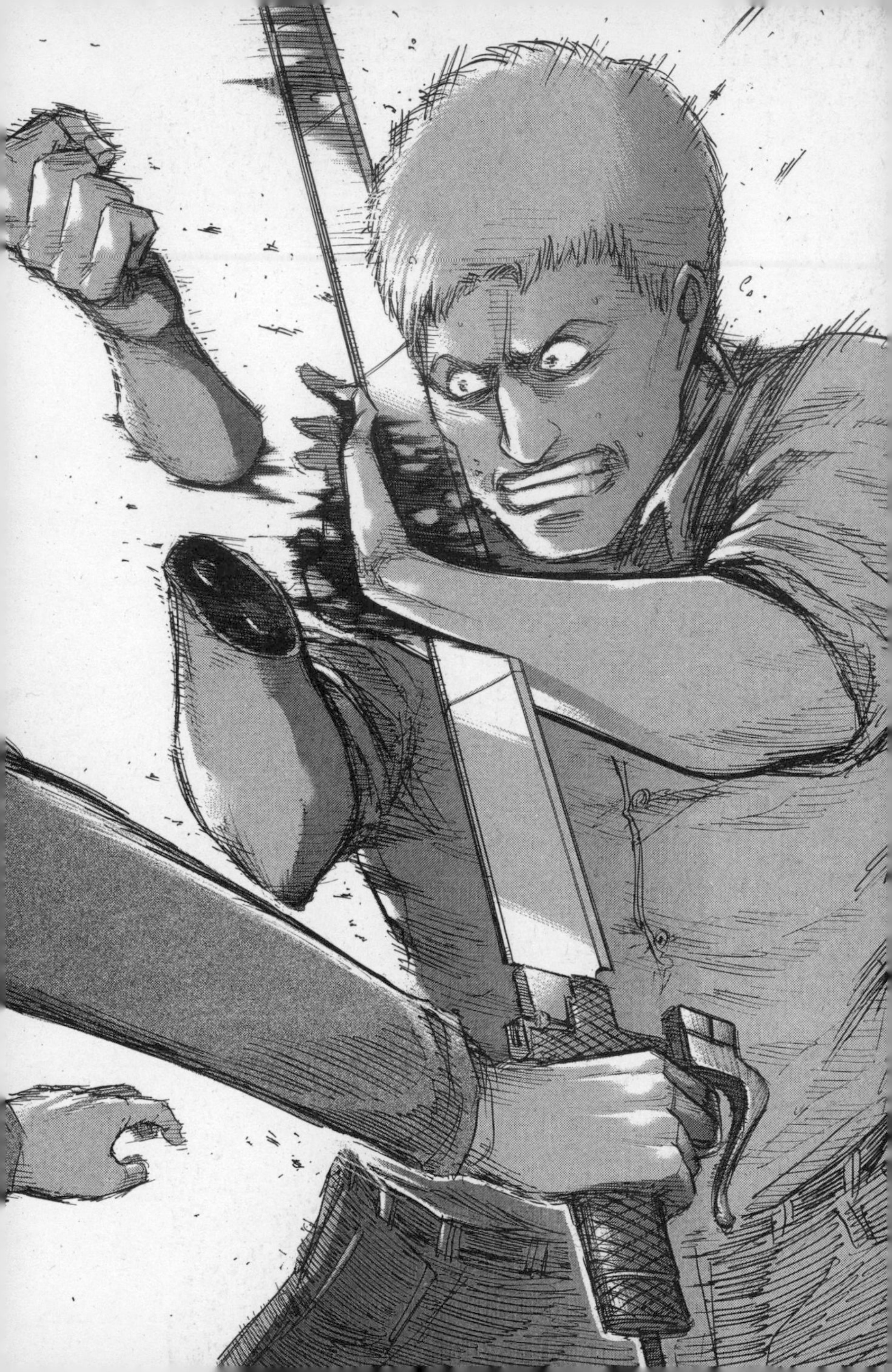

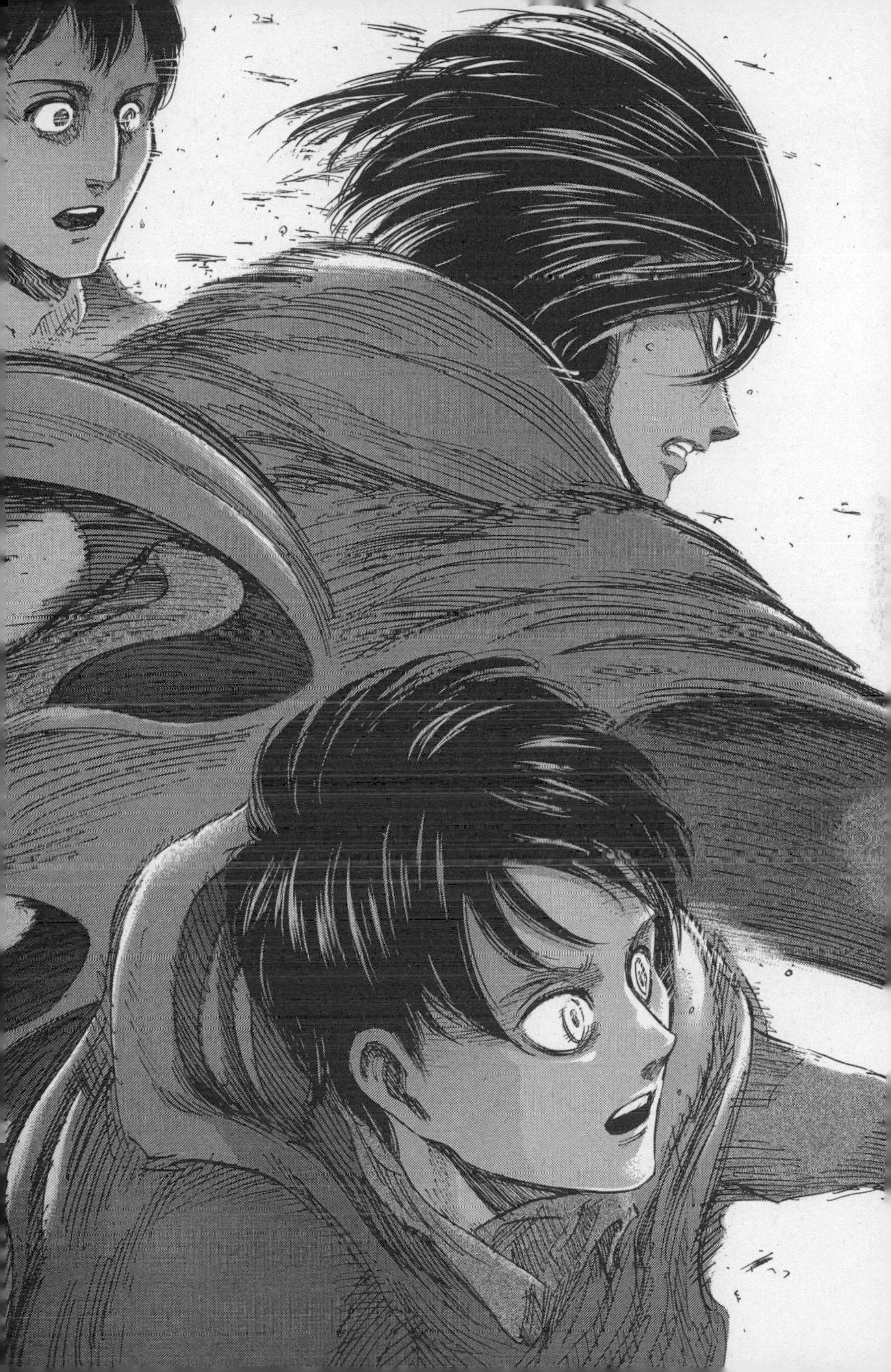

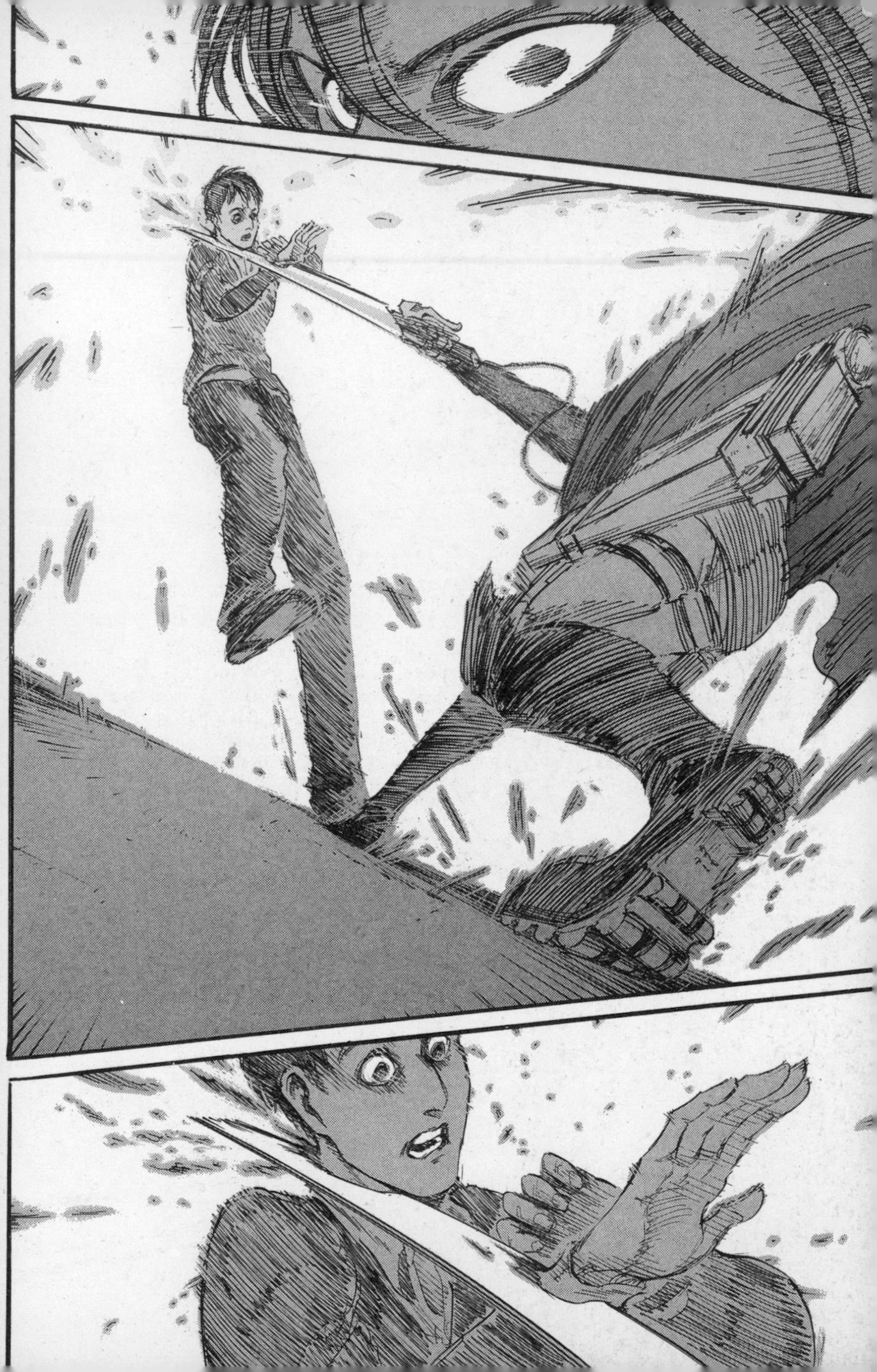

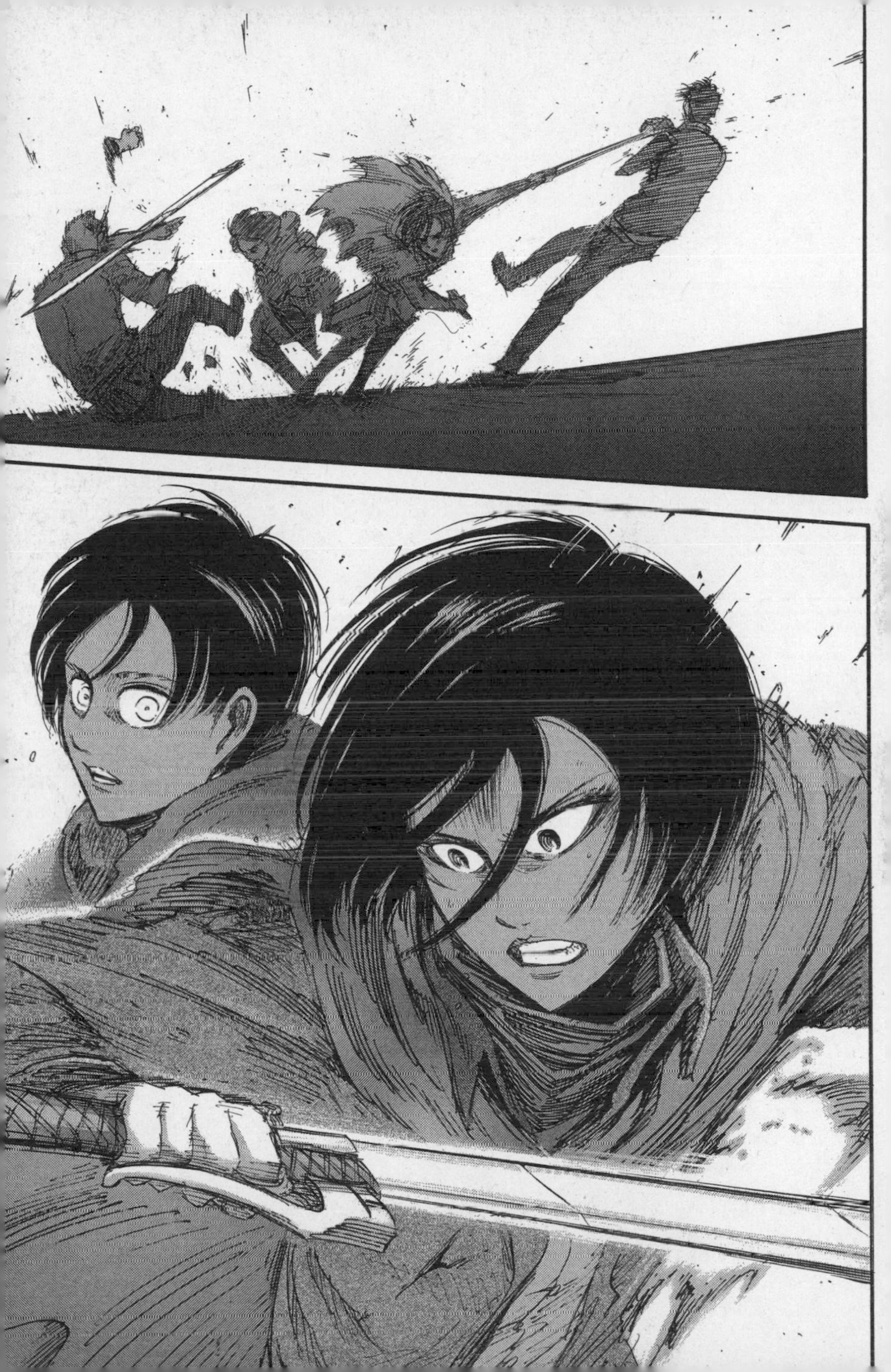

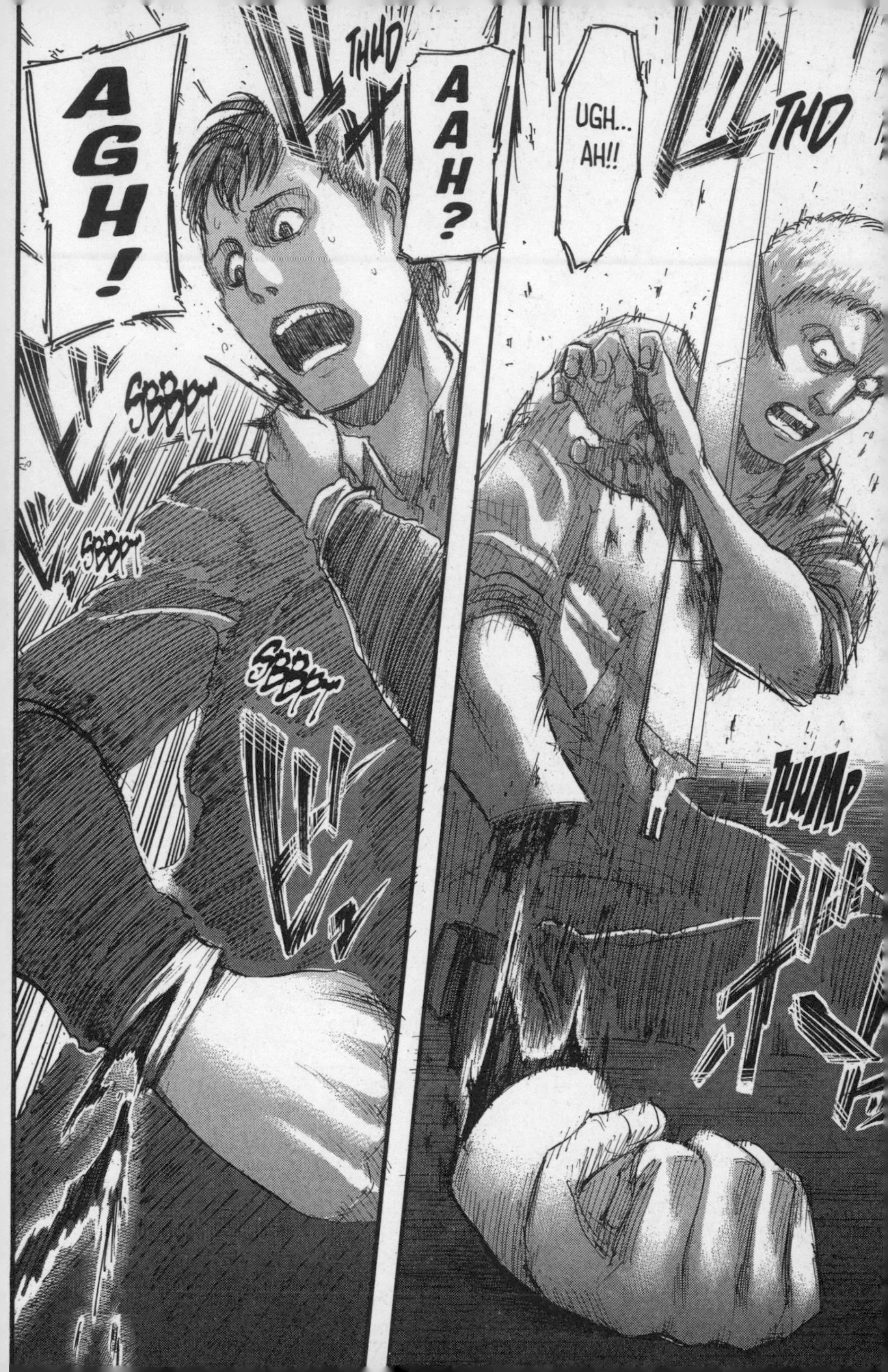
UGH... AH!!
THD
THUMP
AAH?
THUD
AGH!
SBBPT
SBBPT
SBBPT

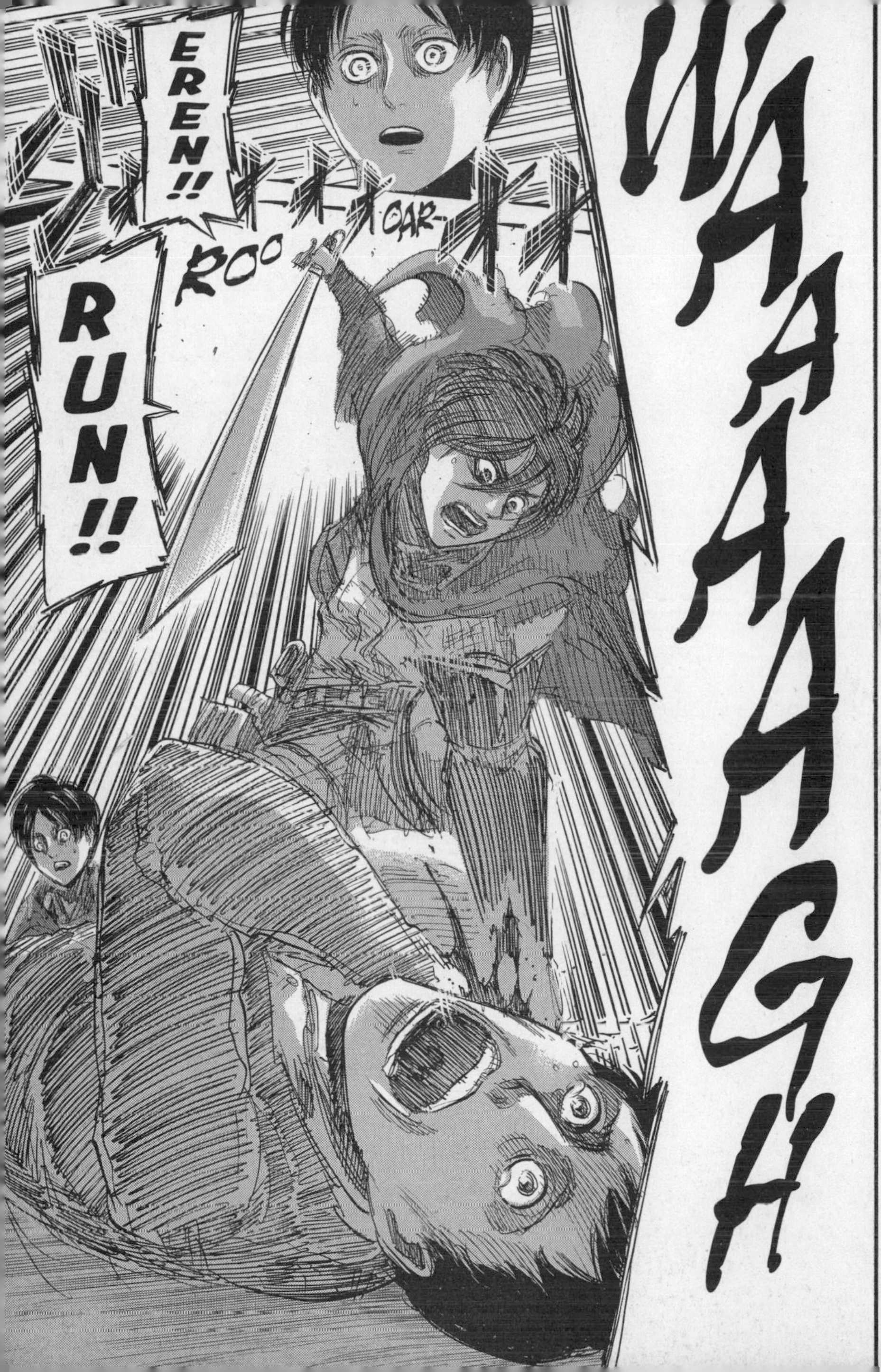
WAAAAAGH
EREN!!
OAR-
ROO
RUN!!

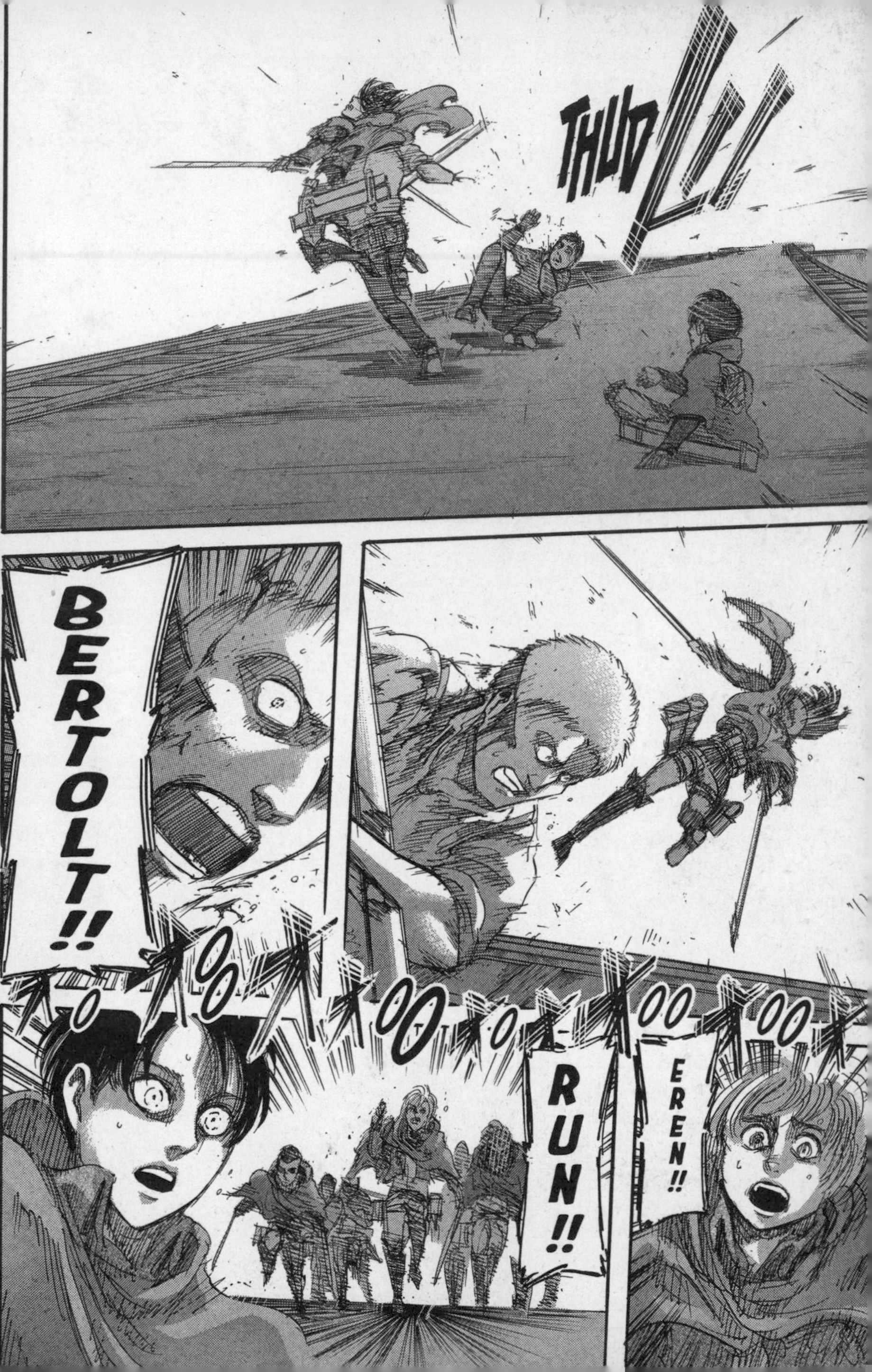
THUD
BERTOLT!!
EREN!!
RUN!!

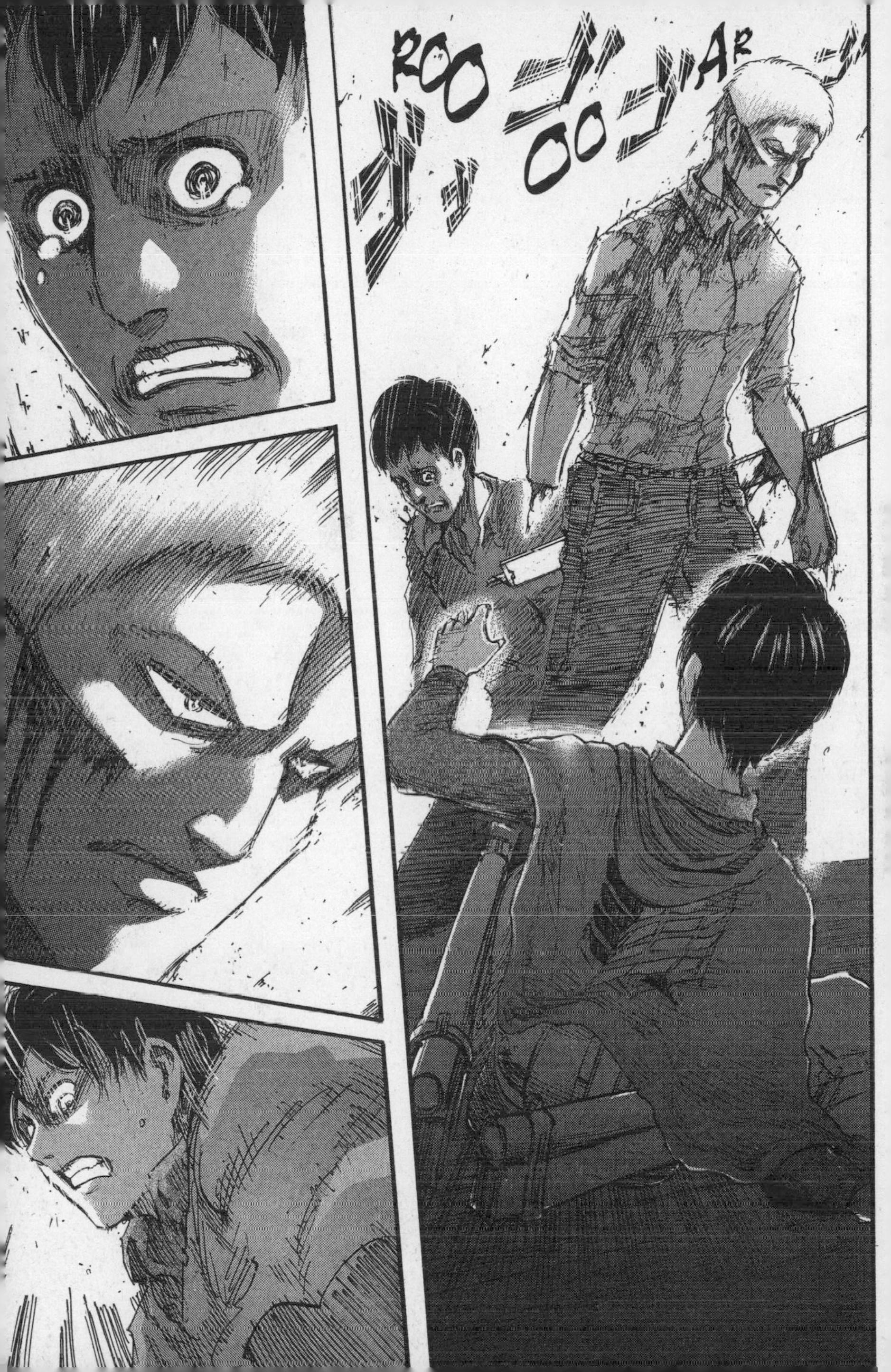
ROOOOAR

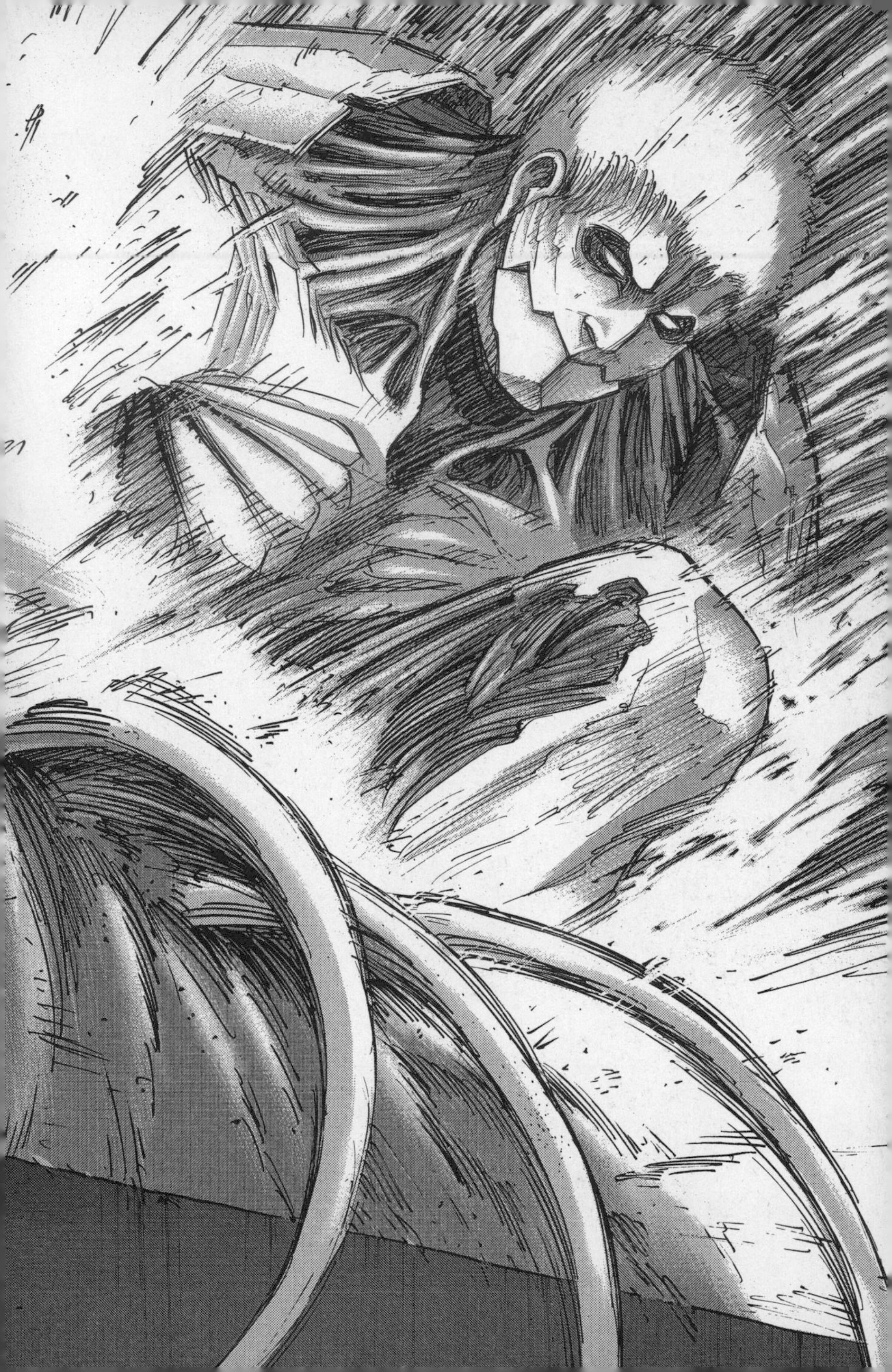

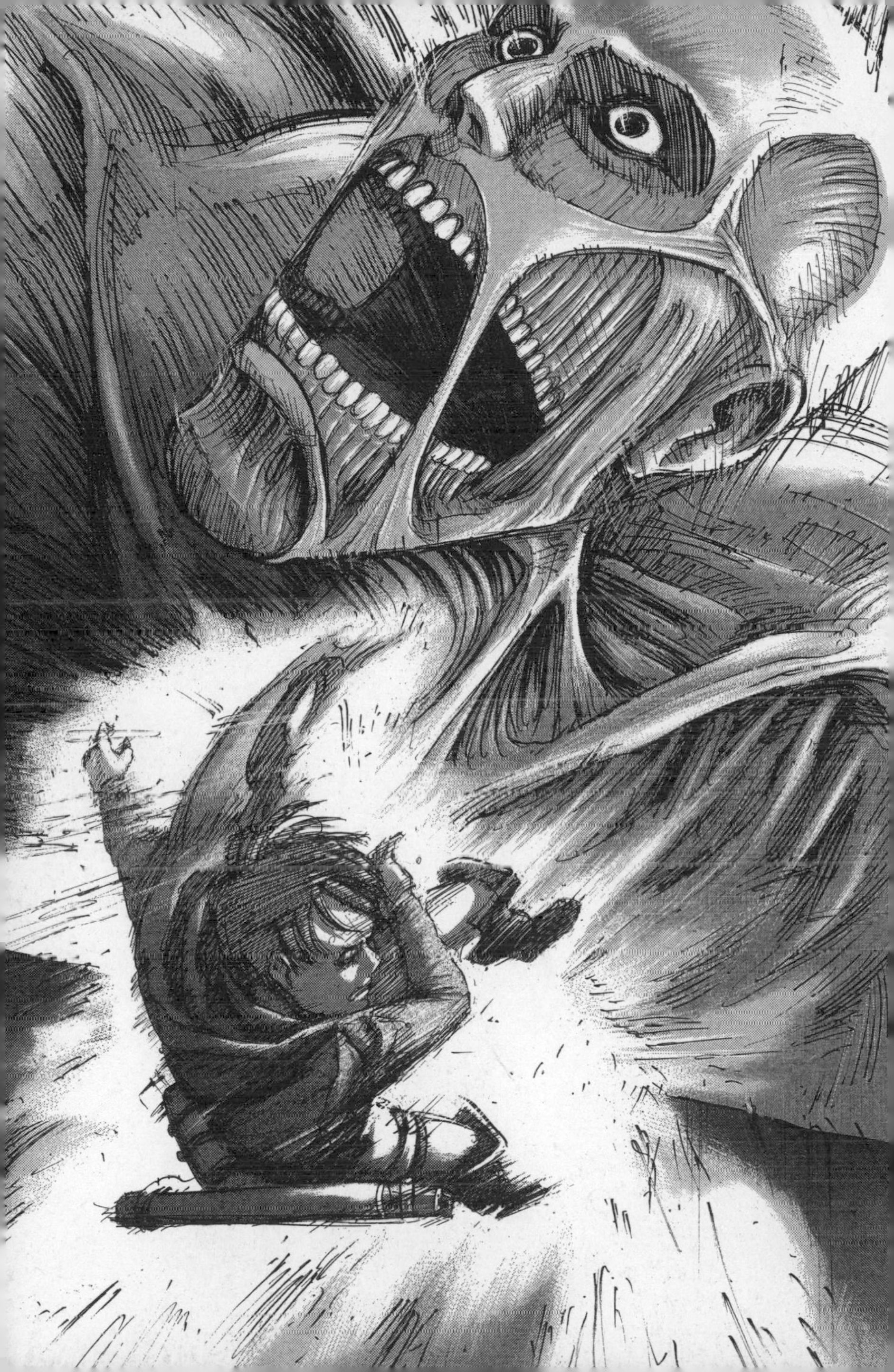

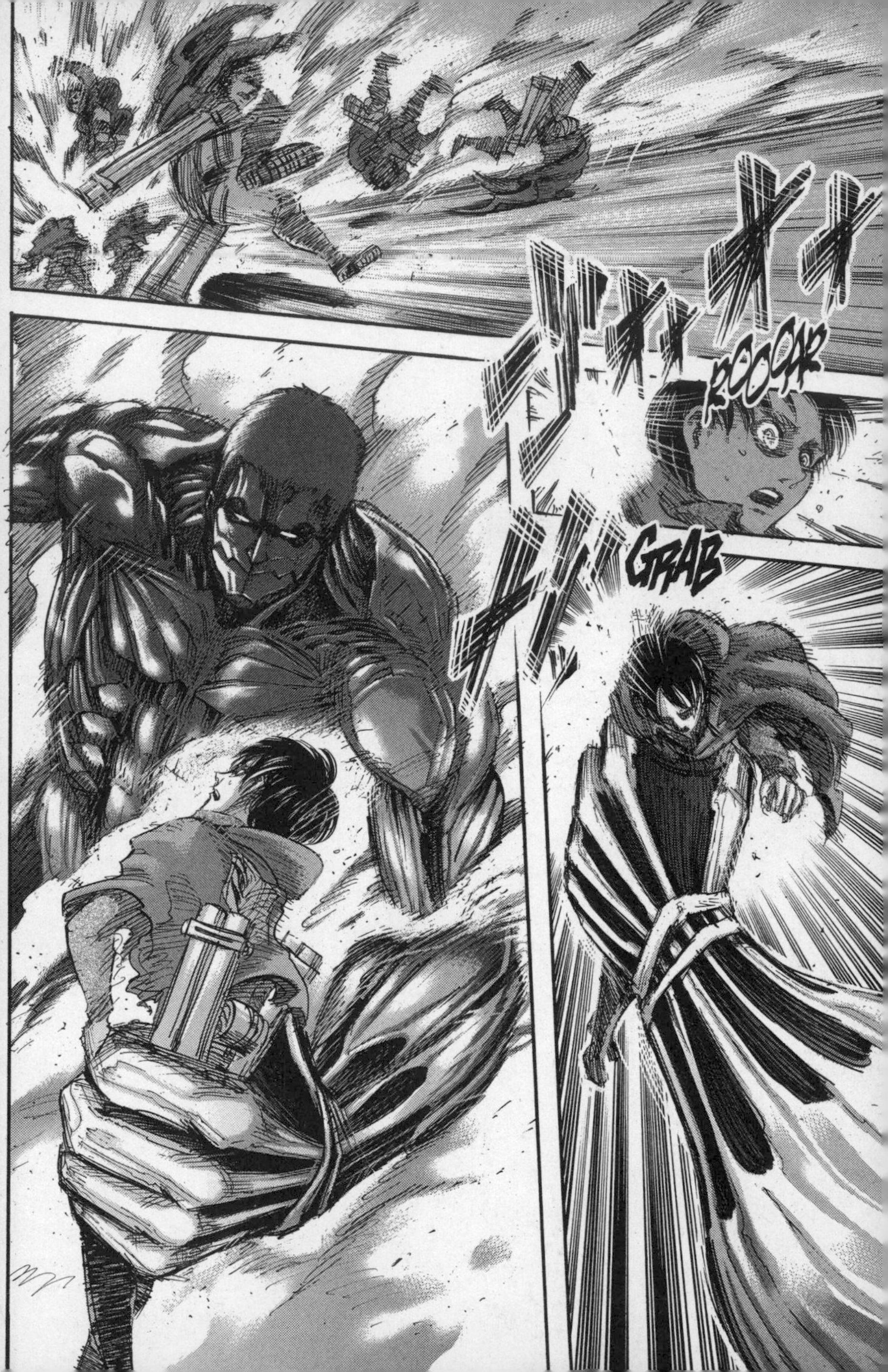
ROOAR
GRAB

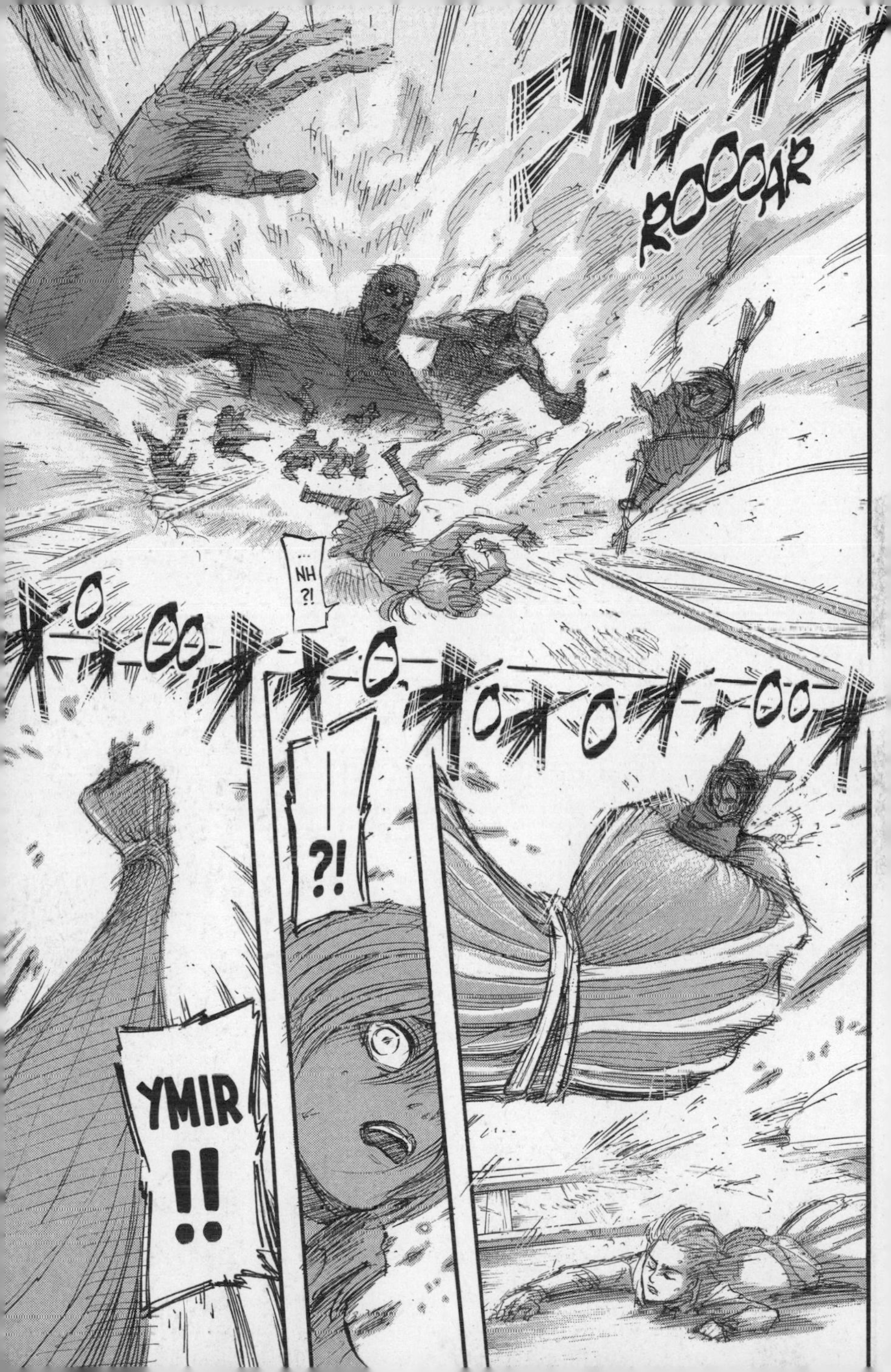
ROOOAR
...NH ?!
O OO O O O OO
?!
YMIR !!

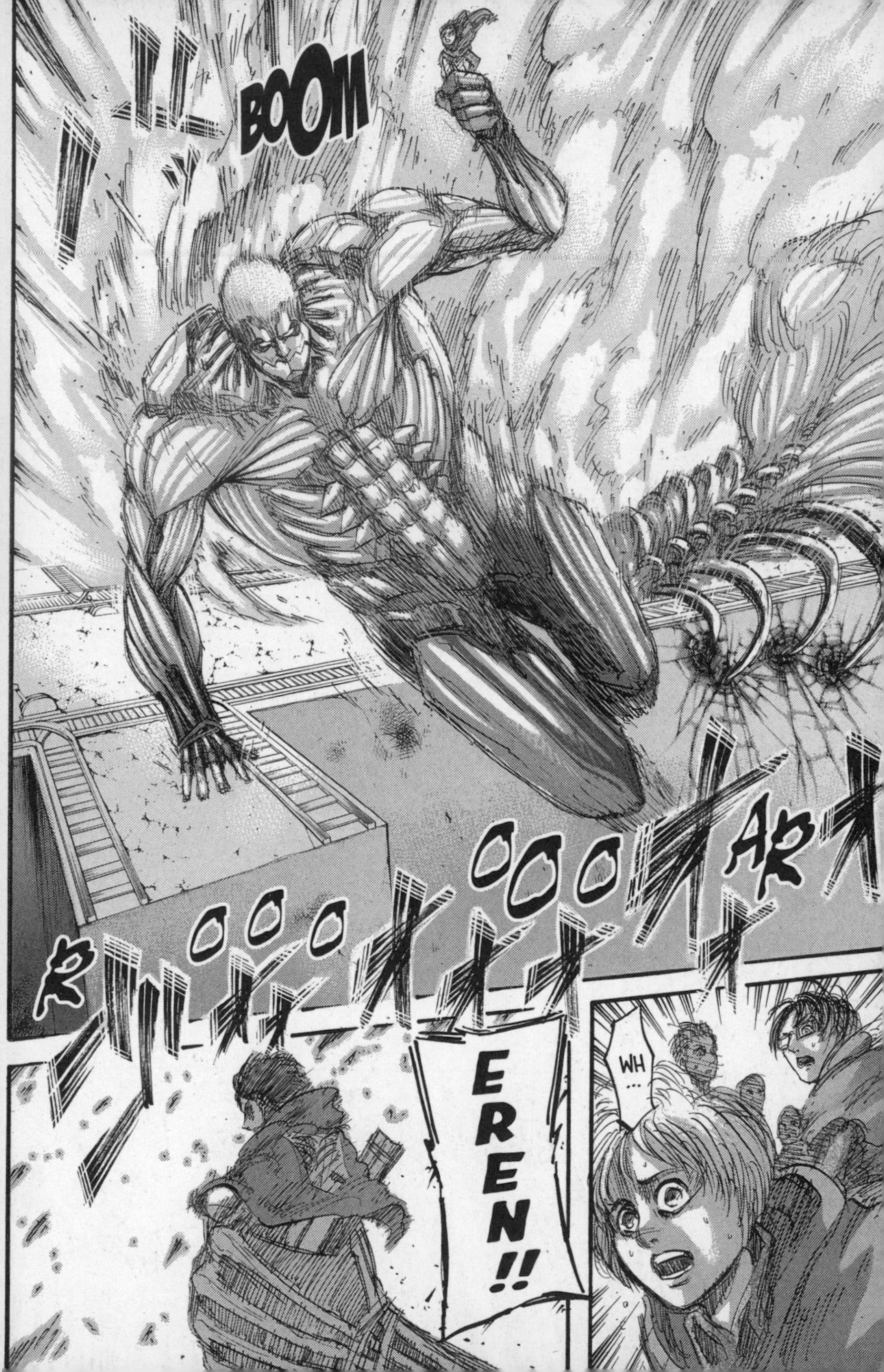
BOOM
ROOOOOOAR
WH...
EREN!!

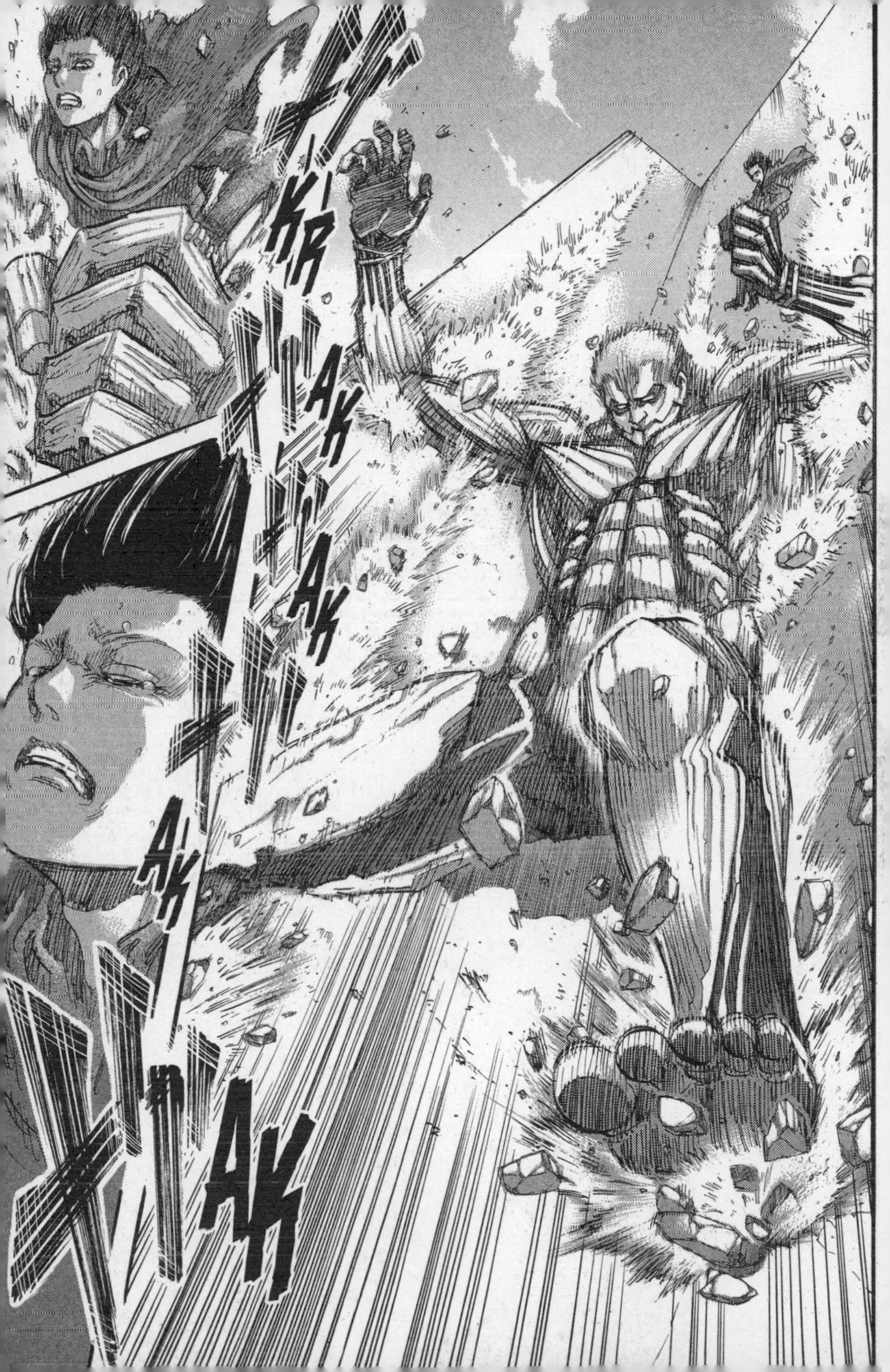
KRAKAKAK
AK
AK

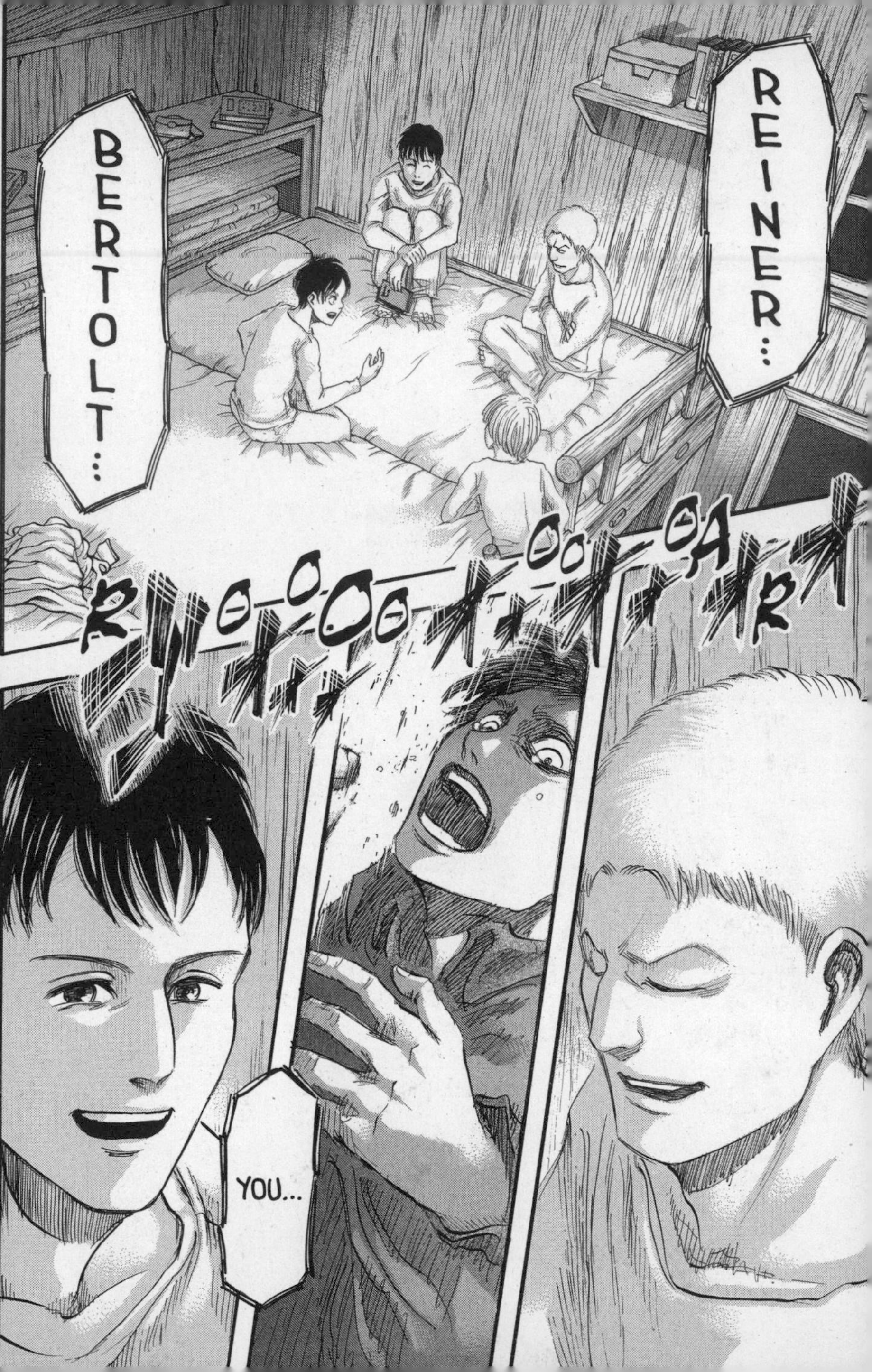
REINER...
BERTOLT...
ROOOOOOOAR
YOU...

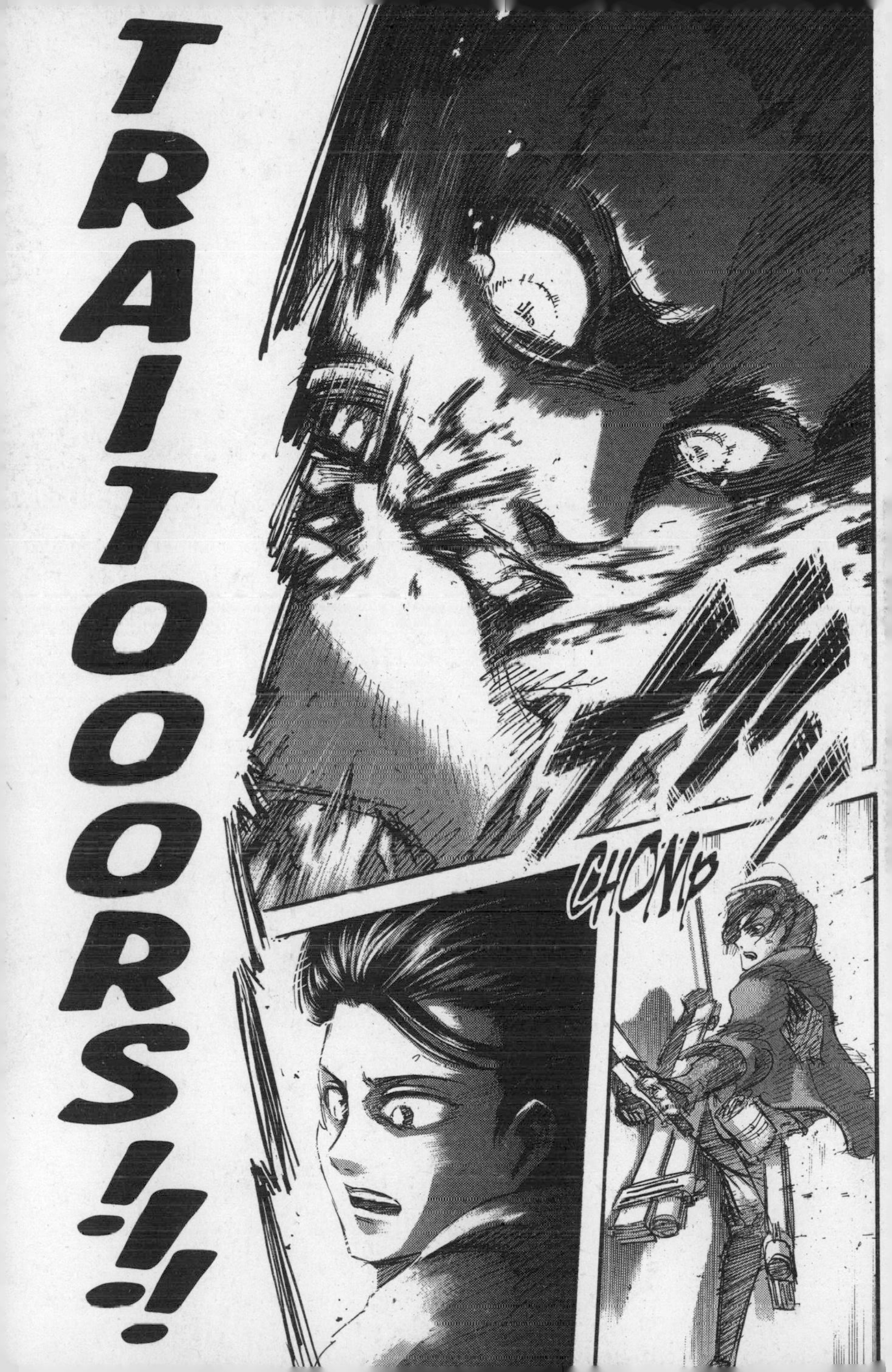

TRAITOORS!!!
CHOMP

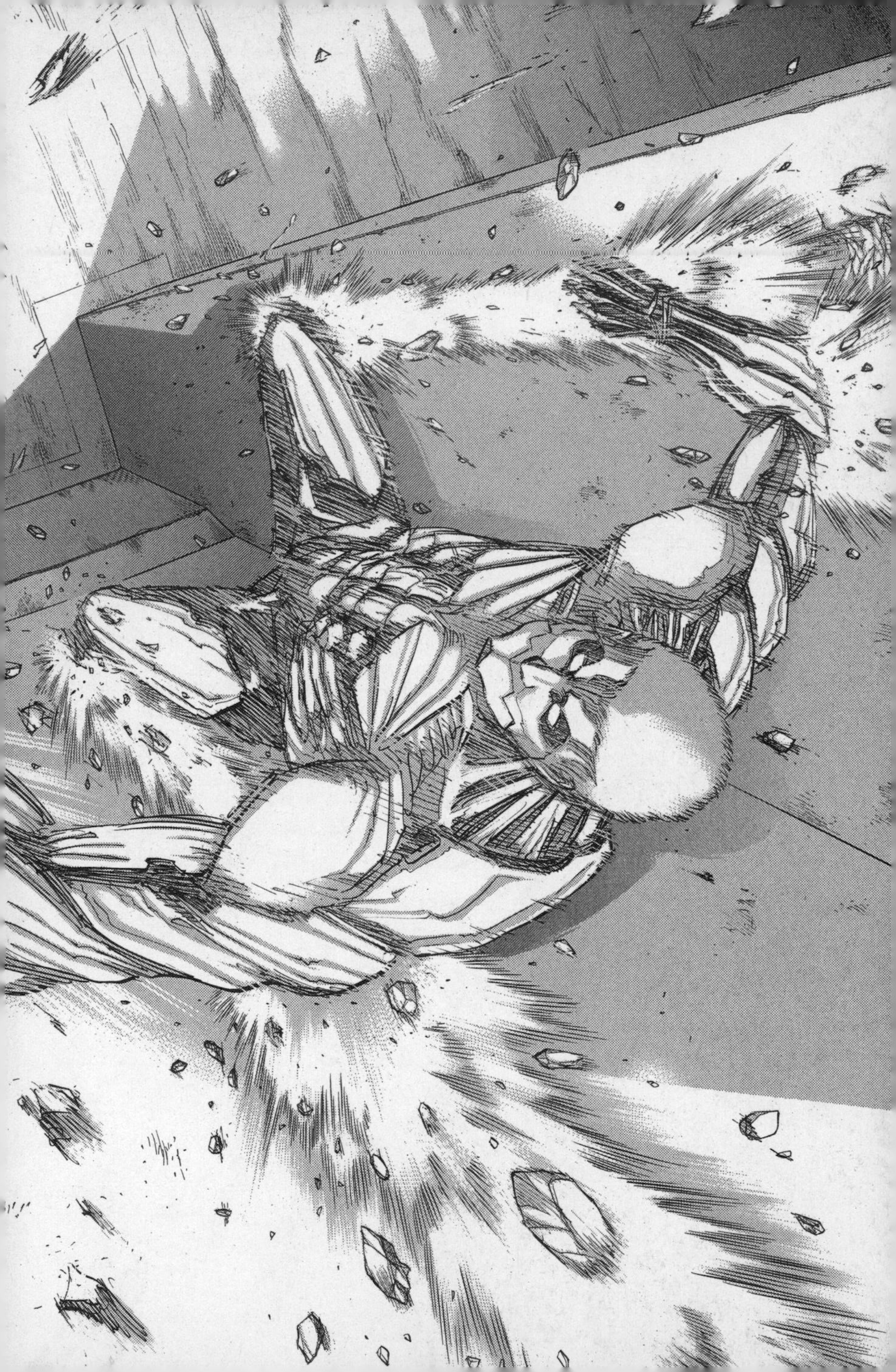

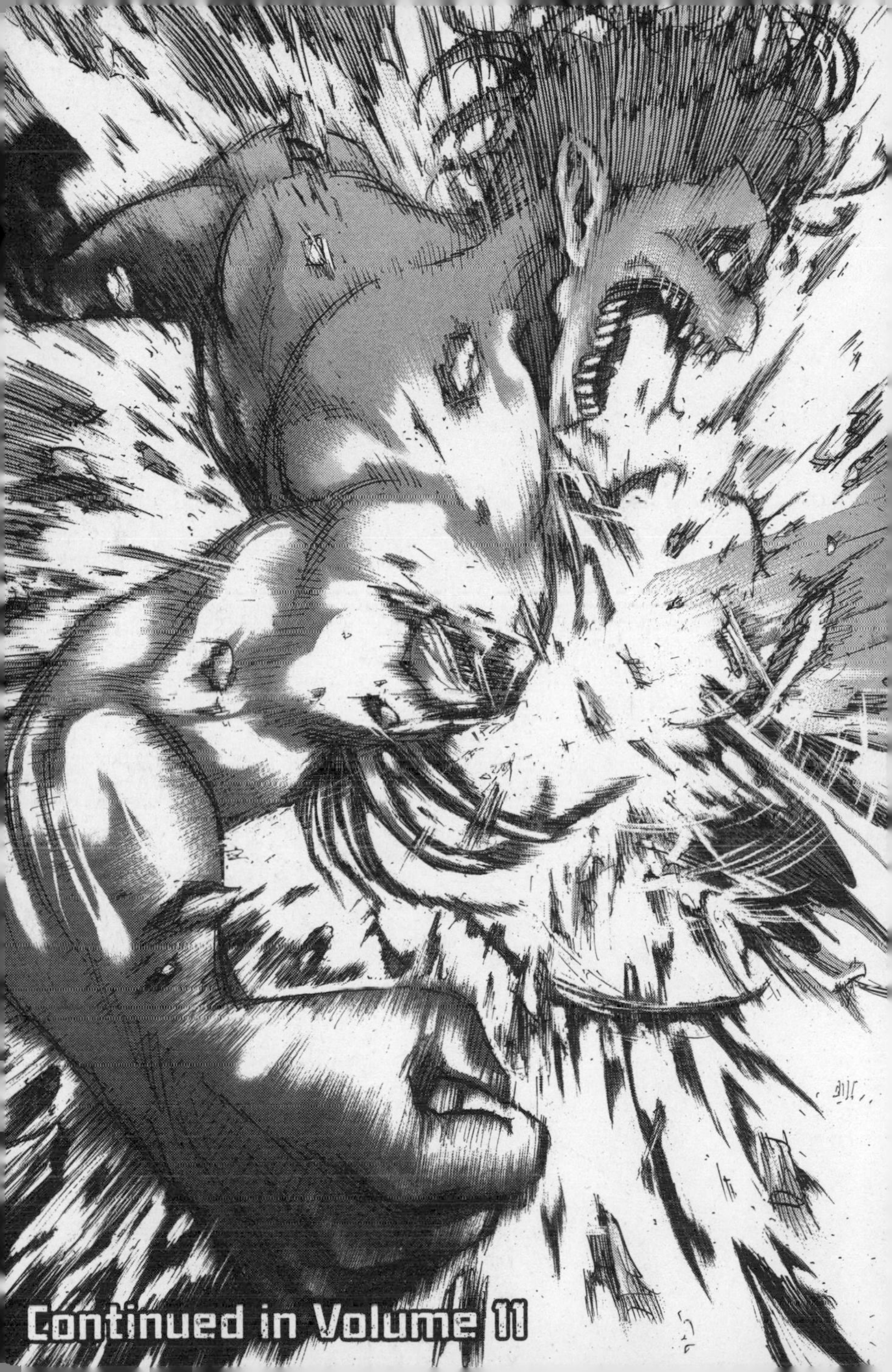

Continued in Volume 11

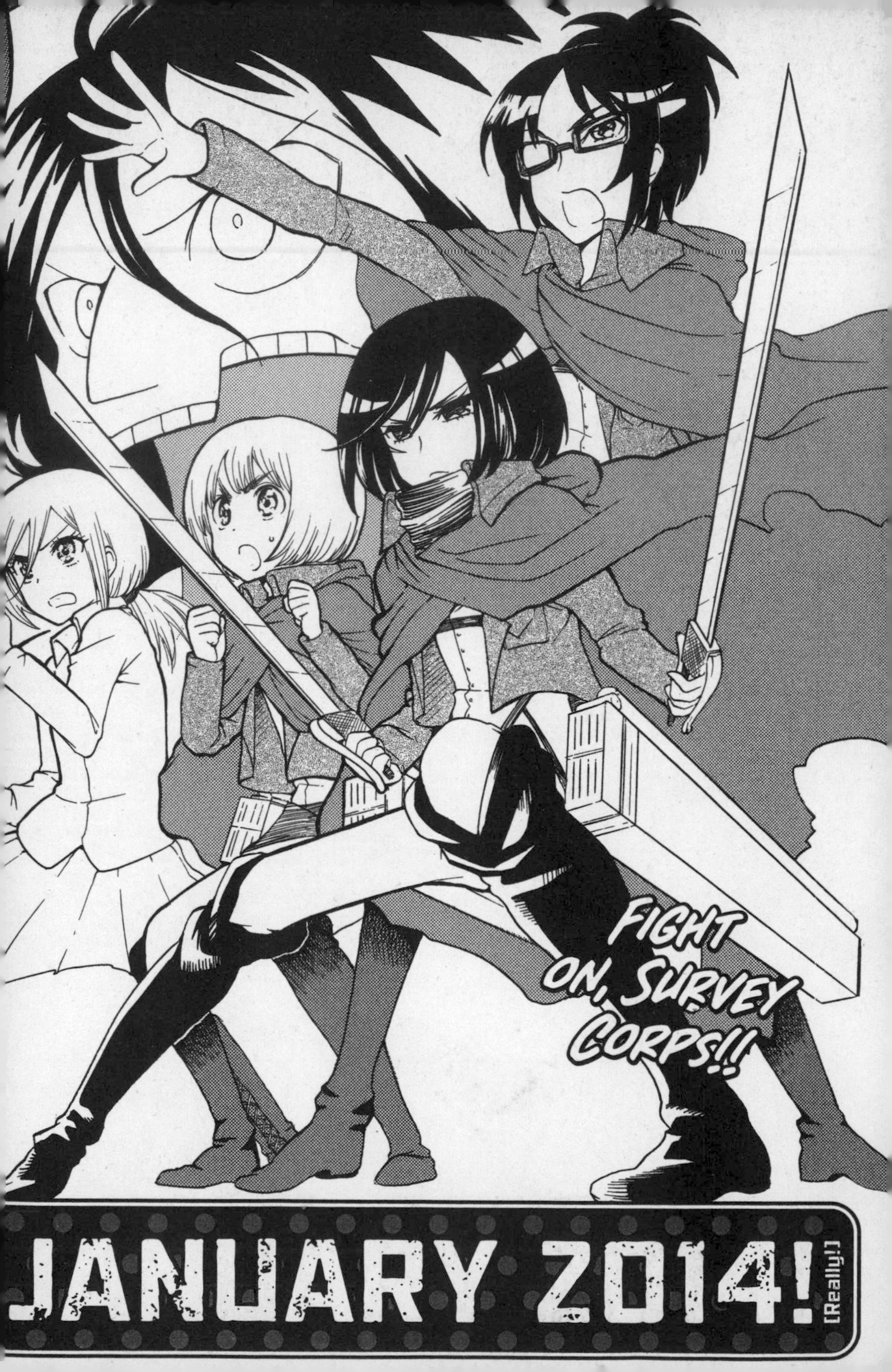
FIGHT ON, SURVEY CORPS!!
JANUARY 2014!
[Really!]

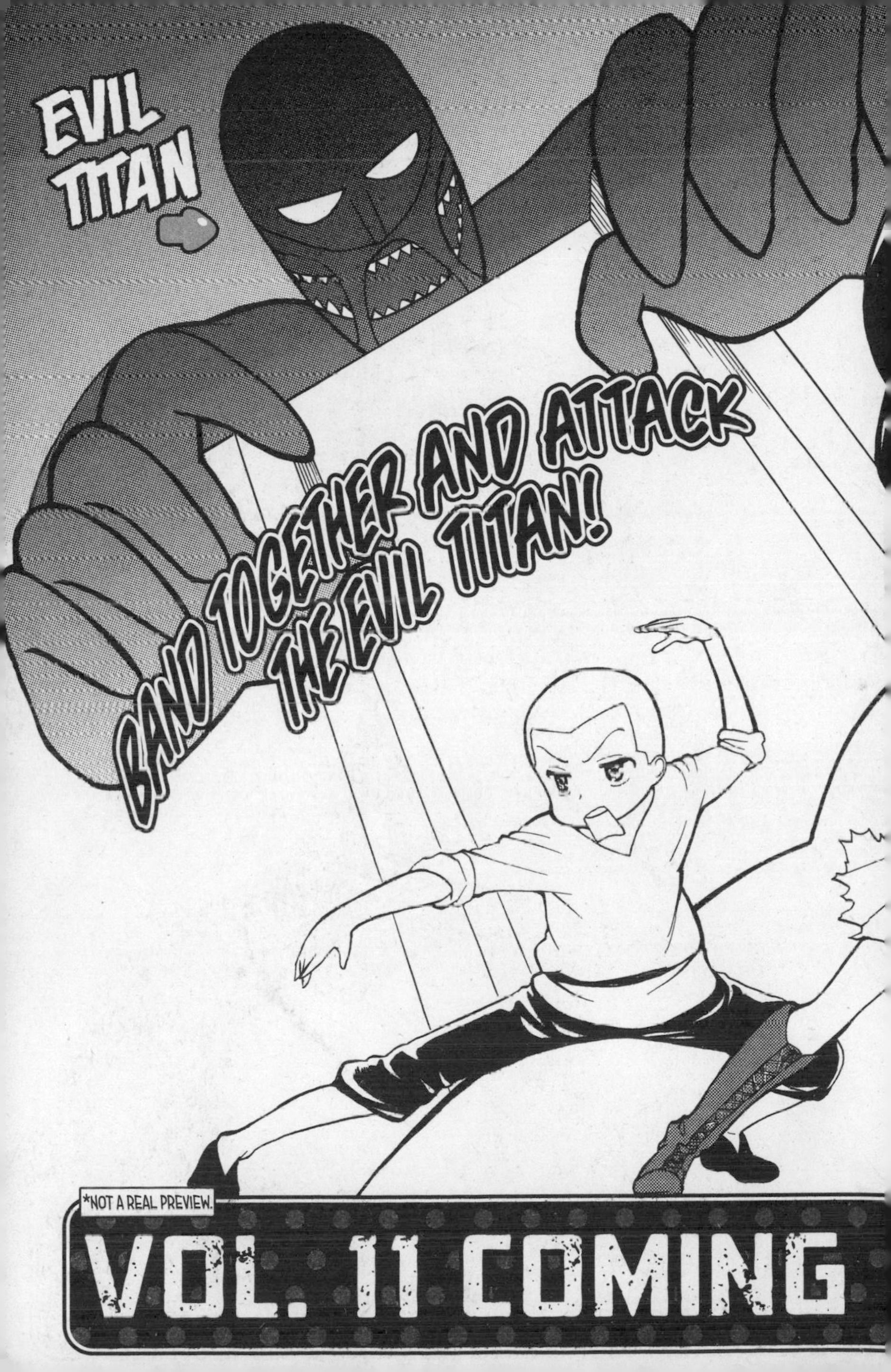
EVIL TITAN
BAND TOGETHER AND ATTACK THE EVIL TITAN!
*NOT A REAL PREVIEW.
VOL. 11 COMING